always up to date

The law changes, but Nolo is on top of it! We offer several
ways to make sure you and your Nolo products are up to date:

1 **Nolo's Legal Updater**
We'll send you an email whenever a new edition of this book
is published! Sign up at **www.nolo.com/legalupdater**.

2 **Updates @ Nolo.com**
Check www.nolo.com/update to find recent changes
in the law that affect the current edition of your book.

3 **Nolo Customer Service**
To make sure that this edition of the book is the most
recent one, call us at **800-728-3555** and ask one of
our friendly customer service representatives.
Or find out at **www.nolo.com**.

please note

We believe accurate, plain-English legal information should help you solve many of your own legal problems. But this text is not a substitute for personalized advice from a knowledgeable lawyer. If you want the help of a trained professional—and we'll always point out situations in which we think that's a good idea—consult an attorney licensed to practice in your state.

7th edition

How to Get a Green Card

By Attorney Ilona Bray

Updated by Attorney Carl Falstrom

Seventh Edition	OCTOBER 2006
Editor	ILONA BRAY
Book Design	TERRI HEARSH
Production	MARGARET LIVINGSTON
Proofreading	SARAH TOLCHIN
Index	BAYSIDE INDEXING SERVICE
Printing	DELTA PRINTING SOLUTIONS, INC.

Lewis, Loida Nicolas.
   How to get a green card / by Loida Nicolas Lewis.--7th ed., updated and rev./by Ilona Bray.
     p. cm.
   ISBN 1-4133-0520-2 (alk. paper)
    1. Aliens--United States--Popular works. 2. Emigration and immigration law--United
States--Popular works. 3. Green cards. I. Bray, Ilona M., 1962- II. Title.

KF4840.Z9L49 2006
342.7308'2--dc22   2006048287

Quantity sales: For information on bulk purchases or corporate premium sales, please contact the Special Sales department. For academic sales or textbook adoptions, ask for Academic Sales, 800-955-4775. Nolo, 950 Parker St., Berkeley, CA 94710.

Acknowledgments

The original authors of this book were Loida Nicolas Lewis and Len Madlansacay. Nolo thanks them for their efforts in producing a work of such ambitious scope, and one that has endured for many years. Of course, changes in immigration laws and practices have necessitated many rewrites and revisions of the original book. For help with this seventh edition, many thanks go to Attorney Carl Falstrom, who not only combed the book for legal and procedural changes, but added many helpful tips for people wanting to get through the process smoothly and quickly.

Table of Contents

Is This Book for You?

1 A Look at Immigration History

2 Overview of Categories

3 Short-Term Alternatives to a Green Card

4 Will Inadmissibility Bar You From Getting a Green Card?

5 How Long You'll Have to Wait

6 Fiancé and Fiancée Visas

7 Green Cards Through Marriage

18 Adjustment of Status

19 Consular Processing

20 Private Bills

21 Inside the Immigration Bureaucracy

22 Immigration Forms: Getting Started

Sample Filled-In Forms

Is This Book For You?

Are you a foreign-born person who's interested in making your home in the United States? If so, this book may be just the ticket to finding out whether you're eligible for permanent U.S. residence, also known as a "green card." A green card gives you the right to live and work in the United States your whole life, travel in and out of the country without too much hassle, sponsor certain family members to join you, and, if all goes well for a few years, apply for U.S. citizenship.

This book will help you learn the application procedures, fill out the various forms, and pick up tips for dealing with often-difficult government officials. However, many types of people won't get the help they need from this book, so read this chapter carefully before you continue!

⚠️ **Green cards also come with certain limitations.** It's not a completely secure status. For example, you can lose your right to your green card if you:

- commit a crime
- don't make your primary home in the United States
- forget to report your change of address to the immigration authorities
- involve yourself in terrorist or subversive activities, or
- otherwise violate the immigration laws.

A. Types of Green Cards We Cover

This book was designed to help the "average" person; for example, someone who doesn't have a million dollars to invest, isn't internationally famous, and hasn't received a job offer from a U.S. employer. That's why we've limited our discussion to the following types of green card opportunities:

- family-based green cards, available to close relatives and adopted children of U.S. citizens and permanent residents
- political asylum and refugee status, available to people fleeing certain types of persecution
- the visa lottery ("diversity visa"), available to people with a certain level of education who win a random drawing
- opportunities for people who have lived in the United States for ten years or more ("registry" and "cancellation of removal").

This book does not cover green cards through employment, investment, the amnesty programs of the 1980s and the followup "NACARA" program, religious workers, or other, more obscure categories. Nor does it cover temporary visas (distinct from green cards in that they expire, usually in a few years). Examples of temporary visas include student, business visitor, H-1B specialty workers, and J-1 exchange visitor visas. (For a quick overview of these temporary visas, see Chapter 3.)

> ⚠️ **Don't confuse green cards with U.S. citizenship.** The highest status you can obtain under the U.S. immigration laws is citizenship. However, with only a very few exceptions, you must get a green card before you can apply for citizenship. For example, an immigrant who marries a U.S. citizen may gain the right to apply for a green card, but not yet to apply for U.S. citizenship.

> 📖 **Are you already eligible for U.S. citizenship?** If you already have a green card and have lived in the United States for five years (or three years if you've been married to a U.S. citizen), you may be eligible for U.S. citizenship. To find out more, see *Becoming a U.S. Citizen: A Guide to the Law, Exam, & Interview,* by Ilona Bray (Nolo).

B. How Much You Can Do Without a Lawyer

The advice given in this book is for simple, straightforward cases. In other words, it's for people who clearly meet the eligibility requirements laid out in this book, and have the education and skills to understand and handle the application requirements. Many tasks can be done yourself, such as filling in forms, collecting documents, and attending interviews.

If your case is more complex, however, you may need to hire a lawyer to advise or represent you, for example if:

- you have been ordered to go before an immigration judge for what are called "removal" proceedings because the immigration authorities do not believe that you have a legal reason to either enter or continue to stay in the United States

- you have a criminal record
- you have some other problems with your immigration paperwork, such as you have submitted forged documents, or
- the bureaucratic requirements are too technical; for example, you must apply for political asylum or labor certification, or you are appealing some decision made in your case by immigration authorities.

(See Chapter 24 for guidance in hiring and working with a lawyer.)

C. Using This Book

You need not read every chapter in this book— only those helpful to your specific situation. Here is some guidance.

Read **Chapter 1** if you're interested in a summary of immigration trends and laws throughout history.

Everyone should read **Chapters 2, 3, and 4**. They describe the basic requirements for obtaining legal permission to stay in the United States.

Everyone should also read **Chapter 5**. It explains the general forms and procedures required for obtaining a green card—and the quotas that may apply to allow set numbers of specific types of immigrants to come to the United States.

> **This book doesn't provide forms, for good reason.** All the application forms you'll need—and we'll tell you exactly which ones they are—are either readily available (www.uscis.gov or 800-870-3676) or will be mailed to you by the immigration authorities when the time is right. Some can even be filled out online. We considered including copies in this book as well, but determined that because the forms get revised so frequently, this might actually be a disservice to our readers. It's best for you to obtain the most up-to-date form when you're ready to use it. We have, however, provided sample filled-in forms to illustrate our advice and show you what the form will look like.

Then comes the time when you can choose and read the specific chapters that concern you. Look over the chapter headings for **Chapters 6 through 17**—and read the ones that make the most sense in your specific situation. For example, if you believe that you might qualify for a green card because you will be marrying or are already married to a U.S. citizen, begin reading **Chapter 7.** It may refer you to other chapters you should read to get a more complete picture.

Each chapter contains samples of most of the forms you'll need to complete.

After reading the information about various rules for specific types of immigrants, if you decide that you qualify to file for yourself or another person, read **Chapters 21 and 22**. They'll help you understand the rules for filling out the necessary forms and getting them into the right hands.

If you lose your green card or need to renew or replace it, read **Chapter 23** to find out how to do so.

Icons Used in the Book

 Caution. This icon alerts you to potential problems.

 See an expert. This icon alerts you to situations where you may need to seek the advice of an attorney.

 Next step. This icon contains information on where to go for the next step in your immigration process.

 Resource. This icon refers you to helpful books or other resources.

 Skip Ahead. This icon tells you when people in certain situations can skip to a later section of the book.

 Tip. This icon gives you a useful tip.

Steps You Must Take to Keep Up to Date

This book was as up to date as we could make it on the day it was printed. However, immigration laws change frequently, and USCIS changes its fees, rules, forms, and procedures even more often—at times without telling anyone.

That's why you must take certain steps on your own, to protect your rights and interests. In particular, be sure to:

- check the USCIS website before turning in any application. Go to the "Immigration Forms, Fees, and Fingerprints" section. Make sure the form you filled out is still the most up to date, and that the fee hasn't gone up.
- check the updates to this book posted on the Nolo website at www.nolo.com. Also see whether we've published a later edition of this book, and read our analysis about who needs to get the new edition.
- listen to the news, particularly for changes by the U.S. Congress. But don't rush to USCIS to apply for something until you're sure it's final. A lot of laws in progress get reported on before the president has actually signed them.

A Look at Immigration History

America: A Nation of Immigrants

To understand current immigration policy, it helps to know about how it came about.

A. America's Earliest Settlers

Long before Cristobal Colon—the Spanish name by which Christopher Columbus referred to himself—opened the Americas to the Europeans in 1492, the first inhabitants of what is now the United States were the Native American Indians, including the Eskimos. Other early settlers included the Vikings, in the northernmost part of North America, and the ancestors of today's Hawaiians.

From the 15th century onward, the continent became a magnet for explorers and colonists from Spain, Holland, France, and England. These people saw the new world as a place to start a new life, to seek better opportunities, to practice their beliefs freely, to seek relief from natural or man-made disasters, or to avoid persecution in their home country.

The pilgrims landed in Massachusetts—although they intended to land in Virginia—where they founded their new Zion, free from the interference of the English government. The Quakers settled in Pennsylvania. Maryland was founded to provide a refuge for the Catholics persecuted in England.

And Spanish Jews, who had settled in Brazil after being expelled from Spain, arrived in New York when the Portuguese took over the former Spanish colony and started the Brazilian inquisition. After the Scottish rebellion was crushed, people from Scotland left for the colonies.

Other immigrants came in groups and provided their special skills to the new cities and settlements: Austrians from Salzburg made silk; Polish and Germans made tar, glass, and tools, and built homes. Later, Italians came and raised grapes. New Jersey was settled by the Swedes; northern Pennsylvania attracted a large number of Germans.

1. Forced Migration

But not everyone who came to the New World did so of their own free will. Many crossed the ocean as indentured servants for landowners in the English colonies.

And as cotton became the most important product in the South, the plantation owners turned to the inhuman trade of African people to create a huge and cheap workforce, while the businessmen of the North conducted the slave trade because it was highly profitable.

By the time the first census of the new republic was taken in 1790, the four million inhabitants were two-thirds English-speaking, and the rest were from other nations—of whom 59,000 were free African-Americans, while 698,000 lived in human bondage, mostly in the South.

Although the U.S. Congress amended the Constitution in 1808 to ban the importation of slaves, it took nearly half a century before the smuggling of human beings stopped.

2. European Exodus

Between 1820 and 1910, Europe experienced the greatest migration of people to the New World. During that time, at least 38 million Europeans arrived in the United States.

Several important events caused this great migration: the Napoleonic Wars; the political disturbances in Germany, Austria-Hungary, Greece, and Poland; the Potato Famine in Ireland; the religious persecutions of Protestants, Catholics, and Jews in Czarist Russia and other parts of Europe; and the Industrial Revolution, which created thousands of unemployed workers and peasants.

3. Growth of the Continental U.S.

At the same time, the United States was expanding into the West and the Southwest all the way to the Pacific Coast. The country grew by purchase, such as the Louisiana Purchase from Napoleon I of France, which bought an expanse of land from the Mississippi to the Rocky Mountains, and the purchase of Florida from Spain. It grew by war, such as the one waged with Mexico for California and Texas, or with Britain in 1812, which ended with a treaty granting the United States parts of Canada. The nation grew by treaty with, purchase from, or the outright massacre of the Native American tribes for the possession of their ancestral lands.

B. Early Immigration Restrictions

In California, the Gold Rush of 1849 brought not only people from all over America but also the Chinese from across the Pacific Ocean. Chinese workers provided cheap labor for the construction of the Union Pacific Railroad. However, they were not granted the right to become American citizens.

By 1882, there were approximately 300,000 low-wage Chinese laborers in America. These new workers were targeted by Americans for antagonism and racial hatred. As a result, the Chinese Exclusion Act was passed in 1882, completely banning noncitizen Chinese from immigrating to the United States. This law remained in effect until 1943.

The Japanese then took the place of the Chinese in agriculture, domestic work, lumber mills, and salmon fisheries. By 1920, approximately 200,000 Japanese immigrants were found on the East Coast and 100,000 more on the sugar plantations in Hawaii. These Japanese workers also were subjected to racial hatred and were excluded from the United States in 1908 and prohibited from becoming U.S. citizens by the Immigration Act of 1924.

Also during this time, when America purchased the Philippines from Spain in 1898, the Filipinos were able to immigrate and were concentrated mostly on the East Coast and Hawaii as laborers on farms and sugar plantations, and in fish canneries and logging camps. These Filipinos were not spared the racial animosity that permeated American society—and they also were excluded from citizenship by the immigration laws passed in 1924.

This great influx of people in the late 19th and early 20th centuries brought the passage of several restrictive immigration laws. At various times, the U.S. Congress forbade people it considered undesirable to enter—paupers, drunkards, anarchists, polygamists, and people of various specific national origins.

In 1917, an Immigration Act was passed to restrict the entry of immigrants, especially the flow of illiterate laborers from central and eastern Europe. This law marked the beginning of a great change in American immigration policy. No immigration was permitted to the United States from the Asiatic Barred Zone. In addition to China and Japan, this zone included India, Siam (Thailand), Indochina (Vietnam, Cambodia, and Laos), Afghanistan, parts of Siberia, Iran, and Arabia, and the islands of Java, Sumatra, Ceylon, Borneo, New Guinea, and Celebes.

After World War I, America faced economic depression and unemployment, and the immigrant became the scapegoat for hard times. In 1921, a tight national-origins quota system was enacted as a temporary measure. Total immigration was limited to about 350,000 per year. Immigration from each country in a given year was limited to 3% of all nationals from that country who were living in the United States during the 1910 census.

This system was made permanent when the U.S. Congress approved the National Origins Act of 1924. Its purpose was "to arrest a trend toward a change in the fundamental composition of the American stock." Based on the ethnic composition of the United States as recorded in the 1920 census, it limited the entry of aliens from any one country to 2% of the number of their people living in the United States. In one stroke, the law reduced the total immigration of aliens from all countries to 150,000 per year.

The object of the law was not simply to limit immigration but to favor certain kinds of immigrants and keep out others. More immigrants were permitted from western Europe and fewer from southern and eastern Europe. The law totally excluded Asians. It was intended mainly to prohibit Chinese, Japanese, and Filipinos from acquiring U.S. citizenship.

The American door, for so long left wide open to "all the tired, the poor, the huddled masses yearning to breathe free," was all but closed against future immigrants for the next 40 years.

After World War II, however, the door would again open—this time, for a few carefully selected groups of immigrants. A new category of naturalized Americans was admitted: thousands of alien soldiers had earned citizenship by serving with the U.S. Armed Forces overseas during the war.

Congress also passed the War Brides Act in 1945 to facilitate the reunion of 118,000 alien spouses and children with members of the U.S. armed forces who had fought and married overseas.

The Displaced Persons Act of 1948 allowed 400,000 refugees to be admitted to the U.S. over the next two years. Most of them had been displaced during the war from Poland, Romania, Hungary, the Baltic area, the Ukraine, and Yugoslavia, and had been placed in refugee camps in Germany, Italy, and Austria.

When the Iron Curtain fell on eastern Europe, the Refugee Relief Act of 1953 allowed 214,000 refugees from the Communist countries to be admitted into the United States. The Anti-Soviet fighters from Hungary, after the suppression of their revolution in 1956, were paroled into the United States—that is, allowed to enter without a visa.

C. Today's Immigration Laws

When the Immigration and Nationality Act was passed in 1952, it wove all the existing immigration laws into one and formed a basic immigration law that's similar to how we know it now. (However, it was not until President Lyndon Johnson signed the 1965 amendments into law that the racially-biased National Origin Quota was abolished.)

The amendments introduced two general ways of becoming an immigrant: by family relationship and by the employment needs of the United States. The legislation established a preference system—giving priority to some groups of immigrants over others. For example, spouses and children of American citizens had higher priority than business workers. The law also provided a separate category for refugees.

1. Preference for Skilled Workers

In 1965, the laws were amended to allow skilled workers to move more easily to the United States. The departure of doctors, lawyers, engineers, scientists, teachers, accountants, nurses, and other professionals caused a "brain drain" not only in Europe, but also in Asia, the Pacific Rim, and developing countries.

This preference for skilled workers remains in effect. Although the laws allow a few unskilled workers to immigrate, the numbers are so limited that the category is useless for many people.

2. Refugees and Political Asylum

The end of the Vietnam War resulted in a flow of refugees from the Indochinese peninsula.

In 1980, Fidel Castro declared that the Port of Mariel was open to anyone who wanted to leave. Cuban refugees arrived on the shores of Florida by the thousands. These included some criminals and mentally ill people who had been forced by Castro to leave the jails and mental hospitals.

In response, the U.S. Congress passed the Refugee Act of 1980, which defined a "refugee" as someone who fears persecution in his or her home country because of religious or political beliefs, race, national origin, or ethnic identity.

3. Undocumented Workers

The door opened wider with the Immigration Reform and Control Act of 1986, more commonly known as the "Amnesty Law." This law benefited a large number of Mexicans and other aliens who had entered and been living without legal status in the United States since January 1, 1982. More than two million aliens were granted legal residency.

At the same time, the Amnesty Law attempted to control the future influx of undocumented aliens into the United States—and those controls still exist today. Any employer who hires or recruits an alien, or who, for a fee, refers an alien to another employer without first verifying the alien's immigration status, is subject to a fine ranging from $200 to $10,000 for each undocumented alien employed.

4. Immigration Acts Since 1990

With the Immigration Act of 1990, the U.S. Congress approved its most comprehensive overhaul of immigration law since 1965.

This act provided for a huge increase of immigrants, to 700,000 annually in 1992, 1993, and 1994, and to 675,000 from 1995. It aimed to attract immigrants who have the education, skills, or money to enhance the economic life of the country, while at the same time maintaining the immigration policy of family reunification. The law therefore makes it easier for scientists, engineers, inventors, and other highly skilled professionals to enter the United States. Millionaire entrepreneurs have their own immigrant classification.

Citizens of nations that have had little immigration to the United States for the past five years are allocated 50,000 immigrant visas yearly under the "lottery" system. The spouses and children of illegal immigrants who were granted amnesty under the 1986 law are also entitled to become permanent residents.

Temporary protections were added for people fleeing war or natural disasters, such as earthquakes. Refugees from the civil war in El Salvador were the first beneficiaries.

Such provisions made the Immigration Act of 1990 the most humane legislation for immigrants in the past century. However, more recent changes again closed America's doors to many immigrants. These changes included 1996's Antiterrorism and Effective Death Penalty Act (AEDPA) and Illegal Immigration Reform and Immigrant Responsibility Act (IIRIRA).

And a variety of legislative and regulatory changes have been added since the terrorist attacks of September 11, 2001, tightening controls on would-be immigrants as well as those who are already here. The most notable of these were the USA PATRIOT Act of 2002, which expanded the definition of terrorism and increased the government's authority to detain and deport immigrants, and the November 2002 legislation establishing the new Department of Homeland Security (DHS) and breaking the Immigration and Naturalization Service (INS) into three agencies under the DHS's power. These three new agencies include the U.S. Citizenship and Immigration Services (USCIS), which took over the most public INS functions, such as deciding on applications for immigration benefits; Immigration and Customs Enforcement (ICE), which now handles enforcement of the immigration laws within the U.S. borders; and the Customs and Border Protection (CBP), which now handles U.S. border enforcement (including at land borders, airports, and seaports). These changes further illustrate that the immigration policy of the United States constantly shifts according to the needs and national purpose of its multiethnic and multiracial people.

D. Looking Forward

Immigration law policies have become a subject of ongoing congressional scrutiny, change, and then reverse change. With every shift in the U.S. economy and sense of security, public attitudes toward immigrants shift as well.

But the opening lines of the Declaration of Independence of the United States of America, so eloquently written by Thomas Jefferson some 200 years ago, remain both an inspiration and a challenge:

We hold these truths to be self-evident, that all men are created equal, that they are endowed by their Creator with certain unalienable Rights, that among these are Life, Liberty, and the pursuit of Happiness. ■

Overview of Green Card Categories

But, It Isn't Even Green!

The official name for the green card is the Alien Registration Receipt Card. It has been called a green card because, when it was first introduced in the 1940s, the color of the plastic identification card with the alien's photo, registration number, date of birth, and date and port of entry was green.

The card was blue in the 1960s through the 1970s. In the 1980s, the government changed it to white. Since the 1990s, it has been pink. Even so, this sought-after plastic card continues to be called the green card.

Front of New-Style Card

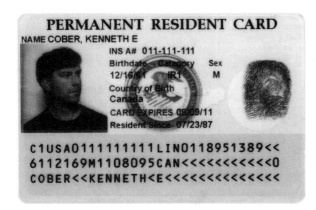

Back of Old-Style Card

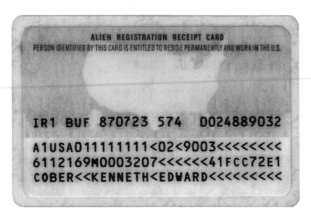

There are several ways an alien can obtain a green card—that is, become a lawful permanent resident. The most popular ones are through family and work. However, there are a number of other ways, such as proving that you're fleeing from persecution, making large investments, or others.

This book covers the green card categories most readily available to ordinary people, with an emphasis on family categories. However, this chapter will tell you a little about the other major green card categories, and tell you where to go next if you're interested in them.

A. Family-Based Relationships

Recognizing that the family is important in the life of the nation, the U.S. Congress has created ways for family members to be reunited with their relatives who are U.S. citizens or lawful permanent residents.

1. Related or Engaged to a U.S. Citizen

If you are the spouse, child, brother, sister, or parent of, or are engaged to be married to, a U.S. citizen, you can become a lawful permanent resident. The person to whom you're related or engaged must start the process by filing a petition with USCIS or the U.S. embassy of your country of residence.

If you are the widow or the widower of a U.S. citizen with whom you have lived for at least two years, you can petition for a green card for yourself, provided you file the application within two years of the death of your spouse.

2. Related to a Lawful Permanent Resident

If you are the spouse or unmarried child of a lawful permanent resident, you can obtain a green card—someday. First, the relative who has the green card must file a petition with USCIS or the U.S. embassy of your country of residence. But you'll have to wait several years, until you reach the top of a waiting list, to apply for the actual green card.

3. Other Relatives

If you are the aunt, uncle, niece, nephew, cousin, grandmother, or grandfather of a U.S. citizen, or if you are the brother, sister, parent, or fiancé of someone who holds a green card, you do not qualify for a green card based on a "family relationship." Understandably, the U.S. Congress had to draw the line on what constitutes a family for the purpose of immigration.

If you believe you qualify for a family-based green card, or are helping someone who does, here's where to go next: Readers who are engaged to U.S. citizens, see Chapter 6. Readers who are married to U.S. citizens or permanent residents, see Chapter 7. Readers who are parents of U.S. citizens, see Chapter 8. Readers who are children of U.S. citizens or permanent residents, see Chapter 9. If you're an Amerasian child born in Korea, Vietnam, Laos, Cambodia, or Thailand, see Chapter 12. For how to bring in an orphan child, see Chapter 10. Readers who are brothers or sisters of U.S. citizens, see Chapter 13.

B. Employment-Based Relationships

If you do not have a close family member who is a U.S. citizen or who holds a green card, you may be able to obtain a green card through a job offer from an employer in the United States—as either a priority or a non-priority worker.

1. Priority Workers

Priority workers are people with extraordinary ability (such as an internationally known artist), outstanding professors and researchers, and multinational executives and managers. Another name for this category is "employment first preference."

Such highly skilled aliens have a relatively easy immigration process. Some do not even need a job offer, and none are required to go through the difficult labor certification process that other immigrating workers do, in which the Department of Labor determines that there are no Americans or lawful permanent residents available and willing to do the same job.

2. Other Workers

Applicants who have been offered jobs that require graduate degrees in the arts or sciences or a profession (such as a law degree), or a master's degree in business administration (MBA), or a bachelor's degree plus five years of specialized experience are eligible for immigrant visas. This category is known as "employment second preference."

These applicants need certification from the Department of Labor to obtain green cards. (Congress was able to meet the objections of the labor unions with this requirement of labor certification by giving the unions the right to notify the Labor Department that an American or permanent resident is available, willing, and able to do the work of the alien.)

Also, ordinary professionals (without graduate degrees), or skilled or unskilled workers (factory workers, plumbers, domestic workers, carpenters, and the like) may apply for labor certification and a green card on the basis of a job offer. This category is known as "employment-based third preference."

If you believe you qualify for any of these employment-based green cards, consult an experienced immigration attorney. As explained earlier, this book doesn't cover employment-based immigration. The employer who has offered you a job (and you must have a job offer in almost all categories described above) may have an attorney it works with regularly. The employer may even be willing to pay the attorney's fees. If you'll be selecting your own attorney, see Chapter 24 for tips.

Be Ready to Wait

It may take you a long time to become a permanent resident under some of the immigrant visa categories described in this chapter. Once you file the first petition form to set the process in motion, however, it may become very difficult for you to come to the United States as a tourist or other nonimmigrant, or to have your status as a nonimmigrant extended.

The only groups who need not be concerned with this warning are diplomats (A visas), employees of international organizations (G visas), intracompany transferees (L-1 or L-2 visas), and workers in specialty occupations that require a bachelor's degree or its equivalent (H-1B visas).

C. Special Immigrants

Certain categories of people may obtain a green card by special laws—in addition to certain provisions of the Immigration Act of 1990—intended to benefit limited groups. These include, for example:

- priests, nuns, pastors, ministers, rabbis, imams, and other workers of recognized religious denominations
- former employees of the U.S. government, commended by the U.S. Secretary of State for having performed outstanding service to the government for at least 15 years
- medical doctors who have been licensed in the United States and have worked and lived in the United States since January 1978
- former employees of the Panama Canal Zone
- retired officers or employees of certain international organizations who have lived in the United States for a certain time, plus their spouses and unmarried children

- foreign workers who have been employees of the U.S. consulate in Hong Kong for at least three years
- foreign children who have been declared dependent in juvenile courts in the United States, and
- international broadcasting employees.

All these people fall into a green card category known as "employment-based fourth preference."

If you believe you fit one of these categories, consult an experienced immigration attorney. Your employer may be willing to hire one for you.

D. Entrepreneur Immigrants

An alien entrepreneur from any country who invests at least one million dollars in a business (or $500,000 if the business is in an economically depressed area) and who employs at least ten U.S. citizens or lawful permanent residents is eligible for a green card. Each year, 10,000 immigrant visas are set aside for this millionaire immigrant category, which is designed to create employment. This category is also known as "employment-based fifth preference."

Are you are financially able to qualify for a green card based on investment? If so, it's well worth hiring an experienced immigration attorney to help.

E. Asylum and Refugee Status

People who can prove that they fled their country for fear of persecution owing to their race, religion, nationality, membership in a particular social or political group, or political opinions may apply for legal status as refugees and asylees. A person who gains U.S. government approval as a refugee or asylee can apply for permanent residence status one year after being admitted to the United States as a refugee or one year after their petition for asylee status is granted. There is no yearly quota or limit on the number of refugees who can be granted permanent residency. But only 10,000 asylees each year can obtain permanent residency. Since the number of asylees applying for permanent residence is currently over 10,000, there is a waiting list.

 For more information on applying for refugee or asylee status, see Chapter 14.

F. Amnesties

Once in a while, Congress gives blanket green card eligibility to people who have been living in the United States illegally. Recent amnesties have covered:

- Aliens who applied for amnesty under the Immigration Reform and Control Act of 1986—having been in the United States out of status since January 1, 1982. Their spouses and unmarried children under 21 years of age were also eligible to become permanent residents.

- Nicaraguans, Cubans, Guatemalans, Salvadorans, and certain Eastern Europeans, under the NACARA law.

While the deadline for both these amnesties have passed, many people's cases are still being decided by USCIS and the courts.

Interested in learning more about a past or upcoming Amnesty? Consult an experienced immigration attorney or a local nonprofit. Do not go to a USCIS office unless you want to risk deportation. ■

Short-Term Alternatives to a Green Card

Temporary Visas for Spending Time in the United States

As you know, this book is only about green cards—or, in legal-speak, U.S. permanent residence. However, you probably also know that many people who want U.S. green cards will never be able to get one. The green card categories are very limited, and the application process is hard to get through successfully. That's why this chapter will briefly tell you about some other—sometimes easier—ways to come to the United States, even if it's for a shorter time.

 Want to learn more about the ways to stay temporarily in the United States? See *U.S. Immigration Made Easy*, by Laurence A. Canter and Martha S. Siegel (Nolo).

A. How Do Foreigners Enter the United States?

The basic rule is that you may enter the United States only after receiving permission from the U.S. government, through the U.S. embassy or consulate in your own country. The permission or authority to enter the United States is called a "visa," and is stamped in your passport by the U.S. consul. The exception is if you are eligible to enter under the Visa Waiver Program; see discussion in Section C, below.

If you enter the United States without permission, without a visa or a visa waiver, and without being examined by the immigration authorities, you are called an "undocumented alien" within the immigration laws and an "illegal alien" by the general public.

B. Types of Visas

There are two kinds of visas an alien can receive from the U.S. embassy or consulate: an immigrant visa and a nonimmigrant visa.

1. Immigrant Visas

Just to avoid confusion, we should mention that even those people who are in the process of getting a green card, as discussed in the rest of this book, must get a visa first if they'll be arriving from another country. They receive what is called an "immigrant visa." They receive the actual green card only after they have arrived in the United States and claimed their permanent residency.

2. Nonimmigrant Visas

Nonimmigrant visas are the main topic we'd like to introduce you to in this short chapter. A nonimmigrant visa gives you the ability to stay in the United States temporarily with limited rights. We understand that a visa that expires in a few years is probably your second choice, given that you're reading a book on green cards. However, a nonimmigrant visa might serve you in two different ways. First, it might allow you to legally visit the United States in order to decide whether you really want a green card, or to make a decision that will lead to your getting a green card. For example, a person might come to the U.S. on a tourist (B-2) visa to visit his or her U.S. citizen boyfriend or girlfriend, to find out whether getting married seems like a good idea.

Second, a nonimmigrant visa might be your only choice for the moment. If your research, using this and other books, leads you to believe that you don't qualify for a green card, then a nonimmigrant visa might allow you to at least live in the United States for a while, hoping that a green card opportunity will open up, or developing U.S. contacts or job skills.

Unfortunately, nonimmigrant visas are not only short-term solutions, but they restrict your life in the United States in other ways. For example, a tourist visa (B-2) does not allow you to work. A student visa (F-1 or M-1) does not allow a student to stop studying to work. A temporary worker's visa (H-1B), given to a professional worker such as an accountant or engineer, does not authorize you to change employers without permission.

3. Nonimmigrant Visa Classifications

You will often hear visa classifications referred to in shorthand by a letter followed by a number. The following list summarizes the nonimmigrant visa classifications available.

A-1   Ambassadors, public ministers, consular officers, or career diplomats, and their immediate families

A-2   Other foreign government officials or employees, and their immediate families

A-3   Personal attendants, servants, or employees, and their immediate families, of A-1 and A-2 visa holders

B-1   Temporary business visitors

B-2   Temporary pleasure visitors

C-1   Foreign travelers in immediate and continuous transit through the U.S.

D-1   Crewmembers (sea or air)

E-1   Treaty traders and their spouses or children

E-2   Treaty investors and their spouses or children

F-1   Academic or language students

F-2   Spouses or children of F-1 visa holders

G-1   Designated principal resident representatives of foreign governments, coming to the U.S. to work for an international organization, and their staff members and immediate families

G-2   Other representatives of foreign governments coming to the U.S. to work for an international organization, and their immediate families

G-3   Representatives of foreign governments and their immediate families, who would ordinarily qualify for G-1 or G-2 visas except that their governments are not members of an international organization

G-4   Officers or employees of international organizations, and their immediate families

G-5   Attendants, servants, and personal employees of G-1 through G-4 visa holders, and their immediate families

H-1B   Aliens working in specialty occupations requiring at least a bachelor's degree or its equivalent in on-the-job experience

H-2A   Temporary agricultural workers coming to the U.S. to fill positions for which a temporary shortage of American workers has been recognized by the U.S. Department of Agriculture

H-2B   Temporary workers of various kinds coming to the U.S. to perform temporary jobs for which there is a shortage of available qualified U.S. workers

H-3   Temporary trainees

H-4   Spouses or children of H-1A/B, H-2A/B, or H-3 visa holders

I   Representatives of the foreign press, coming to the U.S. to work solely in that capacity, and their immediate families

J-1   Exchange visitors coming to the U.S. to study, work, or train as part of an exchange program officially recognized by the U.S. Department of State

J-2   Spouses or children of J-1 visa holders

K-1   Fiancés and fiancées of U.S. citizens coming to the U.S. for the purpose of getting married

K-2   Children of K-1 visa holders

K-3   Spouses of U.S. citizens awaiting approval of their immigrant visa petition or the availability of a green card

K-4   Children of K-3 visa holders

L-1   Intracompany transferees who work as managers, executives, or persons with specialized knowledge

L-2   Spouses or children of L-1 visa holders

M-1   Vocational or other nonacademic students

M-2   Immediate families of M-1 visa holders

N   Children of certain special immigrants

NATO-1   Principal permanent representatives of member states to NATO—including any subsidiary bodies, residents in the U.S., and resident official staff members, secretaries general, assistant secretaries general, and executive secretaries of

NATO, other permanent NATO officials of similar rank, or their immediate families

NATO-2 Other representatives to member states to NATO—including any subsidiary bodies, including its advisers and technical experts of delegations, members of Immediate Article 3, 4 UST 1796 families; dependents of members of forces entering in accordance with the Status-of-Forces Agreement or in accordance with the Protocol on Status of International Military Headquarters; members of such a force if issued

NATO-3 Official clerical staff accompanying representatives of member states to NATO—including any subsidiary bodies, or their immediate families

NATO-4 Officials of NATO—other than those who can be classified as NATO-1, or their immediate families

NATO-5 Experts—other than officials who can be classified as NATO-1, employed on missions in behalf of NATO, and their dependents

NATO-6 Members of civilian components accompanying forces entering in accordance with provisions of the NATO Status-of-Forces Agreement; members of civilian components attached to or employed by allied headquarters under the Protocol on Status of International Military Headquarters set up pursuant to the North Atlantic Treaty; and their dependents

NATO-7 Attendants, servants, or personal employees of NATO-1 through NATO-6 classes, and their immediate families

O-1   Aliens of extraordinary ability in the sciences, arts, education, business, or athletics

O-2   Support staff of O-1 visa holders

O-3   Spouses or children of O-1 or O-2 visa holders

P-1   Internationally recognized athletes and entertainers

P-2   Artists or entertainers in reciprocal exchange programs

P-3   Artists and entertainers coming to the U.S. to give culturally unique performances in a group

P-4   Spouses or children of P-1, P-2, or P-3 visa holders

Q-1   Participants in international cultural exchange programs

Q-3   Immediate family members of Q-1 visa holders

R-1   Aliens in religious occupations

R-2   Spouses or children of R-1 visa holders

S-5   Certain aliens supplying critical information relating to a criminal organization or enterprise

S-6   Certain aliens supplying critical information relating to terrorism

S-7   Immediate family members of S-1 visa holders

T   Women and children who are in the United States because they are victims of trafficking, who are cooperating with law enforcement, and who fear extreme hardship (such as retribution) if returned home

TN   NAFTA professionals from Canada or Mexico

TD   Spouses and children of NAFTA professionals

V   Spouses and children of lawful permanent residents who have been waiting for three years or more to qualify for a green card

C. Tourists Who Can Visit Without a Visa

The Visa Waiver Program allows the citizens of certain countries—that the Department of State (DOS) chooses—to visit the United States for 90 days without first having a tourist visa stamped on their passports.

The Visa Waiver Program was originally set up to eliminate the useless paperwork involved in processing tourist visas for applicants who were clearly temporary visitors. All that visitors require is a passport and a round-trip ticket.

EXAMPLE: You want to visit the United States for two months. If you live in a country that is included in the Visa Waiver Program, you can take a plane to the United States without first visiting a U.S. consulate to get a tourist visa. You will, however, be required to show a round-trip ticket, as evidence that you are simply visiting and that you will return to your country within the 90-day limit.

1. Countries Exempted

Under the Visa Waiver Program, citizens of the following countries who can present a machine-readable passport are exempted from getting visas before entering the United States:

Andorra	Holland	Norway
Australia	(Netherlands)	Portugal
Austria	Iceland	San Marino
Belgium	Ireland	Singapore
Brunei	Italy	Slovenia
Denmark	Japan	Spain
Finland	Liechtenstein	Sweden
France	Luxembourg	Switzerland
Germany	Monaco	
Great Britain	New Zealand	
(United Kingdom)		

To be included in the Visa Waiver Program, the country must have:

- a very low rate of refusals of tourist visa applications, and
- few violations of U.S. immigration laws.

In short, countries whose citizens are least likely to stay too long or work illegally in the United States are most likely to be included in the Visa Waiver Program.

2. Procedure Required

While on the plane to your U.S. destination, you will be handed Form I-94W, Arrival/Departure Record for the Visa Waiver Program, which asks for simple information, including your:

- name
- birthdate
- country of citizenship
- passport number
- airline and flight number
- country where you live
- city where you boarded the airplane, and
- address while staying in the United States.

You must use an ink pen to fill out the form. Print neatly, in all capital letters. The questions on Form I-94W are straightforward, and you should have no trouble answering them. However, if you do have questions or problems when filling out the form, a flight attendant should be able to help you—or ask immigration officers for assistance when you land.

On the bottom half of Form I-94W, you will write in your name, birthdate, and country of citizenship. That portion of the form will later be stamped by immigration officers with the port of entry, the dates you were admitted, and the date by which you must leave the U.S., and the type of visa—and will be attached to your passport.

Disadvantages of Entering Without a Visa

There may be disadvantages to entering the U.S. under the Visa Waiver Program without first getting a visa.

For starters, if you are inadmissible (see Chapter 4) or if you have violated the terms of the Visa Waiver Program in the past, you will probably not be allowed to enter the U.S. on a visa waiver. That means you will be turned around and sent home to apply for a visitor visa at the consulate.

If you are allowed into the U.S., realize that you cannot change your tourist status to another nonimmigrant status, such as that of student or temporary worker, nor can you request an extension of your 90-day stay.

With few exceptions, you also cannot change your status to a lawful permanent resident.

In addition, should the border officials deny you entry into the United States for any reason, you have no right to appeal. Political refugees who are fleeing persecution and who apply for asylum in the United States are the sole exceptions. (See Chapter 14.)

 Need more information on the process of obtaining student or tourist visas? See *Student & Tourist Visas: How to Come to the U.S.*, by Ilona Bray and Richard Boswell (Nolo).

D. The Importance of Staying Legal

If you enter the United States as a tourist, student, temporary worker, entertainer, or any other nonimmigrant category, your chances at a future green card depend on your maintaining your legal status and not violating the conditions of your stay in the United States. Do not overstay the limits of your visa. Do not work when you are not authorized to work. Do not change schools or employers without first requesting and receiving permission from the immigration authorities.

The consequences for breaking the rules controlling immigration may be quite serious: You could be detained in an immigration jail; removal proceedings could be started against you; and, if deported, you could be barred from returning to the United States for the next five years. Even if you are not deported, if you overstay by 180 days (around six months) and then leave the United States, you will have to stay outside for three years before being admitted again. If you overstay by 12 months and then leave, the waiting period is ten years before you will be allowed to return. (See Chapter 4.)

More to the point, by staying within the law, you can make use of almost all the ways enumerated in this book to stay in the United States for as long as your status is legal.

If you are running out of time, one possibility is to apply to extend your stay (if you can show a good reason for needing more time) or change your status, for example from tourist to student or from student to temporary worker. You can apply only if your immigration status is legal, you are not an overstaying visitor, and you have not worked illegally.

If instead you overstay the period written on your I-94 card, your visa will be automatically void—even if it is a multiple entry, indefinite visa. You will then be required to apply for a new visa at the consulate in your home country, unless you can prove "exceptional circumstances."

If there is some question in your case, or to change status, seek professional advice from an immigration support group, specialized clinic, or experienced immigration lawyer. (See Chapter 24.) Do not depend on advice from your friends or relatives.

E. How to Extend a Visitor Visa

Temporary business or tourist visitors—those who hold B-1 or B-2 visas—once admitted to the United States, can apply for an extension of stay. The basis can be business circumstances, other family reasons, or any other good reason consistent with your visa.

For example, if a tourist decides to visit different locations or to spend more time with relatives, he or she can seek an extension. The Application for Extension must be mailed directly to the USCIS Service Center closest to where the applicant lives. (See the USCIS website at www.uscis.gov for contact details.)

The application must include the following:
- Form I-539, Application to Extend/Change Nonimmigrant Status
- Form I-94; a copy may be submitted
- a filing fee (currently $200); either personal check or money order will be accepted
- a company letter or other supporting documentation, stating the reason for the extension request—for example, more business consultations, continuing medical reasons, extended family visit with a complete itinerary
- evidence to show that the visit is temporary— particularly, evidence of continued overseas employment or residence and a return ticket, and
- evidence of financial support, such as the purchase of travelers' checks or a bank letter including amounts in accounts.

Also attach an itinerary or a letter explaining your reasons for requesting the extension.

Be sure you have attached a copy of your Form I-94, Arrival/Departure Record, to your application. It is proof that you arrived in the United States lawfully. Also attach information showing when and how you will depart the United States after your extension, such as a copy of a new plane ticket.

The extension may not give you as much time as you'd like. Extensions of more than six months are rare. However, you are legally allowed to stay until USCIS makes a decision on your extension.

1. When to File

USCIS recommends that you file for an extension at least 45 days before the expiration date of your stay, which is shown on your Form I-94—the white paper attached to your passport when you entered the United States. If you are prone to procrastination, file the request for extension at least 15 days before the expiration date shown on your Form I-94.

2. If Your I-94 Is Missing or Destroyed

Your completed Form I-94 or Form I-95 (Crewman's Landing Permit, issued to crews on ships and airlines)—which is your proof of lawful arrival in the United States—may have been lost, stolen, or damaged. Or perhaps you were not issued the proper form when you entered.

To get the proper documentation, file Form I-102, Application for Replacement/Initial Nonimmigrant Arrival-Departure Document. (See the sample at the end of this chapter.) It currently costs an additional $160 to file this form. This form must accompany your Form I-539, Application to Extend/Change Nonimmigrant Status, if you are asking for this as well.

If you are applying to replace a lost or stolen form, submit a copy of the original Form I-94 or Form I-95 if you have it, or submit a copy of the biographic page from your passport and a copy of the page indicating admission as claimed.

If you have none of these documents because your passport was lost or stolen, you will have to submit other evidence of your admission. USCIS may accept your ticket and an affidavit, which is a written statement that you have sworn to before a notary public, explaining why you cannot provide any of the documents requested. Submit this affidavit with some proof of identity, such as a copy of your work identification card, credit card, or driver's license. If the passport was stolen, be sure to include a copy of the police report with your submission.

If your Form I-94 has been damaged, attach it anyway.

If you were not issued a Form I-94 when you were admitted to the United States, submit a copy of your passport and the page that was stamped by the border officials when you first arrived.

F. Changing Your Reason for Staying

If you wish to request a change of status from one category to another, or apply for a green card, be aware that applying for the change within the first two months after arriving in America may lead to USCIS denying your application based on the theory of "preconceived intent." Preconceived intent simply means that you lied about your reasons for coming to the United States.

For example, if you attempt to change your status from B-2 tourist to H-1B specialty worker soon after arriving in the United States, USCIS may conclude that you had the preconceived intent of working in the United States when you applied for a tourist visa from the U.S. embassy. Your failure to reveal your actual reason for going to the United States when you first requested a visa could be considered to be fraud.

A similar problem can arise for people who want to study in the U.S., but sensibly want to visit some schools and see whether they like them before going through the hassle of filling out application forms. You might think that the logical thing would be to come as a tourist and then, after choosing a school, apply for a change to student status.

However, logic and the immigration laws don't always match up. USCIS may deny this type of applicants' requests to change status, saying that the person lied about his or her intention to be a tourist (the person's real, secret intention was to become a student). Fortunately, this is one of the few immigration law traps that you can get around with advance planning. If, when applying for your tourist visa, you tell the consular official that you may wish to change to student status after looking around, then you can have a "prospective student" notation made in your tourist visa. After that, you'll be free to apply to change status, without worrying that it will look like you lied.

G. What to Do If Your Application Is Denied

If USCIS denies your request for an extension of your stay in the U.S., you could contest the denial. However, this will require help from an experienced immigration lawyer. (See Chapter 24.)

It might be easier to leave the U.S. and apply for a new visa from overseas. This is far safer than staying in the U.S. illegally.

H. Tips on Filling Out Form I-539

Most of Form I-539 is self-explanatory. However, on Part 4 of Form I-539, Additional Information, Questions 3a through f may act as time bombs if you answer "yes" to any one of them—that is, they may explode and prove fatal to your application.

Do not lie and misrepresent your answer as no when the truthful answer is yes. But if you have to answer yes to any of these six questions, it is best to consult with an immigration lawyer or other experienced immigration professional.

EXAMPLE: The first question on this part of the form is: Are you or any other person included in this application an applicant for an immigrant visa or adjustment of status to permanent residence? Do not answer "no" if your U.S. citizen brother filed a relative visa petition for you ten years ago and your immigrant visa is still pending. In all probability, USCIS would find out your fraudulent answer, and you might never get your green card as a result.

Do Not Bring This Book With You

Because this book tells you how to stay and work legally in the United States, you should not have it—or any other book about immigrating to the U.S.—with you when you enter the United States on a tourist or other nonimmigrant visa.

If the border officials suspect that you are not a bona fide tourist, they may detain and question you at the airport or border about your purpose in coming to the United States.

For the same reason, you should not board the plane with letters from your Aunt Mary or cousin John stating that employment has been arranged for you as soon as you arrive in the United States, a wedding dress, or a stack of resumes. Should the border officials find such things when you land, you will not be admitted as a tourist; you may, in fact, be sent back to your home country without being allowed to set foot outside the airport or other port of entry in the United States.

If this happens, you will be unable to return to the U.S. for five years.

Application for Replacement/Initial Nonimmigrant Arrival-Departure Document, Sample Form I-102

OMB No. 1615-0079; Expires 06/30/07

Department of Homeland Security
U.S. Citizenship and Immigration Services

I-102, Application for Replacement/Initial Nonimmigrant Arrival - Departure Document

START HERE - Please type or print in black ink.

For USCIS Use Only

Part 1.   Information about you.

Family Name	Given Name	Middle Name
Khanmohammad	Parirokh	Jamal

Address - In care of -

Hossein Lofti

Street Number and Name
In care of -

	Apt./Suite #
17241 Fulton Street	101

City	State
New York	NY

Zip/Postal Code	Country	Date of Birth (mm/dd/yyyy)
10038	U.S.A.	09/24/68

Country of Birth	Country of Citizenship/Nationality
France	France

A # (if any)	U.S. Social Security # (if any)
None	None

Date (mm/dd/yyyy) and Place of Last Admission	Current Nonimmigrant Status
08/27/06	B-1 Visitor

Status Expires on (mm/dd/yyyy)	I-94, I-94W or I-95 Arrival/Departure Document #
11/26/06	112 113 124

For USCIS Use Only

Returned

Date

Date
Resubmitted

Date

Date
Reloc Sent

Date

Date
Reloc Rec'd

Date

Date

☐ Applicant
Interviewed
on _____

Receipt

New I-94 #

Remarks

Part 2.   Reason for application.

Check the box that best describes your reason for requesting a replacement document. *(Check one box.)*

a.   ☒ I am applying to replace my lost or stolen Form I-94 (or I-94W).

b.   ☐ I am applying to replace my lost or stolen Form I-95.

c.   ☐ I am applying to replace Form I-94 (or I-94W) because it is mutilated. I have attached my original I-94 (or I-94W).

d.   ☐ I am applying to replace Form I-95 because it is mutilated. I have attached my original I-95.

e.   ☐ I was not issued a Form I-94 when I entered as a nonimmigrant, and I am filing this application together with an application for an extension of stay/change of status.

f.   ☐ I was issued a Form I-94, I-94W or Form I-95 with incorrect information, and I am requesting USCIS to correct the document. I have attached my original Form I-94, I-94W or Form I-95.

g.   ☐ I was not issued a Form I-94 when I entered as a nonimmigrant member of the military and I am filing this application for an initial Form I-94.

Action Block

To Be Completed by
Attorney or Representative, if any.
☐ Fill in box if G-28 is attached
to represent the applicant.

ATTY State License #

Form I-102 Form (Rev. 10/26/05)Y

Sample Form I-102 (Page 2)

Part 3.   Processing information.

1. Are you filing this application with any other petition or application?

   ☐ No   ☒ Yes - Form #   I-539

2. Are you now in removal proceedings?

   ☒ No

   ☐ Yes (Give detailed information regarding the proceedings. If you need more space to complete the answer, use a separate sheet(s) of paper. Write your name and A #, if any, and "Part 3, Number 2" at the top of each sheet.)

3. If you are unable to provide the original of your Form I-94, I-94W or I-95, give the following information:

   Your name exactly as it appears on Form I-94, I-94W or I-95, if known *(print clearly)*

   Parirokh J. Khanmohammad

   Class of Admission: Place of Admission:

   B-1   Newark, NJ

Part 4.   Signature.   *Read the information on penalties in the instructions before completing this section. You must file this application while in the United States.*

I certify, under penalty of perjury under the laws of the United States of America, that this application and the evidence submitted with it is all true and correct. I authorize the release of any information from my records that the U.S. Citizenship and Immigration Services needs to determine eligibility for the benefit I am seeking.

Signature   **Daytime Telephone Number** *(with area code)*   **Date** *(mm/dd/yyyy)*

Parirokh J. Khanmohammad   (212) 555-1212   09/19/2006

Part 5.   Signature of person preparing form, if other than above.   *(Sign below.)*

I declare that I prepared this application at the request of the above person and it is based on all information of which I have knowledge.

Signature   **Print or Type Your Name**

Firm Name   **Firm Address** *(Street Number and Name or P.O. Box, City, State, Zip Code)*

Daytime Telephone Number *(with area code)*   **E-Mail Address** *(if any)*   **Date** *(mm/dd/yyyy)*

(   )

Application to Extend/Change Nonimmigrant Status, Sample Form I-539 (page 1)

OMB No. 1115-0093; Expires 11/30/07

Department of Homeland Security
U.S. Citizenship and Immigration Services

**I-539, Application to Extend/
Change Nonimmigrant Status**

START HERE - Please type or print in black ink.

For USCIS Use Only

Part 1.   Information about you.

Family Name	Given Name	Middle Name
Martino	Tony	F.

Address -
In care of -   Antero Martino

Street Number and Name 3746 81st St.	Apt. # 2D

City	State	Zip Code	Daytime Phone #
Jackson Heights	NY	11372	718-555-1212

Country of Birth	Country of Citizenship
Philippines	Philippines

Date of Birth (mm/dd/yyyy) 08/02/69	U. S. Social Security # (if any) None	A # (if any) None

Date of Last Arrival Into the U.S. 02/05/06	I-94 # 334533908 03

Current Nonimmigrant Status B-2	Expires on (mm/dd/yyyy) 08/04/06

For USCIS Use Only

Returned	Receipt
Date	
Resubmitted	
Date	
Reloc Sent	
Date	
Reloc Rec'd	
Date	

Part 2. Application type. *(See instructions for fee.)*

1. I am applying for: *(Check one.)*
   a. ☑ An extension of stay in my current status.
   b. ☐ A change of status. The new status I am requesting is: _____
   c. ☐ Other: *(Describe grounds of eligibility.)* _____

2. Number of people included in this application: *(Check one.)*
   a. ☐ I am the only applicant.
   b. ☑ Members of my family are filing this application with me.
   The total number of people (including me) in the application is: 2
   (Complete the supplement for each co-applicant.)

☐ Applicant
Interviewed
on
_____
Date

☐ *Extension Granted to (Date):*
_____

Change of Status/Extension Granted
New Class: From *(Date)*: _____
_____ To *(Date)*: _____

Part 3. Processing information.

1. I/We request that my/our current or requested status be extended until (mm/dd/yyyy):   01/15/06

2. Is this application based on an extension or change of status already granted to your spouse, child or parent?
☑ No ☐ Yes. USCIS Receipt # _____

3. Is this application based on a separate petition or application to give your spouse, child or parent an extension or change of status? ☑ No ☐ Yes, filed with this I-539.

   ☐ Yes, filed previously and pending with USCIS. Receipt #: _____

4. If you answered "Yes" to Question 3, give the name of the petitioner or applicant: _____

If the petition or application is pending with USCIS, also give the following data:

Office filed at	Filed on (mm/dd/yyyy)

If Denied:
☐ Still within period of stay
☐ S/D to: _____
☐ Place under docket control

Remarks:

Action Block

Part 4. Additional information.

1. For applicant #1, provide passport information: Valid to: (mm/dd/yyyy)
Country of Issuance   Philippines   01/16/08

2. Foreign Address: Street Number and Name   Apt. #
   66 Felix Manalo St.

City or Town Cubao, Quezon City	State or Province

Country Philippines	Zip/Postal Code 1111

To Be Completed by
Attorney or Representative, if any

☐ Fill in box if G-28 is attached to represent the applicant.

ATTY State License #

Form I-539 (Rev. 04/01/06)Y

Sample Form I-539 (page 2)

Part 4. Additional information.

3. Answer the following questions. If you answer "Yes" to any question, explain on separate sheet of paper.	Yes	No
a. Are you, or any other person included on the application, an applicant for an immigrant visa?	☐	☑
b. Has an immigrant petition ever been filed for you or for any other person included in this application?	☐	☑
c. Has a Form I-485, Application to Register Permanent Residence or Adjust Status, ever been filed by you or by any other person included in this application?	☐	☑
d. Have you, or any other person included in this application, ever been arrested or convicted of any criminal offense since last entering the U.S.?	☐	☑
e. Have you, or any other person included in this application, done anything that violated the terms of the nonimmigrant status you now hold?	☐	☑
f. Are you, or any other person included in this application, now in removal proceedings?	☐	☑
g. Have you, or any other person included in this application, been employed in the U.S. since last admitted or granted an extension or change of status?	☐	☑

- If you answered "Yes" to Question 3f, give the following information concerning the removal proceedings on the attached page entitled "**Part 4. Additional information. Page for answers to 3f and 3g.**" Include the name of the person in removal proceedings and information on jurisdiction, date proceedings began and status of proceedings.

- If you answered "No" to Question 3g, fully describe how you are supporting yourself on the attached page entitled "**Part 4. Additional information. Page for answers to 3f and 3g.**" Include the source, amount and basis for any income.

- If you answered "Yes" to Question 3g, fully describe the employment on the attached page entitled "**Part 4. Additional information. Page for answers to 3f and 3g.**" Include the name of the person employed, name and address of the employer, weekly income and whether the employment was specifically authorized by USCIS.

Part 5. Signature. (*Read the information on penalties in the instructions before completing this section. You must file this application while in the United States.*)

I certify, under penalty of perjury under the laws of the United States of America, that this application and the evidence submitted with it is all true and correct. I authorize the release of any information from my records that U.S. Citizenship and Immigration Services needs to determine eligibility for the benefit I am seeking.

Signature _Tony F. Martino_	Print your Name Tony F. Martino	Date 6/29/06
Daytime Telephone Number 718-555-1212	E-Mail Address tonytourist@hotmail.com	

NOTE: *If you do not completely fill out this form or fail to submit required documents listed in the instructions, you may not be found eligible for the requested benefit and this application may be denied.*

Part 6. Signature of person preparing form, if other than above. *(Sign below.)*

I declare that I prepared this application at the request of the above person and it is based on all information of which I have knowledge.

Signature	Print your Name	Date
Firm Name and Address	Daytime Telephone Number *(Area Code and Number)*	
	Fax Number *(Area Code and Number)*	E-Mail Address

Form I-539 (Rev. 04/01/06)Y Page 2

Sample Form I-539 (page 3)

Part 4. Additional information. Page for answers to 3f and 3g.

If you answered "Yes" to Question 3f in Part 4 on Page 3 of this form, give the following information concerning the removal proceedings. Include the name of the person in removal proceedings and information on jurisdiction, date proceedings began and status of procedings.

If you answered "No" to Question 3g in Part 4 on Page 3 of this form, fully describe how you are supporting yourself. Include the source, amount and basis for any income.

My brother, Antero Martino, will provide my lodging and other support. See attached Form I-134, Affidavit of Support.

If you answered "Yes" to Question 3g in Part 4 on Page 3 of this form, fully describe the employment. Include the name of the person employed, name and address of the employer, weekly income and whether the employment was specifically authorized by USCIS.

Sample Supplement to Form I-539

Supplement -1
Attach to Form I-539 when more than one person is included in the petition or application.
(List each person separately. Do not include the person named in the Form I-539.)

Family Name	Given Name	Middle Name	Date of Birth (mm/dd/yyyy)	
Martino	Eduardo	L.	12/01/93	
Country of Birth	County of Citizenship	U.S. Social Security # (if any)	A # (if any)	
Philippines	Philippines	None		None
Date of Arrival (mm/dd/yyyy)		I-94 #		
02/05/06		334 533 909 03		
Current Nonimmigrant Status:		Expires on (mm/dd/yyyy)		
B-2		08/04/05		
Country Where Passport Issued		Expiration Date (mm/dd/yyyy)		
Philippines		03/08/08		
Family Name	Given Name	Middle Name	Date of Birth (mm/dd/yyyy)	
Martino	Miranda	C.		04/02/69
Country of Birth	Country of Citizenship	U.S. Social Security # (if any)	A # (if any)	
Philippines	Philippines	None	None	
Date of Arrival (mm/dd/yyyy)		I-94 #		
02/05/06		334 533 910 03		
Current Nonimmigrant Status:		Expires on (mm/dd/yyyy)		
B-2		08/04/05		
Country Where Passport Issued		Expiration Date (mm/dd/yyyy)		
Philippines		01/16/07		
Family Name	Given Name	Middle Name	Date of Birth (mm/dd/yyyy)	
Country of Birth	Country of Citizenship	U.S. Social Security # (if any)	A # (if any)	
Date of Arrival (mm/dd/yyyy)		I-94 #		
Current Nonimmigrant Status:		Expires on (mm/dd/yyyy)		
Country Where Passport Issued		Expiration Date (mm/dd/yyyy)		
Family Name	Given Name	Middle Name	Date of Birth (mm/dd/yyyy)	
Country of Birth	Country of Citizenship	U.S. Social Security # (if any)	A # (if any)	
Date of Arrival (mm/dd/yyyy)		I-94 #		
Current Nonimmigrant Status:		Expires on (mm/dd/yyyy)		
Country Where Passport Issued		Expiration Date (mm/dd/yyyy)		
Family Name	Given Name	Middle Name	Date of Birth (mm/dd/yyyy)	
Country of Birth	Country of Citizenship	U.S. Social Security # (if any)	A # (if any)	
Date of Arrival (mm/dd/yyyy)		I-94 #		
Current Nonimmigrant Status:		Expires on (mm/dd/yyyy)		
Country Where Passport Issued		Expiration Date (mm/dd/yyyy)		

If you need additional space, attach a separate sheet(s) of paper.
Place your name, A #, if any, date of birth, form number and application date at the top of the sheet(s) of paper.

Form I-539 (Rev. 04/01/06)Y Page 4

Will Inadmissibility Bar You From Getting a Green Card?

Sorry, You're Not Welcome Here

The U.S. government has decided that people with certain histories or conditions are a risk to others and therefore should not be allowed to enter the country. These people are called "inadmissible." Inadmissibility creates problems in green card applications. This chapter explains the conditions that make a person inadmissible—and whether there is any way under the bar of inadmissibility.

A. Inadmissibility Defined

The U.S. government keeps a list of reasons that make a person unwelcome in the United States. The list includes affliction with various physical and mental disorders, commission of crimes, participation in terrorist or subversive activity, and more.

You may be judged inadmissible any time after you have filed an application for a green card, nonimmigrant visa, or other immigration status. Even a permanent resident who departs the United States for more than 180 days may be found inadmissible upon return.

If you are found inadmissible, your immigration application will be denied. The notice of denial will be issued in the same manner as denials for any other reason. Even if you manage to hide your inadmissibility long enough to receive a green card or visa and be admitted into the U.S., if the problem is discovered later—perhaps when you apply for U.S. citizenship—you can be removed or deported.

B. The Possibility of Waiving Inadmissibility

Not everyone who falls into one of the categories of inadmissibility is absolutely barred from getting a green card or otherwise entering the United States. Some grounds of inadmissibility may be legally excused or waived. Others may not.

Below is a chart summarizing all the grounds of inadmissibility, whether or not a waiver is available, and the special conditions you must meet to get a waiver. For more details, see I.N.A. §212, 8 U.S.C. §1182.

C. Reversing an Inadmissibility Finding

There are four ways to overcome a finding of inadmissibility. Each of them is discussed in some detail below. However, you'll most likely need an attorney's help.

- In the case of physical or mental illness only, you may be able to correct the condition.
- You can prove that you really don't fall into the category of inadmissibility USCIS believes you do.
- You can prove that the accusations of inadmissibility against you are false.
- You can apply for a waiver of inadmissibility.

1. Correcting Grounds of Inadmissibility

If you have had a physical or mental illness that is a ground of inadmissibility and you have been cured of the condition by the time you submit your green card application, you will no longer be considered inadmissible for that reason. If the condition is not cured by the time you apply, with certain illnesses you can still get a waiver of inadmissibility.

2. Proving That Inadmissibility Does Not Apply

Proving that inadmissibility does not apply in your case is a method used mainly to overcome criminal and ideological grounds of inadmissibility. When dealing with criminal grounds of inadmissibility, it is very important to consider both the type of crime committed and the nature of the punishment to see whether your criminal activity really constitutes a ground of inadmissibility.

Inadmissibility		
Ground of Inadmissibility	**Waiver Available**	**Conditions of Waiver**
Health Problems		
Communicable diseases, particularly tuberculosis and HIV (AIDS).	Yes	A waiver is available to a person who is the spouse, unmarried son or daughter, or the unmarried minor lawfully adopted child of a U.S. citizen or permanent resident, or of an alien who has been issued an immigrant visa; or to an individual who has a son or daughter who is a U.S. citizen; or a permanent resident or an alien issued an immigrant visa, upon compliance with USCIS's terms and regulations.
Physical or mental disorders that threaten the property, welfare, and safety of the applicant or others.	Yes	Special conditions required by USCIS, at its discretion.
Drug abusers or addicts.	No	
Failure to show that the applicant has been vaccinated against certain vaccine-preventable diseases.	Yes	The applicant must show either that he or she subsequently received the vaccine, that the vaccine is medically inappropriate as certified by a civil surgeon, or that having the vaccine administered is contrary to the applicant's religious beliefs or moral convictions.
Criminal and Related Violations		
Commission of crimes involving moral turpitude.	Yes	Waivers are not available for commission of crimes such as attempted murder or conspiracy to commit murder, or for murder, torture, or drug crimes, or for people previously admitted as permanent residents, if they have been convicted of aggravated felony since such admission or if they have fewer than seven years of lawful continuous residence before deportation proceedings are initiated against them. Waivers for all other offenses are available only if the applicant is a spouse, parent, or child of a U.S. citizen or green cardholder; or the only criminal activity was prostitution; or the actions occurred more than 15 years before the application for a visa or green card is filed, and the alien shows that he or she is rehabilitated and is not a threat to U.S. security.
Convictions for two or more crimes.	Yes	
Prostitutes or procurers of prostitutes.	Yes	
Diplomats or others involved in serious criminal activity who have received immunity from prosecution.	Yes	

	Inadmissibility	
Ground of Inadmissibility	**Waiver Available**	**Conditions of Waiver**
Drug offenders.	No	However, there may be an exception for a first and only offense or for juvenile offenders. There's also a waiver for simple possession of less than 30 grams of marijuana.
Drug traffickers.	No	
Immediate family members of drug traffickers who knowingly benefited from their illicit money within the last five years	No	But note that the problem "washes out" after five years.
National Security and Related Violations		
Spies, governmental saboteurs, violators of export or technology transfer laws.	No	
People intending to overthrow the U.S. government.	No	
Terrorists and members or representatives of foreign terrorist organizations.	No	
People whose entry would have adverse consequences for U.S. foreign policy, unless the applicant is an official of a foreign government, or the applicant's activities or beliefs would normally be lawful in the U.S., under the Constitution.	No	
Members of totalitarian parties.	Yes	An exception is made if the membership was involuntary, or is or was when the applicant was under 16 years old, by operation of law, or for purposes of obtaining employment, food rations, or other "essentials" of living. An exception is also possible for past membership if the membership ended at least two years prior to the application (five years if the party in control of a foreign state is considered a totalitarian dictatorship). If neither applies, a waiver is available for an immigrant who is the parent, spouse, son, daughter, brother, or sister of a U.S. citizen, or a spouse, son, or daughter of a permanent resident.
Nazis	No	

Inadmissibility		
Ground of Inadmissibility	**Waiver Available**	**Conditions of Waiver**
Economic Grounds		
Any person who, in the opinion of a USCIS, border, or consular official, is likely to become a "public charge," that is, receive public assistance or welfare in the United States. The official can consider factors such as the person's age, health, family and work history, and previous use of public benefits.	No	However, the applicant may cure the ground of inadmissibility by overcoming the reasons for it or obtaining an Affidavit of Support from a family member or friend.
Family-sponsored immigrants and employment-sponsored immigrants where a family member is the employment sponsor (or such a family member owns 5% of the petitioning business) whose sponsor has not executed an Affidavit of Support (Form I-864).	No	But an applicant may cure the ground of inadmissibility by subsequently satisfying affidavit of support requirements.
Nonimmigrant public benefit recipients (where the individual came as non-immigrant and applied for benefits when he or she was not eligible or through fraud). Five-year bar to admissibility.	No	But ground of inadmissibility expires after five years.
Labor Certifications & Employment Qualifications		
People without approved labor certifications, if one is required in the category under which the green card application is made.	No	
Graduates of unaccredited medical schools, whether inside or outside of the U.S., immigrating to the U.S. in a second or third preference category based on their profession, who have not both passed the foreign medical graduates exam and shown proficiency in English. (Physicians qualifying as special immigrants who have been practicing medicine in the U.S. with a license since January 9, 1978, are not subject to this rule.)	No	
Uncertified foreign healthcare workers seeking entry based on clinical employment in their field (but not including physicians).	No	But applicant may show qualifications by submitting a certificate from the Commission on Graduates of Foreign Nursing Schools or the equivalent.

Inadmissibility		
Ground of Inadmissibility	**Waiver Available**	**Conditions of Waiver**
Immigration Violators		
People who entered in the U.S. without inspection by U.S. border authorities.	Yes	Available for certain battered women and children who came to the U.S. escaping such battery or who qualify as self-petitioners. Also available for some individuals who had visa petitions or labor certifications on file before January 14, 1998 or before April 30, 2001 if they were in the U.S. on December 21, 2000 ($1,000 penalty required for latter waiver). Does not apply to applicants outside of the U.S.
People who were deported after a hearing and seek admission within ten years.	Yes	Discretionary with USCIS.
People who have failed to attend removal (deportation) proceedings (unless they had reasonable cause for doing so). Five-year bar to reentry.	Yes	Discretionary with USCIS.
People who have been summarily excluded from the U.S. and again attempt to enter within five years.	Yes	Advance permission to apply for readmission. Discretionary with USCIS.
People who made misrepresentations during the immigration process.	Yes	The applicant must be the spouse or child of a U.S. citizen or green card holder. A waiver will be granted if the refusal of admission would cause extreme hardship to that relative. Discretionary with USCIS.
People who made a false claim to U.S. citizenship.	No	
Individuals subject to a final removal (deportation) order under the Immigration and Naturalization Act § 274C (Civil Document Fraud Proceedings).	Yes	Available to permanent residents who voluntarily left the U.S., and to those applying for permanent residence as immediate relatives or other family-based petitions if the fraud was committed solely to assist the person's spouse or child and provided that no fine was imposed as part of the previous civil proceeding.
Student visa abusers (person who improperly obtains F-1 status to attend a public elementary school or adult education program, or transfers from a private to a public program except as permitted). Five-year bar to admissibility.	No	

Inadmissibility		
Ground of Inadmissibility	**Waiver Available**	**Conditions of Waiver**
Certain individuals twice removed (deported) or removed after aggravated felony. Twenty-year bar to admissibility for those twice deported.	Yes	Discretionary with USCIS (advance permission to apply for readmission).
Individuals unlawfully present (time counted only after April 1, 1997 and after the age of 18). Presence for 180–364 days results in three-year bar to admissibility. Presence for 365 or more days creates ten-year bar to admissibility. Bars kick in only when the individual departs the U.S. and seeks reentry.	Yes	A waiver is provided for an immigrant who has a U.S. citizen or permanent resident spouse or parent to whom refusal of the application would cause extreme hardship. There is also a complex body of law concerning when a person's presence will be considered "lawful," for example, if one has certain applications awaiting decisions by USCIS or is protected by battered spouse/child provisions of the immigration laws.
Individuals unlawfully present after previous immigration violations. (Applies to persons who were in the U.S. unlawfully for an aggregate period over one year, who subsequently reenter without being properly admitted. Also applies to anyone ordered removed who subsequently attempts entry without admission.)	No	A permanent ground of inadmissibility. However, after being gone for ten years, an applicant can apply for permission to reapply for admission.
Stowaways.	No	
Smugglers of illegal aliens.	Yes	Waivable if the applicant was smuggling in people who were immediate family members at the time, and either is a permanent resident or is immigrating under a family-based visa petition as an immediate relative; the unmarried son or daughter of a U.S. citizen or permanent resident; or the spouse of a U.S. permanent resident.
Document Violations		
People without required current passports or visas.	No	Except limited circumstance waivers. Under new "summary removal" procedures, border officials may quickly deport people for five years who arrive without proper documents or make misrepresentations during the inspection process.

Inadmissibility		
Ground of Inadmissibility	**Waiver Available**	**Conditions of Waiver**
Draft Evasion and Ineligibility for Citizenship		
People who are permanently ineligible for citizenship.	No	
People who are draft evaders, unless they were U.S. citizens at the time of evasion or desertion.	No	
Miscellaneous Grounds		
Practicing polygamists.	No	
Guardians accompanying excludable aliens.	No	
International child abductors. (The exclusion does not apply if the applicant is a national of a country that signed the Hague Convention on International Child Abduction.)	No	
Unlawful voters (voting in violation of any federal, state, or local law or regulation).	No	
Former U.S. citizens who renounced citizenship to avoid taxation.	No	

For example, with some criminal activity, only actual convictions are grounds of inadmissibility. If you have been charged with a crime and the charges were then dropped, you may not be inadmissible.

Another example involves crimes of moral turpitude. Crimes of moral turpitude are those showing dishonesty or basically immoral conduct. Committing an act that is considered a crime of moral turpitude can make you inadmissible, even if you have not been convicted.

Crimes with no element of moral turpitude, however, are often not considered grounds of inadmissibility. Laws differ from state to state on which crimes are considered to involve moral turpitude and which are not.

Other factors that may work to your benefit are:

- expungement laws that remove the crime from your record
- the length of the prison term
- how long ago the crime was committed
- the number of convictions in your background
- conditions of plea bargaining, and
- available pardons.

Sometimes, a conviction can be erased or vacated if you can show it was unlawfully obtained or you were not advised of its immigration consequences.

Proving that a criminal ground of inadmissibility does not apply in your case is a complicated business. You need to have a firm grasp not only of immigration law, but also the technicalities of criminal law. If you have a criminal problem in your past, you may be able to get a green card, but not without the help of an experienced immigration lawyer. (See Chapter 24.)

3. Proving That an Inadmissibility Finding Is Incorrect

When your green card or nonimmigrant visa application is denied because you are found inadmissible, you can try to prove that the finding of inadmissibility is incorrect. For example, if a USCIS medical examination shows that you have certain medical problems, you can present reports from other doctors stating that the first diagnosis was wrong and that you are free of the problem condition. If you are accused of lying on a visa application, you can present evidence proving you told the truth, or that any false statements were made unintentionally.

4. Applying for a Waiver

In many circumstances, you may be able to get a waiver of inadmissibility. By obtaining a waiver, you don't eliminate or disprove the ground of inadmissibility. Instead you ask USCIS to overlook the problem and give you a green card or visa anyway.

All green card and visa application forms ask questions designed to find out whether any grounds of inadmissibility apply in your case. When the answers to the questions on these forms clearly show that you are inadmissible, you may be authorized to begin applying for a waiver immediately on filing your application. In most cases, however, the consulate or USCIS office insists on having your final visa interview before ruling that you are inadmissible. If the USCIS office or consulate handling your case decides to wait until your final interview before finding you inadmissible, this will delay your ability to file for a waiver. This may delay your getting a green card or visa; waivers can take many months to process.

Once it is determined that a waiver is necessary, you will need to complete Form I-601 and pay a filing fee (currently $265). Note that if you file this with a U.S. consulate abroad, you will have to wait for the consulate to send your application to a USCIS office. The consulate cannot approve the waiver.

Once again, there are many technical factors that control whether or not a waiver of inadmissibility is granted. If you want to get one approved, you stand the best chance of success by hiring a good immigration lawyer.

D. Most Troublesome Grounds of Inadmissibility

The 1996 Immigration Reform law made many changes to the immigration code, most of them restrictive. Although it's been a few years since their passage, these continue to be among the most troublesome of the grounds of inadmissibility for many immigrants. Some of the grounds that have the most significant impact are summarized here.

1. Affidavit of Support for Family-Based Petitions

All family-based immigrants seeking permanent residence must now include an Affidavit of Support, on either Form I-864 or I-864-EZ. This form helps satisfy the requirement that an immigrant show he or she is not likely to become a public charge. (But even with this form, you can still be found inadmissible on public charge grounds.)

There are, however, limited exceptions to this requirement. If the immigrant will qualify for automatic U.S. citizenship upon becoming a permanent resident (discussed in Chapter 9), the I-864 is not necessary. Also, if the beneficiary has already worked in the U.S. for 40 or more work quarters as defined by Social Security (about ten years), Form I-864 is not required. Moreover, the beneficiary can count time worked by a parent while the beneficiary was under the age of 18 or by a spouse toward these 40 quarters.

If you're exempt from the Affidavit of Support requirement due to one of these exceptions, you should fill out Form I-864W instead of the regular Form I-864.

The requirements for this Affidavit of Support are very different from those of its predecessor, Form I-134. The government can rely on the newer form to hold the sponsor responsible if the immigrant receives public benefits. And it is also enforceable by the immigrant-family member against the sponsor for support. Finally, it requires that the sponsor show that he or she has at least 125% of income for a similar household size (including family and dependents), according to the federal Poverty Guidelines level.

Family-based immigrants who file adjustment of status or immigrant visa applications are required to have Form I-864 filed by the person who is sponsoring their immigrant petition. However, another person—a joint sponsor—may add income to the sponsor's if he or she meets the 125% income requirement for the household and is:

- willing to be jointly liable
- a U.S. legal permanent resident or citizen
- over 18 years old, and
- living in the United States.

The joint sponsor files a separate Affidavit of Support. The principal immigrant can have only one joint sponsor. However, if the joint sponsor's income is not sufficient to cover all the derivative beneficiaries (such as children), a second joint sponsor may be added. Two joint sponsors is the limit, however. Other household members may join their income to that of the primary sponsor to help reach the 125% level, but only if they are age 18 or older, and agree to be jointly liable by filing Form I-864A, Contract Between Sponsor and Household Member.

Personal assets of the sponsor or the immigrant—such as property, bank account deposits, and personal property such as automobiles—may also be used to supplement the sponsor's income if the primary sponsor's actual income does not add up to 125% of the federal Poverty Guidelines income levels. The sponsor or immigrant must show assets worth five times the difference between the Poverty Guidelines level and actual household income (or three times for immediate relatives).

The requirements and paperwork burden of the Affidavit are complicated and substantial; most of the requirements are spelled out on the forms. If you have questions about your eligibility or the scope of your legal responsibility, consult an experienced immigration attorney.

2. Summary Exclusion

Another law that has a drastic impact on individuals requesting to enter the United States is the summary exclusion law. This law empowers an inspector at the airport to exclude and deport you at your entry to the U.S. if:

- the inspector thinks you are making a misrepresentation about practically anything connected to your right to enter the U.S.— such as your purpose in coming, intent to return, prior immigration history, or use of false documents, or
- you do not have the proper documentation to support your entry to the U.S. in the category you are requesting.

If the inspector excludes you, you may not request entry for five years, unless a special waiver is granted. For this reason, it is extremely important to understand the terms of your requested status and not make any misrepresentations.

If the inspector looks likely to summarily exclude you, you may request withdrawing your application to enter the U.S. to prevent having the five-year deportation order on your record. The inspector may allow you to do this in some cases.

3. Unlawful Presence and the Overstay Bars

Fairly new grounds of inadmissibility apply to people who were unlawfully present in the United States for 180 days after April 1, 1997, who subsequently left, and who now seek admission through adjustment of status or by applying for an immigrant or nonimmigrant visa. Such people are subject to a three-year waiting period; the period is ten years if they were unlawfully present for one year after April 1, 1997.

Even worse, people who have lived in the United States illegally for more than one year and who then left or were deported but returned to the United States illegally (or were caught trying to) can never get a green card. This is usually referred to as the "permanent bar." (Check with a lawyer before concluding that you're subject to the permanent bar, however—recent case law has carved out a few exceptions.)

4. Limitations on Who Can Adjust Status

The rules concerning adjustment of status—or getting your green card in the U.S.—are somewhat complicated. In general, if you entered the U.S. properly—by being inspected by a border official— and maintained your nonimmigrant status, you can probably get your green card without leaving the United States. Most people who marry U.S. citizens can adjust their status even if they have fallen out of status or worked without authorization, as long as they did not enter without being properly inspected, or as a crewman or stowaway. Those who marry U.S. citizens and who entered without inspection or as crewmen or stowaways need to use a "grandfather clause." (See Chapter 18.)

Unfortunately, the grandfather clause helps only a few people who happened to be in the United States when certain laws were changed (in particular, a law known as § 245(i)). Under the old laws, practically everyone had the right to stay in the United States to adjust their status, simply by paying a $1,000 penalty fee. But under the newer laws, paying this fee is no longer an option.

That means that many people who are just becoming eligible for green cards are in a trap. If they stay in the United States, the fact that they entered illegally or committed certain other violations means that they're not allowed to adjust their status to permanent resident within the United States. But if they leave the United States and attempt to apply for their green card through an overseas consulate, they may well face a three- or ten-year bar to returning to the United States, as punishment for their illegal stay.

If you believe you're in this trap, consult a lawyer to make sure and to see if you might qualify for a waiver of the three- or ten-year bar. All refugees or political asylees can stay in the U.S. to adjust status.

5. Crimes Plus Alcohol or Drugs

If you've committed any sort of crime, you may be found inadmissible, and should consult an experienced immigration attorney. Some attorneys specialize in analyzing the significance of criminal convictions in the immigration context.

However, if you've been convicted of a crime involving alcohol, you've got double trouble. Even if the crime itself doesn't make you inadmissible, USCIS can, and often does, argue that it's a sign that you have a physical or mental disorder associated with harmful behavior—in other words, that you're inadmissible on health, rather than criminal, grounds.

This is most often a problem for people with convictions for DUI or DWI (Driving Under the Influence or Driving While Intoxicated). One DUI alone won't always create a problem, unless there were additional factors, such as someone having been injured, your license having been suspended, or your state treating the crime as a felony. But if USCIS sees a "significant criminal record of alcohol-related driving incidents," it will take a closer look. You may be required to undergo an additional examination by the doctor who filled out your medical report, or by more specialized doctors or psychiatrists.

DUIs aren't the only crime that can lead USCIS to find you inadmissible on health grounds. Crimes such as assaults or domestic violence where alcohol or drugs were contributing factors can lead to the same result. Again, see an attorney if this is an issue in your case—and remember that trying to hide crimes on your green card application will only get you in bigger trouble, after the fingerprint or police report reveals them. ■

How Long You'll Have to Wait

Quota System and Preference Categories

As a U.S. citizen, I filed the papers for my brother five years ago. Why is it taking so long for the U.S. Embassy in India to give him his immigrant visa?

My ten-year-old daughter was born in Hawaii, where I was a graduate student at the University of Hawaii. Since she is a U.S. citizen, when can I get a green card by having her claim me as her mother?

Three years ago, based on my green card, I sponsored my wife, who comes from Mexico. She is still waiting for her green card. What is the problem?

These questions are often asked by people who may have expected some delay in getting their green cards, but who can't believe how many years it's taking.

There are three main causes of common immigration delays. The first type of delay, no one can escape. It's simply the bureaucratic backup caused by an overworked government agency trying to deal with many thousands of applications every year. Even the amount of time you spend waiting for a decision on one application can be shocking—many months or years is "normal." And a fair number of people wait months only to discover that their application got misplaced or lost in the paperwork shuffle. Although USCIS is perpetually launching efforts to fix these problems, no one expects miracles.

The second type of delay is also tough to avoid: the security checks and double checks your name and fingerprints will be run through, sometimes more than once, during the application process. Although security checks were always part of the application process, they've become more rigorous since the terrorist attacks of September 11, 2001. For people with common names, this can create particular problems. Of course, if you've had any arrests or other history that you believe will raise questions in the immigration process, you should consult an attorney.

The third type of delay applies only to applicants in green card categories that have a yearly limit on how many are given out. For example, spouses of U.S. citizens don't have to worry, because as "immediate relatives," the government can grant unlimited numbers of green cards to them, no matter how many apply. But spouses of U.S. permanent residents are less lucky. Their annual limit is 87,934, and far more spouses than that apply every year. Spouses of permanent residents have to wait, usually five years or more, until all the people who applied before them have gotten their green cards. After that, in technical terms, a "visa number" is said to becomes available, and they can continue their application for a green card.

"Visa" and "green card" can have similar meanings. When we're talking about numbers and quotas, the immigration laws always refer to "visas" rather than "green cards," for technical reasons. Part of the reason is that if you come from overseas, you don't become a permanent resident (green card holder) until you receive an "immigrant visa" and use it to enter the United States. But even if you're applying within the United States, you can't become a permanent resident until a "visa number" is allotted to you. So, when you hear about numbers and limits on "visas" in this discussion, assume it means your right to a green card, no matter where you're coming from or whether you use an actual, physical entry visa.

You'll face delays based on limited numbers of visas if you apply for a green card in any of the so-called "preference" categories (which we'll explain below). All the preference categories come with limits, or "quotas," on how many visas or green cards can be passed out in a year. And in every preference category, the demand for green cards always seems to exceed the supply.

To make matters more complicated, no country is allowed to send more than 7% of all preference immigrants (or 25,620 people) to the United States in a year. That means that for certain countries with high rates of immigration to the United States—like Mexico, India, China, and the Philippines—the U.S. government sometimes has to start a separate—and longer—waiting list. This isn't discrimination, so much as it is mathematics.

A. Immediate Relatives of U.S. Citizens: No Waiting

Immigrant visas are immediately available for one group of eligible aliens: immediate relatives of U.S. citizens. They have the highest priority in immigration law because of the congressional intent to encourage families of U.S. citizens to live together and stay together.

Members of this group have to wait only for as long as it takes various government offices to handle their applications. This averages from two to twelve months, depending on various factors such as whether the immigrant is coming from another country or already lives legally in the United States, and how backed up the office serving his or her region is.

For purposes of immigration law, you are the immediate relative and eligible for an immigrant visa without waiting if you are:

- the husband or wife of a U.S. citizen
- the parent of a U.S. citizen, if the citizen is at least 21 years of age
- the child under 21 years of age (including stepchildren and children adopted before they reach the age of 16) of a U.S. citizen, or
- the widow or widower of a U.S. citizen who died after living with you for at least two years.

B. Relatives in Preference Categories: Longer Waits

In all family-based preference categories, petitions from U.S. citizens generally have higher priority than those of lawful permanent residents.

Family first preference: unmarried sons or daughters of U.S. citizens. The children must be 21 years old or older and not married—meaning either single, divorced, or widowed. (A son or daughter who is under 21 years old and not married would be classified as an immediate relative.) A maximum of 23,400 immigrant visas are now available worldwide for the family first preference category.

The current waiting period is approximately five years, but 14 years if you're from Mexico and 15 years from the Philippines.

Family second preference: spouses and unmarried children of permanent residents. This category is divided into two parts, including:

- husbands and wives of a lawful permanent resident and their unmarried children who are under 21 years old (category 2A), and
- unmarried (meaning single, divorced, or widowed) sons or daughters (over 21 years old) of a lawful permanent resident (category 2B, which waits somewhat longer than category 2A).

A total of 114,200 immigrant visas worldwide are given to second preference immigrants. However, 77% (87,934) of the total is intended for the spouses and minor children of green cardholders (2As), while 23% (26,266) of the total is meant for the unmarried children over 21 years of age (2Bs).

The current wait in category 2A is approximately five years, except that applicants from Mexico wait about seven years. In category 2B, the current wait is approximately ten years, except that applicants from Mexico wait about 15 years.

Family third preference: married sons and daughters of U.S. citizens. What if a U.S. citizen's unmarried son or daughter (in the family first preference category) gets married before entering the U.S. as a lawful permanent resident? Or what if he or she is married already? Either way, the third preference category provides a solution, although the waits tend to be long. Only 23,400 visas worldwide are made available every year for married sons and daughters of U.S. citizens.

The current wait in the third preference category is approximately eight years, except that applicants from Mexico wait about 13 years, and those from the Philippines wait as many as 18 years.

Family fourth preference: brothers and sisters of U.S. citizens. The brother or sister of a U.S. citizen has to wait until the American sibling turns 21 years of age before a petition can be filed for the alien brother or sister. A total of 65,000 visas worldwide are available each year for this category. The waiting list is always very long, from ten to 24 years.

C. Dealing With the Wait

If you belong to a preference category in which there are many hopeful immigrants waiting—for example, in Mexico, there are well over 60,000 brothers and sisters of U.S. citizens on file—you may have to wait several years for your immigrant visa number.

If, during these years, you want to come to the United States as a nonimmigrant—as a tourist, businessperson, student, or other category—the U.S. embassy in your country will probably not approve your visa application. This is because you already have an application on file for an immigrant visa. The U.S. government interprets that latter filing as a statement that you intend to live permanently in the United States—which disqualifies you from most short-term visas.

Of course, there are exceptions to every rule. If you can convince the U.S. consul that you will not remain illegally in the United States waiting for your immigrant visa number to come up, and that you will return to your country once the period of your nonimmigrant stay is over, you may be granted a nonimmigrant visa. Also, spouses of U.S. citizens may qualify for the newly expanded "K" visa (see Chapter 7).

However, people who qualify for certain temporary work statuses (H and L visas) need not worry about conflicts with their green card application. Although they may have an approved visa petition by reason of their U.S. citizen spouse, child, parent, brother, or sister, or a lawful permanent resident spouse or parent, the U.S. embassy is supposed to issue them an H or L visa if they qualify for that nonimmigrant visa, while waiting for a visa number to become available.

D. Can You Predict How Long You'll Wait?

No one can tell you for certain how long you'll wait for a visa or green card. If you're an immediate relative, you'll get your best estimate from asking people who work in the office you're dealing with what the current expected processing times are. Processing times are also posted on USCIS's website at https://egov.immigration.gov/cris/jsps/ptimes.jsp. Choose the office at which your case is pending, and you'll be given a list of what types of petitions and applications the office handles and what the oldest pending case is for each type at that office. If you are not in the immediate relative category, you can track how long you're likely to spend on the waiting list if you pay special attention to the Priority Date and the cutoff date that apply to your visa application.

1. The Priority Date

The Priority Date is the date on which your relative began the process by filing a petition for you with USCIS (or INS, as it was formerly called) or with the U.S. embassy.

It is very important to keep the receipt of the fee paid to USCIS and the registered mail return receipt card from the post office. The date on the USCIS receipt is the Priority Date of your application or petition. That date should also be shown on your approval notice, which is the next piece of paper you'll get from USCIS—and which is even more important to keep.

Your relative may wait several years for an answer on the initial visa petition. In 2004, USCIS announced a new policy on handling approvals and denials of Form I-130 visa petitions. Instead of reviewing all petitions in the order received, they're going to start prioritizing those filed on behalf of people whose visas will be available sooner. That means that if you're in a category with long waits, your U.S. citizen or resident relative could receive a receipt notice one year and the approval notice several years later, when it's almost time for you to immigrate. This new policy won't add any delays to your overall wait—it's like having two sources of delay going on simultaneously. It will, however, add uncertainty to your life, since you won't know until the last minute whether the initial visa petition will be approved—or denied.

The Department of State keeps careful count of how many immigrant visas are issued for each country in each preference category. If the quota has been reached in one category before the fiscal year is over (in October), the department will not issue any immigrant visas in that category for the rest of the fiscal year and will, in addition, state that visas are temporarily unavailable for that category, either for a particular country or worldwide.

October 1 of each year marks the beginning of another fiscal year for the federal government—and the count of the immigrant visas issued begins all over again for each country in each preference category.

2. Visa Cutoff Date

Each month, the Department of State issues a *Visa Bulletin,* which sets out the immigrant visa cutoff date of each visa preference.

The cutoff date simply announces which Priority Dates in each category are receiving attention from the Department of State because people holding those numbers have become eligible for an immigrant visa. Anyone whose Priority Date falls before this cutoff date will be given an appointment within a few months if they're overseas, or will be allowed to submit the next part of their application if they're in the U.S. and eligible to "adjust status" there. Anyone whose Priority Date falls after the cutoff date will have to wait.

EXAMPLE: You were born in Poland. Your brother, who is a naturalized U.S. citizen, filed a petition for you on August 2, 1994, which becomes your Priority Date.

You are in the fourth preference category. The *Visa Bulletin* of June 2006 says the State Department is processing siblings with a Priority Date of on or before March 1, 1995. Your appointment for your immigrant visa is currently available.

However, if you were from another country, the waiting period could be longer. For example:

If born in	What was being processed in June 2006
Mexico	August 15, 1993
Philippines	November 1, 1983

The cutoff dates announced in the *Visa Bulletin* may not change much from one month to the next—sometimes one week for one preference and two weeks for another preference. Or it may not move at all for several months in your category. Be prepared to wait.

The *Visa Bulletin* is normally available in each embassy or consulate, or in USCIS offices. You can also call the Department of State in Washington, DC, at 202-663-1541 for a tape-recorded message that gives the cutoff dates for each preference category being processed that month. Or, visit the State Department website at www.state.gov. Click "Travel and Business," then "Visas," then "Visa Bulletins." You can even subscribe to an email service that will automatically send you the latest *Visa Bulletin* every month as it becomes available! Details about how to do this can be found in the bulletin itself.

3. Some People Can Switch Preference Categories

A special rule applies to family-based immigrant visas, which allows applicants to hang onto their Priority Dates if they change from one preference category to another.

If you belong to one family preference, and some event (marriage, divorce, death of spouse, or the simple passage of time) places you in a different preference category, your original Priority Date may remain unchanged—even if you have become eligible for a different preference. That means you won't lose much ground, since your place on the new waiting list will reflect the fact that your petition was filed long before many other people's.

⚠ **Some life changes make you ineligible for any visa at all.** Not everyone who marries, who divorces, or whose petitioning family member dies can switch to another preference category. You can switch only if, at the time, an existing category fits your new situation. So, for example, the child of a U.S. citizen who marries can switch to the third preference category. But the child of a lawful permanent resident who marries is out of luck, because there's no category for married children of permanent residents. Such issues are explained further in Section E, below.

Situations Where You Automatically Convert to Another Visa Category With Your Original Priority Date

- Marriage of the son or daughter (over 21 years old) of U.S. citizen—moves down from first to third preference.
- Marriage of child (under 21 years old) of U.S. citizen—moves down from immediate relative to third preference.
- Divorce of child or son or daughter—moves up from third preference to immediate relative or first preference, depending on child's age at divorce.
- Naturalization of legal resident petitioner—moves up from second preference to immediate relative (if applicant is under 21 years old) or first preference (if applicant is over 21 years old).
- Child of lawful permanent resident reaching age 21 before Priority Date becomes current—drops from category 2A to category 2B of the second preference. However, if the child reaches age 21 after his or her Priority Date has become current but before he has actually been approved for permanent residency, the child can retain 2A status as long as he or she applies within one year of the Priority Date having become current. (This represents a change in the law, as of 2002—formerly such children would have also dropped into category 2B, simply by virtue of not having received their approval on time, and therefore had to wait longer.)

Situations Where Children Are Protected From Switching Categories

The Child Status Protection Act of 2002 allows certain children of U.S. citizens and permanent residents to retain their original visa eligibility even if they turn 21 while they're waiting for the process to finish up. (Formerly, turning 21 would have automatically dropped them into a lower preference category and caused them to have to wait longer for their visa or green card.) Those who benefit include:

- Children of U.S. citizens—will retain immediate relative status even if they turn 21 at any time after a visa petition has been filed on their behalf.
- Children of lawful permanent residents—will retain 2A status if they turn 21 after their Priority Date has become current, so long as they file for a green card within one year of becoming current.

These rules may sound technical and a little hard to follow, but because they can make a big difference in how quickly your application is processed, it is worth your time to understand which rules apply to your situation.

EXAMPLE: Your mother, a permanent resident, filed a family second preference petition for you as her unmarried son on February 10, 2000. But she has recently been naturalized as a U.S. citizen, so you could now move into the family first preference as the unmarried son of an American citizen. If the visa cutoff date for the family first preference is closer to your Priority Date than the cutoff date for the family second preference, you can now receive your immigration visa more quickly.

EXAMPLE: A visa application is filed for the teenaged daughter of a U.S. citizen. When she turns 21 and her Priority Date has not yet become current, she moves into the first preference but keeps the Priority Date assigned to the immediate relative petition filed by her American parent.

You must always call to the attention of the U.S. embassy or USCIS this conversion of your preference category and your right to keep your old Priority Date. Write a letter with copies of the documents to prove your change of preference category. For example, if you're moving up because your spouse or parent became a citizen, include a copy of the signed naturalization certificate. Also, enclose a copy of your previously approved petition (or receipt notice if you haven't yet been approved) to show your old Priority Date.

If your I-130 application is still pending at a service center, check on its procedures—you may be able to email your request.

E. Revocation of a Petition or Application

Here is a bit of scary information, but it's better to know it than not to know: After a petition or application has been filed on behalf of an alien, it can be revoked or canceled—even if it has already been approved by the INS or USCIS. This is usually based on a change in circumstances that makes the immigrant no longer eligible, but it can also be based on fraud.

USCIS will normally revoke a petition if, for example:

- the person who filed the petition decides to withdraw it and informs USCIS of this decision
- the person who filed the petition dies. However, USCIS may decide not to revoke the petition if it is convinced that there are "humanitarian reasons" not to do so.

- in a marriage case, the couple divorces or the marriage is annulled before the green card is approved, or
- in a family second preference case, the unmarried son or daughter gets married before the green card is approved.

Special Rules for Widows and Widowers

If the beneficiary is the spouse of a U.S. citizen, and the couple was married for at least two years, the petition will be granted as long as the widowed beneficiary applies within two years of the spouse's death and has not remarried.

Consider this scenario: A permanent resident mother has brought all her children to the United States except her eldest son, who marries before she could petition for him. After five years, she becomes a U.S. citizen and immediately files a petition for her married son, still living in the foreign country. The petition is approved, but before the son and his family come to the United States, the mother dies. The petition is automatically revoked, and the son remains separated from his brothers and sisters, who have been living in the United States since their mother received her green card.

That application of the regulations seems cruel.

It is precisely for such cases that the regulations have been somewhat liberalized. The beneficiary of a petition filed by a U.S. citizen, or by a permanent resident, who dies before the alien beneficiary could come to the United States is no longer in an entirely hopeless situation.

With a lawyer's help, you may be able to show the immigration authorities that for "humanitarian reasons," revocation would be inappropriate. There is, however, a catch: Because every immigrant to the United States must have a financial sponsor—that is, someone who promises to support the immigrant if he or she is unable to support him or herself—you will need to find a substitute sponsor for the person who died. Only certain people can fill this substitute role, including your spouse, parent, mother-in-law, father-in-law, sibling, son, daughter, son-in-law, or daughter-in-law. As in the case of other sponsors, your sponsor must maintain an annual income equal to at least 125% of the federal Poverty Guidelines.

But you can always try the indirect approach. A little help from a U.S. representative or senator who can intercede on your behalf may prove effective. Call the office of your representative or senator and get the name of the aide in that office who is responsible for handling immigration matters. Write him or her a letter summarizing why he or she should intercede on your behalf with USCIS. This approach may be a long shot, but it may be your last hope. ■

Fiancé and Fiancée Visas

I Left My Heart in San Francisco

The fiancé visa (K-1) was designed to allow people who've become engaged to—but haven't yet married—a U.S. citizen to travel to the U.S. for the wedding. It unfortunately isn't available to the fiancés of U.S. permanent residents (green card holders). Your minor children can go with you to the U.S. After the wedding, you and your children can either apply for a green card or return home—but must do one or the other within 90 days.

→ **If you're already married, see Chapter 7 for how you can speed things up by using a fiancé visa.** Using a fiancé visa to get to the United States is a legitimate way to speed up the process if you're already married. You'll need to first learn the procedural details, however; see Chapter 7, then refer back to this chapter for information on filling out the relevant forms.

A. Who Qualifies for a Fiancé Visa

To qualify for a fiancé visa, you must:
- intend to marry a U.S. citizen (see Section 1, below)
- have met your intended spouse in person within the last two years (though this can be waived based on cultural customs or extreme hardship; see Section 2, below), and
- be legally able to marry (see Section 3, below).

It's important to realize that a fiancé visa is not a green card. It's only a temporary, 90-day right to be in the United States. However, it's included in this book because it's an important first step towards getting a green card. After the immigrant has arrived in the United States and gotten married, he or she can file for a green card—through a process called "adjustment of status"—through a U.S.-based USCIS office. (Or, if the immigrant has no desire for a U.S. green card, he or she can simply return home before the fiancé visa runs out.)

1. You Must Intend to Marry a U.S. Citizen

Of course you want to get married—but how do you plan to prove that to the U.S. government? As part of your application, you'll have to supply proof that you've made actual plans, such as a place, a day, a type of ceremony or proceedings (even if it's only a front of a judge), and more. We'll talk more about this in the sections that discuss paperwork.

💡 **Make your wedding plans flexible.** You can't know exactly how long it will take to get a fiancé visa, but you'll have to hold your wedding within 90 days of entering the United States. Before you sign any contracts for catering, photographic, or other services, discuss the situation with the service providers and build some flexibility into your contracts or agreements in case the date needs to change.

The person you plan to marry must be a citizen, not a permanent resident, of the United States. A U.S. citizen is someone who was:
- born in the United States or its territories
- became a citizen through a process of application and testing (called "naturalization"), or
- acquired or derived citizenship through a family member (for more information, see Nolo's website at www.nolo.com; look for the article entitled "U.S. Citizenship by Birth or Through Parents").

2. You Must Have Met in Person Within the Last Two Years

To protect against sham marriages, the law requires that you and your fiancé have met in person within the last two years. Even a brief meeting may be enough. Perhaps the immigrant can visit the United States on a tourist visa. However, getting approval for a tourist visa may be difficult, because the U.S. consulate may believe that the immigrant actually intends to get married and apply for the green card right away—which would be a misuse of the tourist visa, and could amount to visa fraud. It will probably be easier for the U. S. citizen to visit the immigrant overseas.

If, however, you're from a country where prospective husbands and wives don't meet before the wedding, for religious or cultural reasons, this meeting will obviously be a greater hardship. In such cases, you can ask the immigration authorities to "waive" (overlook) the meeting requirement. You'll need letters from your religious leader, parents, or other relevant people, and other proof of the normal practices in your culture, to succeed with your request. Getting a lawyer's help would be a good idea here.

U.S. Citizen Petitioners Must Now Disclose Criminal Records

Recently Congress became concerned that immigrating fiancés were particularly susceptible to domestic violence and abuse—particularly those whose engagements were arranged through a marriage broker (sometimes called "mail order brides"). In response, Congress passed the International Marriage Brokers Regulation Act of 2005 (IMBRA). As a result of IMBRA, the fiancé visa petition (Form I-129F) now asks whether you and your fiancé or spouse met through an international marriage broker. If you did, the immigrant will be asked, at the visa interview, whether the broker complied with new legal requirements that he or she collect information on the U.S. fiancé or spouse's criminal record and pass it to the immigrant. In addition, Form I-129F now asks all U.S. citizen petitioners whether they have a history of violent crime and crime relating to alcohol or controlled-substance abuse.

---

3. You Must Be Legally Able to Marry

For most people, the requirement that you be legally able to marry won't pose any problems. However, if one of you is already married or too young to legally marry in the state or country where you plan to perform the wedding, or if the two of you are close relatives, such as cousins, and forbidden to marry in the state or country where you plan to hold the wedding, you may not qualify for a fiancé visa.

If possible, take steps to correct the problem—for example, obtain a divorce, figure out a different place to marry, or wait until you're older.

B. Quick View of the Fiancé Visa Application Process

Here's what to plan for on your path to a fiancé visa:

1. The U.S. citizen submits a fiancé visa petition to USCIS (on Form I-129F).
2. USCIS sends the U.S. citizen a receipt notice, after confirming that the application is complete, then (within weeks or months) a notice of its decision, hopefully approving the petition. (Occasionally, USCIS will call in the U.S. citizen petitioner for an interview before deciding on the petition.)
3. USCIS will transfer the file to an intermediary called the National Visa Center (NVC), which then transfers it to the U.S. consulate serving the immigrant's country. The consulate will instruct the immigrating fiancé on what documents to prepare, and schedule him or her for a visa interview.
4. The immigrating fiancé attends the interview, and if all goes well, is approved for a fiancé visa. The visa will usually need to be picked up on a separate day.

C. Detailed Instructions for the Fiancé Visa Application Process

All the immigration forms required and prohibitions explained here are very unromantic. But because the immigration laws have been abused by people who used marriage simply to obtain a green card, romance takes a backseat when it comes to immigration procedures. Obtaining a fiancé visa—also called a K-1 visa—requires time, patience, and paperwork.

1. Documents Required for Fiancé Visa Petition

To start the process, the U.S. citizen must prepare the following:

☐ Form I-129F, Petition for Alien Fiancé(e). (See the sample at the end of this chapter.)

☐ Separate color photographs of the U.S. citizen and the alien fiancé.

☐ Form G-325A, Biographic Information, one for each person. (See the sample at the end of this chapter.)

☐ Proof of your U.S. fiancé's U.S. citizenship, such as a copy of a passport, birth certificate, or naturalization certificate (see Chapter 22, Section D3 for details).

☐ Proof that any previous marriages have been terminated by death, divorce, or annulment.

☐ Written affidavit from the U.S. citizen stating how the couple met, how they decided to get married, and the plans for the marriage and the honeymoon.

☐ Proof that the U.S. citizen and the foreign-born fiancé have met each other within the past two years: photographs, plane tickets, letters, etc.

☐ Proof that the two of you intend to marry within 90 days after the alien fiancé arrives in the United States: letters, long-distance telephone bills, letter from the religious or civil authority who will officiate at the wedding, letter from the place where the reception will be held, and engagement or wedding announcement or invitation.

☐ Filing fee of $170, payable to USCIS, in the form of a money order or bank check.

2. Where and How to Send the Fiancé Visa Petition

Once the U.S. citizen petitioner has prepared everything on the above list, he or she should make two complete photocopies of everything on it, including the check or money order. This will be extremely important in the all-too-common event that USCIS misplaces the petition. Send one copy to the immigrating fiancé, for his or her records. The U.S. citizen should assemble the package neatly, and preferably write a cover letter that lists, in bullet points, everything inside.

The petitioner should send the completed visa petition by certified mail, return receipt requested, to the appropriate USCIS Service Center. (See the USCIS website for contact details; make sure to get the right P.O. box.)

3. Visa Petition Interviews

The U.S. citizen petitioner may be called in for an interview by a USCIS officer. He or she should bring all original documents to the interview. If the documents and the interview convince USCIS that true romance is behind the planned marriage, the petition will be approved and a Notice of Action, Form I-797, will be mailed to the U.S. citizen. The form will contain instructions for the next step to take—and may include a request for additional information or documentation.

4. Transfer to a U.S. Consulate

After USCIS approves the Form I-129F visa petition, it will advise a processing unit called the National Visa Center (NVC). The NVC will send you, the immigrating fiancé, a packet of forms. The immigrant should follow the instructions and fill out the appropriate forms right away, and send them to the U.S. consulate indicated in the instructions. The forms usually include DS-230 Part I, DS-156, and DS-156K.

The forms are mostly pretty simple, asking for biographical information. See the samples at the end of this chapter; but realize that the ones you receive may look a little different. Some consulates customize the forms, for example adding language for the country they're in.

Some of these forms are used for other types of visas—don't be concerned, for example, with questions about whether you plan to work or study in the United States. Though this would be against the rules for people on visitor visas, it's okay for you, on a fiancé visa.

After the consulate receives and reviews your forms, it will send you a packet including an appointment date, additional forms, and instructions for completing the fiancé visa application process.

How the Immigrating Fiancé Can Plan Ahead

You can start gathering all the documents required by the U.S. embassy now so that you are ready to proceed with the case as soon as you're notified.

These documents include:

☐ a current passport for yourself and for all of your unmarried children under 21 years of age, if they are coming with you or following you to the United States

☐ birth certificates for yourself and all children mentioned above

☐ documents to prove termination of any previous marriage (death certificate, divorce decree, annulment decree)

☐ police clearance from all places you have lived for more than six months (except from the United States, where USCIS gathers the information)

☐ originals of all documents, copies of which were submitted by your U.S. citizen fiancé with Form I-129F (see the sample at the end of this chapter)

☐ three photographs of yourself and each of any children applying with you for a visa (see Chapter 22, Section E for photo requirements)

☐ report of your own medical examination and those of all children over 14 years of age to verify that you've had all your vaccinations and no one has a communicable disease (though you might want to wait for the consulate to send you instructions on which doctors do these examinations), and

☐ Form I-134, Affidavit of Support, filled out by your U.S. citizen fiancé. (See the sample at the end of this chapter.)

5. Interview at the Embassy

The U.S. embassy or consulate will schedule the immigrating fiancé for an interview. You should bring all the documents listed in the consulate's instructions. There will be an application fee of $100.

One of the most important of the documents will be Form I-134, Affidavit of Support, along with proof that the U.S. petitioner is willing and able to take financial responsibility for the immigrant. In support of this form, the citizen should add copies of his or her:

- bank statements
- recent tax returns and W-2s
- employment verification (make this an original letter from the employer detailing salary, hours, and whether the position is temporary or permanent), and
- documents showing the value of any of the following property, if owned: bonds and stocks, real estate, and mortgage information or life insurance.

The immigrating fiancé will also need to have a medical exam done. The fiancé can't just go to the family doctor, but will have to go to a clinic specified by the consulate. The doctor will do an exam, ask questions about medical history and drug and alcohol use, take X-rays, and withdraw blood. The fiancé will be asked to show records of having received all appropriate vaccinations, and will have to get any vaccinations that are lacking. The cost is usually around $300.

Most of the forms and documents must be filed for you and for any minor children who will also be going to the United States.

Because of new and increased security procedures, it is unlikely that you will receive your visa on the same day as you attend your interview. It can take several weeks for the consulate to run security checks on you—and even longer if you come from a country that the United States suspects of supporting terrorism.

If the U.S. consular official is ultimately convinced that you and your U.S. citizen fiancé are truly engaged to be married and will marry upon your arrival in the United States, and that you aren't barred from entry for any of the reasons described in Chapter 4, your passport will be stamped with the K-1 visa. The passports of your accompanying minor children will be stamped with the K-2 visa, meaning that they are dependent upon you for their immigration status.

 If you're already married but are applying for a K-3 fiancé visa, most of the advice in this section regarding the visa interview applies to you, too. However, you won't have to worry about convincing anyone that you plan to get married! Your main task will simply be to show that your paperwork is in order, with the understanding that you will complete the green card application after you've arrived in the United States.

The fiancé visa is considered a nonimmigrant visa because you are simply promising to marry a U.S. citizen. You are not yet an immigrant.

6. At the Border

Once you receive your fiancé visa, you'll have six months to use it to enter the United States. At the U.S. port of entry, the border officer will examine the contents of your visa envelope and ask you a few questions. Be careful with this—if the officer spots a reason that you should not have been given the fiancé visa, he or she has the power to deny your entry right there. You would have no choice but to find a flight or other means of transport home. And you might not be allowed back for five years (unless the officer allows you to withdraw the application before it's officially denied, which is entirely at the officer's discretion).

Assuming all goes well, the border officer will stamp your passport with your K-1 fiancé visa status, and give you a small white I-94 card showing the 90-day duration of your status.

7. Permission to Work in the U.S.

When you arrive in the United States, you can apply at once for an Employment Authorization card that will enable you to work legally. The proper paperwork to complete for this is Form I-765. (See the USCIS website, www.uscis.gov.)

However, you'll have to submit your application to a USCIS Service Center, and the service centers are famous for delays of many months. Submitting this application may not be worth the effort since the maximum time the work permit will be good for is three months (based on the length of your fiancé visa). You may be better off getting married, then submitting your green card application together with an application for a work permit. This allows you more time to work before the card expires (it will last for approximately one year).

D. How to Bring Your Children on a Fiancé Visa

Your unmarried children under age 21 are eligible to accompany you on your fiancé visa and apply for green cards after you're in the United States and you have gotten married. This includes biological as well as adopted children. All you have to do at the beginning of the fiancé visa application process is to include your children's names on question 14 of the fiancé visa petition (Form I-129F). The consular officials will then send you extra sets of the required forms for the children to fill out. (If they forget, contact them.) For young children, it's okay for you to fill out these forms on their behalf. Just sign your name, then write "Parent of [name of your child]."

Your children will probably be asked to attend your consular interview with you, although some consulates let younger children stay home. The technical name of their visa will be K-2. For the visa interview, they'll normally be asked to bring:

- filled-out forms provided by the consulate
- birth certificate
- police record (if the child is over age 16)
- passport (unless your country permits the child to be included on your passport)
- four photos, and
- medical exam results.

Even if your children don't accompany you when you first enter the U.S. as a fiancé, they can join you under the same visa for a year after yours was approved. Just make sure they remain unmarried and under the age of 21. They'll need to contact the U.S. consulate for forms and an interview. If they don't plan to immigrate with you, but want to attend your wedding, their other option is a visitor visa.

When it comes time to apply for green cards, you and your children will each have to submit a separate application, before their visa expires.

E. Marriage and After

You must marry within 90 days after arriving in the United States. It's best to get married as soon as possible after you arrive. That's because you've got only 90 days to apply for your green card; and at that time, you'll have to prove to USCIS that you really got married. USCIS won't accept a mere church certificate—it needs the official marriage certificate prepared and stamped by your local government office. However, it can take your local government several weeks to prepare this certificate and get you a copy, so plan ahead.

If you cannot get married because of some emergency or circumstances beyond your control, you must submit an affidavit to USCIS stating the reasons for the delay and request an extension of time to marry.

If you fail to marry your U.S. citizen fiancé at all, USCIS can start removal (deportation) proceedings against you and all children who came with you on a fiancé visa.

If you marry someone other than your U.S. citizen fiancé, you will lose your right to receive your green card in the United States—and so will all of your minor children who are attempting to immigrate with you.

If you do marry your U.S. citizen fiancé within 90 days, there is one more important step you must take in order to get a green card. You must file for Adjustment of Status (see Chapter 18), for yourself and all your minor children who came on the fiancé visa.

Beware of the two-year time limit. Going through the adjustment of status procedure will confer upon you and your minor children conditional permanent residence status, and you will acquire a green card that is valid for only two years. To make it a permanent green card after the two years, follow the procedures for conditional permanent residents laid out in Chapter 7.

Petition for Alien Fiancé(e), Sample Form I-129F (Page 1)

OMB No. 1615-0001; Expires 12/31/06

Department of Homeland Security
U.S. Citizenship and Immigration Services

I-129F, Petition for Alien Fiancé(e)

Do not write in these blocks.   **For USCIS Use Only**

Case ID #	Action Block	Fee Stamp
A #		
G-28 #		
The petition is approved for status under Section 101(a)(5)(k). It is valid for four months from the date of action. _____		**AMCON:** _____ ☐ Personal Interview ☐ Previously Forwarded ☐ Document Check ☐ Field Investigation

Remarks:

Part A.   Start Here. Information about you.

1. Name *(Family name in CAPS)* *(First)* *(Middle)*

| BEACH | Sandra | Leah |

2. Address *(Number and Street)*   Apt. #

| 114 Fulton St. | 6E |

(Town or City)   (State or Country)   (Zip/Postal Code)

| New York | New York | 10038 |

3. Place of Birth *(Town or City)*   (State/Country)

| Horseheads | New York |

4. Date of Birth *(mm/dd/yyyy)*   **5. Gender**

| 12/20/1980 | ☐ Male ☒ Female

6. Marital Status
☐ Married ☒ Single ☐ Widowed ☐ Divorced

7. Other Names Used *(including maiden name)*

| None |

8a. U.S. Social Security Number   8b. A# *(if any)*

| 123-45-6789 | |

9. Names of Prior Spouses   Date(s) Marriage(s) Ended

| None | n/a |
| | |

10. My citizenship was acquired through *(check one)*
☒ Birth in the U.S.   ☐ Naturalization
Give number of certificate, date and place it was issued.

| |

☐ Parents
Have you obtained a certificate of citizenship in your name?
☐ Yes   ☐ No
If "Yes," give certificate number, date and place it was issued.

| |

11. Have you ever filed for this or any other alien fiancé(e) or husband/wife before?
☐ Yes   ☒ No
If "Yes," give name of all aliens, place and date of filing, A# and result.

| |

Part B.   Information about your alien fiancé(e).

1. Name *(Family name in CAPS)* *(First)* *(Middle)*

| Hollis | Nigel | Ian |

2. Address *(Number and Street)*   Apt. #

| 123 Limestone Way | 7 |

(Town or City)   (State or Country)   (Zip/Postal Code)

| Penzance | U.K. | TR197NL |

3a. Place of Birth *(Town or City)*   (State/Country)

| Port Navas | U.K. |

3b. Country of Citizenship

| |

4. Date of Birth *(mm/dd/yyyy)*   **5. Gender**

| 8/17/1978 | ☒ Male ☐ Female

6. Marital Status
☐ Married ☐ Single ☐ Widowed ☒ Divorced

7. Other Names Used *(including maiden name)*

| None |

8. U.S. Social Security #   9. A# *(if any)*

| n/a | |

10. Names of Prior Spouses   Date(s) Marriage(s) Ended

| Jane Simpson | 5/20/2003 |
| | |

11. Has your fiancé(e) ever been in the U.S.?
☒ Yes   ☐ No

12. If your fiancé(e) is currently in the U.S., complete the following:

He or she last arrived as a: *(visitor, student, exchange alien, crewman, stowaway, temporary worker, without inspection, etc.)*

| |

Arrival/Departure Record (I-94) Number

| ☐ ☐ ☐ — ☐ ☐ ☐ ☐ ☐ ☐ ☐ ☐ |

Date of Arrival *(mm/dd/yy)*   **Date authorized stay expired, or will expire as shown on I-94 or I-95**

| | |

INITIAL RECEIPT _____ RESUBMITTED _____ RELOCATED: Rec'd _____ Sent _____ COMPLETED: Appv'd. _____ Denied _____ Ret'd. _____

Form I-129F (Rev. 05/23/06) N

Sample Form I-129F (page 2)

Part B.   Information about your alien fiancé(e).   *(Continued.)*

13. List all children of your alien fiancé(e) *(if any)*

Name *(First/Middle/Last)*	Date of Birth *(mm/dd/yyyy)*	Country of Birth	Present Address
None			

14. Address in the United States where your fiancé(e) intends to live.

(Number and Street)	(Town or City)	(State)
114 Fulton St.	New York	NY

15. Your fiancé(e)'s address abroad.

(Number and Street)	(Town or City)	(State or Province)
123 Limestone Way	Penzance	Cornwall

(Country)	(Phone Number; Include Country, City and Area Codes)
U.K.	1234 123456

16. If your fiancé(e)'s native alphabet uses other than Roman letters, write his or her name and address abroad in the native alphabet.

(Name)	(Number and Street)
n/a	

(Town or City)	(State or Province)	(Country)

17. Is your fiancé(e) related to you?   ☐ Yes   ☒ No

If you are related, state the nature and degree of relationship, e.g., third cousin or maternal uncle, etc.

18. Has your fiancé(e) met and seen you within the two-year period immediately receding the filing of this petition?

☒ Yes   ☐ No

Describe the circumstances under which you met. If you have not personally met each other, explain how the relationship was established. Explain also in detail any reasons you may have for requesting that the requirement that you and your fiancé(e) must have met should not apply to you.

See attached statement.

19. Did you meet your fiancé(e) or spouse through the services of an international marriage broker?

☐ Yes   ☒ No

If you answered yes, please provide the name of the international marriage broker and where the international marriage broker is located. (Attach additional sheets of paper if necessary).

20. Your fiancé(e) will apply for a visa abroad at the American embassy or consulate at:

(City)	(Country)
London	England

NOTE: (Designation of a U.S. embassy or consulate outside the country of your fiancé(e)'s last residence does not guarantee acceptance for processing by that foreign post. Acceptance is at the discretion of the designated embassy or consulate.)

Sample Form I-129F (page 3)

Part C. Other information.

1. If you are serving overseas in the Armed Forces of the United States, please answer the following:

I presently reside or am stationed overseas and my current mailing address is: I plan to return to the United States on or about:

2. Have you ever been convicted by a court of law (civil or criminal) or court martialed by a military tribunal for any of the following crimes. This is required even if your records were sealed or otherwise cleared or if anyone, including a judge, law enforcement officer, or attorney, told you that you no longer have a record. *(Check all that apply. Using a separate sheet(s) of paper, attach information relating to the conviction(s), such as crime involved, date of conviction and sentence.)*

☐ Domestic violence, sexual assault, child abuse and neglect, dating violence, elder abuse and stalking.

☐ Homicide, murder, manslaughter, rape, abusive sexual contact, sexual exploitation, incest, torture, trafficking, peonage, holding hostage, involuntary servitude, slave trade, kidnapping, abduction, unlawful criminal restraint, false imprisonment or an attempt to commit any of these crimes.

☐ Three or more convictions for crimes relating to a controlled substance or alcohol not arising from a single act.

3. If you have provided information about a conviction for a crime listed above and you were being battered or subjected to extreme cruelty by your spouse, parent, or adult child at the time of your conviction, check all of the following that apply to you:

☐ I was acting in self-defense.

☐ I violated a protection order issued for my own protection.

☐ I committed, was arrested for, was convicted of, or plead guilty to committing a crime that did not result in serious bodily injury, and there was a connection between the crime committed and my having been battered or subjected to extreme cruelty.

Part D. Penalties, certification and petitioner's signature.

PENALTIES: You may by law be imprisoned for not more than five years, or fined $250,000, or both, for entering into a marriage contract for the purpose of evading any provision of the immigration laws, and you may be fined up to $10,000 or imprisoned up to five years, or both, for knowingly and willfully falsifying or concealing a material fact or using any false document in submitting this petition.

YOUR CERTIFICATION: I am legally able to and intend to marry my alien fiancé(e) within 90 days of his or her arrival in the United States. I certify, under penalty of perjury under the laws of the United States of America, that the foregoing is true and correct. Furthermore, I authorize the release of any information from my records that U.S. Citizenship and Immigration Services needs to determine eligibility for the benefit that I am seeking.

Moreover, I understand that any criminal conviction information that I am required to provide with this petition, and any related criminal conviction information pertaining to me that U.S. Citizenship and Immigration Services may discover independently in adjudicating this petition will be disclosed to the beneficiary of this petition.

Signature	**Date** *(mm/dd/yyyy)*	**Daytime Telephone Number** *(with area code)*
Sandra L. Beach	8/2/2006	212-555-1212

E-Mail Address (if any)

sandrab@email.com

Part E. Signature of person preparing form, if other than above. *(Sign below.)*

I declare that I prepared this application at the request of the petitioner and it is based on all information of which I have knowledge.

Signature	Print or Type Your Name	G-28 ID Number	Date *(mm/dd/yyyy)*

Firm Name and Address   Daytime Telephone Number *(with area code)*

E-Mail Address (if any)

Sample Fiancé Meeting Statement – Attachment to Form I-129F

Filed by Sandra Beach on Behalf of Nigel Hollis

Question 18

I met my fiancé 18 months ago, while visiting a college friend who has settled in England. My friend Carrie had been telling me for months that she wanted to introduce me to Nigel, because of our offbeat senses of humor and shared interest in long-distance swimming. I've had bad experiences with friends trying to set me up before, so I didn't take it very seriously. But when vacation plans took me to England, I let her arrange for me and Nigel to meet over lunch at a pub.

To my amazement, we clicked right away. We had a lot to talk about—he had completed an English Channel swim a few months before, and I'm hoping to swim the Channel next year. Both of us have built our lives around swimming, which sometimes leaves little time for other things, including relationships. We compared notes on training techniques, equipment, dealing with cold water, rip tides, and more.

Our lunch lasted all afternoon and into the evening. By the end of that evening, I considered Nigel a friend, and someone I could very easily fall in love with.

Nigel and I spent almost all my remaining week's vacation together. Poor Carrie joked that her plan had backfired, because I spent embarrassingly little time at her house. By the end of the week, we both knew this was headed toward a serious relationship.

Since then, Nigel and I have corresponded almost constantly by email, and call each other twice a week. During one long phone call, we decided to get married.

It was difficult deciding where we would live after marrying—Nigel has a beautiful cottage in Cornwall, and I could happily live in England. However, my mother is in poor health, and ever since my father passed away last year, she has relied on my help, so we agreed to make our home in New York.

As proof that Nigel and I are in love and plan to marry, I am attaching copies of his plane tickets to New York; photos of the two of us together; copies of our telephone bills and some of our emails; copies of catering and other contracts showing that the two of us plan to marry in July; and copies of our travel itinerary for New Zealand, where we will honeymoon.

Signed: _Sandra L. Beach_
        Sandra Beach

Date: ___8/2/2006___

Affidavit of Support, Sample Form I-134 (page 1)

OMB No. 1615-0014; Exp. 04-30-07

U.S. Department of Homeland Security
Bureau of Citizenship and Immigration Services

I-134, Affidavit of Support

(Answer All Items: Type or Print in Black Ink.)

I, _Sandra Leah Beach_ residing at _114 Fulton St., Apt. 6E_
(Name)   (Street and Number)

New York   _NY_   _10038_   _U.S.A._
(City)   (State)   (Zip Code if in U.S.)   (Country)

BEING DULY SWORN DEPOSE AND SAY:

1. I was born on _12/20/1981_ at _Horseheads_ _U.S.A._
(Date-mm/dd/yyyy)   (City)   (Country)

If you are **not** a native born United States citizen, answer the following as appropriate:

a. If a United States citizen through naturalization, give certificate of naturalization number _____

b. If a United States citizen through parent(s) or marriage, give citizenship certificate number _____

c. If United States citizenship was derived by some other method, attach a statement of explanation.

d. If a lawfully admitted permanent resident of the United States, give "A" number _____

2. That I am _25_ years of age and have resided in the United States since (date) _birth_

3. That this affidavit is executed on behalf of the following person:

Name (Family Name)	(First Name)	(Middle Name)	Gender	Age
Hollis	Nigel	Ian	M	27

Citizen of (Country)	Marital Status	Relationship to Sponsor
United Kingdom	Divorced	Fiancé

Presently resides at (Street and Number)	(City)	(State)	(Country)
123 Limestone Way #7	Penzance	Cornwall	U.K.

Name of spouse and children accompanying or following to join person:

Spouse	Gender	Age	Child		Gender	Age
Child	Gender	Age	Child		Gender	Age
Child	Gender	Age	Child		Gender	Age

4. That this affidavit is made by me for the purpose of assuring the United States Government that the person(s) named in item **3** will not become a public charge in the United States.

5. That I am willing and able to receive, maintain and support the person(s) named in item **3**. That I am ready and willing to deposit a bond, if necessary, to guarantee that such person(s) will not become a public charge during his or her stay in the United States, or to guarantee that the above named person(s) will maintain his or her nonimmigrant status, if admitted temporarily and will depart prior to the expiration of his or her authorized stay in the United States.

6. That I understand this affidavit will be binding upon me for a period of three (3) years after entry of the person(s) named in item **3** and that the information and documentation provided by me may be made available to the Secretary of Health and Human Services and the Secretary of Agriculture, who may make it available to a public assistance agency.

7. That I am employed as or engaged in the business of _Executive Assistant_ with _Helport Foundation_
(Type of Business)   (Name of Concern)

at _87 W. 57th St._ _New York_ _NY_ _10039_
(Street and Number)   (City)   (State)   (Zip Code)

I derive an annual income of *(if self-employed, I have attached a copy of my last income tax return or report of commercial rating concern which I certify to be true and correct to the best of my knowledge and belief. See instructions for nature of evidence of net worth to be submitted.)* $ _45,000_

I have on deposit in savings banks in the United States $ _8,000_

I have other personal property, the reasonable value which is $ _7,500_

Form I-134 (Rev. 06/17/04)N (Prior versions may be used until 09/30/04)

Sample Form I-134 (page 2)

I have stocks and bonds with the following market value, as indicated on the attached list, which I certify to be true and correct to the best of my knowledge and belief. $ _____ 0 _____

I have life insurance in the sum of $ _____ 0 _____

With a cash surrender value of $ _____

I own real estate valued at $ _____ 0 _____

With mortgage(s) or other encumbrance(s) thereon amounting to $ _____

Which is located at _____

| | (Street and Number) | (City) | (State) | (Zip Code) |

8. That the following persons are dependent upon me for support: *(Place an "x" in the appropriate column to indicate whether the person named is **wholly** or **partially** dependent upon you for support.)*

Name of Person	Wholly Dependent	Partially Dependent	Age	Relationship to Me
None				

9. That I have previously submitted affidavit(s) of support for the following person(s). If none, state *"None."*

Name	Date submitted
None	

10. That I have submitted visa petition(s) to the Bureau of Citizenship and Immigration Services (CIS) on behalf of the following person(s). If none, state none.

Name	Relationship	Date submitted
Nigel Ian Hollis	Fiancé	8/2/2006

11. That I ☐ intend ☒ do not intend to make specific contributions to the support of the person(s) named in item **3**. *(If you check "intend," indicate the exact nature and duration of the contributions. For example, if you intend to furnish room and board, state for how long and, if money, state the amount in United States dollars and state whether it is to be given in a lump sum, weekly or monthly, or for how long.)*

_____

_____

_____

Oath or Affirmation of Sponsor

I acknowledge that I have read Part III of the Instructions, Sponsor and Alien Liability, and am aware of my responsibilities as an immigrant sponsor under the Social Security Act, as amended, and the Food Stamp Act, as amended.

I swear (affirm) that I know the contents of this affidavit signed by me and that the statements are true and correct.

Signature of sponsor _____

Subscribed and sworn to (affirmed) before me this _____ **day of** _____ , _____

at _____ . **My commission expires on** _____

Signature of Officer Administering Oath _____ **Title** _____

If the affidavit is prepared by someone other than the sponsor, please complete the following: I declare that this document was prepared by me at the request of the sponsor and is based on all information of which I have knowledge.

| (Signature) | (Address) | (Date) |

Application for Immigrant Visa and Alien Registration, Sample Form DS-230, Part I (page 1)

U.S. Department of State

OMB APPROVAL NO. 1405-0015
EXPIRES: 07/31/2007
ESTIMATED BURDEN: 1 HOUR*
(See Page 2)

APPLICATION FOR IMMIGRANT VISA AND ALIEN REGISTRATION

PART I - BIOGRAPHIC DATA

INSTRUCTIONS: Complete one copy of this form for yourself and each member of your family, regardless of age, who will immigrate with you. Please print or type your answers to all questions. Mark questions that are **Not Applicable** with "N/A". If there is insufficient room on the form, answer on a separate sheet using the same numbers that appear on the form. Attach any additional sheets to this form.

WARNING: Any false statement or concealment of a material fact may result in your permanent exclusion from the United States.

This form (DS-230 PART I) is the first of two parts. This part, together with Form DS-230 PART II, constitutes the complete Application for Immigrant Visa and Alien Registration.

1. Family Name	First Name	Middle Name
Hollis	Nigel	Ian

2. Other Names Used or Aliases *(If married woman, give maiden name)*

None

3. Full Name in Native Alphabet *(If Roman letters not used)*

4. Date of Birth *(mm-dd-yyyy)*	5. Age	6. Place of Birth		
		(City or town)	*(Province)*	*(Country)*
8/17/79	27	Penzance	Cornwall	England

7. Nationality *(If dual national, give both)*	8. Gender	9. Marital Status
U.K.	[X] Male	[ ] Single *(Never married)* [ ] Married [ ] Widowed [X] Divorced [ ] Separated
	[ ] Female	Including my present marriage, I have been married _____ times.

10. Permanent address in the United States where you intend to live, if known *(street address including zip code)*. Include the name of a person who currently lives there.

Sandra Beach

114 Fulton Street #6E

New York, NY 10038

Telephone number: 212-555-1212

11. Address in the United States where you want your Permanent Resident Card (Green Card) mailed, if different from address in item #10 *(include the name of a person who currently lives there)*.

Telephone number:

12. Your Present Occupation

Sportswear Designer

13. Present Address *(Street Address) (City or Town) (Province) (Country)*

123 Limestone Way

Cornwall, Penzance, U.K. TR197NL

Telephone number: Home 1234 123456   Office 1234 654321

14. Name of Spouse *(Maiden or family name)*   First Name   Middle Name

Date *(mm-dd-yyyy)* and place of birth of spouse:

Address of spouse *(If different from your own)*:

Spouse's occupation: Date of marriage *(mm-dd-yyyy)*:

15. Father's Family Name	First Name	Middle Name
Hollis	Kevin	Andrew

16. Father's Date of Birth *(mm-dd-yyyy)*	Place of Birth	Current Address	If deceased, give year of death
1/12/1951	York, England	83 Herriott Rd., York	

17. Mother's Family Name at Birth	First Name	Middle Name
Chumley	Sarah	Elizabeth

18. Mother's Date of Birth *(mm-dd-yyyy)*	Place of Birth	Current Address	If deceased, give year of death
4/7/1955	York, England	83 Herriott Rd., York	

DS-230 Part I
07-2004

THIS FORM MAY BE OBTAINED FREE AT CONSULAR OFFICES OF THE UNITED STATES OF AMERICA
PREVIOUS EDITIONS OBSOLETE

Page 1 of 4

Sample Form DS-230, Part I (page 2)

19. List Names, Dates and Places of Birth, and Addresses of **ALL** Children.

NAME	DATE (mm-dd-yyyy)	PLACE OF BIRTH	ADDRESS (If different from your own)
None			

20. List below all places you have lived for at least six months since reaching the age of 16, including places in your country of nationality. Begin with your present residence.

CITY OR TOWN	PROVINCE	COUNTRY	FROM/TO (mm-yyyy)
Penzance	Cornwall	U.K.	7/1995-present
Cambridge		U.K.	9/1994-7/1998
York		U.K.	8/1978-9/1994

21a. Person(s) named in 14 and 19 who will accompany you to the United States now.

n/a

21b. Person(s) named in 14 and 19 who will follow you to the United States at a later date.

n/a

22. List below all employment for the last ten years.

EMPLOYER	LOCATION	JOB TITLE	FROM/TO (mm-yyyy)
Outbound Design	Penzance	Sportswear Designer	8/1998-present
Fish & Chips Shop	Cambridge	Fryer	9/1997-6/1998

In what occupation do you intend to work in the United States?_____

23. List below all educational institutions attended.

SCHOOL AND LOCATION	FROM/TO (mm-yyyy)	COURSE OF STUDY	DEGREE OR DIPLOMA
Cambridge Technical College	9/1994-6/1998	design	B.A.

Languages spoken or read: English, French

Professional associations to which you belong: International Design Group

24. Previous Military Service ☐ Yes ☒ No

Branch:_____ Dates (mm-dd-yyyy) of Service: _____

Rank/Position:_____ Military Speciality/Occupation: _____

25. List dates of all previous visits to or residence in the United States. (If never, write "never") Give type of visa status, if known. Give DHS "A" number if any.

FROM/TO (mm-yyyy)	LOCATION	TYPE OF VISA	"A" NO. (If known)
8/1999-8/1999	New York, San Francisco	B-2	None

SIGNATURE OF APPLICANT *Nigel J. Hollis*	DATE (mm-dd-yyyy) 11/20/2006

Privacy Act and Paperwork Reduction Act Statements

The information asked for on this form is requested pursuant to Section 222 of the Immigration and Nationality Act. The U.S. Department of State uses the facts you provide on this form primarily to determine your classification and eligibility for a U.S. immigrant visa. Individuals who fail to submit this form or who do not provide all the requested information may be denied a U.S. immigrant visa. If you are issued an immigrant visa and are subsequently admitted to the United States as an immigrant, the Department of Homeland Security will use the information on this form to issue you a Permanent Resident Card, and, if you so indicate, the Social Security Administration will use the information to issue you a social security number and card.

*Public reporting burden for this collection of information is estimated to average 1 hour per response, including time required for searching existing data sources, gathering the necessary data, providing the information required, and reviewing the final collection. In accordance with 5 CFR 1320 5(b), persons are not required to respond to the collection of this information unless this form displays a currently valid OMB control number. Send comments on the accuracy of this estimate of the burden and recommendations for reducing it to: U.S. Department of State (A/RPS/DIR) Washington, DC 20520.

DS-230 Part I   **Page 2 of 4**

Nonimmigrant Visa Application, Sample Form DS-156, (page 1)

U.S. Department of State
NONIMMIGRANT VISA APPLICATION

Approved OMB 1405-0018
Expires 09/30/2007
Estimated Burden 1 hour
See Page 2

PLEASE TYPE OR PRINT YOUR ANSWERS IN THE SPACE PROVIDED BELOW EACH ITEM

1. Passport Number	2. Place of Issuance:			DO NOT WRITE IN THIS SPACE
22431	City: London	Country: England	State/Province	B-1/B-2 MAX B-1 MAX B-2 MAX

DO NOT WRITE IN THIS SPACE

Other _____ MAX
Visa Classification

3. Issuing Country	4. Issuance Date (dd-mmm-yyyy)	5. Expiration Date (dd-mmm-yyyy)
U.K.	1/18/2005	1/18/2010

Mult or _____
Number of Applications

Months _____
Validity

Issued/Refused

6. Surnames (As in Passport)

Hollis

On _____ By _____

7. First and Middle Names (As in Passport)

Nigel Ian

Under SEC.   214(b)   221(g)

8. Other Surnames Used (Maiden, Religious, Professional, Aliases)

None

Other _____ INA

9. Other First and Middle Names Used	10. Date of Birth (dd-mmm-yyyy)
None	08/17/1979

Reviewed By _____

11. Place of Birth: City	Country	State/Province	12. Nationality
Penzance	England	Cornwall	U.K.

13. Sex	14. National Identification Number (If applicable)	15. Home Address (Include apartment number, street, city, state or province, postal zone and country)
[X] Male / [ ] Female		123 Limestone Way #7 Penzance, Cornwall, U.K. TR197NL

16. Home Telephone Number	Business Phone Number	Mobile/Cell Number
1234 123456	1234 654321	None
Fax Number	Business Fax Number	Pager Number
None	1234 655444	None

17. Marital Status	18. Spouse's Full Name (Even if divorced or separated. Include maiden name.)	19. Spouse's DOB (dd-mmm-yyyy)
[ ] Married [ ] Single (Never Married) [ ] Widowed [X] Divorced [ ] Separated	Jane Simpson	10/31/1980

20. Name and Address of Present Employer or School		
Name: Outbound Design, Inc.	Address: 222 Heather Lane Penzance, U.K. TR198NL	

21. Present Occupation (If retired, write "retired". If student, write "student".)	22. When Do You Intend To Arrive In The U.S.? (Provide specific date if known)	23. E-Mail Address
Sportswear Designer	December 2005	nigel@outbound.com

24. At What Address Will You Stay in The U.S.?

114 Fulton St. #6E
New York, NY 10038

BARCODE

25. Name and Telephone Numbers of Person in U.S. Who You Will Be Staying With or Visiting for Tourism or Business	
Name: Sandra Beach	Home Phone: 212-555-1212
Business Phone: 212-555-1313	Cell Phone: 212-555-1414

DO NOT WRITE IN THIS SPACE

26. How Long Do You Intend To Stay in The U.S.?	27. What is The Purpose of Your Trip?
Permanently after apply for AOS	Get married, apply for adjustment of status

50 mm x 50 mm

PHOTO

staple or glue photo here

28. Who Will Pay For Your Trip?	29. Have You Ever Been in The U.S.? [X] Yes [ ] No
I will	WHEN? August 1999 FOR HOW LONG? 3 weeks

Sample Form DS-156, (page 2)

30. Have You Ever Been Issued a U.S. Visa? ☒ Yes ☐ No	**31. Have You Ever Been Refused a U.S. Visa?** ☐ Yes ☒ No
WHEN? _7/12/99_	WHEN? _____
WHERE? _London_	WHERE? _____
WHAT TYPE OF VISA? _B-2 Tourist_	WHAT TYPE OF VISA? _____
32. Do You Intend To Work in The U.S.? ☒ Yes ☐ No *(If YES, give the name and complete address of U.S. employer.)* _After receipt of a work permit—_ _no employer yet._	**33. Do You Intend To Study in The U.S.?** ☐ Yes ☒ No *(If YES, give the name and complete address of the school.)*

34. Names and Relationships of Persons Traveling With You

None

35. Has Your U.S. Visa Ever Been Cancelled or Revoked? ☐ Yes ☒ No	**36. Has Anyone Ever Filed an Immigrant Visa Petition on Your Behalf?** ☐ Yes ☒ No If Yes, Who?

37. Are Any of The Following Persons in The U.S., or Do They Have U.S. Legal Permanent Residence or U.S. Citizenship?
Mark YES or NO and indicate that person's status in the U.S. (i.e., U.S. legal permanent resident, U.S. citizen, visiting, studying, working, etc.).

☐ YES ☒ NO Husband/Wife _____   ☒ YES ☐ NO Fiance/Fiancee _U.S. citizen_   ☐ YES ☒ NO Brother/Sister _____

☐ YES ☒ NO Father/Mother _____   ☐ YES ☒ NO Son/Daughter _____   Brother/Sister _____

38. IMPORTANT: ALL APPLICANTS MUST READ AND CHECK THE APPROPRIATE BOX FOR EACH ITEM.
A visa may not be issued to persons who are within specific categories defined by law as inadmissible to the United States (except when a waiver is obtained in advance). Is any of the following applicable to you?

- Have you ever been arrested or convicted for any offense or crime, even though subject of a pardon, amnesty or other similar legal action? Have you ever unlawfully distributed or sold a controlled substance (drug), or been a prostitute or procurer for prostitutes? ☐ YES ☒ NO

- Have you ever been refused admission to the U.S., or been the subject of a deportation hearing, or sought to obtain or assist others to obtain a visa, entry into the U.S., or any other U.S. immigration benefit by fraud or willful misrepresentation or other unlawful means? Have you attended a U.S. public elementary school on student (F) status or a public secondary school after November 30, 1996 without reimbursing the school? ☐ YES ☒ NO

- Do you seek to enter the United States to engage in export control violations, subversive or terrorist activities, or any other unlawful purpose? Are you a member or representative of a terrorist organization as currently designated by the U.S. Secretary of State? Have you ever participated in persecutions directed by the Nazi government of Germany; or have you ever participated in genocide? ☐ YES ☒ NO

- Have you ever violated the terms of a U.S. visa, or been unlawfully present in, or deported from, the United States? ☐ YES ☒ NO

- Have you ever withheld custody of a U.S. citizen child outside the United States from a person granted legal custody by a U.S. court, voted in the United States in violation of any law or regulation, or renounced U.S. citizenship for the purpose of avoiding taxation? ☐ YES ☒ NO

- Have you ever been afflicted with a communicable disease of public health significance or a dangerous physical or mental disorder, or ever been a drug abuser or addict? ☐ YES ☒ NO

While a YES answer does not automatically signify ineligibility for a visa, if you answered YES you may be required to personally appear before a consular officer.

39. Was this Application Prepared by Another Person on Your Behalf? (If answer is YES, then have that person complete item 40.)   ☐ Yes ☒ No

40. Application Prepared By:

NAME: _____   Relationship to Applicant: _____

ADDRESS: _____

Signature of Person Preparing Form: _____   DATE *(dd-mmm-yyyy)* _____

41. I certify that I have read and understood all the questions set forth in this application and the answers I have furnished on this form are true and correct to the best of my knowledge and belief. I understand that any false or misleading statement may result in the permanent refusal of a visa or denial of entry into the United States. I understand that possession of a visa does not automatically entitle the bearer to enter the United States of America upon arrival at a port of entry if he or she is found inadmissible.

APPLICANT'S SIGNATURE _Nigel J. Hollis_   DATE *(dd-mmm-yyyy)* _11/20/2006_

Nonimmigrant Fiancé(e) Visa Application, Sample Form DS-156K

U.S. Department of State

NONIMMIGRANT FIANCÉ(E) VISA APPLICATION

USE WITH FORM DS-156

OMB APPROVAL NO.1405-0096
EXPIRES: 07/31/2007
ESTIMATED BURDEN: 1 HOUR*

The following questions must be answered by all applicants for visas to enter the United States as the fiancée or fiancé of a U.S. citizen in order that a determination may be made as to visa eligibility.

This form, together with Form DS-156, Nonimmigrant Visa Application, completed in duplicate, constitutes the complete application for a "K" Fiancé(e) Nonimmigrant Visa authorized under Section 222(c) of the Immigration and Nationality Act.

1. FAMILY NAME	FIRST NAME	MIDDLE NAME
Hollis	Nigel	Ian

2. DATE OF BIRTH (mm-dd-yyyy)	3. PLACE OF BIRTH (City, Province, Country)
08/17/1979	Penzance, Cornwall, England, U.K.

4. MARITAL STATUS
    If you are now married or were previously married, answer the following:

a. Name of spouse: Jane Simpson

b. Date (mm-dd-yyyy) and place of marriage: 6/10/2000   London

c. How and when was marriage terminated: 5/20/2003   Divorce

d. If presently married, how will you marry your U.S. citizen fiancé(e)? Explain:*

    * NOTE: If presently married to anyone, you are **not** eligible for a fiancé(e) visa.

5. LIST NAME, DATE AND PLACE OF BIRTH OF ALL UNMARRIED CHILDREN UNDER 21 YEARS OF AGE

NAME	BIRTH DATE (mm-dd-yyyy)	BIRTH PLACE	WILL ACCOMPANY YOU YES NO	WILL FOLLOW YOU YES NO
None			☐ ☐	☐ ☐
			☐ ☐	☐ ☐
			☐ ☐	☐ ☐
			☐ ☐	☐ ☐
			☐ ☐	☐ ☐

THE FOLLOWING DOCUMENTS MUST BE ATTACHED IN ORDER TO APPLY FOR A FIANCE(E) NONIMMIGRANT VISA

- Your birth certificate
- Birth certificates of all children listed in No. 5
- Death certificate of spouse (if any)
- Marriage certificate (if any)
- Divorce decree (if any)
- Police certificates
- Evidence of engagement to your fiancé(e)
- Evidence of financial support

NOTE: All of the above documents will also be required by the U.S. Citizenship and Immigration Services (USCIS) when you apply for adjustment of status to lawful permanent resident. The USCIS will accept these documents for that purpose.

DO NOT WRITE BELOW THIS LINE
The consular officer will assist you in answering this part.

I understand that I am required to submit my visa to the United States Immigration Officer at the place where I apply to enter the United States, and that the possession of a visa does not entitle me to enter the United States if at that time I am found to be inadmissable under the immigration laws. I further understand that my adjustment of status to permanent resident alien is dependent upon marriage to a U.S. citizen and upon meeting all of the requirements of the U.S. Department of Homeland Security.

I understand that any willfully false or misleading statement or willful concealment of a material fact made by me herein may subject me to permanent exclusion from the United States and, if I am admitted to the United States, may subject me to criminal prosecution and/or deportation.

I hereby certify that I am legally free to marry and intend to marry _____ , a U.S. citizen, within 90 days of my admission into the United States.

I do solemnly swear or affirm that all statements which appear in this application have been made by me and are true and complete to the best of my knowledge and belief.

_____
Signature of Applicant

SUBSCRIBED AND SWORN TO before me this _____ day of _____ , _____ at: _____

_____
United States Consular Officer

*Public reporting burden for this collection of information is estimated to average 1 hour per response, including time required for searching existing data sources, gathering the necessary data, providing the information required, and reviewing the final collection. In accordance with 5 CFR 1320 5(b), persons are not required to respond to the collection of this information unless this form displays a currently valid OMB control number. Send comments on the accuracy of this estimate of the burden and recommendations for reducing it to: U.S. Department of State (A/RPS/DIR) Washington, D.C. 20520.

DS-156K
07-2004

PREVIOUS EDITIONS OBSOLETE

Green Cards Through Marriage

I'm Getting Married in the Morning

Every year, thousands of immigrants fall in love with U.S. citizens or permanent residents. Some couples meet overseas, others meet when the foreigner is studying or traveling in the United States. In a few cases, both members of the couple are foreign born, but one becomes a U.S. citizen or permanent resident. No matter how it came about, your topmost priority right now may be to join each other in the U.S. as soon as possible. This chapter will lay out the possibilities and help you decide the easiest, fastest way to achieve this.

We're assuming that you plan to live in the United States. If not, there's no point in applying for a green card now. You won't get one if the U.S. citizen or permanent resident can't show that he or she is, or soon will be, living and earning income in the U.S., and you'll lose the green card if you don't make the U.S. your home. If you're going to be living overseas for a while, wait until your plans change to apply for the green card.

A. Who Qualifies

You are eligible for a green card if you have entered into a bona fide, legal marriage with a U.S. citizen or lawful permanent resident. Bona fide means that the marriage is based on your desire to create a life together with your new spouse, not merely on your desire to obtain a green card. Legal means that it is valid and recognized by the laws of the state or country in which you live. It doesn't matter whether you hold the marriage ceremony in the United States or overseas, but you do need to abide by local laws—and obtain a document, such as a marriage certificate, to prove that you've done so.

- **Marriage to a U.S. citizen** makes you an immediate relative and eligible to receive a green card just as soon as you can get through the application process.
- **Marriage to a U.S. permanent resident,** unfortunately, will not yield such fast results. Your new spouse can file a visa petition for you

right away, but then you'll be placed in category 2A of the family visa preferences and have to wait, probably several years, before a green card becomes available to you. Only after that waiting period is over and you've applied for your green card will you be legally permitted to live in the United States.

The Inconveniences of Marriages of Convenience

In the early 1980s, the U.S. government came to believe that as many as half the petitions based on marriage were fraudulent, in that the marriages were entered into solely for the purpose of obtaining a green card. In 1986, the U.S. Congress passed a law called the Immigration Marriage Fraud Amendments, to eliminate as many "paper marriages" as possible.

U.S. citizens, permanent residents, and aliens who evade immigration laws by means of a fraudulent marriage can be charged with a federal crime. Those found guilty can be imprisoned for up to five years, fined up to $250,000, or both imprisoned and fined. In addition, permanent residents can be deported, as can those who are undocumented.

If you are even entertaining the idea of entering into a sham marriage, consider the following...

Do you want to live with the possibility of being blackmailed emotionally, psychologically, and financially?

Do you want to be prosecuted for a federal crime with a penalty of five years in prison, a fine of up to $250,000, or both?

If USCIS discovers that you have entered into a marriage or even helped someone else enter into a marriage to evade the immigration laws—or if you have submitted papers to USCIS based on such a marriage—you will almost certainly forever lose the possibility of getting a green card, no matter what relationships you may have in the future.

B. Special Rules in Court Proceedings

Suppose that removal—formerly called deportation or exclusion—proceedings have been started against you, perhaps because the immigration authorities have found that you are out of status or that you entered the U.S. without the proper documentation. While the proceedings are pending, you marry a U.S. citizen. You are now potentially eligible to file your marriage-based petition and the application for adjustment of status with the judge.

However, because you married while removal proceedings were going on, your marital status is suspect. After all, you did get married with the "shotgun" of a possible removal order facing you. You, the newly married alien, will have to provide clear and convincing evidence showing that the marriage was entered into in good faith and not solely for the purpose of getting a green card, and that no fee or financial arrangements were given for filing the petition. (Don't worry about the money you might have paid an attorney or other person to help you, that doesn't count.)

You will have to clearly establish that you married to establish a life together—for love and with a real commitment—not simply to avoid removal from the United States. See Section D4, below, for more guidance on gathering this kind of evidence. Also seek help from an experienced attorney.

C. Quick View of the Marriage-Based Green Card Application Process

Let's start with the general concept: To get a marriage-based green card, the U.S. citizen or permanent resident spouse must begin the process by submitting a "visa petition" (Form I-130). This form serves to prove to the immigration authorities that you're legally married. After that petition is approved, you, the immigrant, complete your half of the process by submitting a green card application and attending an interview, usually with your spouse. Your application serves to prove not only that your marriage is technically legal, but that it's the "real thing," and that you're otherwise eligible for U.S. permanent residence.

However, the details of when and how all this happens depend on two things: first, whether you, the immigrant, are living overseas or in the United States; and second, whether your spouse is a U.S. citizen or a permanent resident. We'll briefly describe each possible situation separately.

Immigrant living overseas, married to a U.S. citizen, option 1. The U.S. citizen submits the visa petition to a USCIS Service Center (unless the citizen also lives overseas, in which case some consulates will accept the visa petition directly). After the service center approves the visa petition, a processing unit called the National Visa Center (NVC) sends the immigrant a package containing forms and instructions. The immigrant fills out some of the forms and send them to the U.S. consulate serving the area where he or she lives. (Note that the forms the immigrant receives are from the U.S. State Department, and are unique to the consular process—that is, different than USCIS forms used by immigrants in the United States.)

After the consulate receives the immigrant's forms, it will send the immigrant a second package containing an interview appointment letter and instructions on getting a medical exam done and obtaining other documents. At the interview (which only the immigrant is required to attend), the immigrant is approved for a visa. He or she must then use the visa to enter the United States within six months to claim his or her permanent residence (or "conditional" residence, if you've been married less than two years at this time; see Section F for details). The entire process usually takes at least a year.

Immigrant living overseas, married to a U.S. citizen, option 2. Because the process of obtaining a green card from overseas based on marriage can take so long, a second method was devised a few years ago. This new method allows the married immigrant to start the application process overseas, but finish it in the U.S., having gained U.S. entry using a modified "fiancé visa." As usual, the U.S. citizen starts the process by submitting a visa petition (on Form I-130) to a USCIS Service Center. However, as soon as the U.S. citizen receives a receipt notice from the service center, he or she must submit a separate, fiancé visa petition (on Form I-129F) to a special USCIS office in the United States.

After this special office approves the fiancé visa petition, it sends word to the National Visa Center (NVC). The NVC conducts some preprocessing procedures, then transfers the case to a U.S. consulate close to where the immigrant lives. The NVC also sends the immigrant a package containing some forms to fill out and return to the consulate. After the consulate receives the immigrant's forms, it will send a package containing an interview appointment letter and some more forms to fill out.

The immigrant attends the interview and presents this latest batch of forms. The consulate approves the immigrant for a K-3, or fiancé, visa. This does not mean that the immigrant has been approved for a green card; the K-3 visa simply allows the immigrant to enter the United States in order to apply for the green card there.

After entering the U.S., the immigrant can prepare and submit an adjustment of status application to a USCIS office. After several months, the immigrant and his or her spouse must attend an interview, at which the immigrant will be approved for permanent residence (or conditional residence if they've been married for less than two years at that time; see Section F for details).

Immigrant living overseas, married to a U.S. permanent resident. The U.S. permanent resident submits the visa petition to a USCIS Service Center. It will stay there until close to the time the immigrant's Priority Date is current (see Chapter 5 for a discussion of Priority Dates). After it's approved, the case will be transferred to a processing unit called the National Visa Center (NVC). The NVC will then send the immigrant a package containing forms and instructions. The immigrant fills out some of the forms and send them to the U.S. consulate serving the area where he or she lives. (Note that the forms the immigrant

receives are from the U.S. State Department, and are unique to the consular process—that is, different than USCIS forms used by immigrants in the United States.)

After the consulate receives the immigrant's forms, it will send the immigrant a package containing an interview appointment letter and instructions on getting a medical exam done and obtaining other documents. At the interview (which only the immigrant is required to attend), the immigrant is approved for a visa, then must enter the United States within six months to claim his or her permanent residence.

Immigrant living in the United States, married to a U.S. citizen. Ideally, the U.S. citizen submits the visa petition together with the immigrant's green card application (adjustment of status packet complete with forms, photos, and the results of a medical exam) to USCIS. The immigrant is sent a fingerprint appointment notice and later an interview appointment notice. Both husband and wife must attend the interview, which will be held at a local USCIS district office. At the interview, the immigrant is approved for permanent residence (or conditional residence, if they've been married less than two years at this time; see Section F for details). However, not all immigrants are eligible to use the adjustment of status procedure—in particular, those whose last entry into the U.S. was illegal cannot. See Chapter 18 for details.

Immigrant living in the United States, married to a U.S. permanent resident. The U.S. permanent resident submits the visa petition to a USCIS Service Center. It will stay there until close to the time the immigrant's Priority Date (discussed in Chapter 5) is current. After it's approved, however, things can get complicated. The only way the immigrant can remain in the United States to adjust status (submit a green card application) is if he or she has either been living legally in the United States during all the intervening years (in which case he or she can adjust status as described in the paragraph above) or started the process when previous laws were in effect. (See Chapter 18 for details on who can adjust status.) The immigrant's alternative is to continue with the case at an overseas U.S. consulate, but if the immigrant has been living illegally in the U.S., this could result in a three- or ten-year bar on reentry (as explained in Chapter 4). See an attorney for a full analysis.

D. Detailed Instructions for the Marriage-Based Green Card Application Process

Now we'll break the application process down into individual procedures, some of which will be covered in this chapter, others of which will be covered in other chapters—we'll tell you exactly where to go to for your situation. We'll start by discussing the visa petition, which all couples must begin by preparing.

Note: The legal term for the U.S. citizen or permanent resident who is signing the immigration papers for the alien spouse is "petitioner." The legal term for the alien spouse is "beneficiary."

1. Beginning the Process: The Visa Petition

No matter what, the U.S. citizen or permanent resident must prepare and collect the following items that make up the visa petition:

❏ Form I-130, Petition for Alien Relative. (See the sample at the end of this chapter. However, if you're also planning to apply for a fiancé visa for speedy entry into the United States, there's one important change to the usual procedures for filling out the form: On Question 22, the U.S. spouse should write "Applicant plans to obtain a K-3 visa abroad and adjust status in the United States," then fill in the lines regarding which city the immigrant plans to adjust status in, and which consulate he or she would return to, if necessary, as a backup.) This form must be signed by the U.S. citizen or permanent resident spouse. It gives information about both the husband and the wife.

❏ Two copies of Form G-325A, Biographic Information—one for the husband and the other for the wife. Each person must fill out a separate form and sign it. (See the sample at the end of this chapter.) The form contains information about the parents, places of residence, employers of both spouses during the past five years, and any previous foreign residences. Both of these forms can be used for checking on the alien spouse's background.

❏ Photos of the immigrant and spouse (one each). These must be passport-style, in color, and taken within 30 days before the filing.

❏ Proof that the American half of the couple (the "petitioner") is either a U.S. citizen or permanent resident. If a citizen, this person should provide a copy of his or her passport, birth certificate, naturalization certificate (don't worry, it's legal to photocopy it for this purpose), or copy of Form FS-20 (Report of Birth Abroad of a Citizen of the United States, issued by a U.S. consulate). If a permanent resident, this person should provide a copy of his or her green card (front and back), passport stamp, or USCIS approval notice.

❏ Documents to prove that there is a valid marriage, including copies of the documents listed below.

Marriage certificate. Submit the civil registry certificate and not the marriage license or the church certificate, unless your country accepts a church marriage certificate as an official document. Marriage by proxy, a cultural practice in certain countries, is not acceptable to the immigration authorities.

Previous marriages. If either of you was previously married, attach proof of the termination of the previous marriage—a divorce decree, annulment decree, or death certificate. Some foreign divorces may not be recognized by USCIS. The law provides that at least one of the parties must be living in the place where the divorce was granted. In addition, when the divorcing pair is living in the U.S., they should obtain a divorce in a local court, not at their embassy.

❑ Filing fee of $190 in the form of a check, money order, or certified check payable to USCIS.

When you've completed and assembled all these items, make two complete copies for yourself and your spouse. What you'll do with it next depends on where you are living, how you entered the U.S. and whether you're eligible to adjust status here, your spouse's status, and where your spouse is living, as detailed on the summary chart below. Look under "Where to Mail the Application."

SUMMARY CHART: From Visa Petition to Green Card Application		
Your situation	**Where to mail the application**	**What's next**
You're living overseas, and your spouse is a U.S. citizen living in the United States.	**Option 1: Standard procedure.** Send the I-130 visa petition via certified mail with a return receipt requested to the USCIS Service Center that serves your spouse's geographic region. Find the correct address and post office box on the USCIS website at www.uscis.gov.	**Option 1: Standard procedure.** As soon as the visa petition is approved, you'll be able to apply for your immigrant visa and green card through an overseas U.S. consulate. (See Chapter 19.)
	Option 2: K-3 visa. Although you're married, you're allowed to use a special type of fiancé visa to get you into the United States, after which you must apply to adjust status in order to become a permanent resident. To take advantage of this option, send Form I-130 as detailed above, but as soon as you can prove that USCIS received it, also send Form I-129F to USCIS, P.O. Box 7218, Chicago, IL 60680-7218.	**Option 2: K-3 fiancé visa procedure.** As soon as USCIS approves the Form I-129F fiancé visa petition, the immigrant will be able to apply for a nonimmigrant visa at an overseas consulate (see Chapter 6, Section A5 for instructions); and after the immigrant enters the United States, for a green card through USCIS (see Chapter 18 for instructions on the adjustment of status application). To avoid USCIS confusion, the immigrant should, as soon as possible after entering the U.S., send a letter to the service center processing the Form I-130 saying that he or she is here and will be adjusting status. (Without such a letter, some service centers have been known to send the case to the overseas consulate for processing.)

SUMMARY CHART: From Visa Petition to Green Card Application (continued)		
Your situation	**Where to mail the application**	**What's next**
You're living overseas, and your spouse is a U.S. lawful permanent resident living in the United States.	Send the I-130 visa petition via certified mail with a return receipt requested to the USCIS Service Center that serves your spouse's geographic region. Find the correct address and post office box on the USCIS website at www.uscis.gov.	Approval of the visa petition will give you a Priority Date, but you'll have to wait until that date is current to apply for your green card. You'll need to wait overseas during that time, after which you'll apply for your immigrant visa and green card through a U.S. consulate. (See Chapter 19.)
You're presently in the U.S., and your spouse is a lawful permanent resident.	Send the I-130 visa petition via certified mail with a return receipt requested to the USCIS Service Center that serves your spouse's geographic region. Find the correct address and post office box on the USCIS website at www.uscis.gov.	Approval of the visa petition will give you a Priority Date, but you'll have to wait until that date is current to apply for your green card. Unless you have a separate visa to remain in the U.S. for those years, or will be eligible to adjust status in the U.S (see Chapter 18), you may have to leave soon to avoid the three- and ten-year time bars for having lived in the U.S. illegally.
You're presently in the U.S., and your spouse is a U.S. citizen. **Situation one:** You entered illegally.	See an immigration attorney for help—you may not be able to adjust status without leaving the United States, which would probably expose you to a three- or ten-year bar on returning.	
Situation two: You entered legally (with a visa or on a visa waiver, no matter if your expiration date passed), but did not misuse your visa to enter in order to get a green card.	You are eligible to adjust status in the United States. Submit your I-130 visa petition in combination with the immigrant's adjustment of status application (described in Chapter 18) to your local USCIS office.	Await fingerprinting and, later, an interview at your local USCIS office.

2. Option for Overseas Spouses of U.S. Citizens: The Fiancé Visa Petition

If you've elected to use the fiancé visa option to get you into the United States more quickly, the U.S. citizen will also need to submit a separate visa petition, consisting of:

❑ Form I-129F, Petition for Alien Fiancé(e). (See the sample for married couples at the end of this chapter.) The most important thing to realize about this form is that it's usually used for people who haven't yet gotten married—who are, in fact, fiancés. Don't be thrown off by instructions or questions directed at people who aren't yet married.

❑ Proof that the American half of the couple (the "petitioner") is a U.S. citizen, such as a copy of his or her passport, birth certificate, naturalization certificate (don't worry, it's legal to photocopy it for this purpose), or copy of Form FS-20 (Report of Birth Abroad of a Citizen of the United States, issued by a U.S. consulate).

❑ Proof that the U.S. citizen spouse has already filed Form I-130, Petition for Alien Relative, with another USCIS Service Center. You may need to wait until the USCIS Service Center sends a Form I-797 receipt notice, then photocopy this and send the copy. However, many people have successfully gotten USCIS to accept other types of proof of filing, including a complete copy of your Form I-130, with a registered letter receipt or similar proof that it was mailed and a copy of the cancelled filing-fee check.

❑ Photos of the immigrant and spouse (one each). These must be in color, passport style, taken within the 30 days before the filing.

❑ Filing fee (currently $170) in the form of a check, money order, or certified check payable to USCIS. Don't send cash.

When you've completed and assembled all these items, make two complete copies for each of your records. Then mail the completed package to: USCIS, P.O. Box 7218, Chicago, IL 60680-7218.

⚠ **Entering the U.S. illegally causes problems.** Except in rare circumstances (described in Chapter 18), people who entered the United States illegally (for example, by crossing the border away from an inspection point) do not have the right to adjust status—that is, apply for a green card—in the United States. Attempting to turn your application in at a local USCIS office could get you deported. Your best course is to get help from an experienced immigration attorney in evaluating and completing your application.

3. Moving the Process Forward

After the U.S. citizen or permanent resident spouse has submitted Form I-130 (and possibly Form I-129F or an adjustment of status packet) to USCIS, it's time to start playing the waiting game. No matter what, you'll probably wait longer than you'd like for a decision on your application. See Chapter 5 for a full explanation of how long you're likely to wait, and why. In particular, spouses of U.S. permanent residents should understand the years-long waits that are caused by limitations on the number of green cards given out in their category every year. If your application seems to be held up due to a simple bureaucratic delay, see Chapter 21 for sample inquiry letters and other instructions on prodding the USCIS into taking action.

For the next step in the process, see the "What's Next" column in the summary chart. For most immigrants, the next step will involve either applying for a green card from outside the United States, through a process called consular processing (discussed in Chapter 19), or from inside the United States, through a process called adjustment of status (discussed in Chapter 18). However, a few unlucky immigrants will get stuck at this point, realizing that because of past illegal entries into the U.S. or other problems, their application cannot go forward. Such persons should consult with an experienced immigration attorney.

Regardless of whether you will be completing your application overseas or in the United States, come back to this chapter for a discussion of materials that only married couples need to prepare in preparation for their interview. (See Section D, below.)

You cannot apply for a green card as a second preference alien until your Priority Date is current. There will be a long waiting period for your Priority Date to become current. For example, as of June 2006, the Department of State listed the waiting period for the second preference 2A category as almost five years. The law expects that you will spend this period outside the United States, and get your visa through a U.S. consulate.

Once your Priority Date is current, and if you are in status and otherwise eligible, you may apply for adjustment of status in the United States. Being "in status" means that the expiration date on your I-94 hasn't passed and you haven't violated the terms of your visa.

However, during the many years you were waiting for your Priority Date to become current, it's very possible you reached the expiration date of your permitted stay in the U.S.—in other words, fell out of status. And, a family member who is out of status or who has worked without authorization or entered the country without inspection is probably not eligible to apply for adjustment of status unless:

- the spouse through which he or she is immigrating becomes a U.S. citizen, or
- the immigrant is covered by the old legal provision that allowed otherwise ineligible applicants to adjust if they agreed to pay a $1,000 penalty. To qualify under this penalty provision, an applicant must have had a visa petition or labor certification on file by January 14, 1998; or have been physically present in the U.S. on December 21, 2000, and had a visa petition or labor certification on file by April 30, 2001.

An additional problem is that if you were out of status for six months after April 1, 1997, leave the United States, and seek to be admitted through a consulate or border, you will be subject to a three-year waiting period; the period is ten years if you were out of status for one year after April 1, 1997. There is a waiver available if you are the spouse or the son or daughter of a U.S. citizen or permanent resident, if you can show the U.S. citizen or resident would suffer extreme hardship. It's very difficult to get this waiver.

4. Documenting Your Bona Fide Marriage

Whether you are applying for adjustment of status or for an immigrant visa at a consulate abroad, start gathering documents for your green card interview. At the interview, you must present not only the standard information that every immigrant does, but also separate documents showing that you have a real, valid marriage. This would include:

- birth certificates for all children of the petitioner and beneficiary
- leases on apartments that the petitioner and beneficiary have occupied, together with rent receipts or cancelled checks
- hospital cards; union books; insurance policies; pay vouchers; joint bank account statements; telephone, gas, and electric bills; or charge cards containing the names of petitioner and beneficiary
- federal income tax returns, signed, dated, and authenticated by the Internal Revenue Service, for the years that the beneficiary and petitioner have been married
- wedding pictures of petitioner and beneficiary, and
- any snapshots of petitioner and beneficiary together taken before the marriage and, more importantly, since the marriage.

Collect and make copies of as many of these documents as possible. If you and your spouse have married for love, you will eventually prevail. Nevertheless, you still have to present the required documentary proof.

E. Bringing Your Children

People immigrating through marriage are often allowed to bring their children with them, even if the children are from a previous marriage or relationship. For immigration purposes, your children must be unmarried and under the age of 21 to immigrate at the same time as you. (Options for older or married children are discussed in Chapter 9.) However, the rules and procedures for having your children immigrate with you vary slightly depending on whether your U.S. spouse is a permanent resident or a citizen.

1. If You're Marrying a U.S. Citizen

If you're marrying a U.S. citizen, each of your children must separately qualify as an "immediate relative" of your spouse in order to immigrate with you.

To qualify as an immediate relative, your child can either be:

- the natural child of the U.S. citizen (if born out of wedlock to a U.S. citizen father, the father must have either legitimated the child while the child was under 18 and living in his custody, or demonstrated a bona fide relationship, through financial or other support), or
- the stepchild of the U.S. citizen, meaning it's legally your (the immigrant's) child, whether by birth or adoption, and you married the U.S. citizen before the child reached the age of 18.

Your spouse will need to submit a separate visa petition (Form I-130) for each one of these children, preferably in the same packet as he or she submits the visa petition for you, the immigrant. (If you have no choice but to submit the visa petitions separately, write a letter to accompany the later ones, explaining that you'd like the cases joined together.) If you're also using a fiancé visa for quicker U.S. entry, your spouse must additionally fill out a separate Form I-129F fiancé visa petition for each child.

2. If You're Marrying a U.S. Permanent Resident

If you're marrying a permanent resident, your children (natural or adopted) who are unmarried and under age 21 are considered "derivative beneficiaries." As a practical matter, this means that your children won't need a separate initial visa petition in order to be included in your immigration process, at least at the beginning—your spouse must simply fill in the blanks on Form I-130 that ask for the children's names. Unlike many other applicants, your children won't need to prove that your spouse is their parent or stepparent.

Your children will be given the same Priority Date as you, and most likely get a visa at the same time (provided they remain unmarried and under the age of 21). If they marry, they lose their chance to immigrate as beneficiaries. If they turn 21 before their Priority Date becomes current, they drop into a separate visa category (2B) and will immigrate later.

3. Final Phases of Children's Green Card Application

After the visa petition has been approved and you and your children are ready to submit your paperwork for your green cards, each child must submit his or her own application, whether to the U.S. consulate overseas or to a U.S. immigration office. These applications are discussed in Chapters 18 and 19.

As a practical matter, however, you can help your child fill out the forms, and even sign them if the child is too young (just write next to your signature, "by [*your name*], the child's [*mother or father*]."

F. If Your Marriage Is Less Than Two Years Old

If you become a resident within two years of the date you were married, whether you were granted status by adjustment of status or by consular processing, your green card is only conditional—in other words, it expires in another two years. You are considered a "conditional permanent resident."

It seems contradictory to be both "permanent" and "conditional" at the same time, but it actually makes sense in this situation. This is because once you remove the conditional basis, your two years of conditional residence will count as unconditional or permanent residence for naturalization (citizenship) and other purposes.

To receive a green card without conditions that will be valid for more than two years, you could wait until you have been married at least two years before becoming a permanent resident. (In fact, if you're overseas, this may mean delaying your date of entry to the United States—because even after you get your immigrant visa from the consulate, you're not a permanent resident until you go through a U.S. port of entry.) (This is because if your marriage is already two years old at the time your permanent residence is granted, you are a full-fledged permanent resident and do not need to file papers to remove any conditions.)

However, most people go ahead and become permanent residents, then wait two years minus 90 days and request the removal of the conditional status. Also, your alien sons or daughters who may have been petitioned by your spouse must likewise apply for removal of their conditional statuses.

⚠️ **The timing of your request is crucial.** Mark on your calendar the third month before your second anniversary of becoming a conditional permanent resident.

EXAMPLE: Your date of admission as a conditional permanent resident was December 7, 2001, the date printed on your conditional green card. The second anniversary of your conditional permanent residence is December 7, 2003. And 90 days (three months) before the second anniversary of December 7, 2003 is September 7, 2003. Therefore, you must file for the removal of the conditional status any time after September 7, 2003 and before December 7, 2003.

1. Forms Required for Removal of Conditions

Within the 90 days before the second anniversary of your conditional permanent residence, you must submit the following:

❏ Form I-751, Petition to Remove the Conditions on Residence, signed by both husband and wife (see the sample at the end of this chapter), or by the alien spouse alone, if seeking a waiver, and

❏ fee (currently $205) in the form of a money order or certified check, payable to USCIS.

You must also present evidence of a true marriage. To do this, submit a sample of as many of the following documents as possible (from within the past two years):

❏ title to house or condo or co-op, or any other real property showing joint ownership

❏ lease to your apartment showing joint tenancy since the time of marriage

❏ telephone or electric and gas bills showing both your names or addressed to you as Mr. and Mrs.

❏ bank books or statements showing evidence of a joint checking or savings account

❏ registration, with both names, of cars or any personal property

❏ insurance policies taken by husband or wife and showing the other as the beneficiary of any insurance benefits

❏ birth certificate of any child born of the marriage, showing both parents' names

❏ current letter from employer of both husband and wife, on the company letterhead, stating present job and salary and the name of a person to be notified in case of emergency

❏ current will showing one spouse as the beneficiary of the other's estate, and

❏ affidavits from your friends or relatives stating that they know your marriage was entered into in good faith and the reasons or facts they have to support this judgment. Your parents, employer, coworker, friend, priest, pastor, rabbi, or imam should give details of times and places at which you appeared as husband and wife. This should be required only if you do not have sufficient proof of a true marriage—or for other unusual cases such as a waiver.

These documents should be sent by certified mail, return receipt requested, to the USCIS Regional Service Center nearest your residence. (See the USCIS website for the address and P.O. box.) You may receive a notice for an interview or it may be approved without one.

While you're waiting, however, the receipt notice that you get from the USCIS Service Center will be your only proof that you are legally in the United States. Your stay will remain legal until a decision is made on your Form I-751. You can use the receipt notice in combination with your expired green card to prove your right to work. If you travel, however, it's best to visit a local USCIS office to get a stamp in your passport with which to reenter the United States.

In any case, with or without an interview, your green card becomes permanent only when UCIS decides to approve your joint petition.

2. If Your Spouse Does Not Sign the Joint Petition

If your spouse will not or cannot sign the joint petition, do not despair. Where certain circumstances are beyond your control, USCIS allows you, as the conditional permanent resident alien, to file without your spouse's signature.

You must fill out the same form, Form I-751, Petition to Remove the Conditions on Residence (see the sample at the end of this chapter), and mail it with the same fee. However, you must also request one of the waivers described on the form. These waivers cover situations where:

- your spouse died
- you were the victim of battery or abuse
- your marriage was valid when it occurred but is now legally terminated, or
- you would suffer extreme hardship if removed.

These waivers require the assistance of an experienced immigration attorney. (See Chapter 24.)

3. People Married Two Years or More

If the original date of your admission as a permanent resident is more than two years after your marriage, you are not considered a conditional permanent resident. You are a full-fledged permanent resident and not subject to the conditions on residence.

> **EXAMPLE:** You married a permanent resident on February 14, 2003, and a visa petition was filed on your behalf shortly thereafter in the second preference category. However, your visa number was not immediately available, and you had to wait a few years. You finally received your green card and were admitted as a permanent—not conditional—resident on July 4, 2005, more than two years after your date of marriage.

G. If You Remarry

If your marriage ends in divorce or annulment after you receive your permanent green card, and then you marry another foreign-born person, it will be difficult for you to sponsor your new spouse for a green card.

To obtain permanent residence for your alien spouse during the first five years after you received your green card through marriage, you'll have to show by "clear and convincing evidence" that your first marriage—the one by which you got your green card—was not fraudulent and was entered into in good faith. Again, this means showing you got married because you wanted to establish a life together, not just to get a green card.

In addition to the other proof required (see Section D, above), you will be asked to explain:

- why and when you got the previous divorce
- how long you lived with your first spouse
- how, when, and where you met your intended spouse, and
- facts about your courtship.

However, after you have been a green card holder for five years—the number of years required for naturalization—you can file a petition for your second spouse without providing such evidence.

Again, Congress provided this restriction because a number of alien couples had obtained green cards fraudulently. One of them would marry either a U.S. citizen or a permanent resident. After getting the immigrant visa, the marriage to the citizen or permanent resident would be ended by divorce or annulment. The immigrant, then in possession of a valid green card, would then marry the original spouse to give him or her a green card, too.

To eliminate this nefarious practice, a law was passed requiring that a green card be valid for five years before a petition to marry another alien, after divorce from a U.S. citizen or green card holder, could be approved, unless the permanent resident can show very clearly that the first marriage was a good one.

Dura lex, sed lex. The law is harsh, but such is the law.

H. Common Questions About Marriage and Immigration

The answers to most immigration questions depend on timing and the specific history of those involved, so it is difficult to give one correct response in solving a problem. There are, however, a number of questions that are asked over and over.

1. Before Marriage

Q: My boyfriend, who is a U.S. citizen, is getting a divorce soon. Can he file a petition for me to get a green card?

A: No—because he has not yet legally ended his previous marriage, he cannot marry you now. He can marry you as soon as his previous divorce petition is finalized.

Q: I intend to marry a U.S. citizen, but because work obligations will require us to live in different states for a while, we will not be living together for the first six months or so after we're married. Can she file for me to get a green card?

A: Yes. But you will have to prove to the USCIS examiner that your marriage is true and not a sham. Good evidence of that would be ticket stubs from visits to one another; telephone bills showing frequent calls to one another; stubs from social events you attended together such as movies, theater performances, and meals; copies of joint bank accounts; and bills bearing both of your names.

2. After Marriage

Q: I entered the U.S. with another name. Now I am married to a U.S. citizen using my real name. Can I get my green card?

A: Yes. But you may need to request that the misrepresentation be waived, or forgiven, before USCIS will approve your case. You should see a lawyer in this case.

Q: I have a minor child living with me in the U.S. and two more young children now living outside the U.S. Can I get green cards for all of them?

A: Yes—if your U.S. citizen spouse files separate petitions for them. If your spouse is a permanent resident, not a citizen, he or she can simply include the children on your visa petition.

Q: What will happen if my marriage legally ends before the conditional status of my green card is removed?

A: A conditional resident can file an application for a Waiver of Condition with USCIS. However, because there are complicated matters of proof, it is best to consult an experienced immigration lawyer for help.

Petition for Alien Relative, Sample Form I-130 (page 1)

Department of Homeland Security
U.S. Citizenship and Immigration Services

OMB # 1615-0012; Expires 01/31/07

I-130, Petition for Alien Relative

DO NOT WRITE IN THIS BLOCK - FOR USCIS OFFICE ONLY..

A#	Action Stamp	Fee Stamp

Section of Law/Visa Category
- [ ] 201(b) Spouse - IR-1/CR-1
- [ ] 201(b) Child - IR-2/CR-2
- [ ] 201(b) Parent - IR-5
- [ ] 203(a)(1) Unm. S or D - F1-1
- [ ] 203(a)(2)(A)Spouse - F2-1
- [ ] 203(a)(2)(A) Child - F2-2
- [ ] 203(a)(2)(B) Unm. S or D - F2-4
- [ ] 203(a)(3) Married S or D - F3-1
- [ ] 203(a)(4) Brother/Sister - F4-1

Petition was filed on: _____ (priority date)
- [ ] Personal Interview
- [ ] Pet. [ ] Ben. " A" File Reviewed
- [ ] Field Investigation
- [ ] 203(a)(2)(A) Resolved
- [ ] Previously Forwarded
- [ ] I-485 Filed Simultaneously
- [ ] 204(g) Resolved
- [ ] 203(g) Resolved

Remarks:

A. Relationship. You are the petitioner. Your relative is the beneficiary.

1. I am filing this petition for my:
[X] Husband/Wife [ ] Parent [ ] Brother/Sister [ ] Child

2. Are you related by adoption?
[ ] Yes [X] No

3. Did you gain permanent residence through adoption?
[ ] Yes [X] No

B. Information about you.

1. Name (Family name in CAPS) (First) (Middle)
NGUYEN   Teo   Thanh

2. Address (Number and Street) (Apt.No.)
1640 Lincoln Park

(Town or City) (State/Country) (Zip/Postal Code)
Beaverton   Oregon   97006

3. Place of Birth (Town or City) (State/Country)
Portland   Oregon

4. Date of Birth (mm/dd/yyyy)
4/12/80

5. Gender
[X] Male [ ] Female

6. Marital Status
[X] Married [ ] Single [ ] Widowed [ ] Divorced

7. Other Names Used (including maiden name)
None

8. Date and Place of Present Marriage (if married)
May 22, 2005 – Salem, Oregon

9. U.S. Social Security Number (if any)
756-91-0637

10. Alien Registration Number

11. Name(s) of Prior Husband(s)/Wive(s)
None

12. Date(s) Marriage(s) Ended

C. Information about your relative.

1. Name (Family name in CAPS) (First) (Middle)
NGUYEN   Lea   Nadres

2. Address (Number and Street) (Apt. No.)
1640 Lincoln Park

(Town or City) (State/Country) (Zip/Postal Code)
Beaverton   Oregon   97006

3. Place of Birth (Town or City) (State/Country)
Quezon City   Philippines

4. Date of Birth (mm/dd/yyyy)
7/18/79

5. Gender
[ ] Male [X] Female

6. Marital Status
[X] Married [ ] Single [ ] Widowed [ ] Divorced

7. Other Names Used (including maiden name)
Pebet

8. Date and Place of Present Marriage (if married)
May 22, 2005 – Salem, Oregon

9. U. S. Social Security Number (if any)

10. Alien Registration Number

11. Name(s) of Prior Husband(s)/Wive(s)

12. Date(s) Marriage(s) Ended

13. If you are a U.S. citizen, complete the following:
My citizenship was acquired through (check one):
- [X] Birth in the U.S.
- [ ] Naturalization. Give certificate number and date and place of issuance.

_____

- [ ] Parents. Have you obtained a certificate of citizenship in your own name?
- [X] Yes. Give certificate number, date and place of issuance. [ ] No

14a. If you are a lawful permanent resident alien, complete the following: Date and place of admission for or adjustment to lawful permanent residence and class of admission.

14b. Did you gain permanent resident status through marriage to a U.S. citizen or lawful permanent resident?
[ ] Yes [X] No

13. Has your relative ever been in the U.S.? [X] Yes [ ] No

14. If your relative is currently in the U.S., complete the following:
He or she arrived as a:: Student
(visitor, student, stowaway, without inspection, etc.)

Arrival/Departure Record (I-94)
| 1 | 4 | 6 | 0 | 7 | 7 | 1 | 2 | 2 | 1 | 0 |

Date arrived (mm/dd/yyyy)
12/23/00

Date authorized stay expired, or will expire, as shown on Form I-94 or I-95   D/S

15. Name and address of present employer (if any)

Date this employment began (mm/dd/yyyy)

16. Has your relative ever been under immigration proceedings?
[X] No [ ] Yes Where _____ When _____
[ ] Removal [ ] Exclusion/Deportation [ ] Recission [ ] Judicial Proceedings

INITIAL RECEIPT _____ RESUBMITTED _____ RELOCATED: Rec'd _____ Sent _____ COMPLETED: Appv'd _____ Denied _____ Ret'd _____

Form I-130 (Rev. 10/26/05) Y

Sample Form I-130 (page 2)

C. Information about your alien relative. (Continued.)

17. List husband/wife and all children of your relative.

(Name)	(Relationship)	(Date of Birth)	(Country of Birth)
N/A			

18. Address in the United States where your relative intends to live.

(Street Address)	(Town or City)	(State)
1640 Lincoln Park	Beaverton	Oregon

19. Your relative's address abroad. (Include street, city, province and country)

1678 Trout Chautoco Roxas District, Q.C., Philippines   Phone Number (if any)

20. If your relative's native alphabet is other than Roman letters, write his or her name and foreign address in the native alphabet.

(Name)   Address (Include street, city, province and country):

N/A

21. If filing for your husband/wife, give last address at which you lived together. (Include street, city, province, if any, and country):

1640 Lincoln Park   Beaverton, Oregon   **From:** 5/05   **To:** Present
                                                        (Month) (Year)   (Month) (Year)

22. Complete the information below if your relative is in the United States and will apply for adjustment of status.

Your relative is in the United States and will apply for adjustment of status to that of a lawful permanent resident at USCIS office in:

Portland Oregon   . If your relative is not eligible for adjustment of status, he or she

(City)   (State)

will apply for a visa abroad at the American consular post in   Manila   Philippines

                                                        (City)   (Country)

NOTE: Designation of an American embassy or consulate outside the country of your relative's last residence does not guarantee acceptance for processing by that post. Acceptance is at the discretion of the designated embassy or consulate.

D. Other information.

1. If separate petitions are also being submitted for other relatives, give names of each and relationship.

2. Have you ever before filed a petition for this or any other alien? ☐ Yes ☒ No
If "Yes," give name, place and date of filing and result.

WARNING: USCIS investigates claimed relationships and verifies the validity of documents. USCIS seeks criminal prosecutions when family relationships are falsified to obtain visas.

PENALTIES: By law, you may be imprisoned for not more than five years or fined $250,000, or both, for entering into a marriage contract for the purpose of evading any provision of the immigration laws. In addition, you may be fined up to $10,000 and imprisoned for up to five years, or both, for knowingly and willfully falsifying or concealing a material fact or using any false document in submitting this petition.

YOUR CERTIFICATION: I certify, under penalty of perjury under the laws of the United States of America, that the foregoing is true and correct. Furthermore, I authorize the release of any information from my records that U.S. Citizenship and Immigration Services needs to determine eligibility for the benefit that I am seeking.

E. Signature of petitioner.

Teo Thanh Nguyen   Date June 11, 2006 Phone Number (503)730-1493

F. Signature of person preparing this form, if other than the petitioner.

I declare that I prepared this document at the request of the person above and that it is based on all information of which I have any knowledge.

Print Name   Signature   Date

Address   G-28 ID or VOLAG Number, if any.

Form I-130 (Rev. 10/26/05) Y Page 2

Petition for Alien Fiancé(e), Sample Form I-129F (When Used by Married Couple) (page 1)

OMB No. 1615-0001; Expires 12/31/06

Department of Homeland Security
U.S. Citizenship and Immigration Services

**I-129F, Petition
for Alien Fiancé(e)**

Do not write in these blocks.   **For USCIS Use Only**

Case ID #	Action Block	Fee Stamp
A #		
G-28 #		**AMCON:** _____
The petition is approved for status under Section 101(a)(5)(k). It is valid for four months from the date of action. _____		☐ Personal Interview ☐ Previously Forwarded ☐ Document Check ☐ Field Investigation
Remarks:		

Part A.   Start Here. Information about you.

1. Name *(Family name in CAPS) (First) (Middle)*

ANDERSON | Christa | Lee

2. Address *(Number and Street)*   Apt. #

123 4th St. | 2

(Town or City) (State or Country) (Zip/Postal Code)

San Diego | CA | 92120

3. Place of Birth *(Town or City)*   (State/Country)

Portland | OR

4. Date of Birth *(mm/dd/yyyy)*   **5. Gender**

4/18/1979 | ☐ Male ☒ Female

6. Marital Status
☒ Married ☐ Single ☐ Widowed ☐ Divorced

7. Other Names Used *(including maiden name)*

None

8a. U.S. Social Security Number 8b. A# *(if any)*

122-33-4444

9. Names of Prior Spouses   Date(s) Marriage(s) Ended

None |

10. My citizenship was acquired through *(check one)*

☒ Birth in the U.S.   ☐ Naturalization
Give number of certificate, date and place it was issued.

_____

☐ Parents
Have you obtained a certificate of citizenship in your name?
☐ Yes   ☐ No
If "Yes," give certificate number, date and place it was issued.

_____

11. Have you ever filed for this or any other alien fiancé(e) or husband/wife before?

☐ Yes   ☒ No

If "Yes," give name of all aliens, place and date of filing, A# and result.

_____

Part B.   Information about your alien fiancé(e).

1. Name *(Family name in CAPS) (First) (Middle)*

CUEVAS | Bernardo | Cristobal

2. Address *(Number and Street)*   Apt. #

123 Calle Centro | 42

(Town or City) (State or Country) (Zip/Postal Code)

Bogota | Colombia |

3a. Place of Birth *(Town or City)*   (State/Country)

Bucaramanga | Colombia

3b. Country of Citizenship

_____

4. Date of Birth *(mm/dd/yyyy)*   **5. Gender**

7/24/1978 | ☒ Male ☐ Female

6. Marital Status
☒ Married ☐ Single ☐ Widowed ☐ Divorced

7. Other Names Used *(including maiden name)*

None

8. U.S. Social Security #   9. A# *(if any)*

None |

10. Names of Prior Spouses   Date(s) Marriage(s) Ended

Sonya Carcamo | 11/2/2001

11. Has your fiancé(e) ever been in the U.S.?

☒ Yes   ☐ No

12. If your fiancé(e) is currently in the U.S., complete the following:

He or she last arrived as a: *(visitor, student, exchange alien, crewman, stowaway, temporary worker, without inspection, etc.)*

_____

Arrival/Departure Record (I-94) Number

☐☐☐ — ☐☐☐☐☐☐☐☐

Date of Arrival *(mm/dd/yy)*   **Date authorized stay expired, or will expire as shown on I-94 or I-95**

_____

INITIAL RECEIPT _____ RESUBMITTED _____ RELOCATED: Rec'd _____ Sent _____ COMPLETED: Appv'd _____ Denied _____ Ret'd _____

Form I-129F (Rev. 05/23/06) N

Sample Form I-129F (page 2)

Part B.   Information about your alien fiancé(e).   *(Continued.)*

13. List all children of your alien fiancé(e) *(if any)*

Name *(First/Middle/Last)*	Date of Birth *(mm/dd/yyyy)*	Country of Birth	Present Address
Jorge Carcamo Cuevas	2/21/2000	Colombia	1100 Calle de Las Montaños, Bogota

14. Address in the United States where your fiancé(e) intends to live.

(Number and Street)	(Town or City)	(State)
123 4th St.	San Diego	CA

15. Your fiancé(e)'s address abroad.

(Number and Street)	(Town or City)	(State or Province)
123 Calle Centro #42	Bogota	

(Country)	(Phone Number; Include Country, City and Area Codes)
Colombia	57 1 2223333

16. If your fiancé(e)'s native alphabet uses other than Roman letters, write his or her name and address abroad in the native alphabet.

(Name)	(Number and Street)
n/a	

(Town or City)	(State or Province)	(Country)

17. Is your fiancé(e) related to you?   ☐ Yes   ☒ No

If you are related, state the nature and degree of relationship, e.g., third cousin or maternal uncle, etc.

(Not a blood relation—we are married, and he will apply for a K-3 visa.)

18. Has your fiancé(e) met and seen you within the two-year period immediately receding the filing of this petition?

☒ Yes   ☐ No

Describe the circumstances under which you met. If you have not personally met each other, explain how the relationship was established. Explain also in detail any reasons you may have for requesting that the requirement that you and your fiancé(e) must have met should not apply to you.

We originally met at a conference and were married in Colombia in 2004.

19. Did you meet your fiancé(e) or spouse through the services of an international marriage broker?

☐ Yes   ☒ No

If you answered yes, please provide the name of the international marriage broker and where the international marriage broker is located. (Attach additional sheets of paper if necessary).

20. Your fiancé(e) will apply for a visa abroad at the American embassy or consulate at:

(City)	(Country)
Bogota	Colombia

NOTE: (Designation of a U.S. embassy or consulate outside the country of your fiancé(e)'s last residence does not guarantee acceptance for processing by that foreign post. Acceptance is at the discretion of the designated embassy or consulate.)

Sample Form I-129F (page 3)

Part C. Other information.

1. **If you are serving overseas in the Armed Forces of the United States, please answer the following:**

   I presently reside or am stationed overseas and my current mailing address is: I plan to return to the United States on or about:

2. **Have you ever been convicted by a court of law (civil or criminal) or court martialed by a military tribunal for any of the following crimes.** This is required even if your records were sealed or otherwise cleared or if anyone, including a judge, law enforcement officer, or attorney, told you that you no longer have a record. *(Check all that apply. Using a separate sheet(s) of paper, attach information relating to the conviction(s), such as crime involved, date of conviction and sentence.)*

   ☐ Domestic violence, sexual assault, child abuse and neglect, dating violence, elder abuse and stalking.

   ☐ Homicide, murder, manslaughter, rape, abusive sexual contact, sexual exploitation, incest, torture, trafficking, peonage, holding hostage, involuntary servitude, slave trade, kidnapping, abduction, unlawful criminal restraint, false imprisonment or an attempt to commit any of these crimes.

   ☐ Three or more convictions for crimes relating to a controlled substance or alcohol not arising from a single act.

3. **If you have provided information about a conviction for a crime listed above and you were being battered or subjected to extreme cruelty by your spouse, parent, or adult child at the time of your conviction, check all of the following that apply to you:**

   ☐ I was acting in self-defense.

   ☐ I violated a protection order issued for my own protection.

   ☐ I committed, was arrested for, was convicted of, or plead guilty to committing a crime that did not result in serious bodily injury, and there was a connection between the crime committed and my having been battered or subjected to extreme cruelty.

Part D. Penalties, certification and petitioner's signature.

PENALTIES: **You may by law be imprisoned for not more than five years, or fined $250,000, or both, for entering into a marriage contract for the purpose of evading any provision of the immigration laws, and you may be fined up to $10,000 or imprisoned up to five years, or both, for knowingly and willfully falsifying or concealing a material fact or using any false document in submitting this petition.**

YOUR CERTIFICATION: I am legally able to and intend to marry my alien fiancé(e) within 90 days of his or her arrival in the United States. I certify, under penalty of perjury under the laws of the United States of America, that the foregoing is true and correct. Furthermore, I authorize the release of any information from my records that U.S. Citizenship and Immigration Services needs to determine eligibility for the benefit that I am seeking.

Moreover, I understand that any criminal conviction information that I am required to provide with this petition, and any related criminal conviction information pertaining to me that U.S. Citizenship and Immigration Services may discover independently in adjudicating this petition will be disclosed to the beneficiary of this petition.

Signature	**Date** *(mm/dd/yyyy)*	**Daytime Telephone Number** *(with area code)*
Christa Anderson	2/28/2006	858-555-1214

E-Mail Address (if any)

christa37@email.com

Part E. Signature of person preparing form, if other than above. *(Sign below.)*

I declare that I prepared this application at the request of the petitioner and it is based on all information of which I have knowledge.

Signature	Print or Type Your Name	G-28 ID Number	Date *(mm/dd/yyyy)*

Firm Name and Address

Daytime Telephone Number *(with area code)*

E-Mail Address (if any)

Petition to Remove Conditions on Residence, Sample Form I-751 (front)

OMB No. 1615-0038; Expires 09/30/05

Department of Homeland Security
U.S. Citizenship and Immigration Services

I-751, Petition to Remove Conditions on Residence

START HERE - Please type or print in black ink.	For USCIS Use Only	

Part 1. Information about you.

	Returned	Receipt
	Date	

Family Name (Last Name): HOLLIS

Given Name (First Name): Nigel

Full Middle Name: Ian

Date

Address: (Street Number and Name): 114 Fulton St.   Apt. #: 6E

Resubmitted

Date

C/O: (In Care Of)

Date

City: New York

State/Province: NY

Reloc Sent

Date

Country: USA

Zip/Postal Code: 10038

Date

Reloc Rec'd

Mailing Address, if different than above: (Street Number and Name)   Apt. #

Date

C/O: (In Care Of)

Date

City

State/Province

☐ Petitioner Interviewed on _____

Country

Zip/Postal Code

Remarks

Date of Birth (mm/dd/yyyy): 8/18/1978

Country of Birth: U.K.

Country of Citizenship: U.K.

Alien Registration Number (#A): A12345678

Social Security # (if any): 888-11-8888

Conditional Residence Expires on (mm/dd/yyyy): 08/07/2008

Daytime Phone # (Area/Country Codes): 212-555-1212

Part 2. Basis for petition. (Check one.)

Action Block

a. ☑ My conditional residence is based on my marriage to a U.S. citizen or permanent resident, and we are filing this petition together.

b. ☐ I am a child who entered as a conditional permanent resident and I am unable to be included in a joint petition to remove the conditional basis of are alien's permanent residence (Form 1-751) filed by my parent(s).

OR

My conditional residence is based on my marriage to a U.S. citizen or permanent resident, but I am unable to file a joint petition and I request a waiver because: **(Check one.)**

c. ☐ My spouse is deceased.

d. ☐ I entered into the marriage in good faith but the marriage was terminated through divorce/annulment.

e. ☐ I am a conditional resident spouse who entered a marriage in good faith, and during the marriage I was battered by or was the subject of extreme cruelty by my U.S. citizen or permanent resident spouse or parent.

f. ☐ I am a conditional resident child who was battered by or subjected to extreme cruelty by my U.S. citizen or conditional resident parent(s).

g. ☐ The termination of my status and removal from the United States would result in an extreme hardship.

To Be Completed by Attorney or Representative, if any.

☐ Fill in box if G-28 is attached to represent the applicant.

ATTY State License #

Form I-751 (Rev. 10/26/05) Y

Petition to Remove Conditions on Residence, Sample Form I-751 (back)

Part 3. Additional information about you.

1. Other Names Used *(including maiden name)*:

None

2. Date of Marriage *(mm/dd/yyyy)*

11/05/2005

3. Place of Marriage

New York, NY

4. If your spouse is deceased, give the date of death *(mm/dd/yyyy)*

5. Are you in removal, deportation or rescission proceedings? ☐ Yes ☑ No

6. Was a fee paid to anyone other than an attorney in connection with this petition? ☐ Yes ☑ No

7. Since becoming a conditional resident, have you ever been arrested, cited, charged, indicted, convicted, fined or imprisoned for breaking or violating any law or ordinance (excluding traffic regulations), or committed any crime for which you were not arrested? ☐ Yes ☑ No

8. If you are married, is this a different marriage than the one through which conditional residence status was obtained? ☐ Yes ☑ No

9. Have you resided at any other address since you became a permanent resident? *(If yes, attach a list of all addresses and dates.)* ☐ Yes ☑ No

10. Is your spouse currently serving with or employed by the U.S. government and serving outside the United States? ☐ Yes ☑ No

If you answered "Yes" to any of the above, provide a detailed explanation on a separate sheet(s) of paper. Place your name and Alien Registration Number (A#) at the top of each sheet and give the number of the item that refers to your response.

Part 4. Information about the spouse or parent through whom you gained your conditional residence.

Family Name	First Name	Middle Name
Beach	Sandra	Leah

Address

114 Fulton St. #6E

Date of Birth *(mm/dd/yyyy)*	Social Security # *(if any)*	A# *(if any)*
12/20/1980	123-456789	None

Part 5. Information about your children. List all your children. *Attach other sheet(s) if necessary.*

Name *(First/Middle/Last)*	Date of Birth *(mm/dd/yyyy)*	A # *(if any)*	If in U.S., give address/immigration status	Living with you?
Nadine Anne Hollis	12/02/2006		U.S. citizen	☑ Yes ☐ No
				☐ Yes ☐ No
				☐ Yes ☐ No
				☐ Yes ☐ No
				☐ Yes ☐ No

Part 6. Signature. *Read the information on penalties in the instructions before completing this section. If you checked block "a" in Part 2, your spouse must also sign below.*

I certify, under penalty of perjury of the laws of the United States of America, that this petition and the evidence submitted with it is all true and correct. If conditional residence was based on a marriage, I further certify that the marriage was entered in accordance with the laws of the place where the marriage took place and was not for the purpose of procuring an immigration benefit. I also authorize the release of any information from my records that the U.S. Citizenship and Immigration Services needs to determine eligibility for the benefit sought.

Signature	Print Name	Date *(mm/dd/yyyy)*
Nigel Hollis	Nigel Hollis	06/01/2008

Signature of Spouse	Print Name	Date *(mm/dd/yyyy)*
Sandra Beach	Sandra Beach	06/01/2008

NOTE: If you do not completely fill out this form or fail to submit any required documents listed in the instructions, you may not be found eligible for the requested benefit and this petition may be denied.

Part 7. Signature of person preparing form, if other than above.

I declare that I prepared this petition at the request of the above person and it is based on all information of which I have knowledge.

Signature	Print Name	Date *(mm/dd/yyyy)*

Firm Name and Address

Daytime Phone Number *(Area/Country Codes)*

E-Mail Address *(If any)*

Form I-751 (Rev. 10/26/05) Y Page 2

Biographic Information, Sample Form G-325A

Department of Homeland Security
U.S. Citizenship and Immigration Services

OMB No. 1615-0008

G-325A, Biographic Information

(Family name) SALONGA	(First name) Fe	(Middle name) Valdez	☐ Male ☑ Female	Birthdate (mm/dd/yyyy) 3-7-63	Citizenship/Nationality Filipino	File Number A

All Other Names Used (Including names by previous marriages) Fe Agnes Salonga	City and Country of Birth Manila, Philippines	U.S. Social Security # (If any) 210-76-9478

	Family Name	First Name	Date, City and Country of Birth (If Known)	City and Country of Residence
Father	SALONGA	Amando	Manila, Philippines, 6-9-39	Manila, Philippines
Mother (Maiden name)	VALDEZ	Lourdes	Manila, Philippines, 12-5-42	-do-

Husband (If none, so state) or Wife	Family Name (For wife, give maiden name) None	First Name	Birthdate	City and Country of Birth	Date of Marriage	Place of Marriage

Former Husbands or Wives(if none, so state) Family Name (For wife, give maiden name) None	First Name	Birthdate	Date and Place of Marriage	Date and Place of Termination of Marriage

Applicant's residence last five years. List present address first.

Street and Number	City	Province or State	Country	From Month	From Year	To Month	To Year
741 12th Ave.	White Plains,	NY	U.S.A.	9	01	Present Time	
676 W. Houston Street	New York,	NY	U.S.A.	8	99	8	99

Applicant's last address outside the United States of more than one year.

Street and Number	City	Province or State	Country	From Month	From Year	To Month	To Year
52-50 MBLA Court, Malaya St.	Marikina	Metro Manila	Philippines	since birth		8	99

Applicant's employment last five years. (If none, so state.) List present employment first.

Full Name and Address of Employer	Occupation (Specify)	From Month	From Year	To Month	To Year
Griffith School, 560 Lexington Avenue, NY, NY 10118	Teacher	3	00	Present Time	
Embassy of Japan, Buendia Ave., Makati, Metro Manila, Philippines	Secretary	5	92	8	99

Show below last occupation abroad if not shown above. (Include all information requested above.)

see above					

This form is submitted in connection with application for: ☐ Naturalization ☑ Status as Permanent Resident ☐ Other (Specify):	Signature of Applicant *Fe Valdez Salonga*	Date 2/26/06

Submit all copies of this form.   If your native alphabet is in other than Roman letters, write your name in your native alphabet below:

Penalties: Severe penalties are provided by law for knowingly and willfully falsifying or concealing a material fact.

Applicant: Be sure to put your name and Alien Registration Number in the box outlined by heavy border below.

Complete This Box (Family Name) SALONGA	(Given Name) Fe	(Middle Name) Valdez	(Alien Registration Number)

(1) Ident.

Form G-325A (Rev. 05/31/05)N (Prior editions may be used until 12/31/05)

Your Parents as Immigrants

I Want My Mama ... And My Papa, Too

If you are a U.S. citizen age 21 or over, but your parents are citizens of another country, your parents are your "immediate relatives" and you may request U.S. green cards for them. They must separately meet the other criteria for green card approval, however. One of the more difficult issues for immigrating parents is that, if they're retired and not working, you may have to prove that you'll be able to find health insurance coverage for them—and that coverage must not include any government support. This could be difficult or impossible if your parents have any serious preexisting health conditions.

Another important issue is whether your parents really want to come to the United States. Many are interested in family togetherness, but don't really want to permanently leave the life they've made for themselves elsewhere. Remember that a green card is not just an easy travel pass—unless your parents are ready to settle down here permanently, they could lose the green card by spending too much time overseas (and all your hard work could go down the drain). Another reason that some parents agree to come is that they can help other family members get green cards; see "Immigration Strategies After Your Parents Get Green Cards," below.

A. Who Qualifies to Petition for Their Parents

To petition to get a green card for your parents, you must meet a couple of basic requirements.

1. You Must Be a U.S. Citizen

You must be a U.S. citizen to file a petition on behalf of your parents. You are a citizen of the United States if you were:

- naturalized by a U.S. federal court (after you applied and passed an exam)
- born in any of the 50 states of the United States or its territories—U.S. Virgin Islands, Puerto Rico, or Guam—or
- born outside the United States or its territories, if one or both of your parents were U.S. citizens when you were born (see the article "U.S. Citizenship by Birth or Through Parents" on the Nolo website, www. nolo.com) or contact the U.S. Embassy; if you are not satisfied, consult a lawyer or other experienced naturalization professional. (See Chapter 24.)

2. You Must Be at Least 21 Years Old

As a U.S. citizen, you must be 21 years old or older to bestow the immigration benefit of a green card on your mother and your father as your immediate relatives.

If you were born in the United States because your parents live there illegally, 21 years will be a frustratingly long time to wait. In fact, because your parents may be ineligible to apply for green cards within the U.S. using the procedure called adjustment of status (see Chapter 18) but may instead have to leave the U.S. and apply through a U.S. consulate (see Chapter 19), your citizenship may turn out to be not much help to them. The reason is that too much time spent in the U.S. illegally can result in bars on returning to the U.S. after they leave (for three or ten years, based on illegal stays of six months or one year or more). If your family is in this situation, see an experienced immigration attorney.

Immigration Strategies After Your Parents Get Green Cards

By becoming permanent residents of the United States, your parents can file for the immigration of all their unmarried children in their home country—as family second preference or 2B petitioners. If they become naturalized as U.S. citizens, they can petition even for their married children—in the family third preference category.

Although as a U.S. citizen, you may have filed for your brothers and sisters in the family fourth preference category, your mother or father, after they become U.S. citizens, could secure a green card for them more quickly.

However, your parents must be aware that getting a green card does not automatically mean that their children can successfully obtain their own green cards. Your parents would also have to live (maintain residence) in the United States until their other children obtained their green cards.

The rules on maintaining residency are complicated and require that the person maintain the United States as their home. While the law allows them to travel overseas, their most important family and business ties should be in the United States. A person in this situation should compile documentation that would prove they maintained permanent residence. Good evidence to support a claim of permanent residency can include:

- a lease, rental agreement, or title to property in the United States.
- utility bills
- a driver's license and/or car registration, and/or
- state and federal tax returns.

If you or your parents have questions about whether you are properly maintaining permanent residence, consult an immigration attorney.

B. Who Qualifies As Your Parent

If you're from a traditional family—that is, you were born and raised by a married couple—you should have no problem petitioning for your parents to immigrate. However, the immigration law also recognizes some variations on the traditional family. Under certain circumstances, you can also petition for unmarried parents, stepparents, and adoptive parents, as described further below. You'll usually have to provide additional documents to prove the relationship, as also described below.

1. Natural Mother

If your mother was not married to your father when you were born, so that your mother's maiden name appears on your birth certificate, you can prove your relationship by presenting a copy of your birth certificate when you file the petition for your mother.

If your mother has changed her maiden name because she has married someone else, then also present her marriage certificate to show her change of name.

2. Natural Father

If your biological father did not marry your mother either before or after you were born, you can still petition for him as your immediate relative. You must also provide some evidence of your relationship.

- Make a copy of your birth certificate, baptismal certificate, or other religious records showing his name as your father. USCIS may require both you and your father to take a blood test as proof of your relationship.
- If you and your father did not live together before you turned 18, you must present proof that, up to the time you turned 21 years of age, he maintained a father-child relationship with you by providing financial support; writing to you or your mother about

your well-being; sending you birthday cards, holiday cards, and photographs; or perhaps naming you as a beneficiary to his life insurance.

- If you lived with your father before your 18th birthday, you must present proof that there was a father-child relationship, as evidenced by school records, photographs, letters, civil records, or written statements from friends and relatives.

If You, the Petitioner, Change Names

If you are a female U.S. citizen filing the petition for your alien parents as your immediate relatives, you may have changed your maiden name, which appears on your birth certificate. You may now be using your married name—that is, your husband's surname.

Therefore, in addition to your birth certificate to prove the parent-child relationship, you must also attach your marriage certificate to show your change of name when you send the Petition for Alien Relative, Form I-130, for your mother or father.

If you have changed your name by petitioning the court, you must attach the final court judgment as proof of that change.

3. Stepmother or Stepfather

If your father or mother marries somebody other than your biological parent before you turn 18 years of age, the person he or she marries becomes your stepmother or stepfather.

When you file a petition for your stepmother or stepfather as your immediate relative (by submitting the usual petition Form I-130), add to it the following documents:

- your birth certificate showing the name of your mother or father, and
- the marriage certificate of your mother or father to show the name of her husband or his wife, who has become your stepparent.

For you to petition for your stepparent, the marriage must have occurred before your 18th birthday. If the marriage happened after your 18th birthday, then say, "I love you, but I cannot claim you as my immediate relative for immigration into the United States."

But all is not lost.

Your natural mother or father, after qualifying as your immediate relative and obtaining a green card, can petition for your stepparent, as the spouse of a permanent resident—2A, the second preference beneficiary. Unfortunately, however, the stepparent will have to wait a few years until a visa becomes available in this category.

4. Adopted Mother and Father

Suppose you were adopted by a non-U.S. citizen before your 16th birthday. If you are a U.S. citizen and you are now 21 years or older, you can petition for your adopted mother and father as your immediate relatives.

When you file the visa petition (or Form I-130), you must also submit:

- the court decree of your adoption
- your birth certificate showing the name of your adopting parents as your father and mother, and
- a statement showing the dates and places you have lived together.

Adopted children cannot petition for their natural parents. When you were adopted, your natural parents gave up all parental ties with you. Therefore, you will never be able to petition for your natural parents as your immediate relatives. The adoption decree cuts off all legal ties between you and your natural parents.

C. Quick View of the Application Process

To get a green card for your parent, you must begin the process by submitting a visa petition (Form I-130, together with certain documents). Form I-130 serves to prove to the immigration authorities that your parents are truly and legally yours. After that petition is approved, your parents must complete their half of the process by submitting a green card application and attending an interview, sometimes but not always with you accompanying them. Their application serves to prove that not only do they qualify as parents of a U.S. citizen, but that they're otherwise eligible for U.S. permanent residence.

However, the details of when and how your parents complete their half of the process depend on whether your parents are living overseas or in the United States, as described in Section D, below.

D. Detailed Instructions for the Application Process

Now we'll break the application process down into individual procedures, some of which will be covered in this chapter, others of which will be covered in other chapters—we'll tell you exactly where to go to for your situation.

1. The Visa Petition

We'll start by discussing the visa petition, which all people petitioning for their parents must begin by preparing. You'll need to assemble:

- ❏ Form I-130, Petition for Alien Relative (see the sample at the end of this chapter).
- ❏ Documents showing your U.S. citizenship.
- ❏ A copy of your birth certificate, showing your name as well as your mother's name, if filing for your mother; and the names of both parents, if filing for your father.

- ❏ A copy of the marriage certificate of your parents if you are filing for your father; your stepparents' marriage certificate, if you are filing for either stepparent.
- ❏ A copy of your adoption decree, if you are filing for your adoptive parent.

Once you've assembled all these items, make a copy for your records. It's also a good idea to write a cover letter, explaining what type of visa petition it is (for example, saying "I am a U.S. citizen, filing the enclosed visa petition on behalf of my parents." The letter should include a bulleted list, much like the one above, of everything you're sending. This will help USCIS see that you're organized. It will help you, too, make sure that nothing has been forgotten.

If your parents are not in the United States, mail all these documents and the fee by certified mail to the appropriate USCIS Service Center. (See the USCIS website for contact details.) If they are in the United States, they may be able to file directly for adjustment of status (see Chapter 18).

Be sure to include the filing fee, currently $190, in a certified check or money order payable to the Department of Homeland Security. Don't send cash.

2. The Green Card Application

The next step in your parents' immigration process depends on where they're located. If they're in the United States, you need to start by figuring out whether they are eligible to adjust status (apply for their green card) here. See Chapter 18, Section A, to determine this. (If they are on valid visas, then they are probably eligible. However, they must be careful—if they obtained a tourist or other visa with the secret intention of applying for a green card after they got here, that could be visa fraud. They can be denied the green card based on this fraud.)

If they are allowed to adjust status in the U.S.: You can submit the I-130 visa petition in combination with an adjustment of status application to a USCIS service center as also described in Chapter 18. Eventually they will be fingerprinted, called in for an interview at a local USCIS office, and hopefully approved for U.S. residency.

If your parents do not qualify to adjust status but are currently in the U.S.: See a lawyer if any of that time has been unlawful—that is, after an illegal entry, past the date of their Form I-94 or in violation of their status. If so, leaving the U.S. could result in them being prevented from reentering for three or ten years, depending on the length of their unlawful stay.

If your parent's current stay in the U.S. has been lawful and they plan to leave on time, or if they're already living overseas: Their next step is to await USCIS approval of the Form I-130 visa petition and then go through consular processing, as described in Chapter 19. Eventually they will be called in for an interview at their local U.S. consulate, at which time they will hopefully be approved for an immigrant visa to enter the United States and claim their permanent residency.

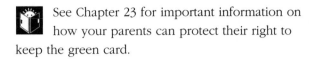 See Chapter 23 for important information on how your parents can protect their right to keep the green card.

In Defense of the Elderly

If your mother or father is elderly, take some time to help them get acquainted with the customs and cultural habits of the country.

Introduce them to the senior citizen center located in their new neighborhood. Teach them how to use the public transportation system, including precautions to be taken if you live in a big city. Bring them to the cultural or popular entertainment activities available in your area.

It is unfair to make your parents mere babysitters for your young children. They have already done all the childrearing they were responsible for when they raised you. Pay them a decent amount if they take care of your children. Do not abuse their kindness by taking advantage of their presence in your home to do the work you should be doing.

Petition for Alien Relative, Sample Form I-130 (when used for parents) (page 1)

Department of Homeland Security U.S. Citizenship and Immigration Services	OMB # 1615-0012; Expires 01/31/07 **I-130, Petition for Alien Relative**

DO NOT WRITE IN THIS BLOCK - FOR USCIS OFFICE ONLY..

A#	Action Stamp	Fee Stamp
Section of Law/Visa Category ☐ 201(b) Spouse - IR-1/CR-1 ☐ 201(b) Child - IR-2/CR-2 ☐ 201(b) Parent - IR-5 ☐ 203(a)(1) Unm. S or D - F1-1 ☐ 203(a)(2)(A)Spouse - F2-1 ☐ 203(a)(2)(A) Child - F2-2 ☐ 203(a)(2)(B) Unm. S or D - F2-4 ☐ 203(a)(3) Married S or D - F3-1 ☐ 203(a)(4) Brother/Sister - F4-1		Petition was filed on: _____ (priority date) ☐ Personal Interview ☐ Previously Forwarded ☐ Pet. ☐ Ben. " A" File Reviewed ☐ I-485 Filed Simultaneously ☐ Field Investigation ☐ 204(g) Resolved ☐ 203(a)(2)(A) Resolved ☐ 203(g) Resolved

Remarks:

A. Relationship. You are the petitioner.   Your relative is the beneficiary.

1. I am filing this petition for my:	2. Are you related by adoption?	3. Did you gain permanent residence through adoption?
☐ Husband/Wife ☒ Parent ☐ Brother/Sister ☐ Child	☐ Yes ☒ No	☐ Yes ☒ No

B. Information about you.	**C. Information about your relative.**
1. Name (Family name in CAPS) (First) (Middle) SOLOMOS Evadne Helia	**1. Name** (Family name in CAPS) (First) (Middle) ADAMIDIS Halimeda Madora
2. Address (Number and Street) (Apt.No.) 121 3rd St.	**2. Address** (Number and Street) (Apt. No.) Galanou 25
(Town or City) (State/Country) (Zip/Postal Code) Baton Rouge LA/USA 70808	(Town or City) (State/Country) (Zip/Postal Code) Athens Greece 105 53
3. Place of Birth (Town or City) (State/Country) Athens Greece	**3. Place of Birth** (Town or City) (State/Country) Santorini Greece
4. Date of Birth (mm/dd/yyyy) **5. Gender** **6. Marital Status** 7/3/72 ☐ Male ☒ Female ☒ Married ☐ Single ☐ Widowed ☐ Divorced	**4. Date of Birth** (mm/dd/yyyy) **5. Gender** **6. Marital Status** 10/12/54 ☐ Male ☒ Female ☐ Married ☐ Single ☒ Widowed ☐ Divorced
7. Other Names Used (including maiden name) Evadne Helia ADIMIDIS	**7. Other Names Used** (including maiden name) Halimeda Madora MAMALIS
8. Date and Place of Present Marriage (if married) 3/17/95, New Orleans, LA	**8. Date and Place of Present Marriage** (if married)
9. U.S. Social Security Number (if any) **10. Alien Registration Number** 111-22-3333 n/a	**9. U. S. Social Security Number** (if any) **10. Alien Registration Number** None None
11. Name(s) of Prior Husband(s)/Wive(s) **12. Date(s) Marriage(s) Ended**	**11. Name(s) of Prior Husband(s)/Wive(s)** **12. Date(s) Marriage(s) Ended** Cyrus Danous ADIMIDIS 11/4/99
13. If you are a U.S. citizen, complete the following: My citizenship was acquired through (check one): ☐ Birth in the U.S. ☒ Naturalization. Give certificate number and date and place of issuance. 321234, 12/3/01, New Orleans ☐ Parents. Have you obtained a certificate of citizenship in your own name? ☐ Yes. Give certificate number, date and place of issuance. ☐ No	**13. Has your relative ever been in the U.S.?** ☐ Yes ☐ No **14. If your relative is currently in the U.S., complete the following:** He or she arrived as a:: (visitor, student, stowaway, without inspection, etc.) Arrival/Departure Record (I-94) Date arrived (mm/dd/yyyy) | | | ▬ | | | | | | Date authorized stay expired, or will expire, as shown on Form I-94 or I-95
14a. If you are a lawful permanent resident alien, complete the following: Date and place of admission for or adjustment to lawful permanent residence and class of admission.	**15. Name and address of present employer** (if any) None Date this employment began (mm/dd/yyyy)
14b. Did you gain permanent resident status through marriage to a U.S. citizen or lawful permanent resident? ☒ Yes ☐ No	**16. Has your relative ever been under immigration proceedings?** ☒ No ☐ Yes Where _____ When _____ ☐ Removal ☐ Exclusion/Deportation ☐ Recission ☐ Judicial Proceedings

INITIAL RECEIPT _____ RESUBMITTED _____ RELOCATED: Rec'd _____ Sent _____ COMPLETED: Appv'd _____ Denied _____ Ret'd _____

Form I-130 (Rev. 10/26/05) Y

Sample Form I-130 (page 2)

C. Information about your alien relative. (Continued.)

17. List husband/wife and all children of your relative.

(Name)	(Relationship)	(Date of Birth)	(Country of Birth)
Kadmus ADIMIDIS	Son	8/7/74	Greece

18. Address in the United States where your relative intends to live.

(Street Address)	(Town or City)	(State)
131 3rd St.	Baton Rouge	Louisiana

19. Your relative's address abroad. (Include street, city, province and country)

Galanou 25, 105 53 Athens, Greece   Phone Number (if any)

20. If your relative's native alphabet is other than Roman letters, write his or her name and foreign address in the native alphabet.

(Name)   Address (Include street, city, province and country):

21. If filing for your husband/wife, give last address at which you lived together. (Include street, city, province, if any, and country):

	From: (Month) (Year)	To: (Month) (Year)

22. Complete the information below if your relative is in the United States and will apply for adjustment of status.

Your relative is in the United States and will apply for adjustment of status to that of a lawful permanent resident at USCIS office in:

_____ . If your relative is not eligible for adjustment of status, he or she

(City)   (State)

will apply for a visa abroad at the American consular post in _____

(City)   (Country)

NOTE: Designation of an American embassy or consulate outside the country of your relative's last residence does not guarantee acceptance for processing by that post. Acceptance is at the discretion of the designated embassy or consulate.

D. Other information.

1. If separate petitions are also being submitted for other relatives, give names of each and relationship.

2. Have you ever before filed a petition for this or any other alien?   ☐ Yes   ☒ No
If "Yes," give name, place and date of filing and result.

WARNING: USCIS investigates claimed relationships and verifies the validity of documents. USCIS seeks criminal prosecutions when family relationships are falsified to obtain visas.

PENALTIES: By law, you may be imprisoned for not more than five years or fined $250,000, or both, for entering into a marriage contract for the purpose of evading any provision of the immigration laws. In addition, you may be fined up to $10,000 and imprisoned for up to five years, or both, for knowingly and willfully falsifying or concealing a material fact or using any false document in submitting this petition.

YOUR CERTIFICATION: I certify, under penalty of perjury under the laws of the United States of America, that the foregoing is true and correct. Furthermore, I authorize the release of any information from my records that U.S. Citizenship and Immigration Services needs to determine eligibility for the benefit that I am seeking.

E. Signature of petitioner.

Evadne H. Solomos   Date 7/9/06   Phone Number 225-555-1313

F. Signature of person preparing this form, if other than the petitioner.

I declare that I prepared this document at the request of the person above and that it is based on all information of which I have any knowledge.

Print Name _____   Signature _____   Date _____

Address _____   G-28 ID or VOLAG Number, if any. _____

Form I-130 (Rev. 10/26/05) Y Page 2

Child Immigrants

What Child Is This?

When Congress writes laws regulating immigration, it aims to keep families together. Foreign-born children of U.S. citizens or permanent residents are eligible to get a green card when a parent files a petition for them. However, you need to look carefully at who qualifies as a "child."

Note: This chapter addresses only children whose parents have already immigrated to the United States. The situation of children accompanying an immigrating parent is covered in other chapters of this book.

A. Who Qualifies

A person is eligible for a green card if he or she is the child of:

- a U.S. citizen parent, under 21 years of age (immediate relative)
- a U.S. citizen parent, if the child is over 21 and not married (family first preference)
- a U.S. citizen parent, if the child is over 21 and married (family third preference), or
- a lawful permanent resident, if the child is not married and is under 21 (family second 2A preference). If the child is over 21 years old and not married, then he or she would come under the family second 2B preference. If the child was formerly married, but is now divorced or a widow or widower, or if the marriage has been annulled, the parent can still petition for the now-unmarried child in the 2B category.

Children of Permanent Residents Wait Longer

The Immigration Act of 1990 allocated around 88,000 immigrant visas per year worldwide to the spouses and unmarried children under 21 years of age of green card holders—and only around 26,000 visas per year to their unmarried children over 21 years of age. And the demand in both categories is far greater than supply. The law placed no time limits on processing the applications.

The current waiting period for a spouse and unmarried children under the age of 21 is about five years. Children over 21 should be prepared to wait nine years or more for their immigrant visas.

The green card–holding parent or spouse may be able to hurry the process along by becoming a U.S. citizen.

Cautions for children who get married or turn 21 before receiving their green cards: The visa categories described above must fit the children not only when the visa application process is begun, but at the very end. This "end" may be years later, when the child attends the interview at which he or she is approved for the green card, and also, if coming from overseas, when the child actually enters the United States. If, for example, the child of a permanent resident gets married, his or her green card eligibility will be destroyed (at least until the parent becomes a U.S. citizen and starts the petition process all over again). Tell your children to consider not getting married if they want to protect their right to immigrate.

Of course, children have less control over getting older, and ultimately turning 21. A law called the Child Status Protection Act helps some, though not all children facing this problem. For details, see Chapter 5, Section D5, "Situations Where Children Are Protected From Switching Categories."

B. Definition of "Child"

Immigration law recognizes many different meanings of the word "child" as it relates to obtaining a green card. This definition is important because it determines what kind of documents USCIS will require when the visa petition is filed.

1. Child of Married Parents

When a child is born to a man and a woman who are married to each other, the child is, in legal terms, their legitimate child. To establish the relationship of mother and child, the only document necessary is the birth certificate showing the name of the mother and of the child.

To show the relationship of father and child, two documents are necessary:

- the birth certificate, which shows the name of the father and the child, and
- the marriage certificate, which shows that the mother and the father were married before the birth of the child.

2. Child of Unmarried Parents

A woman and man who conceive a child are that child's natural parents. Proving this relationship for immigration purposes requires extra steps if the woman and man are not married to one another.

Proving through mother. When a child is born of a woman who is not married to the child's father, the child is her natural child.

To establish the relationship of mother and child, the only document necessary is the birth certificate showing the name of the mother and the name of the child.

If the mother's maiden name as shown on the birth certificate of her child differs from her present name, the mother must present the document showing that her name was changed. Usually, she has changed her name after marrying. The marriage certificate will then verify that the mother named on the birth certificate and the mother on the immigration form are the same person.

Similarly, if the child is a daughter who has changed her name after marriage, her marriage certificate must be submitted with the immigration papers to show that the child on the birth certificate and the child on the immigration form are the same person.

Proving through father. Even if the father of the child is not married to the mother when the child is born, both the father and mother can petition for the child to immigrate into the United States.

But it may become complicated to prove the father-child relationship. First, the father must establish that he is really the biological father of the child. The birth certificate is the best proof, if his name appears as the father of the child.

If his name is not on the birth certificate, the father should apply to his civil registry requesting that his name be added to the birth certificate as the father of the child. He should do this before the child turns 18.

In some countries, the father may have to acknowledge before a civil court, government agency, or civil registry that he is the father of the child. USCIS requires such acknowledgment to occur before the child turns 18 years old.

If none of this proof is available, a blood test, accompanied by an affidavit from the mother stating that the man is the father of the child, may be acceptable.

In addition, the father must show that he was not simply the biological father, but that there was a father-child relationship. There must be proof that:

- the father and child lived together before the child turned 18, or
- there was a true father-child relationship before the child turned 18 or got married.

This relationship can be shown by letters written by one to the other; canceled checks or other proof of money sent regularly to support the child; photos of both of them together; school records showing the father's name; affidavits from at least two people who know of the father-child relationship; U.S. income tax returns showing the child listed as a dependent; birthday cards; or

Valentine, Christmas, or other holiday cards sent and received.

In short, almost any evidence may help show that the father did not abandon the child, but kept up paternal ties before the child turned 18 years old.

Some Countries Require No Proof

The governments in some countries, such as China, Haiti, Trinidad and Tobago, and Jamaica, have passed laws erasing the legal distinction between children born to parents who are married to one another and those whose parents are not married.

But the father has to show USCIS that the law was changed before the child turned 18 years of age. If he can show this, he need not submit all those letters, affidavits, school records, and other proof mentioned above.

---

3. Legitimated Child of Recently Married Parents

When a child is born to a man and a woman who are not married to each other when the child was born but who marry each other before the child turned 18 years of age, the child is considered to be a legitimated child.

To prove the relationship of mother and child, only the birth certificate is necessary.

To prove the relationship of father and child, two documents are needed: the birth certificate and the marriage certificate.

4. Stepchild

When the mother or the father of a child marries a person who is not the biological parent of that child, a step-relationship is created between the new parent and the child.

For there to be any immigration benefit, the marriage between the child's parent and stepparent must occur before the child turns 18 years of age. A U.S. citizen or green card-holding spouse can petition for a foreign-born spouse's children as his or her stepchildren at any time as long as the children were under 18 years of age at the time of the marriage.

In addition to the birth certificate of the child, a marriage certificate is necessary to show that the step-relationship was created by a marriage that occurred before the child's 18th birthday.

5. Adopted Child

For immigration purposes, an adopted child is a child who has been adopted according to the laws of the country of his or her birth, or the U.S. state of the adopting parents, as long as the adoption occurs before the child turns 16 years of age. Unlike an orphan child (discussed in Chapter 10), the adopted child is neither orphaned nor abandoned by his or her natural parents.

> **EXAMPLE:** If you were 17 years old when you were adopted by your naturalized American uncle, you may inherit his wealth, but you will not be able to obtain a green card as the adopted child of a U.S. citizen.

USCIS requires two additional circumstances before an adopted child can become eligible for a green card.

- The petitioner—who may be either a U.S. citizen or a permanent resident—must have had legal custody of the adopted child for at least two years. This means that either a legal guardianship or an actual adoption decree must have been issued two years before the immigrant petition was filed.
- The adopted child must have lived with the adopting parents at least two years before the petition was filed.

Because of these requirements, the only way the adopted child can get an immigrant visa is for one or both of the adopting parents to live in the foreign country with the alien child. This is practically impossible for lawful permanent resident parents, who must maintain their U.S.

residences in order to keep their green cards. The other alternative may be to process the immigration papers required for an orphan child. (See Chapter 10.)

New Adoption Opportunities on the Way?

In October 2000, President Clinton signed into law the Intercountry Adoption Act of 2000, which implements the Hague Convention on International Adoption. This is expected to streamline and broaden opportunities for adoption of children from overseas. However, before this law is actually implemented, the U.S. government must first set up a Central Adoption Authority and issue regulations—all of which is moving very slowly.

The child may live with the adopting parent, or may be under the legal custody of the adopting parent for two years, either before or after the adoption becomes final by court decree. It does not matter. However, the child must live with the adopting parents for two years and must be in the legal custody of the adopting parents for two years. When these two periods have occurred, either at the same time or one after the other, the immigrant petition can be filed.

The only other way to petition for a child under this provision is for the child to enter the United States as a nonimmigrant, such as a visiting student. Adoption proceedings may then be initiated in the United States. However, the adopting parents cannot file a petition for the child as a relative until two years after the adoption.

C. Quick View of the Application Process

For someone to get a green card as a child, his or her U.S. citizen or permanent resident parent must begin the process, by submitting what's called a "visa petition" (using Form I-130). We're going to assume that the person reading this is the parent. Form I-130 serves to prove to the immigration authorities that your children are truly and legally yours. After that petition is approved, your children complete their half of the process (with your help, of course) by submitting a green card application and attending an interview, most likely with you accompanying them. Their application serves to prove that not only do they qualify as children of a U.S. citizen or permanent resident, but that they're otherwise eligible for U.S. permanent residence.

However, the details of when and how your children complete their half of the process depend on whether they are living overseas or in the United States, as described in Section D, below.

D. Detailed Instructions for the Application Process

Now we'll break the application process down into individual procedures, some of which will be covered in this chapter, others of which will be covered in other chapters—we'll tell you exactly where to go to for your situation.

1. Preparing the Form I-130 Visa Petition

We'll start by discussing the visa petition, which all parents of immigrating children must begin by preparing. You'll need to assemble:

- ❑ Form I-130, Petition for Alien Relative, (see sample at the end of this chapter)
- ❑ Form G-325A, Biographic Information (signed by child)
- ❑ birth certificate of child
- ❑ parents' marriage certificate
- ❑ documents proving the parent's U.S. citizenship or permanent residence (see Chapter 22), and
- ❑ filing fee for Form I-130, currently $190.

In cases where the child is adopted, the following documents must also be presented:

- ❑ the adoption decree showing adoption prior to 16 years of age

❑ documents showing legal custody for at least two years

❑ documents proving that the adopted child has resided with the adopting parent or parents for at least two years

❑ a birth certificate of the child showing the adopting parent as mother or father by reason of the adoption decree, and

❑ documents showing the marital status of the petitioning parent.

Once you've assembled all these items, make a copy for your records. It's also a good idea to write a cover letter, explaining what type of visa petition it is (for example, saying "I am a U.S. citizen, filing the enclosed visa petition on behalf of my married daughter."). The letter should include a bulleted list, much like the one above, of everything you're sending. This will help USCIS see that you're organized. It will help you, too, make sure that nothing has been forgotten.

2. Where to Submit the I-130 Visa Petition

Once you've assembled and copied everything, your next step and where to send the visa petition depends on which visa category your child will be applying in, and where the child is now, as detailed below.

Next step for unmarried children under age 21 of U.S. citizens (immediate relatives), if the children live overseas: The parent should mail the visa petition to the USCIS Service Center appropriate for the parent's geographical area. Soon after the visa petition is approved, the U.S. consulate serving the country where the child lives will take over. The child will apply for the immigrant visa and green card through "consular processing," described in Chapter 19.

Next step for unmarried children under age 21 of U.S. citizens (immediate relatives), if the children live in the United States: If the child is eligible for adjustment of status (as explained in

Chapter 18), then the parent shouldn't file the visa petition by itself, but should combine it with the adjustment of status application, according to the instructions in Chapter 18. If, however, the child is not eligible to adjust status, and has spent any time in the U.S. illegally or out of status, consult an experienced immigration attorney.

Next step for all children of U.S. permanent residents, and married or over-21 children of U.S. citizens (preference relatives) if the children live overseas: The parent should mail the visa petition to the USCIS Service Center appropriate for the parent's geographical area. After the visa petition is approved, the child will be put on a waiting list, based on his or her Priority Date. When the Priority Date becomes "current," the U.S. consulate serving the country where the child lives will take over. The child will apply for the immigrant visa and green card through "consular processing," described in Chapter 19.

Next step for all children of U.S. permanent residents and married or over-21 children of U.S. citizens (preference relatives) if the children live in the United States: The parent should mail the visa petition to the appropriate USCIS Service Center for the parent's geographical area. After the visa petition is approved, the child will be put on a waiting list, based on his or her Priority Date. It will be many years before the Priority Date becomes "current," during which time the mere filing of a visa petition gives the child no rights to remain in the United States (though many do, illegally). After the child's Priority Date becomes current, then:

• If the child is still living in the U.S. and is eligible for adjustment of status (unlikely), see Chapter 18 for instructions.

• If the child is living in the U.S. and is not eligible for adjustment of status, or has left the U.S. but spent more than six months here illegally before leaving, see an experienced immigration attorney for help.

- If the child left the U.S. without having spent too much time there illegally, you can safely continue the process, and the U.S. consulate serving the country where the child lives will take over. The child will apply for the immigrant visa and green card through consular processing, described in Chapter 19.

E. Automatic Citizenship for Some Children

In 2000, Congress passed important new legislation allowing many children living in the U.S. with green cards to become citizens automatically, if they have at least one U.S. citizen parent. Natural born as well as adopted children can benefit from these new laws.

The law is slightly less helpful for children living overseas, who must go through an application process in order to claim their U.S. citizenship.

1. Children Living in the United States

For natural born children to qualify for automatic citizenship, one parent needs to be a U.S. citizen, the child must have a green card and be living in the legal and physical custody of the U.S. citizen parent, and the child must still be under age 18 when all of these conditions are fulfilled.

For adopted children to qualify, one of the parents must be a U.S. citizen, a full and final adoption must have occurred, the child must be living in the United States after having entered on an immigrant visa (meaning the child would now be a green card holder), and the child must still be under age 18 at the time that all these things become true.

Though the process is automatic—and USCIS tries to send such children certificates of citizenship within six weeks of when they get their green cards—it's an excellent idea for such children to also apply for U.S. passports as proof of their U.S. citizen status.

EXAMPLE: Lorna is 16 years old and living in Mexico. Some years ago, her father, a U.S. permanent resident, petitioned for her to immigrate. Even before her Priority Date became current, however, he became a U.S. citizen, so the process was speeded up. Lorna successfully applies for an immigrant visa through consular processing, and enters the United States to live with her father.

Almost as soon as Lorna enters the U.S., she automatically becomes a U.S. citizen, because she 1) has a U.S. citizen parent, 2) has a green card, 3) is living in the citizen parent's legal and physical custody, and 4) was still under 18 when the first three things became true. USCIS should, recognizing her status, automatically send her a citizenship certificate. (Note: If Lorna's father had become a citizen after she got her green card and came to the U.S. but before she turned 18, USCIS wouldn't realize she'd become an automatic citizen, and Lorna would have to request a certificate to prove it.)

2. Children Living Overseas

For children who are living overseas, the process is somewhat more complex. Either natural born or adopted children may qualify, but they need to have one U.S. citizen parent; that parent or the parent's parent must have been physically present in the U.S. for five years after the age of 14; the child must be visiting the U.S. on a temporary visa or other lawful means of entry; the child must live in the legal and physical custody of the U.S. citizen parent in their overseas home; and the child must remain under the age of 18 and in valid visa status until USCIS makes its decision on the citizenship application.

In practice, these conditions are very hard to meet. You might wish to consult with a lawyer. The application is made on Form N-600 for natural born children and N-600K for adopted children. For a sample of Form N-600, see the end of the chapter. For further instructions, see the USCIS website at www.uscis.gov.

Petition for Alien Relative, Sample Form I-130 (when used for a child) (page 1)

Department of Homeland Security
U.S. Citizenship and Immigration Services

OMB # 1615-0012; Expires 01/31/07

I-130, Petition for Alien Relative

DO NOT WRITE IN THIS BLOCK - FOR USCIS OFFICE ONLY..

A#	Action Stamp	Fee Stamp

Section of Law/Visa Category
- [ ] 201(b) Spouse - IR-1/CR-1
- [ ] 201(b) Child - IR-2/CR-2
- [ ] 201(b) Parent - IR-5
- [ ] 203(a)(1) Unm. S or D - F1-1
- [ ] 203(a)(2)(A)Spouse - F2-1
- [ ] 203(a)(2)(A) Child - F2-2
- [ ] 203(a)(2)(B) Unm. S or D - F2-4
- [ ] 203(a)(3) Married S or D - F3-1
- [ ] 203(a)(4) Brother/Sister - F4-1

Petition was filed on: _____ (priority date)
- [ ] Personal Interview   [ ] Previously Forwarded
- [ ] Pet. [ ] Ben. " A" File Reviewed   [ ] I-485 Filed Simultaneously
- [ ] Field Investigation   [ ] 204(g) Resolved
- [ ] 203(a)(2)(A) Resolved   [ ] 203(g) Resolved

Remarks:

A. Relationship. You are the petitioner. Your relative is the beneficiary.

1. I am filing this petition for my:
[ ] Husband/Wife [ ] Parent [ ] Brother/Sister [X] Child

2. Are you related by adoption?
[ ] Yes [X] No

3. Did you gain permanent residence through adoption?
[ ] Yes [X] No

B. Information about you.

1. Name (Family name in CAPS) (First) (Middle)
CARLTON   Derek   Andrew

2. Address (Number and Street) (Apt.No.)
575 7th St.
(Town or City) (State/Country) (Zip/Postal Code)
Champaign   IL/USA   61820

3. Place of Birth (Town or City) (State/Country)
Chicago IL/USA   Saraburi Thailand

4. Date of Birth (mm/dd/yyyy) 6/18/72
5. Gender [X] Male [ ] Female
6. Marital Status [X] Married [ ] Single [ ] Widowed [ ] Divorced

7. Other Names Used (including maiden name)

8. Date and Place of Present Marriage (if married)
4/12/04

9. U.S. Social Security Number (if any)
656-56-5656
10. Alien Registration Number
None

11. Name(s) of Prior Husband(s)/Wive(s)
None
12. Date(s) Marriage(s) Ended

13. If you are a U.S. citizen, complete the following:
My citizenship was acquired through (check one):
[X] Birth in the U.S.
[ ] Naturalization. Give certificate number and date and place of issuance.

[ ] Parents. Have you obtained a certificate of citizenship in your own name?
[ ] Yes. Give certificate number, date and place of issuance. [ ] No

14a. If you are a lawful permanent resident alien, complete the following: Date and place of admission for or adjustment to lawful permanent residence and class of admission.

14b. Did you gain permanent resident status through marriage to a U.S. citizen or lawful permanent resident?
[ ] Yes [ ] No

C. Information about your relative.

1. Name (Family name in CAPS) (First) (Middle)
SRISAI   Kanya   Lawan

2. Address (Number and Street) (Apt. No.)
14 Sri Ayudayha Road
(Town or City) (State/Country) (Zip/Postal Code)
Bangkok   Thailand

3. Place of Birth (Town or City) (State/Country)

4. Date of Birth (mm/dd/yyyy) 2/2/06
5. Gender [ ] Male [X] Female
6. Marital Status [ ] Married [ ] Single [ ] Widowed [ ] Divorced

7. Other Names Used (including maiden name)
none

8. Date and Place of Present Marriage (if married)
N/A

9. U.S. Social Security Number (if any)
None
10. Alien Registration Number
None

11. Name(s) of Prior Husband(s)/Wive(s)
None
12. Date(s) Marriage(s) Ended

13. Has your relative ever been in the U.S.?
[ ] Yes [X] No

14. If your relative is currently in the U.S., complete the following: He or she arrived as a::
(visitor, student, stowaway, without inspection, etc.)

Arrival/Departure Record (I-94)   Date arrived (mm/dd/yyyy)
| | | | ▬ | | | | | | | | |

Date authorized stay expired, or will expire, as shown on Form I-94 or I-95

15. Name and address of present employer (if any)
None

Date this employment began (mm/dd/yyyy)

16. Has your relative ever been under immigration proceedings?
[X] No [ ] Yes Where _____ When _____
[ ] Removal [ ] Exclusion/Deportation [ ] Recission [ ] Judicial Proceedings

INITIAL RECEIPT _____ RESUBMITTED _____ RELOCATED: Rec'd _____ Sent _____ COMPLETED: Appv'd _____ Denied _____ Ret'd _____

Form I-130 (Rev. 10/26/05) Y

Sample Form I-130 (page 2)

C. Information about your alien relative. (Continued.)

17. List husband/wife and all children of your relative.

(Name)	(Relationship)	(Date of Birth)	(Country of Birth)
None			

18. Address in the United States where your relative intends to live.

(Street Address)	(Town or City)	(State)
575 7th St.	Champaign	Illinois

19. Your relative's address abroad. (Include street, city, province and country)

14 Sri Ayudayha Road, Bangkok, Thailand

Phone Number (if any)   None

20. If your relative's native alphabet is other than Roman letters, write his or her name and foreign address in the native alphabet.

(Name)   Address (Include street, city, province and country):

21. If filing for your husband/wife, give last address at which you lived together. (Include street, city, province, if any, and country):

From: (Month) (Year)   To: (Month) (Year)

22. Complete the information below if your relative is in the United States and will apply for adjustment of status.

Your relative is in the United States and will apply for adjustment of status to that of a lawful permanent resident at USCIS office in:

_____ . If your relative is not eligible for adjustment of status, he or she

(City)   (State)

will apply for a visa abroad at the American consular post in

(City)   (Country)

NOTE: Designation of an American embassy or consulate outside the country of your relative's last residence does not guarantee acceptance for processing by that post. Acceptance is at the discretion of the designated embassy or consulate.

D. Other information.

1. If separate petitions are also being submitted for other relatives, give names of each and relationship.

Chosita Chanakarn SRISAI, wife

2. Have you ever before filed a petition for this or any other alien? ☐ Yes ☒ No

If "Yes," give name, place and date of filing and result.

WARNING: USCIS investigates claimed relationships and verifies the validity of documents. USCIS seeks criminal prosecutions when family relationships are falsified to obtain visas.

PENALTIES: By law, you may be imprisoned for not more than five years or fined $250,000, or both, for entering into a marriage contract for the purpose of evading any provision of the immigration laws. In addition, you may be fined up to $10,000 and imprisoned for up to five years, or both, for knowingly and willfully falsifying or concealing a material fact or using any false document in submitting this petition.

YOUR CERTIFICATION: I certify, under penalty of perjury under the laws of the United States of America, that the foregoing is true and correct. Furthermore, I authorize the release of any information from my records that U.S. Citizenship and Immigration Services needs to determine eligibility for the benefit that I am seeking.

E. Signature of petitioner.

Derek A. Carlton   Date 8/19/06   Phone Number (217) 555-1313

F. Signature of person preparing this form, if other than the petitioner.

I declare that I prepared this document at the request of the person above and that it is based on all information of which I have any knowledge.

Print Name   Signature   Date

Address   G-28 ID or VOLAG Number, if any.

Form I-130 (Rev. 10/26/05) Y Page 2

Application for Certificate of Citizenship, Sample Form N-600 (page 1)

OMB No. 1615-0057; Expires 10/31/05
You may continue to use this form after expiration date.

Department of Homeland Security
U.S. Citizenship and Immigration Services

N-600, Application for Certificate of Citizenship

Print clearly or type your answers, using CAPITAL letters in black ink. Failure to print clearly may delay processing of your application.

Part I. Information About You. *(Provide information about yourself, if you are a person applying for the Certificate of Citizenship. If you are a U.S. citizen parent applying for a Certificate of Citizenship for your minor child, **provide information about your child**).*

If your child has an "A" Number, write it here:

A

For USCIS Use Only

A. Current legal name
Family Name *(Last Name)*

REYNOLDS

Given Name *(First Name)*

Besa

Full Middle Name *(If applicable)*

Najada

B. Name exactly as it appears on your Permanent Resident Card *(If applicable).*
Family Name *(Last Name)*

REYNOLDS

Given Name *(First Name)*

Besa

Full Middle Name *(If applicable)*

Najada

C. Other names used since birth

Family Name *(Last Name)*	Given Name *(First Name)*	Middle Name *(If applicable)*

D. U.S. Social Security # *(If applicable)*

None

E. Date of Birth *(mm/dd/yyyy)*

3/9/97

F. Country of Birth

Albania

G. Country of Prior Nationality

Albania

H. Gender

☐ Male   ☒ Female

I. Height

4'1"

Returned	Receipt
Date	
Date	
Resubmitted	
Date	
Date	
Reloc Sent	
Date	
Date	
Reloc Rec'd	
Date	
Date	

Remarks

Part 2. Information About Your Eligibility. *(Check only one).*

A. I am claiming U.S. citizenship through:

☐   A U.S. citizen father or a U.S. citizen mother.

☐   Both U.S. citizen parents.

☐   A U.S. citizen adoptive parent(s).

☐   An alien parent(s) who naturalized.

B. ☒ **I am a U.S. citizen parent applying for a certificate of citizenship on behalf of my minor (under 18 years) BIOLOGICAL child.**

C. ☐ **I am a U.S. citizen parent applying for a certificate of citizenship on behalf of my minor (less than 18 years) ADOPTED child.**

D. ☐   **Other** *(Please explain fully)*

Action Block

To Be Completed by
☐ *Attorney or Representative*, if any.
Fill in box if G-28 is attached to represent the applicant.

ATTY State License #

Form N-600 (Rev. 10/26/05) Y

Sample Form N-600 (page 2)

Part 3. Additional Information About You. *(Provide additional information about* **yourself**, *if you are the person applying for the Certificate of Citizenship. If you are a U.S. citizen parent applying for a Certificate of Citizenship for your* **minor child**, *provide the additional information about your* **minor child**).

A. Home Address - Street Number and Name *(Do not write a P.O. Box in this space)*

	Apartment Number
122 Dyrrah Way	

City	County	State/Province	Country	Zip/Postal Code
Durres			Albania	

B. Mailing Address - Street Number and Name *(If different from home address)*

	Apartment Number

City	County	State/Province	Country	Zip/Postal Code

C. Daytime Phone Number *(If any)*

Daytime Phone Number *(If any)*	Evening Phone Number *(If any)*	E-Mail Address *(If any)*
(355) 04 223322	(355) 04 112233	besa37@durres.com

D. Marital Status

[X] Single, Never Married   [ ] Married   [ ] Divorced   [ ] Widowed

[ ] Marriage Annulled or Other *(Explain)* _____

E. Information about entry into the United States and current immigration status

1. I arrived in the following manner:

Port of Entry *(City/State)*	Date of Entry *(mm/dd/yyyy)*	Exact Name Used at Time of Entry:
Buffalo, NY	04/02/05	Besa Najada REYNOLDS

2. I used the following travel document to enter:

[X] Passport

[ ]

Passport Number	Country Issuing Passport	Date Passport Issued *(mm/dd/yyyy)*
1234567	Albania	06/07/04

Other *(Please Specify Name of Document and Dates of Issuance)*

3. I entered as:

[ ] An immigrant (lawful permanent resident) using an immigrant visa

[X] A nonimmigrant

[ ] A refugee

[ ] Other *(Explain)* _____

4. I obtained lawful permanent resident status through adjustment of status *(If applicable)*:

Date you became a Permanent Resident *(mm/dd/yyyy)*	USCIS (or former INS) Office where granted adjustment of status

F. Have you previously applied for a certificate of citizenship or U.S. passport?   [X] No   [ ] Yes *(Attach Explanation)*

Sample Form N-600 (page 3)

Part 3. Additional Information About You. *(Provide additional information about **yourself**, if you are the person applying for the Certificate of Citizenship. If you are a U.S. citizen parent applying for a Certificate of Citizenship for your **minor child**, provide the additional information about your **minor child**). Continued.*

G. Were you adopted? [X] No   [ ] Yes *(Please complete the following information)*:

Date of Adoption *(mm/dd/yyyy)*

Place of Final Adoption *(City/State or Country)*

Date Legal Custody Began *(mm/dd/yyyy)*

Date Physical Custody Began *(mm/dd/yyyy)*

H. Did you have to be re-adopted in the United States?   [ ] No   [ ] Yes *(Please complete the following information)*:

Date of Final Adoption *(mm/dd/yyyy)*

Place of Final Adoption *(City/State)*

Date Legal Custody Began *(mm/dd/yyyy)*

Date Physical Custody Began *(mm/dd/yyyy)*

I. Were your parents married to each other when you were born (or adopted)?   [ ] No   [ ] Yes

J. Have you been absent from the United States since you first arrived? *(Only for persons born before October 10, 1952, who are claiming U.S. citizenship at time of birth; otherwise, do not complete this section.)*   [ ] No   [ ] Yes

If yes, complete the following information about all absences, beginning with your most recent trip. If you need more space, use a separate sheet of paper.

Date You Left the United States *(mm/dd/yyyy)*	Date You Returned to the United States *(mm/dd/yyyy)*	Place of Entry Upon Return to the United States

Part 4. Information About U.S. Citizen Father (or Adoptive Father). *(Complete this section if you are claiming citizenship through a U.S. citizen father. If you are a U.S. citizen father applying for a Certificate of Citizenship on behalf of your minor biological or adopted child, provide information about **yourself** below.)*

A. Current legal name of U.S. citizen father.

Family Name *(Last Name)*
REYNOLDS

Given Name *(First Name)*
Joseph

Full Middle Name *(If applicable)*
Lee

B. Date of Birth *(mm/dd/yyyy)*
7/10/71

C. Country of Birth
USA

D. Country of Nationality

E. Home Address - Street Number and Name *(If deceased, so state and enter date of death)*
122 Dyrrah Way

Apartment Number

City
Durres

County

State/Province

Country
Albania

Zip/Postal Code

Sample Form N-600 (page 4)

Part 4. Information About U.S. Citizen Father (or Adoptive Father). *(Complete this section if you are claiming citizenship through a U.S. citizen father. If you are a U.S. citizen father applying for a Certificate of Citizenship on behalf of your minor biological or adopted child, provide information about **yourself** below.)* **Continued.**

F. U.S. citizen by:

- [X] Birth in the United States
- [ ] Birth abroad to U.S. citizen parent(s)
- [ ] Acquisition after birth through naturalization of alien parent(s)
- [ ] Naturalization

Date of Naturalization *(mm/dd/yyyy)*   Place of Naturalization *(Name of Court and City/State or USCIS or Former INS Office Location)*

Certificate of Naturalization Number   Former "A" Number *(If known)*

G. Has your father ever lost U.S. citizenship or taken any action that would cause loss of U.S. citizenship?

- [X] No   [ ] Yes *(Provide full explanation on a separate sheet(s) of paper.)*

H. Dates of Residence and/or Physical Presence in the United States *(Complete this only if you are an applicant claiming U.S. citizenship at time of birth abroad)*

Provide the dates your U.S. citizen father resided in or was physically present in the United States. If you need more space, use a separate sheet(s) of paper.

From *(mm/dd/yyyy)*	To *(mm/dd/yyyy)*
7/10/71	11/1/95

I. Marital History

1. How many times has your U.S. citizen father been married (including annulled marriages)?

2. Information about U.S. citizen father's **current spouse:**

Family Name *(Last Name)*	Given Name *(First Name)*	Full Middle Name *(If applicable)*
MANESH	Saranda	Venera

Date of Birth *(mm/dd/yyyy)*	Country of Birth	Country of Nationality
4/15/73	Albania	Albania

Home Address - Street Number and Name: 122 Dyrrah Way   Apartment Number:

City	County	State or Province	Country	Zip/Postal Code
Durres			Albania	

Date of Marriage *(mm/dd/yyyy)*	Place of Marriage *(City/State or Country)*
8/7/96	Tirana, Albania

Spouse's Immigration Status:

- [ ] U.S. Citizen   [ ] Lawful Permanent Resident   [X] Other *(Explain)*   Resides in Albania

3. Is your U.S. citizen father's current spouse also your mother?   [ ] No   [X] Yes

Sample Form N-600 (page 5)

Part 5. Information About Your U.S. Citizen Mother (or Adoptive Mother). *(Complete this section if you are claiming citizenship through a U.S. citizen mother (or adoptive mother). If you are a U.S. citizen mother applying for a Certificate of Citizenship on behalf of your minor biological or adopted child, provide information about **yourself** below).*

A. Current legal name of U.S. citizen mother.

Family Name *(Last Name)*	Given Name *(First Name)*	Full Middle Name *(If applicable)*

B. Date of Birth *(mm/dd/yyyy)*	**C. Country of Birth**	**D. Country of Nationality**

E. Home Address - Street Number and Name *(If deceased, so state and enter date of death)*   Apartment Number

City	County	State/Province	Country	Zip/Postal Code

F. U.S. citizen by:

☐ Birth in the United States

☐ Birth abroad to U.S. citizen parent(s)

☐ Acquisition after birth through naturalization of alien parent(s)

☐ Naturalization

Date of Naturalization *(mm/dd/yyyy)*	Place of Naturalization *(Name of Court and City/State or USCIS or Former INS Office Location)*

Certificate of Naturalization Number	Former "A" Number *(If known)*

G. Has your mother ever lost U.S. citizenship or taken any action that would cause loss of U.S. citizenship?

☐ No   ☐ Yes *(Provide full explanation on a separate sheet(s) of paper.)*

H. Dates of Residence and/or Physical Presence in the United States *(Complete this only if you are an applicant claiming U.S. citizenship at time of birth abroad)*

Provide the dates your U.S. citizen father resided in or was physically present in the United States. If you need more space, use a separate sheet(s) of paper.

From *(mm/dd/yyyy)*	To *(mm/dd/yyyy)*

I. Marital History

1. How many times has your U.S. citizen mother been married (including annulled marriages)?

2. Information about U.S. citizen mother's **current spouse:**

Family Name *(Last Name)*	Given Name *(First Name)*	Full Middle Name *(If applicable)*
Date of Birth *(mm/dd/yyyy)*	Country of Birth	Country of Nationality

Sample Form N-600 (page 6)

Part 5. Information About Your U.S. Citizen Mother (or Adoptive Mother). *(Complete this section if you are claiming citizenship through a U.S. citizen mother (or adoptive mother). If you are a U.S. citizen mother applying for a Certificate of Citizenship on behalf of your minor biological or adopted child, provide information about **yourself** below).* **Continued.**

2. Information about U.S. citizen mother's **current spouse**: *(Continued.)*

Home Address - Street Number and Name | Apartment Number

City | County | State or Province | Country | Zip/Postal Code

Date of Marriage *(mm/dd/yyyy)* | Place of Marriage *(City/State or Country)*

Spouse's Immigration Status:

☐ U.S. Citizen   ☐ Lawful Permanent Resident   ☐ Other *(Explain)*

3. Is your U.S. citizen mother's current spouse also your father?   ☐ No   ☐ Yes

Part 6. Information About Military Service of U. S. Citizen Parent(s). *(Complete this only if you are an applicant claiming U.S. citizenship at time of birth abroad)*

1. Has your U. S. citizen parent(s) served in the armed forces?   ☐ No   ☐ Yes

2. If "Yes," which parent?   ☐ U.S. Citizen Father   ☐ U.S. Citizen Mother

3. Dates of Service. *(If time of service fulfills any of required physical presence, submit evidence of service.)*

From *(mm/dd/yyyy)* | To *(mm/dd/yyyy)* | From *(mm/dd/yyyy)* | To *(mm/dd/yyyy)*

4. Type of discharge.   ☐ Honorable   ☐ Other than Honorable   ☐ Dishonorable

Part 7. Signature.

I certify, under penalty of perjury under the laws of the United States, that this application and the evidence submitted with it is all true and correct. I authorize the release of any information from my records, or my minor child's records, that U.S. Citizenship and Immigration Services needs to determine eligibility for the benefit I am seeking.

Applicant's Signature | Printed Name | Date *(mm/dd/yyyy)*

Joseph Reynolds | Joseph Reynolds | 4/6/06

Part 8. Signature of Person Preparing This Form, If Other Than Applicant.

I declare that I prepared this application at the request of the above person. The answers provided are based on information of which I have personal knowledge and/or were provided to me by the above-named person in response to the questions contained on this form.

Preparer's Signature | Preparer's Printed Name | Date *(mm/dd/yyyy)*

Name of Business/Organization *(If applicable)* | Preparer's Daytime Phone Number

(   )

Preparer's Address - Street Number and Name

City | County | State | Zip Code

Sample Form N-600 (page 7)

NOTE: Do not complete the following parts unless a USCIS officer instructs you to do so at the interview.

Part 9. Affidavit.

I, the (applicant, parent or legal guardian) _____ do swear or affirm, under penalty of perjury laws of the

United States, that I know and understand the contents of this application signed by me, and the attached supplementary pages number (___) to

(___) inclusive, that the same are true and correct to the best of my knowledge, and that corrections number (___) to (___) were made by me or

at my request.

Signature of parent, guardian or applicant   Date *(mm/dd/yyyy)*

Subscribed and sworn or affirmed before me upon examination of the applicant (parent, guardian) on _____ at

_____ .

Signature of Interviewing Officer   Title

Part 10. Officer Report and Recommendation on Application for Certificate of Citizenship.

On the basis of the documents, records and the testimony of persons examined, and the identification upon personal appearance of the underage

beneficiary, I find that all the facts and conclusions set forth under oath in this application are ☐ true and correct; that the applicant did ☐

derive or acquire U.S. citizenship on _____ *(mm/dd/yyyy)*, through *(mark "X" in appropriate section of law or, if*

section of law not reflected, insert applicable section of law in "Other" block):   ☐ **section 301 of the INA**   ☐ **section 309 of the INA**

☐ **section 320 of the INA**   ☐ **section 321 of the INA**   ☐ **Other** _____

and that (s)he ☐ *has* ☐ *has not* been expatriated since that time. I recommend that this application be ☐ *granted* ☐ *denied* and that

☐ *A or* ☐ *AA* Certificate of Citizenship be issued in the name of _____ .

District Adjudication Officer's Name and Title   District Adjudication Officer's Signature

I do ☐   do not ☐   concur in recommendation of the application.

District Director or Officer-in-Charge Signature   Date *(mm/dd/yyyy)*

Orphan Immigrants

Little Orphan Annie

If you've read the chapter on adopted children, you realize that the immigration rules around adoption are difficult, requiring not only legal custody, but two years of living together before the parent can petition for the child. Adopting an orphan is easier, in that these requirements are dropped. In fact, many of the U.S. citizens you know who've adopted from overseas probably adopted orphans.

There are two types of orphan immigrant visas: an IR-3 visa classification, for orphans who have met the parents and whose adoptions were completed abroad, and an IR-4 classification, for orphans who, although in the legal custody of the U.S. citizen parent or parents, still need to be legally adopted after reaching the United States, or who need to be readopted because the U.S. parents haven't yet seen the child. In either case, the application process includes a number of complexities.

Because of these complexities, most Americans who adopt from overseas use an agency that specializes in international adoptions, although direct adoption is also possible. Even with an agency, expect the process to take at least six to twelve months. Although we can't provide you with a list of reputable agencies, two California-based groups that Nolo lawyers have had good experiences with are Adopt International, at 415-934-0300, www.adopt-intl.org; and Adoption Connection, at 800-972-9225, 415-359-2494, www.adoptionconnection.org.

Be selective in choosing an adoption agency—look for one that has been doing adoptions for a number of years, successfully completes a comparatively large number per year, serves the countries in which you're interested, and is happy to show you evidence that it's licensed and comes with good references. The U.S. government also provides a centralized information source, the National Adoption Information Clearinghouse, at http://naic.acf.hhs.gov.

You'll also need to follow the rules of the country you're adopting from. Not every country allows international adoptions, and those that do usually impose various requirements on the parents. For example, some countries refuse to allow single-parent adoptions, or require that adopting parents be of a certain age. This chapter covers only the U.S. requirements; you'll need to research the international requirements on your own, or with the help of your adoption agency.

A. Who Qualifies as an Orphan Child

A child under 16 years of age (or under 18, if he or she is being adopted along with a brother or sister under 16) is considered an orphan if he or she meets any of the following conditions:
- both parents have died or have disappeared
- the sole or surviving parent is incapable of providing the proper child care and has, in writing, released the child for adoption and emigration, or
- both father and mother have abandoned the child, or have become separated or lost from the child—and the legal authorities in the child's country, recognizing the child as abandoned, have granted legal custody of the child to an orphanage.

However, if the child has been placed with other people, or temporarily in the orphanage, or if one or both parents continue to maintain contact—for example, sending gifts, writing letters, or showing that they have not ended their parental obligations to the child—the child will not be considered an orphan by the U.S. government. You also can't get around the requirements by having the overseas parent or parents "abandon" the child into the hands of the adopting U.S. couple or person.

B. Who Can Petition for an Orphan Child

Only U.S. citizens are allowed to file a visa petition for an orphan child; lawful permanent residents may not do so. A number of other regulations also apply.

- If a married couple is adopting, only one of them need be a U.S. citizen (but both have to be age 21 or over and sign the petition).
- If the U.S. citizen is not married, then he or she must be at least 25 years of age before filing the petition. In addition, if the citizen was under 25 when the foreign adoption took place, the adoption will be considered invalid, and he or she will have to readopt the child after the child reaches the United States (if allowed in his or her state of residence).
- The orphan child must be less than 16 years of age when the petition is filed (or under 18, if the parents are also petitioning for the child's brother or sister who is under 16).
- The adopting married couple, or single person, must have completed certain pre-adoption requirements before filing the petition. (See Section C, below.)
- The adopting married couple, or single person, must have seen the child in the orphan's country before or during the adoption proceedings, or show that they'll be able to "readopt" the child in the United States.

Beware of the lawbreakers. In some developing countries, kidnapping poor children and then selling them for adoption to childless couples in the United States and Europe has become scandalously rampant.

Your search for a child of your own should not cause the kidnapping or sale of another person's child. Before you sign up with any adoption organization, check its references with friends who have worked with the organization—or ask for the names of some former clients. Above all, avoid direct arrangements with the surviving parent or private individuals acting as brokers for a fee.

C. Pre-Adoption Requirements

To protect the child and to ensure that the adopting parent or parents will care for the child properly, the immigration laws require what's called a "home study" before an adoption decree is finalized or before a petition for an orphan child will be approved. Many couples take care of this first, as part of an Advance Processing application, described below in Section D1.

The purpose of the home study is to allow the state agency handling adoptions to investigate the future home of the child (and any adult living it in) and verify whether the adopting couple, or the single person, is psychologically and economically fit to adopt a child. Most home studies take about three months.

The home study must result in a favorable report recommending the proposed adoption. The report must be signed by an official of a state agency, or an agency licensed by the state in which the child will live with the adopting parent or parents. It's good for only six months.

This report must contain the following information:

- the financial ability of the parent or parents to raise and educate the child
- a discussion of possible negative factors, such as a history of substance abuse, child abuse, sexual abuse, domestic violence, criminal behavior, or past denials of adoptions or unfavorable home study reports
- a detailed description of the living accommodations including special accommodations for a child with disabilities or medical issues, and
- a factual evaluation of the physical, mental, and moral ability of the adopting parent or parents, including observations made during personal interviews.

In addition to the home study, other pre-adoption conditions may be required by some states before an adoption petition may be filed with local courts. Therefore, if you are planning to adopt the orphan child in the United States, you must first comply with these state rules.

In every state, there is one main agency that oversees adoptions. To contact the local representative of your state agency, check your state government website or look in the telephone book under Adoption, Child Welfare, or Social Services.

International Adoption for Lesbians and Gays

Currently, no foreign country allows adoption by same-sex couples or by any openly gay person. Most countries strongly prefer that the adopting parents be married. If a country requires adoptive parents to be married, then neither a same-sex couple nor a lesbian or gay individual can adopt there. It's doubtful that the ability to marry in Massachusetts will have any impact on the host country's policy.

At least one country (China) is so determined not to grant adoptions to lesbians and gays that it requires adoptive parents to sign an affidavit swearing that they are heterosexual. Apparently undeterred, a large number of same-sex couples have successfully adopted Chinese girls who were being raised in orphanages.

If you are proceeding with a foreign adoption, you may opt to keep your sexual orientation—and your relationship with your partner—hidden from the host country. It is a judgment call whether or not you tell the agency helping you with the adoption. Many agencies operate on a wink-and-nod basis—they are fully aware of the nature of your relationship with your partner, but refer to the partner as a "roommate" in their reports to the host country, and simply ignore the issue of sexual orientation.

No agency will advertise that it works with same-sex couples or lesbian/gay individuals on international adoptions, so word of mouth is the best way to find an agency to help you.

For more about adoption and parenting for same-sex couples, check out *A Legal Guide for Lesbian & Gay Couples,* by Hayden Curry, Denis Clifford, and Frederick Hertz (Nolo).

D. Starting the Adoption Process

The first steps toward adoption depend in part on whether or not the orphan child has been identified.

1. When the Child Is Not Yet Identified

If the child has not yet been identified and those who wish to adopt are going abroad to locate an orphan child for adoption, or for adoption after arrival in the United States, they should file an Advance Processing application, as follows:

❑ Form I-600A, Application for Advance Processing of Orphan Petition, signed by the U.S. citizen and, if married, the spouse. (See sample at end of this chapter.)

❑ Proof of petitioner's U.S. citizenship. (See Chapter 22.)

❑ If married, evidence of the spouse's U.S. citizenship or lawful legal status in the United States.

❑ Marriage certificate, divorce or annulment decree, or death certificate, as evidence of present and previous marital status.

❑ Fees of $70 each for fingerprints of the U.S. citizen and, if married, of the spouse. Also, all adults aged 18 years old or older who live in the household must be fingerprinted. (See Chapter 22, Section F.)

❑ Evidence of petitioner's age, if unmarried.

❑ A favorable home study report. If the home study report is not yet available, it must be submitted within one year from the date of filing the advance application. Otherwise, the application will be considered to have been abandoned.

❑ Proof of compliance with any pre-adoption requirements of the state in which the child will live if the adoption is to be completed in the United States (see Section C).

❑ A filing fee (currently $545). However, no filing fee is required if an Application for Advance Processing has been previously filed and if the petition has been filed within one year of the approval of the advance application. A copy of the receipt showing the filing fee has been paid is sufficient. Also include a copy of the approval notice.

If the adopting parents are unsuccessful in locating an orphan child within one year, the application will be considered abandoned. If the prospective parents wish to continue the process of adopting an alien child, they'll have to submit a new Advance Processing application (with a new filing fee of $545) if the child has not yet been identified, or a petition as described below (which also requires a filing fee of $545) if the child has been identified.

Can you Bring the Child to the U.S. First?

It's frustrating for parents eager to bring an orphan child into their home to have to wait for all the immigration procedures to be completed. In light of this, the U.S. government tries to give high priority to orphan petitions. However, the government doesn't smile upon efforts by parents to get around the U.S. immigration laws, for example by bringing the child in on a tourist or student visa, and attempting to complete the adoption and immigration processes afterward. Basically, this won't work. In rare cases, however, USCIS will grant humanitarian parole to allow an orphan into the U.S. even before the immigration procedures have been finished—most often because of a medical or similar emergency. You're best off consulting an experienced immigration attorney for help in requesting humanitarian parole.

2. When the Child Is Identified

When the adopting parent or parents have identified the orphan child they wish to adopt, they can immediately file a petition for the child at the appropriate USCIS Service Center. (See the appendix for contact details and the USCIS website at www.uscis.gov for the exact P.O. box.).

This can be done even if the Advance Processing application has not yet been approved or has not yet been filed. If the Advance Processing application has been filed but not approved, include a copy of the filing receipt with the petition. If it has already been approved, include a copy of the approval notice.

You must file all the documents listed in Section D1 above (except Form I-600A), as well as:

❏ Form I-600, Petition to Classify Orphan as an Immediate Relative

❏ the birth certificate of the orphan child, who must be under 16 years of age when the petition is filed

❏ death certificates of the parents of the child or proof of legal abandonment by both the father and mother of the child, and

❏ the adoption decree or evidence that you have legal custody of the orphan and are working toward adoption.

E. Where to File

The petition may be filed either with a USCIS Service Center or, if the U.S. citizen will be overseas to adopt or locate the orphan, with the U.S. consulate in the country of the child's residence.

F. After the Petition Is Approved

If the petition is filed and approved by USCIS in the United States, the entire file is sent to the U.S. consulate in the country in which the child lives.

The consular officer then investigates the child. This may take either a few days or several months. The investigation aims to confirm that the child:

• meets the legal definition of an orphan, and

• does not have an illness or disability that has not been described in the orphan petition.

A long delay in the adoption process of an orphan child can cause would-be parents much anxiety. However, keep in mind that the investigation is performed as a service to protect adopting parents from the heartbreaking situation that could develop if the child later proved not to be available for adoption.

G. Filing for a Visa

When the petition is approved, the case will be transferred to the U.S. consulate in the orphan child's country of residence, for immigrant visa processing. (See Chapter 19 on consular processing.) In addition to the documents ordinarily required for consular processing, you'll need to bring the child's final adoption decree or proof of custody from the foreign government.

After receiving an immigrant visa, the orphan child can then enter the United States as a permanent resident. If the child has not yet been adopted in the foreign country, the U.S. citizen, or couple, can proceed to adopt the child according to the laws of the state in which they live.

Meeting Face-to-Face

The American individual or couple who wish to adopt need not have seen the child personally before filing the visa petition if the adoption is to be done in the United States. However, if you are going to adopt a child to raise as your own for the rest of your life, you will likely want to find out what the child looks like, how you react to one other, what his or her physical condition is, and other imperceptible factors that only a face-to-face encounter can provide. Most people prefer to visit the child abroad before beginning adoption proceedings.

H. Automatic Citizenship for Adopted Orphans

Under the Child Citizenship Act of 2000, orphans who enter on IR-3 visas become citizens as soon as they enter the United States, and should receive a citizenship certificate by mail from USCIS within about six weeks. Orphans who enter the U.S. on IR-4 visas will become U.S. citizens as soon as their adoptions are complete. To obtain proof of their citizenship, the parents will need to apply to their local USCIS office, using Form N-643K.

Application for Advance Processing of Orphan Petition, Sample Form I-600A (page 1)

OMB No. 1615-0028; Expires 08/31/08

Department of Homeland Security
U.S. Citizenship and Immigration Services

I-600A, Application for Advance Processing of Orphan Petition

---

Do not write in this block.   **For USCIS Use Only.**

It has been determined that the:

☐ Married   ☐ Unmarried

prospective adoptive parent will furnish proper care to a beneficiary orphan if admitted to the United States.
There:

☐ are   ☐ are not

preadoptive requirements in the State of the child's proposed residence.

The following is a description of the preadoption requirements, if any, of the State of the child's proposed residence:

The preadoption requirements, if any,:
☐ have been met.   ☐ have not been met.

Fee Stamp

DATE OF FAVORABLE DETERMINATION

DD

DISTRICT

File number of applicant, if applicable.

Please type or print legibly in black ink.

This application is made by the named prospective adoptive parent for advance processing of an orphan petition.

BLOCK I - Information about the prospective adoptive parent.

1. My name is: (Last)   (First)   (Middle)
LERNER   Cora   Lynn

2. Other names used (including maiden name if appropriate):
ADAMS, Cora Lynn

3. I reside in the U.S. at: (C/O if appropriate)   (Apt. No.)

(Number and Street)   (Town or City)   (State)   (Zip Code)
444 5th St.   Fremont   CA   94536

4. Address abroad (If any):   (Number and Street)   (Apt. No.)

(Town or City)   (Province)   (Country)

5. I was born on: *(mm/dd/yyyy)*
September 16 1972

In: (Town or City)   (State or Province)   (Country)
Fort Bragg   CA   USA

6. My telephone number is: (Include Area Code)
510-555-1212

7. My marital status is:
☒ Married
☐ Widowed
☐ Divorced
☐ Single
  ☐ I have never been married.
  ☐ I have been previously married _____ time(s).

8. If you are now married, give the following information:

Date and place of present marriage *(mm/dd/yyyy)*
October 4, 2001, Fremont, CA

Name of present spouse (include maiden name of wife)
LERNER, Kenneth Jon

Date of birth of spouse *(mm/dd/yyyy)*   Place of birth of spouse
July 8, 1971   Buffalo, NY

Number of prior marriages of spouse
None

My spouse resides ☒ With me   ☐ Apart from me (provide address below)

(Apt. No.)   (No. and Street)   (City)   (State)   (Country)

9. I am a citizen of the United States through:
☒ Birth   ☐ Parents   ☐ Naturalization

If acquired through naturalization, give name under which naturalized, number of naturalization certificate, and date and place of naturalization.

If not, submit evidence of citizenship. See Instruction 2.a(2).

If acquired through parentage, have you obtained a certificate in your own name based on that acquisition?
☐ No   ☐ Yes

Have you or any person through whom you claimed citizenship ever lost United States citizenship?
☒ No   ☐ Yes (If Yes, attach detailed explanation.)

Received	Trans. In	Ret'd Trans. Out	Completed

Form I-600A (Rev. 10/26/05) Y

Sample Form I-600A (page 2)

BLOCK II - General information.

10. Name and address of organization or individual assisting you in locating or identifying an orphan
(Name)

Adopt International

(Address)

3705 Haven AVe., Menlo Park CA

11. Do you plan to travel abroad to locate or adopt a child?

[X] Yes   [ ] No

12. Does your spouse, if any, plan to travel abroad to locate or adopt a child?

[X] Yes   [ ] No

13. If the answer to Question **11** or **12** is "Yes," give the following information:

a. Your date of intended departure   February 10, 2006

b. Your spouse's date of intended departure   February 10, 2006

c. City, province   Datong, Shanxi

14. Will the child come to the United States for adoption after compliance with the preadoption requirements, if any, of the State of proposed residence?

[ ] Yes   [X] No

15. If the answer to Question **14** is "No," will the child be adopted abroad after having been personally seen and observed by you and your spouse, if married?

[X] Yes   [ ] No

16. Where do you wish to file your orphan petition?

The USCIS office located at

The American Embassy or Consulate at

Beijing, China

17. Do you plan to adopt more than one child?

[ ] Yes   [X] No

If "Yes," how many children do you plan to adopt?

Certification of prospective adoptive parent.
I certify, under penalty of perjury under the laws of the United States of America, that the foregoing is true and correct and that I will care for an orphan/orphans properly if admitted to the United States.

Cora Lynn Lerner

(Signature of Prospective Adoptive Parent)

July 15, 2005

Executed on (Date)

Certification of married prospective adoptive parent spouse.
I certify, under penalty of perjury under the laws of the United States of America, that the foregoing is true and correct and that my spouse and I will care for an orphan/orphans properly if admitted to the United States.

Kenneth Jon Lerner

(Signature of Prospective Adoptive Parent Spouse)

July 15, 2005

Executed on (Date)

Signature of person preparing form, if other than petitioner.
I declare that this document was prepared by me at the request of the petitioner and is based entirely on information of which I have knowledge.

(Signature)

Street Address and Room or Suite No./City/State/Zip Code

Executed on (Date)

Form I-600A (Rev. 10/26/05) Y Page 2

The Diversity Visa Lottery

In 1990, Congress created a new green card category to help balance out the numbers of immigrants coming from different countries, by opening up green card opportunities for people from countries that don't send many immigrants to the United States. Although the official name for this category is the "diversity visa," most people know it as the "visa lottery," because winners—50,000 in total—are selected through a random drawing. (The drawing is done by a computer.)

The visa lottery is held once a year. Every year the U.S. government looks to see which countries have sent the fewest immigrants to the United States in the last five years, and accordingly adds to or subtracts from the list of countries whose natives are allowed to put their names into the drawing. Each qualifying country is limited to 3,850 lottery green cards per year.

You can enter the lottery if you are a native of one of the listed countries and meet certain other requirements. One of the latest requirements is purely technological—all applicants must now submit their applications through the Internet and attach a digital photo.

If you win the lottery, you've won the right to apply for green cards for yourself, your spouse, and your unmarried children under age 21—but no more than the right to apply. You can still be refused a green card for many reasons, including because of delays by the U.S. government causing you to miss the deadline, or because you've failed to meet the educational, health, or financial criteria for the diversity visa and green card.

Certain risks come with applying for the lottery. For example, if you win the lottery but are ultimately refused a green card, you've announced to the U.S. government that you're hoping to get a green card. That can make it very difficult to obtain or extend short-term visas to the United States—such as student or visitor visas. (Most short-term visas require you to assure the U.S. government that you have every intention of returning home afterward.) Even entering the lottery and losing is something you must declare on any later applications for U.S. visas, and it may be taken into account in considering whether you'll really return home on time.

⚠️ **The lottery changes every year.** It is an annual event, with a slightly different set of rules, including qualifying countries, every year. Although this chapter will give you the basics, you'll need to double check with the U.S. State Department during the year in which you'll be applying. The rules are usually announced around September, and posted on the State Department's website at www.state.gov.

Details of the Lottery That Began in 2005

At the time this book went to print, the most recent lottery had begun in 2005 (which the government calls "DV-2007"). Applications were accepted between October 10, 2005 and December 4, 2005. Winners were to be notified between May and July 2006. Natives of the following countries were not eligible (meaning that people who were natives of any other country in the world were allowed to enter):

Canada	Mexico
China (mainland, not including Macau, Taiwan, or Hong Kong)	Pakistan
	Philippines
	Poland
Colombia	Russia
Dominican Republic	South Korea
El Salvador	United Kingdom
Haiti	(except Northern
India	Ireland) and its
Jamaica	dependent territories
	Vietnam

A. Who Qualifies for the Lottery

Whether or not you're allowed to enter the lottery depends on whether:

- you are a native of one of the countries that is eligible that year, and
- you meet the educational requirements.

It doesn't matter if you've already got an application for a green card underway in another category, for example through a family member or employer—you can still enter the diversity visa lottery.

1. What Country—or Countries—You're a Native Of

Lottery applicants should make sure that they can actually claim what the law describes as "nativity" in an eligible country. Nativity is usually based on having been born in the country. Living in a country is not enough, even if you have residence rights there.

You may, however, be a native of more than one country. This can be helpful for lottery purposes if you were born in one of the ineligible countries, or if your native country has a lot of people applying for the lottery from it. There are two ways to gain nativity in a country other than having been born there:

- If your spouse was born in an eligible country, you can claim your spouse's country of birth for lottery purposes.
- If neither of your parents was born in your birth country or made a home there at the time of your birth, you may be able to claim nativity in one of your parents' countries of birth.

And remember, the list of eligible countries changes slightly every year, so check the State Department's instructions before you apply.

⚠️ **You must choose which country to apply based on.** Even if you're a native of more than one eligible country, you can't apply for the lottery more than once within a single year.

2. The Educational Requirements

Applicants from qualifying countries must have either:

- a high school diploma or its equivalent, meaning a successfully completed twelve-year course of elementary plus secondary education that would qualify you to enter a U.S. college or university, or
- a minimum of two years' work experience (within the last five years) in a job that normally requires at least two years' training or experience. American job offers are not necessary. However, you won't be allowed to argue about how much experience your job requires—this judgment will be made based on a list of job titles and descriptions kept by the U.S. government in an online database called O*NET, at http://online.onetcenter. org. (To check this out yourself, go to the website and click "Find Occupations," then fill in the appropriate blank spaces to bring up various reports. Either the "summary" or "details" report will tell you how many years of experience your job needs, under the heading "Job Zone.")

You won't be asked to prove your educational qualifications on the lottery application—but that doesn't mean you can puff up the truth. If you win the lottery, you will have to come up with proof of your education as part of the green card application.

B. How to Apply for the Lottery

A new application period starts every year, usually in late fall or early winter. You can submit one application—and only one. People who try to apply more than once will have all their lottery visa applications tossed out of the running. Husbands, wives, and children in the same family can, however, submit separate applications if each one who applies separately meets the educational and other eligibility criteria.

No fee is charged for applying, so watch out for websites and consultants who claim that there is, or who charge you a lot of money for supposed "special" handling. The application is fairly simple and can be done by yourself, or with minimal help from another person.

⚠️ **Registrations submitted one year are not held over to the next.** So if you are not selected one year, you need to reapply the next year to be considered.

1. The Application Form

We can't give you a sample application form, because there isn't one—the one and only way to apply is online, using a computer. (In previous years, paper applications were allowed, but no longer.)

The Web address at which to apply is www.dvlottery.state.gov. It doesn't matter what country you're in when you submit the online application. You can start the application and then stop without submitting it, for example if you realize you're missing a piece of information—but you cannot save or download your work. And if you try to submit an application and the system rejects it, you can try again until you succeed.

Once you start your application, the system will give you only an hour in which to submit it before it erases all the information you've entered. So, you'll need to assemble all the needed information ahead of time, and plan for a time when you can complete the entire application within that hour.

Here's what you'll probably be asked when you go to the State Department website to apply:

FULL NAME – Last name (family or surname), first name, middle name.

DATE OF BIRTH - Day, month, year.

GENDER - Male or female.

CITY/TOWN OF BIRTH.

COUNTRY OF BIRTH (Use your country's current name, even if it had a different name when you were born there—for example, Myanmar instead of Burma.)

ONE DIGITAL (JPEG FORMAT) PHOTOGRAPH OF YOU AND EACH OF YOUR LISTED SPOUSE AND CHILDREN (You'll need to create or scan a color photo, with your face straight into the camera, your head covering about 50% of the area of the photo, and a neutral or light background. See the State Department's instructions for more details on the technical and visual photo requirements. Note that you cannot submit a family group photo; each person named in your application must have his or her own photo attached.)

MAILING ADDRESS - Address, city/town, district/country/province/state, postal code/zip code, country.

PHONE NUMBER (Optional.)

EMAIL ADDRESS (Optional.)

COUNTRY OF ELIGIBILITY IF YOUR NATIVE COUNTRY IS DIFFERENT FROM YOUR COUNTRY OF BIRTH (For example, if you're claiming a native country through your spouse or parents.)

MARITAL STATUS - Unmarried, married, divorced, widowed, or legally separated.

NUMBER OF CHILDREN THAT ARE UNMARRIED AND UNDER 21 YEARS OF AGE (No need to mention children who are either U.S. legal permanent residents or U.S. citizens.)

SPOUSE INFORMATION - Name, date of birth, gender, city/town of birth, country of birth, photograph.

CHILDREN INFORMATION - Name, date of birth, gender, city/town of birth, country of birth, photograph.

⚠️ **Be extra careful not to make typing errors.** If your application contains a typing error, particularly in the spelling of your name, the State Department may throw it out. The reason is that it believes that people try to cheat the system by submitting more than one application with their name spelled slightly differently.

After you've successfully completed and submitted your online application, you'll get a confirmation screen, showing your name, other personal information, and a date/time stamp. It may take several minutes before you receive this screen. The confirmation doesn't mean you've won, it simply means your application went through okay. Print out the confirmation screen for your records.

2. Notification of Winners

About five to seven months after submitting your online application, you'll be notified by mail if your name has been drawn (you "won"). If your name wasn't chosen, you won't hear anything. Keep track of the State Department's intended notification date, so that you'll know when to keep a close eye on your mail—and when to give up.

C. After You Win—The Green Card Application

Unfortunately, winning the lottery doesn't guarantee you a green card. The government always declares more than 50,000 winners—but gives out only 50,000 green cards. This means if you don't follow up quickly or receive your interview on time, the supply of green cards could run out. You'll have to complete the process and have received your visa or green card by September 30th of the year following your selection. (For example, applicants in 2005, who will be notified in 2006, will lose their chance if they can't complete the process by September 30, 2007.)

This is a serious problem. The State Department and U.S. Citizenship and Immigration Services (USCIS, formerly called the INS) are so backed up that months can go by with no action, causing you to miss your opportunity altogether. Some people's applications get stalled while their security checks are being completed by the FBI (Federal Bureau of Investigation) and CIA (Central Intelligence

Agency). Even if you've never done anything wrong, just having a common name can lead to delays, as the FBI and CIA check and double check your name and fingerprints against various databases.

Another problem is that, as with all green card applications, if you win the lottery, you still must prove that you are not "inadmissible" to the United States. For example, if you have been arrested for committing certain crimes, are considered a security risk, have spent too much time in the United States illegally, or are afflicted with certain physical or mental illnesses, you may be prevented from receiving a green card. (For more on inadmissibility, see Chapter 4.)

Proving that you'll be able to support yourself financially in the U.S. can be a huge challenge for lottery winners. If you can't show this, you'll be considered inadmissible as a potential "public charge"—that is, someone who may need government financial assistance. You will need to show that you are either self-supporting, have sufficient skills and/or education to find employment, or have friends or family who will support you once you're living in the United States. In 2006, for example, the U.S. government said that a family of four would be presumed to need government assistance unless their income was $25,000 per year or more.

Don't miss your chance—get professional help. If you've been declared a lottery winner, we strongly recommend seeking an experienced immigration lawyer's help. A good lawyer will know the latest ways to get your application through the system quickly, and who and when to ask for speeded up handling.

The exact procedures for applying for the green card depend on where you're living now, and whether you've spent any time illegally in the United States. If you're currently overseas, see Chapter 19 regarding consular processing. If you're in the United States, see Chapter 18 regarding adjustment of status. If you've got a choice, consular processing is usually a faster bet than adjusting status. Also, if you're in the United States illegally, realize that it's very unlikely you'll be allowed to apply for the green card unless you've got a valid, unexpired visa or other status—again, you should see a lawyer for assistance.

> ⚠ **Don't forget to pay the extra fees.** Lottery winners must pay a "diversity visa surcharge" in addition to the regular fees for applying for a green card. At the time this book was published, the fee was $375.

D. How to Bring Your Spouse and Children

For the lottery application itself, it's very simple to include your spouse and children—in fact, you're required to name them on your application, unless you and your spouse are legally separated (by court order) or divorced, or your children are U.S. citizens or permanent residents. Simply include your spouse and children's names, and remember to attach a digital photograph of each one to your lottery submission. (And remember that your spouse may, if eligible, submit a separate lottery application for him or herself, which includes your name and those of your children.)

It doesn't matter whether your spouse and children plan to come with you to the U.S. or not—you must still list their names and provide their photos with your lottery application. If you don't list them, they'll lose their chance to immigrate with you if you win. In fact, even if you and your spouse are no longer living together, you must provide his or her photo unless you're either legally separated (by court order) or divorced—a requirement that causes problems for some applicants.

What if you give birth to a child or get married after submitting the lottery application? That's okay—your new child and spouse will be allowed to immigrate with you if you win. However, you may be asked to provide extra proof that this relationship wasn't created fraudulently, to get the newly added person a green card.

If you win the lottery, the rules and paperwork for your family get more complicated. First, you need to figure out which family members are allowed to immigrate with you. Your spouse will be allowed, so long as you're legally married. Your children will also be allowed, so long as they're under 21 years of age and remain unmarried up to the date you're approved for green cards. Warn your children that they must remain unmarried until they've entered the U.S., or they'll lose their eligibility!

Next, each family member must submit a separate green card application, as described in either Chapter 19 (discussing consular processing for people coming from overseas) or Chapter 18 (discussing adjustment of status for people already in the United States and lucky enough to have a right to apply for a green card without leaving). No matter where you apply, the application will consist of several forms, expensive fees, medical examination results, and more.

Fortunately, only the lead person—the one who won the lottery—is required to meet the educational and work requirements of the lottery. However, each of your family members must separately prove that he or she doesn't have any of the health, criminal, or other problems that make people inadmissible to the United States. And you'll have to show that the family as a whole isn't likely to need government assistance.

⚠ **Be careful if you have a child about to turn 21.** Getting older is, of course, something your children have no control over. But a child who turns 21 before being approved for a green card is, technically, no longer eligible. Fortunately, the law contains some protections for children in this situation. When and if you are approved for green cards, your child will be allowed to subtract from his or her age the amount of time between the date you could have first applied for the lottery and the date you got the letter saying you'd won.

EXAMPLE: Jorge applies for the DV-2007 lottery program. The first date for applying was October 10, 2005 (although Jorge didn't get around to applying until November 17th). Jorge receives a congratulatory letter dated May 31, 2006, telling him that he's been selected. A total of 233 days passed between October 10th and May 31. Jorge, as well as his wife and daughter, submit immigrant visa (green card) applications through their local U.S. consulate. They attend their interview on September 5, 2007. The consular officer notices that Jorge's daughter already turned 21, on July 5, 2007. However, the daughter can subtract 233 days from her age, which brings her back to age 20. (An easy way to look at this is that the daughter has been 21 for less than 233 days). The consular officer grants the entire family their immigrant visas. ∎

Amerasian Immigrants

I Am a GI Baby

In Vietnam, they are called "bui-doi," which means "dust of life."

In Korea, they are called "hon-hul," which means "mixed blood."

They are the children of American servicemen who have returned to the United States leaving behind the human results of the liaisons they had with the children's mothers. The children are often unclaimed, unrecognized, and unwanted.

The U.S. Congress passed a law on October 22, 1982 allowing Amerasians to come to the United States as the sons or daughters of a U.S. citizen. (See I.N.A. § 204.4.) Because the shadow of the Vietnam War has receded with the passing of time, and most of those able to come to the United States have already come, the emigration of Amerasians to the United States has been reduced to a trickle. (In fact, this chapter no longer mentions requirements for Amerasians under 18, because no more could qualify at that age.)

A. Who Qualifies as an Amerasian

An Amerasian is a person who was:
- born in Korea, Vietnam, Laos, Cambodia, or Thailand
- born after December 31, 1950 and before October 22, 1982, and
- fathered by a U.S. citizen.

The Amerasian's spouse and minor, unmarried children are eligible to immigrate along with him or her.

B. Who Can Start the Process

To begin the process of allowing the Amerasian to immigrate, someone must first submit what's called a "visa petition" to USCIS. Unlike many other types of visas, there are several options as to who submits this petition, as follows:

- If over 18 years of age, the Amerasian can file the petition on his or her own behalf.
- Any person of legal age (18 or over), regardless of citizenship, can file the petition on behalf of the Amerasian.
- A business incorporated in the United States can also file the petition on behalf of the Amerasian.

The person filing the petition is called the "petitioner." The Amerasian is called the "beneficiary."

 The father need not be involved. Contrary to what you might assume, the American father does not have to be the petitioner. In fact, the American father's real name need not even be known as long as it can be proven that he was a U.S. citizen.

C. Who Will Serve as a Sponsor?

The Amerasian must have a sponsor who is either:
- a U.S. citizen, at least 21 years of age and of good moral character
- a permanent resident in the United States who is at least 21 years of age and of good moral character, or
- an American organization that will arrange to place the Amerasian with a sponsor in the United States. The American organization filing the petition must be able to show that:
  - it is licensed in the United States and experienced in arranging to place Amerasian children, and
  - a sponsor has been identified, and is willing and able to accept the Amerasian in his or her home.

Sponsors are essential. If the Amerasian cannot find an American family or citizen or permanent resident to sponsor his or her stay in the United States—someone who will take financial, emotional, cultural, and social responsibility for him or her—the petition cannot be granted.

D. How to File

The paperwork required to petition for an Amerasian can be done in one stage or two. You might prefer to start with the first stage, simply to make sure USCIS will accept that the Amerasian is really the child of a U.S. citizen before you go through the added effort of identifying a sponsor and gathering documents proving the sponsor's financial and other capacity. On the other hand, if the sponsor is ready and eager to provide all the necessary documents, you'll probably get a faster green card approval by submitting everything at once.

To do the processing in two stages, submit the items listed in Section 1, below, and then wait for the go-ahead from USCIS (or for further questions, which you'll need to deal with) before submitting the items listed in Section 2.

1. Preliminary Processing

No filing fee is required for Amerasians. The petitioner should prepare the following documents:

- ❏ Form I-360, Petition for Amerasian, Widow(er), or Special Immigrant. (See the sample form at the end of this chapter.)
- ❏ Birth certificate of the Amerasian.
- ❏ The identification card issued by the Vietnamese government if the Amerasian was born there. If the identification card is not available, an affidavit—a written statement sworn to before a notary public—should explain why.
- ❏ Marriage certificate of the Amerasian, if any, and proof of the termination of any prior marriages (through divorce or death).
- ❏ Photograph of the Amerasian.
- ❏ Documents to prove that the Amerasian was fathered by an American citizen. The name of the father is not required. The documents may include:
  - ❏ the Amerasian's birth certificate, baptismal certificate, or any religious documents or church records

  - ❏ vital statistics on family members maintained by local civil authorities
  - ❏ affidavits from knowledgeable witnesses
  - ❏ letters, notes, or proof of financial support from the father
  - ❏ photographs of the father, especially those taken with the Amerasian, and
  - ❏ evidence of the father's U.S. citizenship, such as military serial number.

2. Stage Two of the Processing

After the petition is approved, or if you're submitting everything together, the next phase involves the sponsor, who must prepare the following documents:

- ❏ Form I-361, Affidavit of Financial Support and Intent to Petition for Legal Custody for Public Law 97-359 Amerasian, signed by the sponsor. (Ask for a copy of this form from the nearest USCIS office or download it from www.uscis.gov.) Upon signing the affidavit, the sponsor becomes legally responsible for financially supporting the Amerasian. Therefore, unless the sponsor dies or becomes bankrupt, the attorney general can sue the sponsor in federal court for enforcement of the support. This affidavit, which must be signed before an immigration or consular officer, states that the sponsor agrees:
  - to file for legal custody of the Amerasian through a state court within 30 days of the arrival of the child, if under 18 years of age, and
  - to financially support the Amerasian and any of his or her family members at 125% of the current official poverty line for the next five years, or until the Amerasian turns 21 years of age, whichever is longer.
- ❏ Proof that the sponsor is over age 21.
- ❏ Proof of the sponsor's financial capability to support and maintain the Amerasian, such as income tax returns and bank statements.

❑ Proof of U.S. citizenship or lawful permanent residency of the sponsor.

❑ Fee of $70 for fingerprinting the sponsor.

Filing for Amerasians under 21. If the Amerasian is under 21 years of age, he or she is classified, for visa coding purposes, as an immediate relative of a U.S. citizen. Therefore, if the Amerasian is already legally in the U.S., he or she may be entitled to submit the documents mentioned above together with the immigration papers required for adjustment of status (see Chapter 18).

Filing for Amerasians 21 and over or married. If the Amerasian is 21 years of age or older, or married, he or she qualifies as an applicant in the family first preference (unmarried son or daughter of an American citizen) or family third preference (married son or daughter of an American citizen) discussed in Chapter 5. He or she will have to wait for a current Priority Date to complete the green card application process.

E. Where to File

Two places will accept the petition for the Amerasian: the USCIS office closest to the future residence of the Amerasian in the United States, and the U.S. embassy or consulate in the country where the Amerasian now lives.

For a complete list of U.S. consulates, with links to their websites, go to http://usembassy.state.gov.

What's next, after the Amerasian's petition has been approved and, if the Amerasian is over 21 or married, his or her Priority Date has become current? The Amerasian will need to complete an application for a green card, like every other applicant. For complete instructions, see either Chapter 18 (for the lucky few eligible to adjust status while living in the U.S.) or Chapter 19 (which discusses consular processing).

Petition for Amerasian, Widow(er), or Special Immigrant, Sample Form I-360 (page 1)

OMB No. 1615-0020; Expires 07/31/07

I-360, Petition for Amerasian, Widow(er) or Special Immigrant

Department of Homeland Security
U.S. Citizenship and Immigration Services

START HERE - Please type or print in black ink.

	For USCIS Use Only

Part 1. Information about person or organization filing this petition. (Individuals should use the top name line; organizations should use the second line.) If you are a self-petitioning spouse or child and do not want USCIS to send notices about this petition to your home, you may show an alternate mailing address here. If you are filing for yourself and do not want to use an alternate mailing address, skip to part 2.

Family Name	Given Name	Middle Name
Stuart Alicia J.		

Company or Organization Name

Address - C/O
Alicia and Sam Stuart

Street Number and Name	Apt.
4602 G Street, NW	# 4

City	State or Province
Washington	District of Columbia

Country	Zip/Postal Code
United States	20004

U.S. Social Security #	A #	IRS Tax # (if any)
464-56-9217	n/a	n/a

For USCIS Use Only:
Returned _____ Receipt
Resubmitted _____
Reloc Sent _____
Reloc Rec'd _____

☐ Petitioner/Applicant Interviewed
☐ Beneficiary Interviewed
☐ I-485 Filed Concurrently
☐ Bene "A" File Reviewed
Classification
Consulate
Priority Date
Remarks:

Part 2. Classification Requested (check one):

a. ☑ Amerasian
b. ☐ Widow(er) of a U.S. citizen who died within the past two (2) years
c. ☐ Special Immigrant Juvenile
d. ☐ Special Immigrant Religious Worker
e. ☐ Special Immigrant based on employment with the Panama Canal Company, Canal Zone Government or U.S. Government in the Canal Zone
f. ☐ Special Immigrant Physician
g. ☐ Special Immigrant International Organization Employee or family member
h. ☐ Special Immigrant Armed Forces Member
i. ☐ Self-Petitioning Spouse of Abusive U.S. Citizen or Lawful Permanent Resident
j. ☐ Self-Petitioning Child of Abusive U.S. Citizen or Lawful Permanent Resident
k. ☐ Other, explain: _____

Part 3. Information about the person this petition is for.

Family Name	Given Name	Middle Name
Nguyen	Sean	T.

Address - C/O
Bangkok Home

Street Number and Name	Apt. #
7 Singla Mai Road	

City	State or Province
Bangkok	

Country	Zip/Postal Code
Thailand	

Date of Birth (mm/dd/yyyy)	Country of Birth
10/1/1981	Thailand

U.S. Social Security #	A # (if any)
none	none

Marital Status: ☑ Single ☐ Married ☐ Divorced ☐ Widowed

Complete the items below if this person is in the United States:

Date of Arrival (mm/dd/yyyy)	I-94#

Current Nonimmigrant Status	Expires on (mm/dd/yyyy)

Action Block

To Be Completed by
☐ *Attorney or Representative,* if any
Fill in box if G-28 is attached to represent the applicant

VOLAG#

ATTY State License #

Form I-360 (Rev. 10/26/05)Y

Sample Form I-360 (page 2)

Part 4. Processing Information.

Below give information on U.S. Consulate you want notified if this petition is approved and if any requested adjustment of status cannot be granted.

American Consulate: City Bangkok	Country Thailand

If you gave a United States address in **Part 3**, print the person's foreign address below. If his or her native alphabet does not use Roman letters, print his or her name and foreign address in the native alphabet.

Name	Address

Gender of the person this petition is for. ☑ Male ☐ Female

Are you filing any other petitions or applications with this one? ☑ No ☐ Yes (How many? _____)

Is the person this petition is for in deportation or removal proceedings? ☑ No ☐ Yes (Explain on a separate sheet of paper)

Has the person this petition is for ever worked in the U.S. without permission? ☑ No ☐ Yes (Explain on a separate sheet of paper)

Is an application for adjustment of status attached to this petition? ☑ No ☐ Yes

Part 5. Complete only if filing for an Amerasian.

Section A. Information about the mother of the Amerasian

Family Name Nguyen	Given Name Mali	Middle Name

Living? ☑ No (Give date of death October 14, 1993) ☐ Yes (complete address line below) ☐ Unknown (attach a full explanation)

Address

Section B. Information about the father of the Amerasian: If possible, attach a notarized statement from the father regarding parentage. Explain on separate paper any question you cannot fully answer in the space provided on this form.

Family Name Adamczek	Given Name Sean	Middle Name C.
Date of Birth *(mm/dd/yyyy)* November 20, 1963	Country of Birth United States	

Living? ☐ No (give date of death _____) ☐ Yes (complete address line below) ☐ Unknown (attach a full explanation)

Home Address   n/a

Home Phone # ( ) n/a	Work Phone # ( ) n/a

At the time the Amerasian was conceived:

The father was in the military (indicate branch of service below - and give service number here): unknown

☐ Army ☐ Air Force ☐ Navy ☑ Marine Corps ☐ Coast Guard

☐ The father was a civilian employed abroad. Attach a list of names and addresses of organizations which employed him at that time.

☐ The father was not in the military, and was not a civilian employed abroad. (Attach a full explanation of the circumstances.)

Part 6. Complete only if filing for a Special Immigrant Juvenile Court Dependent.

Section A. Information about the Juvenile

List any other names used.

Answer the following questions regarding the person this petition is for. If you answer "No," explain on a separate sheet of paper.

Is he or she still dependent upon the juvenile court or still legally committed to or under the custody of an agency or department of a state? ☐ No ☐ Yes

Does he or she continue to be eligible for long term foster care? ☐ No ☐ Yes

Sample Form I-360 (page 3)

Part 7. Complete only if filing as a Widow/Widower, a Self-petitioning Spouse of an Abuser, or as a Self-petitioning Child of an Abuser.

Section A. Information about the U.S. citizen husband or wife who died or about the U.S. citizen or lawful permanent resident abuser.

Family Name	Given Name	Middle Name

Date of Birth *(mm/dd/yyyy)*	Country of Birth	Date of Death *(mm/dd/yyyy)*

He or she is now, or was at time of death a (check one):

☐ U.S. citizen through Naturalization *(Show A #)* _____

☐ U.S. citizen born in the United States.　　☐ U.S. lawful permanent resident (Show A #) _____

☐ U.S. citizen born abroad to U.S. citizen parents.　　☐ Other, explain

Section   B. Additional Information about you.

How many times have you been married?	How many times was the person in Section A married?	Give the date and place where you and the person in Section A were married. *(If you are a self-petitioning child, write: "N/A")*

When did you live with the person named in **Section A**? From *(Month/Year)* _____　　until *(Month/Year)* _____

If you are filing as a widow/widower, were you legally separated at the time of the U.S citizens's death?　☐ No　☐ Yes, *(attach explanation)*.

Give the last address at which you lived together with the person named in **Section A**, and show the last date that you lived together with that person at that address:

If you are filing as a self-petitioning spouse, have any of your children filed separate self-petitions?　☐ No　☐ Yes *(show child(ren)'s full names)*:

Part 8. Information about the spouse and children of the person this petition is for.

A widow/widower or a self-petitioning spouse of an abusive citizen or lawful permanent resident should also list the children of the deceased spouse or of the abuser.

A. Family Name	Given Name	Middle Name	Date of Birth *(mm/dd/yyyy)*
Country of Birth	Relationship　☐ Spouse ☐ Child		A #
B. Family Name	Given Name	Middle Name	Date of Birth *(mm/dd/yyyy)*
Country of Birth	Relationship　☐ Child		A #
C. Family Name	Given Name	Middle Name	Date of Birth *(mm/dd/yyyy)*
Country of Birth	Relationship　☐ Child		A #
D. Family Name	Given Name	Middle Name	Date of Birth *(mm/dd/yyyy)*
Country of Birth	Relationship　☐ Child		A #
E. Family Name	Given Name	Middle Name	Date of Birth *(mm/dd/yyyy)*
Country of Birth	Relationship　☐ Child		A #
F. Family Name	Given Name	Middle Name	Date of Birth *(mm/dd/yyyy)*
Country of Birth	Relationship　☐ Child		A #

Form I-360 (Rev. 10/26/05)Y Page 3

Sample Form I-360 (page 4)

Part 8. Information about the spouse and children of the person this petition is for. (Continued.)

G. Family Name	Given Name	Middle Name	Date of Birth *(mm/dd/yyyy)*
Country of Birth	Relationship ☐ Child		A #
H. Family Name	Given Name	Middle Name	Date of Birth *(mm/dd/yyyy)*
Country of Birth	Relationship ☐ Child		A #

Part 9. Signature.

Read the information on penalties in the instructions before completing this part. If you are going to file this petition at a USCIS office in the United States, sign below. If you are going to file it at a U.S. consulate or USCIS office overseas, sign in front of a USCIS or consular official.

I certify, or, if outside the United States, I swear or affirm, under penalty of perjury under the laws of the United States of America, that this petition and the evidence submitted with it is all true and correct. If filing this on behalf at an organization, I certify that I am empowered to do so by that organization. I authorize the release of any information from my records, or from the petitioning organization's records, that the U.S. Citizenship and Immigration Services needs to determine eligibility for the benefit being sought.

Signature *Alicia J. Stuart*	Alicia J. Stuart	Date 9/6/05
Signature of USCIS or Consular Official	Print Name	Date

NOTE: If you do not completely fill out this petition or fail to submit required documents listed in the instructions, the person(s) filed for may not be found eligible for a requested benefit and the petition may be denied.

Part 10. Signature of person preparing form, if other than above. (Sign below.)

I declare that I prepared this application at the request of the above person and it is based on all information of which I have knowledge.

Signature	Print Your Name	Date
Firm Name and Address		

Your Brothers and Sisters as Immigrants

My Brothers and Sisters All Over This Land

If you are a U.S. citizen, whether by birth, naturalization, or some other means, you can petition for your brothers and sisters to immigrate—but you must be at least 21 years old when you file the petition.

What's more, your brothers and sisters will be put in the family fourth preference visa category, which is so overloaded with applicants that they'll face a wait of at least ten years, and up to 24 years for applicants from some countries. (See Chapter 5 for more information on waiting periods in visa preference categories.) Nevertheless, the years can pass surprisingly quickly, so it may be worthwhile to get the petition in and reserve your brother or sister's place on the waiting list.

Once a visa number becomes available, your brother or sister will also be able to bring in his or her spouse and any unmarried children under age 21.

 Other people can petition for your brother and sister at the same time. There's no limit on the number of visa petitions that can be filed for a person—and it can be good to have more than one pending, in case one petitioner dies, for example. Let's say your parents are or become permanent residents—in that case, they could file visa petitions for your siblings (if they're unmarried) in the second preference visa category, which moves much faster than the fourth preference. But you could file for your siblings as well, as a backup.

A. Who Counts As Your Brother or Sister

The immigration laws contain specific definitions setting out who qualifies as a brother and sister in every family.

When it comes time to submit the paperwork for your brothers or sisters (the "visa petition"), you'll need to prove that they fit into one of these relationship categories. The sections below will explain the different possibilities and list the documentation that you'll need to provide as proof.

1. Legitimate Brother and Sister

If your mother and father were married and had other children, all of them are your legitimate brothers and sisters.

Be sure to add the following to your visa petition:

- your birth certificate, and
- your brothers' and sisters' birth certificates (to show that you have the same mother and father).

EXAMPLE: Your parents raised your cook's baby as their own child. But to file a petition for that baby, you would have to present proof that your birth certificate and the other child's birth certificate show the same father and mother. Of course, you cannot do this. There is no way you can petition for this person as your brother or your sister.

The only way around this strict rule is for someone in the family to legally adopt the child before the child turns 16. If that is not possible, you will have to look for another way for the child to immigrate to the United States, such as an employment visa.

2. Half-Brother and Half-Sister

If you and another person have the same mother or father, but not both parents in common, that other person is your half-brother or half-sister.

It does not matter when the relationship of half-brother or half-sister occurred. As far as the immigration law is concerned, you can petition for them just as if they were your full-blooded brothers or sisters.

Be sure to add the following to your visa petition:

- your birth certificate, and
- your half-brothers' or sisters' birth certificates (showing that you have one parent in common).

3. Stepbrother and Stepsister

If your mother or father has married somebody who had children from a previous marriage or relationship, the children of your stepfather or stepmother would be your stepbrothers and stepsisters.

However, for purposes of immigration into the United States, you can file a petition for them only on one condition: Your mother or father must have married your stepparent before your 18th birthday.

Be sure to include the following documents with your visa petition:

- your birth certificate
- the birth certificates of your stepbrothers or stepsisters, and
- the marriage certificate of your mother or father and your stepparent, or documents showing that the marriage ended by death, divorce, or annulment.

4. Adopted Brother and Adopted Sister

If your mother and father have adopted a child according to the laws of the state or country they are in, that child is your adopted brother or adopted sister. Or, you may have been adopted by parents who may have other legitimate children of their own. Their children became your brothers and sisters when you were adopted into their family.

However, you can petition for your adoptive sibling only if the adoption decree occurs before the 16th birthday of your adopted brother or sister if they are the petitioners, or before your own 16th birthday if you were the adopted child.

Be sure to include the following with your visa petition:

- the adoption decree, and
- your and your siblings' birth certificates to show you had the same parents.

B. Quick View of the Application Process

To get a green card as a brother or sister, the U.S. citizen must begin the process by submitting what's called a "visa petition" (using Form I-130). We're going to assume that the person reading this is the U.S. citizen. Form I-130 serves to prove to the immigration authorities that your siblings are truly and legally yours. After that petition is approved, your siblings must complete their half of the process (with your help, of course) by submitting green card applications and attending interviews, sometimes but not always with you accompanying them. Their applications serve to prove that not only do they qualify as the brothers or sisters of a U.S. citizen, but that they're otherwise eligible for U.S. permanent residence.

However, the details of when and how your brothers or sisters complete their half of the process depend on whether they are living overseas or in the United States, as described in Section D, below.

C. Detailed Instructions for the Application Process

Now we'll break the application process down into individual procedures, some of which will be covered in this chapter, others of which will be covered in other chapters—we'll tell you exactly where to go to for your situation. We'll start by discussing the visa petition, which the U.S. citizen must always begin by preparing.

1. Preparing the Form I-130 Visa Petition

To prepare the visa petition, the U.S. citizen will need to assemble and prepare the following:

- ❑ Form I-130, Petition for Alien Relative (see the sample at the end of this chapter)
- ❑ copy of a document proving your U.S. citizenship, such as a birth certificate, naturalization certificate, or passport

❏ copy of your birth certificate

❏ copy of your immigrating brother or sister's birth certificate

❏ any other required proof of your relationship as detailed in Section A, above

❏ if you or any of your brothers and sisters have changed your name from the name that appears on the birth certificate, a copy of a marriage certificate or court document that explains the change, and

❏ filing fee (currently $190, but double check the USCIS website at www.uscis.gov). Pay this by check or money order—don't send cash.

2. Submitting the Form I-130 Visa Petition

When you've prepared and assembled all the items on the above list, make a complete copy of everything for yourself (even the check or money order—your copy will be helpful if USCIS loses the application, which happens more often than it should). Then send it to the appropriate USCIS Service Center—you can find this information on the USCIS website, www.uscis.gov. (Go to the section on forms and fees and scroll down until you find Form I-130. Then follow the links until you find the post office box that handles I-130 petitions.)

After the service center receives your application and determines that you haven't left anything out, it will send you a receipt notice. Don't expect a final decision on the visa petition for many years, however. USCIS often decides to wait until a visa will soon be available to the immigrants before making a decision on the application—which, in the case of brothers and sisters, could be ten or more years away.

D. What Happens After Filing Form I-130

And now, your brothers or sisters must sit back and wait. There is no way to hurry up the process—see Chapter 5 for details on the visa preference system, and for information on how to track your brothers' or sisters' progress on the waiting list (using their Priority Dates).

Having a visa petition on file does not give your brothers or sisters any right to stay in the United States. In fact, it could cause them problems when they apply for tourist or other temporary visas, because the State Department will know that they also have plans to stay in the U.S. permanently.

If your brothers or sisters are already in the United States, they cannot become permanent residents unless they remain in legal status during all the time that they are in the country. They will probably have to return to their home country and proceed with consular processing (see Chapter 19), unless they're lucky enough to qualify for adjustment of status in the U.S. (see Chapter 18).

If your brothers or sisters are in the U.S. illegally, or have spent six or more months here illegally since 1997, they should talk to a lawyer about whether they'll be found inadmissible and barred from returning.

Once the immigrant visa is available to your brothers or sisters, they can extend the immigration privilege to their spouses and all unmarried children under 21 years of age at the same time, as "accompanying relatives."

⚠ **A brother or sister who wants to come to the United States to visit during the waiting period must tell the U.S. consul when applying for a tourist or business visa that he or she has an approved visa petition.** To be silent about this important fact will be looked upon as fraud in an immigrant visa file—and may mean a lost chance for a green card in the future. On the other hand, to be approved for the visa, he or she will need plenty of evidence of intent to return on time.

Petition for Alien Relative, Sample Form I-130 (when used for sibling) (page 1)

Department of Homeland Security
U.S. Citizenship and Immigration Services

OMB # 1615-0012; Expires 01/31/07

I-130, Petition for Alien Relative

DO NOT WRITE IN THIS BLOCK - FOR USCIS OFFICE ONLY..		
A#	Action Stamp	Fee Stamp

Section of Law/Visa Category
- [ ] 201(b) Spouse - IR-1/CR-1
- [ ] 201(b) Child - IR-2/CR-2
- [ ] 201(b) Parent - IR-5
- [ ] 203(a)(1) Unm. S or D - F1-1
- [ ] 203(a)(2)(A)Spouse - F2-1
- [ ] 203(a)(2)(A) Child - F2-2
- [ ] 203(a)(2)(B) Unm. S or D - F2-4
- [ ] 203(a)(3) Married S or D - F3-1
- [ ] 203(a)(4) Brother/Sister - F4-1

Petition was filed on: _____ (priority date)
- [ ] Personal Interview
- [ ] Pet. [ ] Ben. " A" File Reviewed
- [ ] Field Investigation
- [ ] 203(a)(2)(A) Resolved
- [ ] Previously Forwarded
- [ ] I-485 Filed Simultaneously
- [ ] 204(g) Resolved
- [ ] 203(g) Resolved

Remarks:

A. Relationship. You are the petitioner. Your relative is the beneficiary.

1. I am filing this petition for my:
[ ] Husband/Wife [ ] Parent [X] Brother/Sister [ ] Child

2. Are you related by adoption?
[ ] Yes [X] No

3. Did you gain permanent residence through adoption?
[ ] Yes [X] No

B. Information about you.

1. Name (Family name in CAPS) (First) (Middle)
GRAY Alexandria Elaine

2. Address (Number and Street) (Apt.No.)
555 Glasgow Road

(Town or City) (State/Country) (Zip/Postal Code)
Mission Hills Kansas/USA 66208

3. Place of Birth (Town or City) (State/Country)
Brussels Belgium

4. Date of Birth (mm/dd/yyyy)
3/22/80

5. Gender
[ ] Male [ ] Female

6. Marital Status
[ ] Married [ ] Single [ ] Widowed [ ] Divorced

7. Other Names Used (including maiden name)
BOFFIN, Alexandria Elaine none

8. Date and Place of Present Marriage (if married)
6/15/00, Bird City, Kansas

9. U.S. Social Security Number (if any)
123-12-1234

10. Alien Registration Number
N/A

11. Name(s) of Prior Husband(s)/Wive(s)
N/A

12. Date(s) Marriage(s) Ended

13. If you are a U.S. citizen, complete the following:
My citizenship was acquired through (check one):
- [ ] Birth in the U.S.
- [X] Naturalization. Give certificate number and date and place of issuance.
  14532, 12/13/04, Kansas City, MO
- [ ] Parents. Have you obtained a certificate of citizenship in your own name?
  [ ] Yes. Give certificate number, date and place of issuance. [ ] No

14a. If you are a lawful permanent resident alien, complete the following: Date and place of admission for or adjustment to lawful permanent residence and class of admission.

14b. Did you gain permanent resident status through marriage to a U.S. citizen or lawful permanent resident?
[X] Yes [ ] No

C. Information about your relative.

1. Name (Family name in CAPS) (First) (Middle)
BOFFIN Ignace Anton

2. Address (Number and Street) (Apt. No.)
Van Cuppenstraat 85

(Town or City) (State/Country) (Zip/Postal Code)
Antwerp Belgium B-222

3. Place of Birth (Town or City) (State/Country)
Brussels Belgium

4. Date of Birth (mm/dd/yyyy)
7/29/75

5. Gender
[ ] Male [ ] Female

6. Marital Status
[ ] Married [ ] Single [ ] Widowed [ ] Divorced

7. Other Names Used (including maiden name)

8. Date and Place of Present Marriage (if married)
7/19/98, Antwerp, Belgium

9. U. S. Social Security Number (if any)
None

10. Alien Registration Number
None

11. Name(s) of Prior Husband(s)/Wive(s)
N/A

12. Date(s) Marriage(s) Ended

13. Has your relative ever been in the U.S.? [X] Yes [ ] No

14. If your relative is currently in the U.S., complete the following: He or she arrived as a:: (visitor, student, stowaway, without inspection, etc.)

Arrival/Departure Record (I-94) Date arrived (mm/dd/yyyy)

Date authorized stay expired, or will expire, as shown on Form I-94 or I-95

15. Name and address of present employer (if any)
The Belgian Observer

Date this employment began (mm/dd/yyyy) 4/20/95

16. Has your relative ever been under immigration proceedings?
[X] No [ ] Yes Where _____ When _____
[ ] Removal [ ] Exclusion/Deportation [ ] Recission [ ] Judicial Proceedings

| INITIAL RECEIPT _____ | RESUBMITTED _____ | RELOCATED: Rec'd _____ | Sent _____ | COMPLETED: Appv'd _____ | Denied _____ | Ret'd _____ |

Form I-130 (Rev. 10/26/05) Y

Sample Form I-130 (page 2)

C. Information about your alien relative. (Continued.)

17. List husband/wife and all children of your relative.

(Name)	(Relationship)	(Date of Birth)	(Country of Birth)
Eline Margaux BOFFIN	Wife	8/1/76	Belgium
Justine Chloe BOFFIN	Daughter	9/4/01	Belgium

18. Address in the United States where your relative intends to live.

(Street Address)	(Town or City)	(State)
555 Glasgow Road	Mission Hills	Kansas

19. Your relative's address abroad. (Include street, city, province and country)

Van Cuppenstraat 85, B-222 Antwerp, Belgium

Phone Number (if any)
02-123 45 67

20. If your relative's native alphabet is other than Roman letters, write his or her name and foreign address in the native alphabet.

(Name)   Address (Include street, city, province and country):

21. If filing for your husband/wife, give last address at which you lived together. (Include street, city, province, if any, and country):

From: To:
(Month) (Year)   (Month) (Year)

22. Complete the information below if your relative is in the United States and will apply for adjustment of status.

Your relative is in the United States and will apply for adjustment of status to that of a lawful permanent resident at USCIS office in:

_____ . If your relative is not eligible for adjustment of status, he or she

(City)   (State)

will apply for a visa abroad at the American consular post in _____

(City)   (Country)

NOTE: Designation of an American embassy or consulate outside the country of your relative's last residence does not guarantee acceptance for processing by that post. Acceptance is at the discretion of the designated embassy or consulate.

D. Other information.

1. If separate petitions are also being submitted for other relatives, give names of each and relationship.

2. Have you ever before filed a petition for this or any other alien?   ☐ Yes   ☒ No
If "Yes," give name, place and date of filing and result.

WARNING: USCIS investigates claimed relationships and verifies the validity of documents. USCIS seeks criminal prosecutions when family relationships are falsified to obtain visas.

PENALTIES: By law, you may be imprisoned for not more than five years or fined $250,000, or both, for entering into a marriage contract for the purpose of evading any provision of the immigration laws. In addition, you may be fined up to $10,000 and imprisoned for up to five years, or both, for knowingly and willfully falsifying or concealing a material fact or using any false document in submitting this petition.

YOUR CERTIFICATION: I certify, under penalty of perjury under the laws of the United States of America, that the foregoing is true and correct. Furthermore, I authorize the release of any information from my records that U.S. Citizenship and Immigration Services needs to determine eligibility for the benefit that I am seeking.

E. Signature of petitioner.

Alexandra E. Gray   Date 8/5/05   Phone Number (310) 555-1515

F. Signature of person preparing this form, if other than the petitioner.

I declare that I prepared this document at the request of the person above and that it is based on all information of which I have any knowledge.

Print Name _____ Signature _____   Date _____

Address _____   G-28 ID or VOLAG Number, if any. _____

Form I-130 (Rev. 10/26/05) Y Page 2

Refugees and Political Asylees

America: A Safe Haven

Since the Refugee Act of 1980 was passed by the U.S. Congress, many people fleeing persecution from their own countries have found a permanent haven in the United States. Those who made it to the U.S. on their own applied for what's called "political asylum." An unlimited number of people can apply for asylum every year. Others were granted refugee status and a right to come to the U.S. while they were overseas. The U.S. president limits the number of refugees who'll be accepted every year—in recent years, the maximum has been set at between 70,000 and 90,000. Those fleeing natural disasters or war do not receive this permanent protection, but may receive what is called Temporary Protected Status. (See Section I, below.)

Consult an expert. This chapter explains the basic procedures and describes the immigration forms required for those claiming status as refugees and political asylees. However, the full legal process is full of possible pitfalls. If, after reading the chapter, you decide that you may qualify as a refugee or political asylee, it is best to consult an experienced immigration lawyer or other immigration professional. Many nonprofit organizations offer free or low-cost services to people fleeing persecution. (See Chapter 24.)

A. Who Qualifies

To apply to be a refugee, you must be outside your country of nationality or country of residence but not within the borders of the United States. To apply to be a political asylee, you must be either at the border or already inside the United States.

In addition, the president of the United States is empowered to recognize as a refugee any person who is still residing in his or her own country.

However, both the refugee and the political asylee have one important thing in common: They are unable or unwilling to return to their countries because of actual persecution or a well-founded fear of persecution on account of their:

- race
- religion
- nationality
- membership in a particular social group, or
- political opinion.

Persecution can include such things as threats, violence, torture, inappropriate access or imprisonment, or a failure by the government to protect you from such things.

You do not have to provide evidence that you would be singled out individually for persecution if you can establish that:

- there is a pattern or practice in your country of persecuting groups of people similarly situated to you
- you belong to or identify with the groups of people being persecuted so that your fear is reasonable, and
- your government persecutes its nationals or residents so that you had to leave your country without authorization or you have sought asylum in another country.

The persecution may have been by your government, or you can claim asylum by showing that you were persecuted by a group that your government is unable or unwilling to control, or that you fear such persecution.

The biggest challenge in applying, especially for asylees, is proving that you were, in fact, persecuted. You can't just say "I was persecuted" and expect to get a green card. But you probably didn't come to the U.S. with a lot of documents to prove what happened, if indeed any such documents exist. Succeeding with your application will depend a great deal on your own ability to tell a detailed, compelling story of what occurred, including names, dates, places, and more. If you underwent torture or suffered other medical or psychological stress, it may help to get a written evaluation by a doctor who is trained in this area and can verify that you suffer from the effects of these things.

You'll also need to show that your own story matches up with accounts by independent sources of what goes on in your country. A good asylum application is accompanied by a thick stack of newspaper clippings, human rights reports, and more, all containing information about the kind of human rights violation you're describing. If, for example, you fled because local government officials were threatening to imprison you because you sent a letter to the editor protesting a political matter, you'd need to provide evidence that others who expressed similar political opinions have been imprisoned or threatened with prison.

New Rules for Asylum Applicants

In our post-9/11 world, Congress has been concerned that terrorists could use our asylum application process to gain a "safe harbor" in the United States. In response to this and other concerns, Congress passed the REAL ID Act of 2005. Among other things, REAL ID:

- requires asylum applicants to prove at least one of the central motives of their persecutors
- obliges asylees to at least attempt to obtain corroborating evidence of their persecution, and
- allows judges to take into account the asylees' demeanor when testifying about their experiences, as well as their statements not made under oath, when making their decisions.

Many immigration advocates believe these changes will make asylum much harder to obtain in the future. However, it remains to be seen how REAL ID will truly affect our asylum process.

B. Who Is Barred From Qualifying

A number of people are prohibited from becoming refugees or asylees in the United States.

1. Those Who Have Assisted in Persecution

The opportunity for refugee or political asylum status is not open to anyone who has ordered, incited, assisted, or participated in the persecution of any other person owing to that person's race, religion, nationality, membership in a particular social group, or political opinion.

For example, this rule is often used against military or police officials who assisted in persecuting minority or guerrilla groups (even though they may, indeed, fear for their life because members of those groups are seeking revenge against them).

2. Those Who Threaten U.S. Safety or Security

No one who has been convicted of a "particularly serious crime" and is therefore a danger to the community of the United States will be granted refugee or asylee status. There is no list of particularly serious crimes—the decision is made case by case, depending on the facts surrounding the crime. However, all "aggravated felonies" are considered particularly serious crimes—and, because of the immigration laws' strict definitions of aggravated felonies, some crimes that may have been called misdemeanors when committed will be looked upon as aggravated felonies.

In addition, no person who has been convicted of a serious nonpolitical crime in a country outside the United States will be granted refugee or asylee status. However, people whose crimes were nonserious or political in nature may still qualify.

Furthermore, no person who has been involved in terrorist activity or who can reasonably be regarded as a threat to U.S. security will be granted refugee or asylee status.

3. Those Who Have Resettled

Refugee status is also denied to refugees or political asylees who have become "firmly resettled" in another country. A person is usually regarded as firmly resettled if he or she has:

- been granted permanent residency or citizenship by that country
- made permanent housing arrangements and has traveled in and out of the adopted country, or
- achieved economic independence because of education, employment, or the exercise of profession or business affairs in the adopted country.

C. How to Apply for Refugee Status

If you believe you qualify as a refugee, there are a number of documents you are required to file—and a number of steps you must follow.

1. Filing the Application

You must prepare and submit the following forms:

- ❑ Form I-590, Registration for Classification as Refugee
- ❑ documentation of persecution or a detailed affidavit supporting your request for classification as a refugee
- ❑ Form G-325C, Biographical Information—for applicants 14 years old or over
- ❑ Form I-134, Affidavit of Financial Support, from a sponsor (a responsible person or organization) for your transportation to the place of resettlement in the United States, and
- ❑ a medical examination report to ascertain that you are mentally sound and do not have a serious communicable disease.

The date on which you file the refugee status application is called your "Priority Date," and shall be the basis for determining when you will be allowed to enter the United States as a refugee. As stated earlier, the number of refugees allowed each year is limited and fixed by the U.S. president.

2. Interview

After submitting your application, you will be interviewed by an overseas immigration officer who will decide whether you have been persecuted or you have a well-founded fear of persecution because of your race, religion, nationality, political opinion, or membership in a particular social group.

3. Action on Your Application

If the overseas immigration officer decides that you meet the requirements and may be designated as a refugee, the application will be granted and you will be given a "parole visa." After your application is approved, you have four months in which to enter the United States.

If the application is denied, there is no appeal. You have no further recourse because you are outside the United States and its legal mechanism of judicial review.

Once you have been granted status as a refugee, you will be granted work authorization for one year as soon as you enter the United States.

4. When You Can Apply for a Green Card

After one year of physical presence in the United States, during which you must not have violated certain laws or regulations, you, your spouse, and your children may apply for permanent residence (a green card).

If you are found to be eligible, you and your family will be given lawful permanent resident status. The date of your permanent residence will be the date that you first arrived in the United States as a refugee. You will be eligible to apply for citizenship five years from that date.

5. Removal Proceedings

If you are found ineligible for permanent residency, removal proceedings may be started against you and your family, and you will have to present your cases before an immigration judge. If this happens, consult with an experienced immigration lawyer who specializes in removal cases. (See Chapter 24.)

D. How to Apply for Political Asylum

For people interested in applying for political asylum, you must fill out various forms and explain your case to a USCIS officer or judge.

1. Where to Request Asylum

You can request asylum:

- upon arrival at the border or port of entry, if you are an alien stowaway, a crewman, or a passenger seeking admission into the United States
- at a removal hearing before the immigration judge, or
- by sending an application to USCIS, after which you'll be interviewed at one of the USCIS Asylum Offices. You can apply for asylum even if you're in the U.S. illegally—but understand that your application will be acted on within a matter of weeks, and if it's denied, you'll probably be deported.

⚠ **Don't delay in preparing your application (if you're already in the U.S. and not in removal proceedings).** The law says that applications for asylum must be submitted within one year of your entry into the United States. USCIS policy favors people who entered the United States legally, by not counting any of the time they spend here with an unexpired I-94 as part of that year. Similarly, time during which you had Temporary Protected Status (discussed in Section I, below) does not count toward your one year. If you've already spent more than a year here, talk to an immigration attorney. Exceptions are possible in rare cases, based on changed country conditions or other compelling reasons.

2. Applications at the Border or Port of Entry

If you arrive at a U.S. border or port of entry and the officer says your visa isn't valid or you can't be admitted to the U.S., you can request political asylum. The officer is supposed to refer you to another officer who is trained to understand, based on very little information, whether you have a valid claim. Unfortunately, these officers do not act consistently, and there are many tragic reports of people being turned around and sent back to places where they were physically harmed.

If the officer denies your entry despite your request for asylum, you won't be allowed to reapply for U.S. entry for five years. You can, however, get around this by withdrawing your request for entry—in other words, by saying you changed your mind and don't want to enter the U.S. after all. But the border official has the option of deciding whether to allow you to get around the system in this way.

If the officer with whom you meet thinks you have a possible asylum case, you'll be placed in removal proceedings, where an immigration judge will consider your asylum claim (and any other relevant claims for immigration benefits you want to make). At this point, you'll have to prepare the application described in Section 3, below—but should, if at all possible, get an attorney's help.

3. Preparing and Filing Your Asylum Application

The following documents should be mailed to a USCIS Regional Service Center, if you are not in removal proceedings, or to the Immigration Court, if you are already in proceedings:

- ❑ Form I-589, Application for Asylum and for Withholding of Removal—one original and two copies. (See the sample at the end of this chapter.) Also make two copies of all supplementary documents. There is no filing fee for this form, though you will be charged $70 if they decide to fingerprint you. Your spouse and children may be included in the application, as long as you supply an additional copy of your filled-out Form I-589 and attached documents for each. If you include your family members, they will either be granted asylum when you win—or be placed in removal proceedings with you when you lose. (Regardless of whether you take the required steps to officially include them, you must provide their names and other requested information on your Form I-589.)

❑ One color photo of you and each family member applying with you, passport style. Write the person's name in pencil on the back.

❑ Copies (three) of your passports (if you have them) and any other travel documents (including from USCIS or the border authorities, such as an I-94 card).

❑ Copies (three) of documents to prove your identity, such as a birth certificate, driver's license, or national identity document ("cedula").

❑ Copies (three) of documents to prove the relationships between the family members applying, such as birth and marriage certificates.

❑ Documentation (three copies) of your experience in your country, showing why you fear to return, supported by your own detailed written statement.

❑ If possible, also include statements (three copies) of any witnesses, doctors, friends, relatives, or respected leaders of your community; news reports; or letters from people in your country.

⚠️ **Documents not in English must be translated.** You'll have to provide a word-for-word English translation of any document in another language. Any capable person can do this, but should, on their translation, add the following text at the bottom: "I certify that I am competent in both English and [your language], and that the foregoing is a full and accurate translation into English, to

the best of my knowledge and ability." The person should sign his or her name and add the date under this statement.

Not long after receiving your application, USCIS will call you in to have your fingerprints taken (if you're over age 14). This is to make sure that you don't have a record of criminal or terrorist acts and that you haven't applied for asylum before.

4. USCIS Asylum Offices—Where to File

There are four regional service centers that handle all asylum applications. Where you file depends on where you live. (See the USCIS website at www. uscis.gov for complete office addresses, including the correct post office box. Click "Field Office Addresses and Information.")

- **California Service Center:** If you reside in Arizona; the California counties of Imperial, Los Angeles, Orange, Riverside, San Bernardino, San Diego, Santa Barbara, San Luis Obispo, or Ventura; Guam; Hawaii; or the Nevada counties of Clark, Esmerelda, Nye, or Lincoln.

- **Nebraska Service Center:** If you reside in Alaska, Idaho, Illinois, Indiana, Iowa, Kansas, Kentucky, Michigan, Minnesota, Missouri, Montana, Nebraska, North Dakota, Ohio, Oregon, South Dakota, Washington, Wisconsin, or a county in California or Nevada not listed above.

- **Texas Service Center:** If you reside in Alabama, Arkansas, Colorado, Puerto Rico, District of Columbia, Florida, Georgia, Louisiana, Maryland, Mississippi, New Mexico, North Carolina, Tennessee, Texas, Virgin Islands, Utah, Virginia, West Virginia, Wyoming, or the Western Pennsylvania counties of Allegheny, Armstrong, Beaver, Bedford, Blair, Bradford, Butler, Cambria, Clarion, Clearfield, Crawford, Elk, Erie, Fayette, Forest, Greene, Indiana, Jefferson, Lawrence, McKean, Mercer, Somerset, Venango, Warren, Washington, and Westmoreland.

- **Vermont Service Center:** If you reside in Connecticut, Delaware, Maine, Massachusetts, New Hampshire, New Jersey, New York, Rhode Island, Vermont, or a county in Pennsylvania not listed above. Mark your application "Attention: Asylum."

Applying for a Work Permit

Some years ago, people were eligible for a work permit as soon as they submitted an application for political asylum—but no more. Now, in order to be given a work permit, you have to either win your case—which may take several years and many appeals—or be lucky enough to be left waiting for an unusually long time (150 days or more) with no initial decision on your application. This obviously creates hardships for asylum applicants, who have to find money to live on, and potentially pay their lawyers with, until the case is won. For this reason, you may want to find help from the lawyers at a nonprofit organization, who, if you're financially needy, will charge little or no fees.

If you get lucky and the 150 days pass with no decision, or if your application for asylum is approved, you'll need to take steps to apply for a work permit (more formally known as an Employment Authorization Document, or EAD.) Do so by filling out Form I-765 (available on the USCIS website). Most of this form is self-explanatory. On Question 16, applicants who've been waiting for 150 days or more with no decision should enter "(c)(8)." Those whose asylum application has already been approved should enter "(a)(5)." Follow the instructions on the form regarding what to include and where to take or send it.

If your asylum application is denied before a decision has been made on your EAD application, USCIS will deny this application. If USCIS has already sent a work permit, however, your work permission terminates when the card is marked to expire or 60 days after asylum is denied, whichever is later.

5. USCIS Interview

After your papers have been processed at the USCIS Service Center, you will be called in to have your fingerprints taken, then, within a few weeks, get an appointment at one of the USCIS Asylum Offices. There, you will be interviewed to determine whether you are eligible for political asylum. Interviews last around 30 minutes.

If you aren't comfortable in English, you'll need to bring your own translator. This doesn't have to be a hired professional—a family member or friend will do. But if your friends and family aren't truly fluent in both English and your own language, it's worth spending the money on a professional. Many asylum interviews have gone badly because the translator wasn't fully competent and the asylum officer, not knowing of the problem, assumed that the applicant couldn't get his or her story straight. For example, we know of a case in which the interpreter repeatedly translated the Spanish word "padres" (which means parents) as "father." The applicant was testifying about the death of both his parents in Guatemala, and the interviewer became very suspicious when he suddenly appeared to be talking about only his father.

Expect the interviewer to begin by reviewing some of the basic items in your application, such as your name, address, and date of entry into the U.S., then to move quickly into open-ended questions such as "Why are you afraid to return to your country?" The interviewer may interrupt you at any point. He or she may also ask questions you never expected, sometimes to test whether you are who you claim to be. For example, if you claim to be a member of a persecuted Christian minority in a Middle Eastern country, you might be asked questions about Christian doctrine. These interviewers are highly trained in the human rights situations of countries around the globe, and many of them have law degrees, so expect some intelligent, probing questions.

Whether the interviewer will behave courteously is another matter. Many of them are sympathetic people who took this job because they're interested in human rights issues—others are government bureaucrats whose first concern is to ferret out cases of fraud. You won't be able to choose your interviewer. Women who have been raped or experienced similar trauma can, however, request a female interviewer.

6. Comments of the Department of State

When USCIS receives your application, the officer may send a copy to the Bureau of Human Rights and Humanitarian Affairs (BHRHA) of the U.S. Department of State for comments on:

- the accuracy of the assertions on the conditions in the foreign country and the experiences described
- how an applicant who returned to the foreign country would be likely to be treated
- whether people who are similarly situated as the applicant are persecuted in the foreign country and the frequency of such persecution, and
- whether one of the grounds for denial may apply to the applicant.

However, these comments are less important than they used to be, since the process usually goes faster than the BHRHA's ability to provide comments.

Protection Under the U.N. Convention Against Torture

Even if you don't qualify for asylum, you may be protected from deportation by the United Nations Convention Against Torture. This prohibits deporting anyone who can show that he or she is more likely than not to suffer torture at the hands of his or her home country's government. The asylum application has a place to mention whether you feel you qualify for this protection. However, it won't get you a green card—it will just stop USCIS from deporting you. Whether USCIS will also allow you a work permit is up to its discretion.

---

7. Decision by the Asylum Officer

After interviewing you, the asylum officer has full discretion to approve or deny your application for political asylum. However, you won't be told the decision that day. You'll have to return to the USCIS Asylum Office at an appointed time to pick up your decision from the front desk.

⚠ You may have friends who applied for asylum years ago and are still waiting for an interview. Because of a huge backlog of applications, USCIS has started acting quickly on the cases of people who are just now applying, while it tries to deal with the older, backlogged cases a few at a time. Your case will probably be decided in six months or less—but you may know people who've waited six years or more.

If you're approved, you'll be given a document stating this. Take good care of this document, and make copies to keep in safe places. You'll need it to apply for your Social Security card, work permit, and green card (permanent resident) status in a year.

 Need to travel after you've gained asylum? Don't leave the U.S. without first obtaining a refugee travel document allowing you to return. The application is made on Form I-131; see the USCIS website for the form and instructions. Allow several weeks for the document to be approved. Also, if at all possible, do not return to the country that persecuted you—this will be taken as a sign that you aren't really in danger there after all, and you may not be allowed to return to the United States. If you feel you have no choice but to return to your home country, talk to an experienced immigration attorney before you leave.

E. If Your Asylum Application Is Denied

If the asylum officer denies your application for political asylum, he or she will also serve you with papers to start your removal proceedings before the immigration court. Get an attorney to help you.

⚠️ **Missing the hearing: an expensive mistake.** If, after you have been notified orally and in writing of the time, place, and date of the hearing, you fail to attend an asylum hearing before an immigration judge, you will be ordered deported and will never be able to adjust your status, be given voluntary departure, or be granted suspension of deportation.

Thus, when you fail to appear at your asylum hearing, the immigration judge may hold the hearing without you being present—and issue an order of deportation if the evidence presented by USCIS supports it. You will be unable to request any green card until after five years from the date of the asylum hearing that you failed to attend.

Only "exceptional circumstances beyond your control," such as your own serious illness or the death of an immediate relative, are considered to be valid excuses for failing to appear before the immigration judge. Your lawyer will need to file a motion to reopen the order of your deportation.

If the immigration judge denies your case, you are free to pursue the case to the Board of Immigration Appeals (BIA) and from there to the federal district court. In the meantime, while your case or your appeal is pending, you are able to remain in the United States. If you have already received work authorization, it will continue to be granted for one year at a time.

Some people turn around after they've been denied asylum and try to apply for it again. This won't work. First of all, it's not allowed; and second, USCIS has your fingerprints on file, and will check them, so even if you change your name, you'll get caught.

F. Asylees Can Bring Overseas Spouses and Children to the United States

If you're granted political asylum, and you have a husband, wife, or unmarried minor (under age 21) child still living in the country that persecuted you, you have the right to request asylum for them, too. But you must act within two years of when you're granted asylum, or they'll miss their chance (at least, until you're a permanent resident or U.S. citizen and can petition for them, but this takes years). No other relatives are eligible—you cannot, for example, bring your parents or grandchildren.

⚠️ **Getting married after you've won asylum won't do it.** As an asylee, you can bring in your spouse only if you and he or she were already married when you were granted asylum. If, however, your wife gave birth to a child after you won asylum, you can bring the child in so long as it was in the womb when you were granted asylum.

The procedure for bringing your spouse and children to join you is to prepare and assemble the following:

❏ Form I-730, Refugee/Asylee Relative Petition, available from USCIS or on its website at www.uscis.gov (see the sample at the end of this chapter).
❏ a copy of the document granting you asylum
❏ a clear photograph of your family member
❏ a copy of proof of the relationship between you and the person you're applying for—a marriage certificate for your spouse, or a birth certificate for your child (or an adoption certificate, but the adoption must have occurred before the child was 16), plus a marriage certificate if you're the child's father or stepparent—and
❏ if your child is adopted, evidence that he or she has been living in your legal custody for the last two years.

For more detailed information, see the instructions that come with Form I-730. After you've finished preparing the application, make a complete copy for your records and send it the USCIS Nebraska Service Center, P.O. Box 87730, Lincoln, NE 68501-7730.

Despite your status as an asylee, be aware that your family members can be denied entry to the U.S. if they've committed serious nonpolitical crimes, been affiliated with terrorism, or otherwise violated the provisions of the immigration law at I.N.A. § 208(b)(2), 8 U.S.C. § 1158.

⚠️ **Your children must remain unmarried and under age 21 until they enter the United States.** Warn them not to get married, or they'll ruin their chance to claim asylum and join you. Of course, turning 21 is something your children have no control over. Fortunately, a 2002 law called the Child Status Protection Act (CSPA) now offers them some protection. The law says that if your child was under age 21 when you filed your Form I-589 with USCIS, he or she will still be considered 21 years of age when you file the Form I-730 for him or her and he or she comes to claim U.S. asylee status.

G. Getting a Green Card After Asylum Approval

One year after your asylum application has been approved, you and your family may apply to become permanent residents. (You can also wait more than a year, but it's safest to apply as soon as you can.) You are eligible for a green card if you:

- have remained physically in the United States for one full year after being granted asylum
- continue to be a refugee or asylee or the spouse or child of such a refugee or asylee (as defined in Section A, above; if conditions in your country have improved a lot, see an attorney), and
- have not violated certain criminal laws of the United States.

If you meet these criteria, it's time to prepare and submit an application for adjustment of status, as described in Chapter 18. You can skip the sections of that chapter that discuss whether or not you're truly eligible to use the adjustment of status procedure—as an asylee, you are. You also don't need to worry about proving that you entered the U.S. legally, like some applicants do.

One problem you may run into, however, is that only a limited number of asylees can be granted green cards every year. That doesn't mean your green card application will be denied—but it's very likely to be delayed until the next year or a later year. While you wait, USCIS may interview you and review your case from time to time to see whether you're still eligible for asylum. If conditions in your home country improve, you could be removed from the United States. If not, your asylee status—and right to work—will continue until your adjustment of status (green card) application is finally approved. (However, you'll need to regularly apply for renewals of your work permit card.)

H. Revocation of Asylee Status

Beware that if your country's political situation has improved or has changed so that you are no longer in danger of being persecuted, USCIS may revoke your asylee status. However, it must first notify you and then convince an asylum officer that you either:

- no longer have a well-founded fear of persecution upon your return, due to a change of conditions in your country
- were guilty of fraud in your application so that you were not eligible for asylum when it was granted, or
- have committed any of the acts that would have caused your asylum application to be denied—such as a serious felony.

The Immigration Act of 1990 saved the day for asylees from Nicaragua, Poland, Panama, and Hungary; USCIS would have revoked their asylum status because their respective oppressive governments had been overthrown before the Act was passed on November 29, 1990. Thus, if you were granted asylum in the United States prior to November 29, 1990 and are no longer a refugee due to a change in circumstances in the country where you fear persecution, you may still apply for adjustment of status without proving that you still fear returning to your country.

I. Temporary Protected Status (TPS)

Temporary Protected Status (TPS) is a new legal category that was fashioned by the U.S. Congress to respond to situations when natural disasters, such as earthquakes, volcanic eruptions, or tidal waves occur, or when war is being waged in a foreign country. It is a form of temporary asylum or safe haven for aliens whose country is in turmoil. Congress responded with this humanitarian gesture to avoid the deportation of aliens to countries where their personal safety is threatened or in which normal living conditions are substantially disrupted. It does not, however, lead to permanent residence or a green card.

1. TPS Benefits

Temporary Protected Status offers several short-term benefits.

- **Stay of deportation.** You will not be placed in removal proceedings. If a removal case is already underway, you can claim TPS, and the proceedings will be adjourned until the end of the disruption period.
- **Work authorization.** You will receive work authorization as long as the TPS is in effect.
- **Temporary Treatment (TT).** When you file for TPS, so long as it is complete with such documentary proof as a birth certificate showing that you are a national of the designated country, the benefits of a stay of deportation and work authorization will be

granted immediately, and won't be taken away until either the TPS designation is ended or your application is denied.

2. Who Designates the TPS Aliens

The U.S. attorney general, working through USCIS, will designate the countries whose nationals deserve Temporary Protected Status. The following situations may give rise to this designation:

- ongoing armed conflict and civil war that pose a serious threat to the lives and personal safety of deported aliens who are nationals of that country
- earthquakes, floods, droughts, epidemics, or other environmental disasters, resulting in a substantial disruption of living conditions and an inability to handle the return of its nationals, in a foreign country that has requested a TPS designation, or
- extraordinary and temporary conditions in the foreign country preventing its nationals in the United States from returning safely to their country.

3. Period of Protected Status

The attorney general will designate the initial period of protection as being not less than six months or more than 18 months. Sixty days before the end of the period, the attorney general will review the conditions of the foreign country to determine whether to end the TPS, or to extend it for a period of six, 12, or 18 months.

The termination or the extension will be published in the *Federal Register*. Termination will be effective 60 days after publication.

4. Who Qualifies for TPS

Nationals or native-born citizens of the designated foreign countries may apply for Temporary Protected Status if they:

- have been physically present in the United States continuously since the date of the designation
- have continuously resided in the United States since a certain date
- register for TPS during a registration period of not less than 180 days, and
- pay the filing fee.

TPS-Designated Countries

At the time this book went to print, citizens from the countries on the list below could apply for TPS. However, this list changes rapidly, so keep your eyes on the news and USCIS website at www.uscis.gov.

Burundi	Nicaragua
El Salvador	Somalia
Honduras	Sudan
Liberia	

---

5. Who Is Not Eligible for TPS

TPS is not available to nationals or native-born citizens of a designated foreign country who are outside the United States. In addition, even if you are already in the United States, your application for TPS will be denied if you:

- have been convicted of any felony, or at least two misdemeanors, in the United States
- have ordered, incited, assisted, or participated in persecuting any person
- have committed a serious nonpolitical crime outside the United States, or
- are regarded as a terrorist or danger to the security of the United States.

6. No Departure From the U.S. Allowed

If a person who has been granted TPS leaves the United States without getting advance permission from USCIS, the agency may treat the TPS status as having been abandoned.

Brief, casual, and innocent absences from the United States—a few hours or days—shall not be considered as failure to be physically present in the United States. For humanitarian reasons, USCIS recognizes emergency and extenuating circumstances, and may give Advance Parole or permission to depart for a brief and temporary trip without affecting the TPS.

7. How to Apply for TPS

The following forms should be filed with the USCIS local office nearest the applicant's place of residence. Most applicants will file these with the USCIS. However, citizens of El Salvador, Honduras, and Nicaragua must mail their applications to either a service center or lockbox (see the USCIS website at www.uscis.gov and the appendix for contact details):

- Form I-821, Application for Temporary Protected Status. The filing fee is $50, plus an additional $70 for fingerprinting if you are age 14 or older.
- If you plan to work, Form I-765, Employment Authorization Application, with filing fee of $180. Work authorization, effective until TPS is ended, is granted for the TPS period or one year, whichever is shorter. The fee must be paid each time.
- Copies of documents showing your physical presence during the period designated: passport used in entering the United States, Form I-94 (Record of Departure), rent receipts, school records, hospital records, pay stubs, banking records, employment records, and affidavits of responsible members of your community (such as a religious officer, school director, or employer).
- Two kinds of documents showing personal identity: birth certificate, a passport, driver's license, employment ID, or school ID.
- Two photographs, passport style.

8. Termination of TPS

After the U.S. government decides that the situation in the foreign country has improved and there is no longer any reason to retain the Temporary Protective Status for nationals of that country, it will announce that the TPS designation will be lifted. Your work authorization will continue until the TPS expiration date.

If you do not have any other legal right to be in the United States, you are expected to leave at that time. However, it does not appear that the immigration authorities will make special efforts to deport people at the end of the TPS period—though there are no guarantees.

9. Deferred Enforced Departure (DED)

Another benefit that may be available for people from countries that have political or civil conflicts is known as Deferred Enforced Departure (DED). This is a temporary form of relief that allows designated individuals to work and stay in the United States for a certain period of time, during which the authorities will not try to deport them.

At the time this book went to print, no countries were currently designated under the DED program.

Certain people are ineligible for DED, including those who have committed certain crimes; persecuted others; or been previously deported, excluded, or removed from the United States.

If you are already in removal proceedings, you may ask the immigration judge to defer action on your case based on DED. If your case is already up on appeal after a decision by an immigration judge at the Board of Immigration Appeals, you should receive notice automatically about the administrative or temporary closure of your proceeding.

Application for Asylum and for Withholding of Removal, Sample Form I-589 (page 1)

Bureau of Citizenship and Immigration Services
U.S. Department of Justice
Executive Office for Immigration Review

OMB No. 1615-0067; Expires 11/30/06

Application for Asylum and for Withholding of Removal

Start Here - Please Type or Print. **USE BLACK INK. SEE THE SEPARATE INSTRUCTION PAMPHLET FOR INFORMATION ABOUT ELIGIBILITY AND HOW TO COMPLETE AND FILE THIS APPLICATION.** (Note: There is NO filing fee for this application.)

Please check the box if you also want to apply for withholding of removal under the Convention Against Torture.   ☒

PART A. I.   INFORMATION ABOUT YOU

1. Alien Registration Number(s)(A#'s)*(If any)* A54750557	2. Social Security No. *(If any)* 999-99-9999

3. Complete Last Name Romero	4. First Name Luiz	5. Middle Name Manuel

6. What other names have you used? *(Include maiden name and aliases.)*   None

7. Residence in the U.S. C/O	Telephone Number 510-555-2222
Street Number and Name 156 Arbol Lane	Apt. No.

City Richmond	State CA	ZIP Code 94666

8. Mailing Address in the U.S., if other than above (same as above)	Telephone Number
Street Number and Name	Apt. No.

City	State	ZIP Code

9. Sex ☒ Male   ☐ Female   10. Marital Status: ☐ Single   ☒ Married   ☐ Divorced   ☐ Widowed

11. Date of Birth *(Mo/Day/Yr)* 4/7/65	12. City and Country of Birth Quetzaltenango, Guatemala		

13. Present Nationality *(Citizenship)* Guatemalan	14. Nationality at Birth Guatemalan	15. Race, Ethnic or Tribal Group Hispanic	16. Religion Catholic

17.   *Check the box, a through c that applies:*   a. ☒   I have never been in immigration court proceedings.
b. ☐ I am now in immigration court proceedings.   c. ☐   I am **not** now in immigration court proceedings, but I have been in the past.

18. *Complete 18 a through c.*
a.   When did you last leave your country? *(Mo/Day/Yr)* Oct. 4, 2002   b. What is your current I-94 Number, if any? 02654000102

c.   Please list each entry to the U.S. beginning with your most recent entry.
  List date (Mo/Day/Yr), place, and your status for each entry. (Attach additional sheets as needed.)

Date	Place	Status	Date Status Expires
Oct. 4, 02	San Francisco, CA	B-2	April 4, 2003
May 7, 99	Los Angeles, CA	B-2	

19. What country issued your last passport or travel document? Guatemala	20. Passport # Travel Document # 775824	21. Expiration Date *(Mo/Day/Yr)* 1/1/07

22. What is your native language? Spanish	23. Are you fluent in English? ☐ Yes ☒ No	24. What other languages do you speak fluently? None

FOR EOIR USE ONLY	**FOR BCIS USE**
	Action:
Interview Date: _____

Decision:
__ Approval Date: _____

— Denial Date: _____

— Referral Date: _____

Asylum Officer ID#   _____ |

Form I-589 (Rev. 07/03/03)Y

Sample Form I-589 (page 2)

PART A. II.   INFORMATION ABOUT YOUR SPOUSE AND CHILDREN
Your Spouse. ☐ I am not married. (Skip to *Your Children, below.*)

1. Alien Registration Number (A#) *(If any)*	2. Passport/ID Card No. *(If any)*	3. Date of Birth *(Mo/Day/Yr)*	4. Social Security No. *(If any)*
A54571570	775825	5/9/68	774-26-4954

5. Complete Last Name	6. First Name	7. Middle Name	8. Maiden Name
Romero	Maria	Beatriz	Carcamo

9. Date of Marriage *(Mo/Day/Yr)*	10. Place of Marriage	11. City and Country of Birth
Nov. 7, 1989	Antigua, Guatemala	Panajachel, Guatemala

12. Nationality *(Citizenship)*	13. Race, Ethnic or Tribal Group	14. Sex ☐ Male ☒ Female
Guatemalan	Hispanic	

15. Is this person in the U.S.?   ☒ Yes *(Complete blocks 16 to 24.)*   ☐ No *(Specify location)*

16. Place of last entry in the U.S. ?	17. Date of last entry in the U.S. *(Mo/Day/Yr)*	18. I-94 No. *(If any)*	19. Status when last admitted *(Visa type, if any)*
San Francisco, CA	10/4/02	02654000103	B-2 visitor

20. What is your spouse's current status?	21. What is the expiration date of his/her authorized stay, if any? *(Mo/Day/Yr)*	22. Is your spouse in immigration court proceedings?	23. If previously in the U.S., date of previous arrival *(Mo/Day/Yr)*
B-2	4/4/03	☐ Yes ☒ No	None

24. If in the U.S., is your spouse to be included in this application? *(Check the appropriate box.)*

☒ Yes *(Attach one (1) photograph of your spouse in the upper right hand corner of page 9 on the extra copy of the application submitted for this person.)*
☐ No

Your Children. Please list **ALL** of your children, regardless of age, location, or marital status.

☒ I do not have any children. *(Skip to Part A. III., **Information about Your Background.**)*
☐ I do have children. Total number of children _____

(Use Supplement A Form I-589 or attach additional pages and documentation if you have more than four (4) children.)

1. Alien Registration Number (A#) *(If any)*	2. Passport/ID Card No. *(If any)*	3. Marital Status *(Married, Single, Divorced, Widowed)*	4. Social Security No. *(If any)*

5. Complete Last Name	6. First Name	7. Middle Name	8. Date of Birth *(Mo/Day/Yr)*

9. City and Country of Birth	10. Nationality *(Citizenship)*	11. Race, Ethnic or Tribal Group	12. Sex ☐ Male ☐ Female

13. Is this child in the U.S.?   ☐ Yes *(Complete blocks 14 to 21.)*   ☐ No *(Specify Location)*

14. Place of last entry in the U.S.?	15. Date of last entry in the U.S.? *(Mo/Day/Yr)*	16. I-94 No. *(If any)*	17. Status when last admitted *(Visa type, if any)*

18. What is your child's current status?	19. What is the expiration date of his/her authorized stay, if any? *(Mo/Day/Yr)*	20. Is your child in immigration court proceedings?
		☐ Yes ☐ No

21. If in the U.S., is this child to be included in this application? *(Check the appropriate box.)*
☐ Yes *(Attach one (1) photograph of your child in the upper right hand corner of page 9 on the extra copy of the application submitted for this person.)*
☐ No

Form I-589 (Rev. 07/03/03)Y Page 2

Sample Form I-589 (page 3)

PART A. II.   INFORMATION ABOUT YOUR SPOUSE AND CHILDREN Continued

1. Alien Registration Number (A#) *(If any)*	2. Passport/IDCard No. *(If any)*	3. Marital Status *(Married, Single, Divorced, Widowed)*	4. Social Security No. *(If any)*
5. Complete Last Name	6. First Name	7. Middle Name	8. Date of Birth *(Mo/Day/Yr)*
9. City and Country of Birth	10. Nationality *(Citizenship)*	11. Race, Ethnic or Tribal Group	12. Sex ☐ Male ☐ Female

13. Is this child in the U.S.?   ☐ Yes *(Complete blocks 14 to 21.)*   ☐ No *(Specify Location)*

14. Place of last entry in the U.S.?	15. Date of last entry in the U.S. ? *(Mo/Day/Yr)*	16. I-94 No. *(If any)*	17. Status when last admitted *(Visa type, if any)*
18. What is your child's current status?	19. What is the expiration date of his/her authorized stay,*(if any)? (Mo/Day/Yr)*	20. Is your child in immigration court proceedings? ☐ Yes ☐ No	

21. If in the U.S., is this child to be included in this application?   *(Check the appropriate box.)*
   ☐ Yes *(Attach one (1) photograph of your child in the upper right hand corner of page 9 on the extra copy of the application submitted for this person.)*
   ☐ No

1. Alien Registration Number (A#) *(If any)*	2. Passport/ID Card No.*(If any)*	3. Marital Status *(Married, Single, Divorced, Widowed)*	4. Social Security No. *(If any)*
5. Complete Last Name	6. First Name	7. Middle Name	8. Date of Birth *(Mo/Day/Yr)*
9. City and Country of Birth	10. Nationality *(Citizenship)*	11. Race, Ethnic or Tribal Group	12. Sex ☐ Male ☐ Female

13. Is this child in the U.S. ?   ☐ Yes *(Complete blocks 14 to 21.)*   ☐ No *(Specify Location)*

14. Place of last entry in the U.S.?	15. Date of last entry in the U.S.? *(Mo/Day/Yr)*	16. I-94 No. *(If any)*	17. Status when last admitted *(Visa type, if any)*
18. What is your child's current status?	19. What is the expiration date of his/her authorized stay, if any? *(Mo/Day/Yr)*	20. Is your child in immigration court proceedings? ☐ Yes ☐ No	

21. If in the U.S., is this child to be included in this application?   *(Check the appropriate box.)*
   ☐ Yes *(Attach one (1) photograph of your child in the upper right hand corner of page 9 on the extra copy of the application submitted for this person.)*
   ☐ No

1. Alien Registration Number (A#) *(If any)*	2. Passport/ID Card No. *(If any)*	3. Marital Status *(Married, Single, Divorced, Widowed)*	4. Social Security No. *(If any)*
5. Complete Last Name	6. First Name	7. Middle Name	8. Date of Birth *(Mo/Day/Yr)*
9. City and Country of Birth	10. Nationality *(Citizenship)*	11. Race, Ethnic or Tribal Group	12. Sex ☐ Male ☐ Female

13. Is this child in the U.S.?   ☐ Yes *(Complete blocks 14 to 21.)*   ☐ No *(Specify Location)*

14. Place of last entry in the U.S.?	15. Date of last entry in the U.S.? *(Mo/Day/Yr)*	16. I-94 No. (If any)	17. Status when last admitted *(Visa type, if any)*
18. What is your child's current status?	19. What is the expiration date of his/her authorized stay, if any? *(Mo/Day/Yr)*	20. Is your child in immigration court proceedings? ☐ Yes ☐ No	

21. If in the U.S., is this child to be included in this application?   *(Check the appropriate box.)*
   ☐ Yes *(Attach one (1) photograph of your child in the upper right hand corner of page 9 on the extra copy of the application submitted for this person.)*
   ☐ No

Form I-589 (Rev. 07/03/03)Y Page 3

Sample Form I-589 (page 4)

PART A. III.   INFORMATION ABOUT YOUR BACKGROUND

1. Please list your last address where you lived before coming to the U.S. If this is not the country where you fear persecution, also list the last address in the country where you fear persecution. *(List Address, City/Town, Department, Province, or State, and Country.) (Use Supplement B Form I-589 or additional sheets of paper if necessary.)*

Number and Street *(Provide if available)*	City/Town	Department, Province or State	Country	Dates From *(Mo/Yr)*	To *(Mo/Yr)*
123 Avenida 7	Guatemala City	Guatemala City	Guatemala	11/14/85	10/4/02

2. Provide the following information about your residences during the last five years. List your present address first. *(Use Supplement Form B or additional sheets of paper if necessary.)*

Number and Street	City/Town	Department, Province or State	Country	Dates From *(Mo/Yr)*	To *(Mo/Yr)*
123 Avenida 7	Guatemala City	Guatemala City	Guatemala	11/14/85	10/4/02
321 Calle de la Paz	Quetzaltenango		Guatemala	birth	11/4/85

3. Provide the following information about your education, beginning with the most recent. *(Use Supplement B Form I-589 or additional sheets of paper if necessary.)*

Name of School	Type of School	Location (Address)	Attended From *(Mo/Yr)*	To *(Mo/Yr)*
San Carlos University	College	Guatemala City	9/82	6/86
Quetzal High School	High School	Quetzaltenango	9/78	6/82
Sta. Maria Academy	Elementary/Middle	Quetzaltenango	9/70	6/78

4. Provide the following information about your employment during the last five years. List your present employment first. *(Use Supplement Form B or additional sheets of paper if necessary.)*

Name and Address of Employer	Your Occupation	Dates From *(Mo/Yr)*	To *(Mo/Yr)*
Jose Torres Ramirez, Attorney	Legal Assistant	8/7/94	10/2/02

5. Provide the following information about your parents and siblings (brother and sisters). Check box if the person is deceased. *(Use Supplement B Form I-589 or additional sheets of paper if necessary.)*

	Name	City/Town and Country of Birth		Current Location
Mother	Gloria Alcala de Romero	Quetzaltenango, Guatemala	☐ Deceased	Quetzaltenango, Guatemala
Father	Jorge Romero	Quetzaltenango, Guatemala	☒ Deceased	
Siblings	Felipe Romero	Quetzaltenango, Guatemala	☒ Deceased	
	Laura Romero	Quetzaltenango, Guatemala	☐ Deceased	Antigua, Guatemala

Form I-589 (Rev. 07/03/03)Y Page 4

Sample Form I-589 (page 5)

PART B.   INFORMATION ABOUT YOUR APPLICATION

(Use Supplement B Form I-589 or attach additional sheets of paper as needed to complete your responses to the questions contained in PART B.)

When answering the following questions about your asylum or other protection claim (withholding of removal under 241(b)(3) of the Act or withholding of removal under the Convention Against Torture) you should provide a detailed and specific account of the basis of your claim to asylum or other protection. To the best of your ability, provide specific dates, places, and descriptions about each event or action described. You should attach documents evidencing the general conditions in the country from which you are seeking asylum or other protection and the specific facts on which you are relying to support your claim. If this documentation is unavailable or you are not providing this documentation with your application, please explain why in your responses to the following questions. Refer to Instructions, Part 1: Filing Instructions, Section II, "Basis of Eligibility," Parts A - D, Section V, "Completing the Form," Part B, and Section VII, "Additional Documents that You Should Submit" for more information on completing this section of the form.

1.   Why are you applying for asylum or withholding of removal under section 241(b)(3) of the Act, or for withholding of removal under the Convention Against Torture? Check the appropriate box (es) below and then provide detailed answers to questions A and B below:

    I am seeking asylum or withholding of removal based on

        ☐ Race
        ☐ Religion
        ☐ Nationality
        ☒ Political opinion
        ☒ Membership in a particular social group
        ☒ Torture Convention

    A.   Have you, your family, or close friends or colleagues ever experienced harm or mistreatment or threats in the past by anyone?

        ☐ No ☒ Yes If your answer is "Yes," explain in detail:

        1) What happened;
        2) When the harm or mistreatment or threats occurred;
        3) Who caused the harm or mistreatment or threats; and
        4) Why you believe the harm or mistreatment or threats occurred.

During the months of July through September 2004, jeeps with darkened windows have been circling our office and followed me home on at least two occasions. The neighbors told me that a military officer has been asking questions about me. I received a phone call on September 4, in which an anonymous voice said "drop the Diaz case or your wife will be a widow."

    B.   Do you fear harm or mistreatment if you return to your home country?

        ☐ No ☒ Yes If your answer is "Yes," explain in detail:

        1) What harm or mistreatment you fear;
        2) Who you believe would harm or mistreat you; and
        3) Why you believe you would or could be harmed or mistreated.

I believe that members of the Guatemalan military would torture, imprison, or kill me because of my work assisting victims of human rights abuses to gain judicial relief.

Form I-589 (Rev. 07/03/03)Y Page 5

Sample Form I-589 (page 6)

PART B.   INFORMATION ABOUT YOUR APPLICATION Continued

2. Have you or your family members ever been accused, charged, arrested, detained, interrogated, convicted and sentenced, or imprisoned in any country other than the United States?

☒ No   ☐ Yes If "Yes," explain the circumstances and reasons for the action.

3. A. Have you or your family members ever belonged to or been associated with any organizations or groups in your home country, such as, but not limited to, a political party, student group, labor union, religious organization, military or paramilitary group, civil patrol, guerrilla organization, ethnic group, human rights group, or the press or media?

☐ No   ☒ Yes If "Yes," describe for each person the level of participation, any leadership or other positions held, and the length of time you or your family members were involved in each organization or activity.

I was a member of Students United for Free Speech from 1983 to 1986. I was a member of the Legal Committee for Redress from 1998 until I left Guatemala in 2004.

B. Do you or your family members continue to participate in any way in these organizations or groups?

☒ No   ☐ Yes If "Yes," describe for each person, your or your family members' current level of participation, any leadership or other positions currently held, and the length of time you or your family members have been involved in each organization or group.

4. Are you afraid of being subjected to torture in your home country or any other country to which you may be returned?

☐ No   ☒ Yes If "Yes," explain why you are afraid and describe the nature of the torture you fear, by whom, and why it would be inflicted.

Other human rights activists, including a former clerk at the office where I work, have been questioned and tortured by members of the Guatemalan police and military.

Form I-589 (Rev. 07/03/03)Y Page 6

Sample Form I-589 (page 7)

PART C.   ADDITIONAL INFORMATION ABOUT YOUR APPLICATION

(Use Supplement B Form I-589 or attach additional sheets of paper as needed to complete your responses to the questions contained in Part C.)

1.   Have you, your spouse, your child(ren), your parents, or your siblings ever applied to the United States Government for refugee status, asylum, or withholding of removal?   ☒ No ☐ Yes

    If "Yes" explain the decision and what happened to any status you, your spouse, your child(ren), your parents, or your siblings received as a result of that decision. Please indicate whether or not you were included in a parent or spouse's application. If so, please include your parent or spouse's A- number in your response. If you have been denied asylum by an Immigration Judge or the Board of Immigration Appeals, please describe any change(s) in conditions in your country or your own personal circumstances since the date of the denial that may affect your eligibility for asylum.

2.   A.   After leaving the country from which you are claiming asylum, did you or your spouse or child(ren), who are now in the United States, travel through or reside in any other country before entering the United States?   ☒ No ☐ Yes

    B. Have you, your spouse, your child(ren), or other family members such as your parents or siblings ever applied for or received any lawful status in any country other than the one from which you are now claiming asylum?   ☒ No ☐ Yes

    If "Yes" to either or both questions (2A and/or 2B), provide for each person the following: the name of each country and the length of stay; the person's status while there; the reasons for leaving; whether the person is entitled to return for lawful residence purposes; and whether the person applied for refugee status or for asylum while there, and, if not, why he or she did not do so.

3.   Have you, your spouse, or child(ren) ever ordered, incited, assisted, or otherwise participated in causing harm or suffering to any person because of his or her race, religion, nationality, membership in a particular social group or belief in a particular political opinion?

    ☒ No ☐ Yes If "Yes," describe in detail each such incident and your own or your spouse's or child(ren)'s involvement.

Form I-589 (Rev. 07/03/03)Y Page 7

Sample Form I-589 (page 8)

PART C.   ADDITIONAL INFORMATION ABOUT YOUR APPLICATION Continued

4.   After you left the country where you were harmed or fear harm, did you return to that country?

☒ No   ☐ Yes   If "Yes," describe in detail the circumstances of your visit (for example, the date(s) of the trip(s), the purpose(s) of the trip(s), and the length of time you remained in that country for the visit(s)).

5.   Are you filing the application more than one year after your last arrival in the United States?

☒ No   ☐ Yes   If "Yes," explain why you did not file within the first year after you arrived.   You should be prepared to explain at your interview or hearing why you did not file your asylum application within the first year after you arrived. For guidance in answering this question, see Instructions, Part 1: Filing Instructions, Section V. "Completing the Form," Part C.

6.   Have you or any member of your family included in the application ever committed any crime and/or been arrested, charged, convicted and sentenced for any crimes in the United States?

☒   No   ☐   Yes If "Yes," for each instance, specify in your response what occurred and the circumstances; dates; length of sentence received; location; the duration of the detention or imprisonment; the reason(s) for the detention or conviction; any formal charges that were lodged against you or your relatives included in your application; the reason(s) for release. Attach documents referring to these incidents, if they are available, or an explanation of why documents are not available.

Form I-589 (Rev. 07/03/03)Y Page 8

Sample Form I-589 (page 9)

PART D.   YOUR SIGNATURE

After reading the information regarding penalties in the instructions, complete and sign below. If someone helped you prepare this application, he or she must complete Part E.

I certify, under penalty of perjury under the laws of the United States of America, that this application and the evidence submitted with it are all true and correct. Title 18, United States Code, Section 1546, provides in part: "Whoever knowingly makes under oath, or as permitted under penalty of perjury under Section 1746 of Title 28, United States Code, knowingly subscribes as true, any false statement with respect to a material fact in any application, affidavit, or knowingly presents any such application, affidavit, or other document required by the immigration laws or regulations prescribed thereunder, or knowingly presents any such application, affidavit, or other document containing any such false statement or which fails to contain any reasonable basis in law or fact - shall be fined in accordance with this title or imprisoned not more than five years, or both." I authorize the release of any information from my record which the Bureau of Citizenship and Immigration Services needs to determine eligibility for the benefit I am seeking.

Staple your photograph here or the photograph of the family member to be included on the extra copy of the application submitted for that person.

***WARNING:* Applicants who are in the United States illegally are subject to removal if their asylum or withholding claims are not granted by an Asylum Officer or an Immigration Judge. Any information provided in completing this application may be used as a basis for the institution of, or as evidence in, removal proceedings even if the application is later withdrawn. Applicants determined to have knowingly made a frivolous application for asylum will be permanently ineligible for any benefits under the Immigration and Nationality Act. See 208(d)(6) of the Act and 8 CFR 208.20.**

Print Complete Name	Write your name in your native alphabet
Luiz Manuel Romero	n/a

Did your spouse, parent, or child(ren) assist you in completing this application?   ☒ No   ☐ Yes *(If "Yes," list the name and relationship.)*

_____   _____   _____   _____
(Name)   *(Relationship)*   *(Name)*   *(Relationship)*

Did someone other than your spouse, parent, or child(ren) prepare this application?   ☒ No   ☐ Yes *(If "Yes," complete Part E)*

Asylum applicants may be represented by counsel. Have you been provided with a list of persons who may be available to assist you, at little or no cost, with your asylum claim?   ☐ No   ☒ Yes

Signature of Applicant *(The person in Part A. I.)*

[*Luiz Manuel Romero*   ]   December 12, 2006
       Sign your name so it all appears within the brackets   Date *(Mo/Day/Yr)*

PART E.   DECLARATION OF PERSON PREPARING FORM IF OTHER THAN APPLICANT, SPOUSE, PARENT OR CHILD

I declare that I have prepared this application at the request of the person named in Part D, that the responses provided are based on all information of which I have knowledge, or which was provided to me by the applicant and that the completed application was read to the applicant in his or her native language or a language he or she understands for verification before he or she signed the application in my presence. I am aware that the knowing placement of false information on the Form I-589 may also subject me to civil penalties under 8 U.S.C. 1324(c).

Signature of Preparer	Print Complete Name		
Daytime Telephone Number ( )	Address of Preparer: Street Number and Name		
Apt. No.	City	State	ZIP Code

PART F.   TO BE COMPLETED AT INTERVIEW OR HEARING

You will be asked to complete this Part when you appear before an Asylum Officer of the U.S. Department of Homeland Security, Bureau of Citizenship and Immigration Services (BCIS), or an Immigration Judge of the U.S. Department of Justice, Executive Office for Immigration Review (EOIR) for examination.

I swear (affirm) that I know the contents of this application that I am signing, including the attached documents and supplements, that they are all true to the best of my knowledge taking into account correction(s) numbered _____ to _____ that were made by me or at my request.

Signed and sworn to before me by the above named applicant on:

_____   _____
            Signature of Applicant   Date *(Mo/Day/Yr)*

_____   _____
     Write Your Name in Your Native Alphabet   Signature of Asylum Officer or Immigration Judge

Form I-589 (Rev. 07/03/03)Y Page 9

Sample Form I-589 (page 10)

A # *(If available)*	Date
Applicant's Name	Applicant's Signature

LIST ALL OF YOUR CHILDREN, REGARDLESS OF AGE OR MARITAL STATUS.
(Use this form and attach additional pages and documentation as needed to your application if you have more than four (4) children.)

1. Alien Registration Number (A#)*(If any)*	2. Passport/ID Card No. *(If any)*	3. Marital Status *(Married, Single, Divorced, Widowed)*	4. Social Security No. *(If any)*
5. Complete Last Name	6. First Name	7. Middle Name	8. Date of Birth *(Mo/Day/Yr)*
9. City and Country of Birth	10. Nationality *(Citizenship)*	11. Race, Ethnic or Tribal Group	12. Sex ☐ Male ☐ Female

13. Is this child in the U.S.? ☐ Yes *(Complete blocks 14 to 21.)* ☐ No *(Specify Location)*

14. Place of last entry in the U.S.?	15. Date of last entry in the U.S.? *(Mo/Day/Yr)*	16. I-94 No. *(If any)*	17. Status when last admitted *(Visa type, if any)*
18. What is your child's current status?	19. What is the expiration date of his/her authorized stay, if any? *(Mo/Day/Yr)*	20. Is your child in immigration court proceedings? ☐ Yes ☐ No	

21. If in the U.S., is this child to be included in this application? *(Check the appropriate box.)*
   ☐ Yes *(Attach one (1) photograph of your child in the upper right hand corner of page 9 on the extra copy of the application submitted for this person.)*
   ☐ No

1. Alien Registration Number (A#)*(If any)*	2. Passport/ID Card No. *(If any)*	3. Marital Status *(Married, Single, Divorced, Widowed)*	4. Social Security No. *(If any)*
5. Complete Last Name	6. First Name	7. Middle Name	8. Date of Birth *(Mo/Day/Yr)*
9. City and Country of Birth	10. Nationality *(Citizenship)*	11. Race, Ethnic or Tribal Group	12. Sex ☐ Male ☐ Female

13. Is this child in the U.S.? ☐ Yes *(Complete blocks 14 to 21.)* ☐ No *(Specify Location)*

14. Place of last entry in the U.S.?	15. Date of last entry in the U.S.? *(Mo/Day/Yr)*	16. I-94 No. *(If any)*	17. Status when last admitted *(Visa type, if any)*
18. What is your child's current status?	19. What is the expiration date of his/her authorized stay, if any? *(Mo/Day/Yr)*	20. Is your child in immigration court proceedings? ☐ Yes ☐ No	

21. If in the U.S., is this child to be included in this application? *(Check the appropriate box.)*
   ☐ Yes *(Attach one (1) photograph of your child in the upper right hand corner of page 9 on the extra copy of the application submitted for this person.)*
   ☐ No

Form I-589 Supplement A (Rev. 07/03/03)Y

Sample Form I-589 (page 11)

ADDITIONAL INFORMATION ABOUT YOUR CLAIM TO ASYLUM.

A # *(If available)*	Date
Applicant's Name	Applicant's Signature

Use this as a continuation page for any information requested. Please copy and complete as needed.

PART _____

QUESTION _____

Form I-589 Supplement B (Rev. 07/03/03)Y

Refugee/Asylee Relative Petition, Sample Form I-730 (page 1)

| Department of Homeland Security
U.S. Citizenship and Immigration Services | OMB No.1615-0037; Expires 06/30/2006
I-730, Refugee/Asylee Relative Petition |

START HERE - Please type or print legibly in black ink.

Part 1. Information about you.

| Family Name (Last Name)
BERA | Given Name (First Name)
John | Middle Name
Paul |

Address - C/O

| Street Number and Name
876 5th St | Apt. #
14 |

| City
Providence | State or Province
Rhode Island |

| Country
USA | Zip/Postal Code
02901 | Gender: a. [X] Male
b. [ ] Female |

| Date of Birth (mm/dd/yyyy)
12/15/68 | Country of Birth
Nigeria | Country of Citizenship/Nationality |

| E-Mail Address
(If any.) | Telephone Number
(With area code.) (   ) |

| Alien Registration Number(A#)
12345555 | U.S. Social Security # (If applicable.)
123-44-5555 |

Other names used (including maiden name)
None

1a. [ ] Refugee   2a. [ ] Lawful Permanent Resident based on previous Refugee status
1b. [X] Asylee   2b. [ ] Lawful Permanent Resident based on previous Asylee status

Date (mm/dd/yyyy) and Place Refugee or Asylee was granted:
3/20/05, Newark, NJ

If Granted Refugee Status, Date (mm/dd/yyyy) and Place Admitted to the United States:

If Married, Date (mm/dd/yyyy) and place of Present Marriage:

If Previously Married, Name(s) of Prior Spouse(s):

Date(s) Previous Marriage(s) Ended: (mm/dd/yyyy)

Part 2. Information about the relationship.

The alien relative is my: a. [X] Spouse   .
   b. [ ] Unmarried child under 21 years of age
Number of relatives I am filing for: _____ (_____ of _____)

Part 3. Information about your alien relative.

(If you are petitionioning for more than one family member you must complete and file a separate Form I-730 for each additional family member.)

| Family Name
BERA | Given Name
Gladys | Middle Name
Mary |

Address - C/O

| Street Number and Name
17 Ozumba Mbadicue Avenue | Apt. #
2 |

| City
Lagos | State or Province |

For USCIS Use Only ...

Returned

Receipt

Submitted

Reloc Sent

Reloc Rec'd

[ ] Petitioner Interviewed

[ ] Beneficiary Interviewed

Consulate

Sections of

[ ] 207 (c) (2) Spouse
[ ] 207 (c) (2) Child
[ ] 208 (b) (3) Spouse
[ ] 208 (b) (3) Child

Remarks

Action Block

To Be Completed by Attorney or Representative, If any
[ ] Fill in box if G-28 is attached to represent the applicant.

Volag #

Atty State License #

Form I-730 (Rev. 04/29/05) N

Sample Form I-730 (page 2)

Part 3. Information about your alien relative. (Continued.)

Country	Zip/Postal Code	Gender:
Nigeria		a. ☐ Male b. ☒ Female

Date of Birth (mm/dd/yyyy)	Country of Birth	Country of Citizenship/Nationality
7/24/70	Nigeria	

E-Mail Address (If any.)	Telephone Number (With country and and city/area codes.)

Alien Registration Number (If any.)	U. S. Social Security # (If any.)
None	None

Other Name(s) Used (Including maiden name)

Gladys Mary ODEKU

If Married, Date (mm/dd/yyyy) and Place of Present Marriage:

7/18/90, Lagos, Nigeria

If Previously Married, Name(s) of Prior Spouse(s):

Date(s) Previous Marriage(s) Ended: (mm/dd/yyyy)

Name and address of your alien relative in the alphabet of the language (if other than Roman letters) spoken in the country where he or she now lives.

Family Name	Given Name	Middle Name

Address - C/O

Street Number and Name/Apt. #

City/State or Province

Country/Zip/Postal Code

Part 4. Processing Information.

1. Check One: a. ☐ The person named in **Part 3** is now in the United States.

   b. ☒ The person named in **Part 3** is now outside the United States. (Please indicate the location of the American Consulate or Embassy where your relative will apply for a visa.)

   American Consulate/Embassy at: Lagos, Nigeria
   _____
   City and Country

2. Is the person named in **Part 3** in deportation or removal proceedings in the United States?

   a. ☒ No

   b. ☐ Yes (Please explain below or on a separate sheet(s) of paper.)

Sample Form I-730 (page 3)

Part 5. Signature.

*Read the information on penalties in the instructions before completing this section and sign below. If someone helped you to prepare this petition, he or she must complete **Part 6**.*

I certify or, if outside the United States, I swear or affirm, under penalty of perjury under the laws of the United States of America, that this petition and the evidence submitted with it, is all true and correct. I authorize the release of any information from my record which U.S. Citizenship and Immigration Services needs to determine eligibility for the benefit I am seeking.

Signature	Print Name	Date	Daytime Telephone Number
			( )

NOTE: *If you do not completely fill out this form or fail to submit the required documents listed in the instructions, your relative may not be found eligible for the requested benefit and this petition may be denied.*

Part 6. Signature of person preparing form, if other than petitioner above. (Sign below.)

I declare that I prepared this petition at the request of the above person and it is based on all of the information of which I have knowledge.

Signature	Print Full Name	Date	Daytime Telephone Number
John Paul Bera	John Paul Bera	3/30/06	(401) 555-2121
Firm Name and Address			E-Mail Address (If any.)

Veterans and Enlistees

Green Card for Sinbad the Sailor

The Armed Forces Immigration Adjustment Act of 1991 was enacted to recognize "the patriotism and valor of aliens who, by virtue of their military service, have clearly demonstrated a commitment to support and defend the Constitution and laws of the United States."

This Act favors aliens who entered military service under the American flag by special agreements between the U.S. and the Philippines, Micronesia, the Marshall Islands, and Palau. Most of those who enlisted under this executive agreement are in the U.S. Navy and are from the Philippines.

However, some veterans don't need to use this law at all, but can jump directly to becoming U.S. citizens. For details, see Section C, below.

A. Who Qualifies

In general, the law allows two classes of alien military personnel to get permanent residence—and then gives green cards under the employment-based classification of "special immigrant."

The spouse and minor children under 21 years of age who are joining or accompanying the veteran or enlistee are also entitled to immigrant visas.

1. Veterans

An alien veteran of the U.S. Armed Forces can apply for permanent residence if he or she:

- has served honorably
- has served on active duty
- has served after October 15, 1978
- is recommended for a special immigrant visa by the U.S. Armed Forces or Navy officer under whom he or she serves
- originally enlisted outside the United States
- has served for an aggregate of 12 years, and
- was honorably discharged when separated from the service.

2. Enlistees

An alien enlistee in the U.S. Armed Forces can apply for permanent residence if he or she:

- originally enlisted outside the United States for six years
- is on active duty when applying for adjustment of status under this law
- has reenlisted for another six years, giving a total of 12 years active duty service, and
- is recommended for a special immigrant visa by the U.S. Armed Forces or Navy officer under whom he or she serves.

A Break for Illegal Workers

Because of this special law for alien members of the U.S. Armed Forces, the Act allows the applicant—and his or her spouse and children—to get permanent residence even if they may have worked illegally in the United States.

B. How to File

The following forms must be completed and filed, along with a filing fee of $190 for the application and $70 for fingerprints in money order or certified check made payable to USCIS:

- Form I-360, Petition for Amerasian, Widow(er), or Special Immigrant (see sample at the end of this chapter)
- Form N-426, Request for Certification for Military or Naval Service
- Form G-325A/G-325B, Biographic Information
- certification of past active duty status of 12 years for the veteran or certified proof of reenlistment after six years of active duty service for the enlistee, issued by an authorized Armed Forces official, and

- birth certificate of the applicant to show that he or she is a national of the country that has an agreement with the United States allowing the enlistment of its nationals in the U.S. Armed Forces.

These papers have to be filed with either:

- the USCIS office having jurisdiction over the veteran or enlistee's current residence or intended place of residence in the United States, or
- the overseas USCIS office having jurisdiction over the residence abroad.

If the veteran is in the U.S., he or she may apply directly for adjustment of status (see Chapter 18), and so may the spouse and children under 21 years of age. Form I-360 and accompanying materials should be included with the rest of the adjustment of status application.

If the spouse and children are outside the United States, the veteran or enlistee may file Form I-824, Application for Action on an Approved Application or Petition, to be sent to the U.S. consulate where the spouse and children will apply for immigrant visas as derivative relatives of a special immigrant.

⚠ **USCIS will automatically revoke the petition and bar the enlistee from getting a green card if he or she:**

- fails to complete the period of reenlistment, or
- receives other than an honorable discharge.

The enlistee's spouse and children will also be barred from getting green cards. If any of them already have green cards, USCIS will begin proceedings to have them taken away.

C. Becoming a U.S. Citizen

The highest immigration benefit available is U.S. citizenship. Some veterans won't need to wait for green cards to apply for citizenship, as described in Section 1, below. Others will need to wait until they've gotten a green card and satisfied other eligibility requirements, as described in Section 2, below.

1. Who Qualifies to Apply for Citizenship Without a Green Card

If the alien war veteran has honorably and actively served the U.S. military in a time of war or conflict, he or she is exempt from all green card requirements and qualifies for immediate citizenship. This special benefit depends, however, on the war or conflict in which the veteran fought under the U.S. Armed Forces. It includes:

- World War I.
- World War II, specifically between September 1, 1939 and December 31, 1946. A special provision was signed into law extending anew the Filipino war veterans' rights to U.S. citizenship. This special provision allows Filipino war veterans to file applications for citizenship until February 3, 2001.
- The Korean War, specifically between June 25, 1950, and July 1, 1955.
- The Vietnam War, specifically between February 28, 1961 and October 15, 1978.
- The Persian Gulf Conflict, specifically between August 2, 1990 and April 11, 1991.
- The "War on Terror" (also called "Operation Enduring Freedom"), which began on September 11, 2001 and will end on a date to be determined by the U.S. president.

2. Who Qualifies to Apply for Citizenship After Getting a Green Card

If you got your green card as a veteran or enlistee, you're only a few short steps away from being eligible for U.S. citizenship. Although most people must wait five years after getting their green card to apply, servicepeople who got their green cards under the Armed Forces Immigration Adjustment Act described in Section A, above, are immediately able to apply for citizenship.

Servicepeople who got their green cards in other ways can apply as soon as they've served honorably for one year; it doesn't matter how long they've had the green card for—one day is enough. However, if they've been discharged, the discharge must have been honorable, and they must apply for citizenship within six months of the discharge date.

To file for naturalization, you must file the following forms and documents with USCIS together with a $330 filing fee plus $70 for fingerprints:

❑ Form N-400, Application for Citizenship
❑ Form N-426, Request for Certification for Military or Naval Service
❑ a copy of your green card
❑ Form G-325A/G-325B, Biographic Information, and
❑ two photographs.

Want complete information on the application process for U.S. citizenship, including special exceptions applying to members of the military? See *Becoming a U.S. Citizen: A Guide to the Law, Exam & Interview*, by Ilona Bray (Nolo).

Petition for Amerasian, Widow(er), or Special Immigrant, Sample Form I-360 (page 1)

OMB No. 1615-0020; Expires 07/31/07

Department of Homeland Security
U.S. Citizenship and Immigration Services

I-360, Petition for Amerasian, Widow(er) or Special Immigrant

START HERE - Please type or print in black ink.

For USCIS Use Only

Part 1. Information about person or organization filing this petition. (Individuals should use the top name line; organizations should use the second line.) If you are a self-petitioning spouse or child and do not want USCIS to send notices about this petition to your home, you may show an alternate mailing address here. If you are filing for yourself and do not want to use an alternate mailing address, skip to part 2.

Family Name ZAPATO	Given Name Dante	Middle Name Diego

Company or Organization
Name

Address - C/O

Street Number and Name 122 Jupiter St.	Apt. # 3

City Makati	State or Province Metro Manila

Country Philippines	Zip/Postal Code

U.S. Social Security # 123-45-6767	A # None	IRS Tax # *(if any)* None

Returned

Resubmitted

Reloc Sent

Reloc Rec'd

☐ Petitioner/ Applicant
☐ Interviewed
Beneficiary Interviewed

☐ I-485 Filed Concurrently
☐ Bene "A" File Reviewed

Receipt

Part 2. Classification Requested (check one):

a. ☐ Amerasian
b. ☐ Widow(er) of a U.S. citizen who died within the past two (2) years
c. ☐ Special Immigrant Juvenile
d. ☐ Special Immigrant Religious Worker
e. ☐ Special Immigrant based on employment with the Panama Canal Company, Canal Zone Government or U.S. Government in the Canal Zone
f. ☐ Special Immigrant Physician
g. ☐ Special Immigrant International Organization Employee or family member
h. ☑ Special Immigrant Armed Forces Member
i. ☐ Self-Petitioning Spouse of Abusive U.S. Citizen or Lawful Permanent Resident
j. ☐ Self-Petitioning Child of Abusive U.S. Citizen or Lawful Permanent Resident
k. ☐ Other, explain: _____

Classification

Consulate

Priority Date

Remarks:

Part 3. Information about the person this petition is for.

Family Name ZAPATO	Given Name Dante	Middle Name Diego

Address - C/O

Street Number and Name 122 Jupiter St.	Apt. # 3

City Makati	State or Province Metro Manila

Country Philippines	Zip/Postal Code

Date of Birth *(mm/dd/yyyy)* 4/6/62	Country of Birth Philippines

U.S. Social Security # 123-45-6767	A # *(if any)* none

Marital Status: ☐ Single ☑ Married ☐ Divorced ☐ Widowed

Complete the items below if this person is in the United States:

Date of Arrival *(mm/dd/yyyy)*	I-94#

Current Nonimmigrant Status	Expires on *(mm/dd/yyyy)*

Action Block

To Be Completed by

☐ *Attorney or Representative,* **if any**
Fill in box if G-28 is attached to represent the applicant

VOLAG#

ATTY State License #

Form I-360 (Rev. 10/26/05)Y

Sample Form I-360 (page 2)

Part 4. Processing Information.

Below give information on U.S. Consulate you want notified if this petition is approved and if any requested adjustment of status cannot be granted.

American Consulate: City	Country
Manila	Philippines

If you gave a United States address in **Part 3**, print the person's foreign address below. If his or her native alphabet does not use Roman letters, print his or her name and foreign address in the native alphabet.

Name	Address

Gender of the person this petition is for.	☑ Male	☐ Female
Are you filing any other petitions or applications with this one?	☑ No	☐ Yes (How many? _____)
Is the person this petition is for in deportation or removal proceedings?	☑ No	☐ Yes (Explain on a separate sheet of paper)
Has the person this petition is for ever worked in the U.S. without permission?	☑ No	☐ Yes (Explain on a separate sheet of paper)
Is an application for adjustment of status attached to this petition?	☑ No	☐ Yes

Part 5. Complete only if filing for an Amerasian.

Section A. Information about the mother of the Amerasian

Family Name	Given Name	Middle Name

Living? ☐ No (Give date of death _____)   ☐ Yes (complete address line below)   ☐ Unknown (attach a full explanation)

Address

Section B. Information about the father of the Amerasian: If possible, attach a notarized statement from the father regarding parentage. Explain on separate paper any question you cannot fully answer in the space provided on this form.

Family Name	Given Name	Middle Name

Date of Birth *(mm/dd/yyyy)*	Country of Birth

Living? ☐ No (give date of death _____)   ☐ Yes (complete address line below)   ☐ Unknown (attach a full explanation)

Home Address

Home Phone # ( )	Work Phone # ( )

At the time the Amerasian was conceived:

The father was in the military (indicate branch of service below - and give service number here): _____

☐ Army   ☐ Air Force   ☐ Navy   ☐ Marine Corps   ☐ Coast Guard

☐ The father was a civilian employed abroad. Attach a list of names and addresses of organizations which employed him at that time.

☐ The father was not in the military, and was not a civilian employed abroad. (Attach a full explanation of the circumstances.)

Part 6. Complete only if filing for a Special Immigrant Juvenile Court Dependent.

Section A. Information about the Juvenile

List any other names used.

Answer the following questions regarding the person this petition is for. If you answer "No," explain on a separate sheet of paper.

Is he or she still dependent upon the juvenile court or still legally committed to or under the custody of an agency or department of a state?	☐ No	☐ Yes
Does he or she continue to be eligible for long term foster care?	☐ No	☐ Yes

Sample Form I-360 (page 3)

Part 7. Complete only if filing as a Widow/Widower, a Self-petitioning Spouse of an Abuser, or as a Self-petitioning Child of an Abuser.

Section A. Information about the U.S. citizen husband or wife who died or about the U.S. citizen or lawful permanent resident abuser.

Family Name	Given Name	Middle Name

Date of Birth *(mm/dd/yyyy)*	Country of Birth	Date of Death *(mm/dd/yyyy)*

He or she is now, or was at time of death a (check one):

☐ U.S. citizen through Naturalization *(Show A #)* _____

☐ U.S. citizen born in the United States.   ☐ U.S. lawful permanent resident (Show A #) _____

☐ U.S. citizen born abroad to U.S. citizen parents.   ☐ Other, explain _____

Section   B. Additional Information about you.

How many times have you been married?	How many times was the person in Section A married?	Give the date and place where you and the person in Section A were married. *(If you are a self-petitioning child, write: "N/A")*

When did you live with the person named in **Section A**? From *(Month/Year)* _____ until *(Month/Year)* _____

If you are filing as a widow/widower, were you legally separated at the time of the U.S citizens's death?   ☐ No   ☐ Yes, *(attach explanation)*.

Give the last address at which you lived together with the person named in **Section A**, and show the last date that you lived together with that person at that address:

If you are filing as a self-petitioning spouse, have any of your children filed separate self-petitions?   ☐ No   ☐ Yes *(show child(ren)'s full names)*:

Part 8. Information about the spouse and children of the person this petition is for.

A widow/widower or a self-petitioning spouse of an abusive citizen or lawful permanent resident should also list the children of the deceased spouse or of the abuser.

A. Family Name	Given Name	Middle Name	Date of Birth *(mm/dd/yyyy)*
ZAPATO	Isabella	Aday	7/12/65
Country of Birth: Philippines	Relationship ☒ Spouse ☐ Child		A # None
B. Family Name ZAPATO	Given Name Ricardo	Middle Name Jesus	Date of Birth *(mm/dd/yyyy)* 6/12/90
Country of Birth Philippines	Relationship ☒ Child		A # None
C. Family Name	Given Name	Middle Name	Date of Birth *(mm/dd/yyyy)*
Country of Birth	Relationship ☐ Child		A #
D. Family Name	Given Name	Middle Name	Date of Birth *(mm/dd/yyyy)*
Country of Birth	Relationship ☐ Child		A #
E. Family Name	Given Name	Middle Name	Date of Birth *(mm/dd/yyyy)*
Country of Birth	Relationship ☐ Child		A #
F. Family Name	Given Name	Middle Name	Date of Birth *(mm/dd/yyyy)*
Country of Birth	Relationship ☐ Child		A #

Form I-360 (Rev. 10/26/05)Y Page 3

Sample Form I-360 (page 4)

Part 8. Information about the spouse and children of the person this petition is for. (Continued.)

G. Family Name	Given Name	Middle Name	Date of Birth (mm/dd/yyyy)
Country of Birth	Relationship ☐ Child		A #
H. Family Name	Given Name	Middle Name	Date of Birth (mm/dd/yyyy)
Country of Birth	Relationship ☐ Child		A #

Part 9. Signature.

Read the information on penalties in the instructions before completing this part. If you are going to file this petition at a USCIS office in the United States, sign below. If you are going to file it at a U.S. consulate or USCIS office overseas, sign in front of a USCIS or consular official.

I certify, or, if outside the United States, I swear or affirm, under penalty of perjury under the laws of the United States of America, that this petition and the evidence submitted with it is all true and correct. If filing this on behalf at an organization, I certify that I am empowered to do so by that organization. I authorize the release of any information from my records, or from the petitioning organization's records, that the U.S. Citizenship and Immigration Services needs to determine eligibility for the benefit being sought.

Signature	Date
Signature of USCIS or Consular Official	Print Name	Date

NOTE: If you do not completely fill out this petition or fail to submit required documents listed in the instructions, the person(s) filed for may not be found eligible for a requested benefit and the petition may be denied.

Part 10. Signature of person preparing form, if other than above. (Sign below.)

I declare that I prepared this application at the request of the above person and it is based on all information of which I have knowledge.

Signature	Print Your Name	Date

Firm Name
and Address

Registry: For Those in the U.S. Since 1972

Green Cards for Old-Timers

If you are one of the few people who, for one reason or another, did not take advantage of the amnesty opportunities in the 1980s, and if you have been living continuously in the United States since January 1, 1972, you have one final avenue available to get a green card. It is called "registry."

The 1972 date may change. Congress has been talking about moving the January 1, 1972 eligibility date forward. Keep your eye on Nolo's website (www.nolo.com) for updates.

A. How You Got Here Is Irrelevant

You can apply for registry no matter how you entered the United States and no matter what your current immigration status. For example, it doesn't matter that you crossed the border from Mexico, or that you came as a tourist for the World's Fair and stayed longer than your visa allowed, or that you were a transit passenger on your way to London. You won't be barred from registering if you cannot find your passport showing your date of entry, or if USCIS cannot find its own records of your entry.

Although you normally would be denied a green card if you entered the U.S. without inspection by a border official, or if you were transit passengers or stowaways, this application is special. In a sense, you are being rewarded for having been able to stay for so long without getting in trouble with the U.S. government.

B. Short Absences Allowed

If you went for a short trip across the Mexican border or took a month's vacation in your home country, your departure will probably not be considered an interruption of your required "continuous residence" in the United States. Such absence must be "brief, casual, and innocent." This means that you must have done nothing either before or during your absence to show that you intended to abandon your residence in the United States.

Of course, if you quit your job, gave up the lease on your apartment, were feted at good-bye parties, stopped paying your bills, and left the United States with all your belongings, your departure is no longer casual or innocent, however brief it may have been. If there is enough evidence that you intended to leave permanently, USCIS is likely to deny your registry application because you interrupted your continuous residence in the United States.

Medical personnel beware. Foreign medical graduates who have come to the United States on a J-1 visa and who must fulfill the two-year home country residence requirement, and other foreign medical graduates, may encounter resistance from USCIS in applying for registry. If you are in this situation, seek legal counsel before proceeding.

C. How to File

There is no immigration form specifically for registry. To file, you must complete Form I-485, Application to Register Permanent Residence or Adjust Status (as explained in detail in Chapter 18), and attach the documents described below.

D. Additional Documentation Required

Registry is basically a paper chase. Simply saying that you have lived in the United States since January 1, 1972—without providing any documents to substantiate your testimony and those of your witnesses—is useless. To prove your continuous residence in the United States, you must submit as many of the following documents as possible with your adjustment of status application:

- your passport and Form I-94, which shows your date of arrival into the United States

- any certificate issued by the government showing birth, death, or marriage of any member of your immediate family in the United States
- any government-issued license, such as a driver's license, business license, fishing license, car license, or professional license
- lease to your apartment and business, rent receipts, or, if you owned your own home, title to your home, mortgage contract, and deed of sale
- bills showing use of gas and electricity, telephone, and fuel oil for each of your home addresses during the years you have been living in the United States
- bank statements, bank book, deposit box agreement, or credit union savings account
- pay stubs, job identification card, union membership, W-2 forms, letters of recommendation from previous employers, daily attendance sheets, and job memos addressed to you
- subscriptions to magazines and newspapers or cable and Internet service
- proof of membership in health or private clubs, churches, or social organizations
- any photos showing you at events that indicate precise dates, such as marriage or religious ceremonies, with invitations showing when and where they occurred
- medical and dental records
- credit card statements or statements from credit institutions showing payment of longstanding debts, such as car loans, student loans, and vacation loans
- letters addressed to you with clear postmarks, and
- written statements from relatives, friends, employers, a pastor or a priest, a school officer, or a police precinct attesting to the fact that you have lived continuously in the United States since January 1, 1972.

E. Approval of Registry

If you have concrete evidence that you have been living in the United States all these years, USCIS will grant your application. You will be registered in USCIS records as having entered the United States as a permanent resident as of January 1, 1972.

If you are unable to convince USCIS of your long stay and it decides to start removal proceedings against you, you may wish to avail yourself of cancellation of removal relief. (See Chapter 17.) ■

Cancellation of Removal

Do Ten Illegal Years Equal One Green Card?

Immigration law does provide a green card as a form of relief from deportation to a person who has been in the United States for more than ten years. However, the process is long and arduous, and can normally be started only if you're already in immigration court proceedings, facing removal from the United States. This relief is called "cancellation of removal;" it was formerly called "suspension of deportation." When granted, an alien immediately becomes a lawful permanent resident—and receives a green card soon after the court hearing.

This area of immigration law has changed drastically in recent years. The rules controlling who qualifies have become much tougher since Congress passed changes in 1996. Some people can still qualify under the former, more flexible rules; others will qualify only if they meet the more restrictive rules passed more recently.

A. Applying in Court Proceedings

You cannot file an application to begin cancellation of removal directly with USCIS, as you can other immigration applications. This process is available only when you are in immigration court, under removal proceedings. (The only exception to this rule is for people who qualify for benefits under the Nicaraguan Adjustment and Central American Relief Act.)

Being in removal proceedings means that USCIS has learned of your illegal status and has served you with a summons called a Notice to Appear (which used to be called an Order to Show Cause). The notice is a formal order giving you the time, date, and place to appear for a hearing on whether or not you should be deported.

If USCIS has not started removal proceedings against you, your sole possibility is to turn yourself in to USCIS—and it may then start removal proceedings against you. But you should not do this before consulting an experienced immigration attorney. The attorney can help evaluate whether you qualify for relief and assess the chances that

USCIS is likely to cooperate with you. More often, USCIS just lets your application sit in their files for years and years, perhaps waiting for the laws to turn against you.

B. Who Qualifies for Cancellation

If you have actually been in the United States for ten years, you are of good moral character, and your deportation would cause hardship to your U.S. citizen and permanent resident family members, there is a chance that your application for cancellation of removal will be granted.

If you were present in the United States for only seven years but USCIS issued your Order to Show Cause after you accumulated those seven years, you may qualify for the old suspension of deportation which didn't require you to show hardship to your relatives.

Consult an expert. It is very risky to ask to be placed in removal proceedings solely to request cancellation. If you are contemplating turning yourself in to USCIS, discuss your situation first with an immigration attorney who specializes in cancellation issues, an immigration law clinic, or a group that specializes in counseling on immigration matters.

C. Who Is Not Eligible for Cancellation

A number of aliens cannot apply for cancellation of removal. They include:

- aliens who entered the United States as crewmen after June 30, 1964
- J-1 visa holders who have not fulfilled a two-year home country residency requirement if they are required to do so, and those who came to the U.S. to receive graduate medical education or training
- those who belong to certain categories of inadmissible aliens, including those who

the U.S. government believes are coming to the U.S. to engage in espionage, unlawful activities to overturn the U.S. government, or terrorist activities, and those who have been members of totalitarian or some communist parties

- people who are deportable for offenses involving national security, espionage, or terrorism
- people who have participated in persecuting others
- certain people previously given relief from removal or deportation
- people who have been convicted of certain crimes involving morally bad conduct or illegal drugs
- people convicted of a crime involving morally bad conduct in the five years after being admitted to the U.S. if the crime may be punished by a sentence of one year or more
- people who have been convicted of certain offenses involving failure to comply with alien registration or change of address requirements, or who have been convicted of certain offenses involving document fraud, and
- people convicted of an aggravated felony. This includes murder, rape, sexual abuse of a minor, illegal trafficking in drugs or firearms, money laundering, crimes of violence, theft, or burglary—or other offenses with possible prison terms of one year or more. If you have been convicted of a crime, get advice from an experienced attorney to see if you can clear your criminal record.

D. Preparing a Convincing Case

If you decide that your best approach is to file for cancellation of removal, know that you will have some difficult times ahead. Your first task will be to explain your situation to a lawyer—and convince him or her that you are eligible. In making your case, you must have strong evidence of several

things. Before you consult with a lawyer, try to collect as many of the following documents as possible. (See Chapter 24 for advice on finding a good lawyer.)

1. Proof of Good Moral Character

You must show that you've been a person of good moral character for at least the last ten years. You may be able to secure a certificate of good conduct from your local police station. This certificate will attest that, according to computer records, you have never been in trouble with the police. Although USCIS will also send your fingerprints to the Federal Bureau of Investigation in Washington, DC, submitting your own record from the local police will help prove to the court that you are a person of good moral character.

You can also submit declarations from relatives, friends, and community members verifying that you have participated in religious institutions, volunteered at schools or other civic places, or in any other way demonstrated that you are a good person.

If you have committed any serious crime during the ten years you were in the United States, the immigration judge may find that you lack good moral character. Ten years must pass from the time you committed the crime until the time you can apply for a suspension of deportation. However, committing certain serious crimes will make you ineligible forever.

2. Proof That You Stayed in the U.S. Ten Years

You must show also that you have lived in the United States continuously for at least ten years. A copy of your passport and the I-94 (Record of Arrival and Departure) that was attached to your passport when you first arrived in the United States are the best proof of this.

In addition, copies of your apartment lease, bank statements, and income tax returns are good evidence that you have been in the United States for ten years. School and medical records, subscriptions and memberships, and statements from friends, landlords, or coworkers are also useful.

What Does "Continuous Physical Presence" Mean?

The court will consider that you have been continuously present in the U.S. even if you departed from the country as long as your absences did not exceed more than 90 days per trip or 180 days total. There are exceptions for individuals who served honorably in the Armed Forces for at least two years. Also, the time that can be used toward the ten-year presence period will be cut short if you commit an act that makes you deportable or inadmissible, or USCIS issues you a Notice to Appear.

---

3. Proof of Hardship

You must convince the court that if you are deported from the United States, it would cause exceptional and extremely unusual hardship to your spouse, child, or parent who is a U.S. citizen or a permanent resident. (The law in effect before 1996 allowed an individual to qualify by showing extreme hardship to himself or herself as well as to one of those family members, but this no longer works.)

Of course, if your spouse, parent, or adult child (21 or over) is a U.S. citizen, you qualify as a candidate for an immigrant visa as an immediate relative or as a family preference beneficiary (see Chapter 4). The relief of cancellation of removal is often a delaying tactic that your lawyer will resort to when, for some reason, you cannot immediately obtain your green card through any one of those immediate relatives.

Because the relief of cancellation of removal depends almost completely on the discretion of the judge, you can only hope for a judge who is compassionate and humane. You and your lawyer must convince the judge that leaving the United States and returning to your own country would cause exceptional and extremely unusual hardship for your family members due to any combination of personal, economic, sociocultural, and psychological reasons.

Personal reasons. The immigration court will need the birth certificate of your child, your marriage certificate, and your own birth certificate if your parents are U.S. citizens or permanent residents who will suffer hardship should you leave the United States.

For starters, your relatives should be prepared to testify in court about how much you mean to them, how much they depend on you, and how empty life would be for them if you were not allowed to remain in the United States. However, this sort of testimony is not enough by itself, since nearly every family would face similar pain. The judge wants to see that the hardship your family would face is "exceptional and extremely unusual."

If your American-born children are under 14, the judge will normally not ask to hear their testimony. However, the testimony of such young children, detailing their affection for you and the hardships they would endure if they accompanied you to your native country—problems with language, problems being uprooted from friend and schools—could strengthen your case.

Although testimony by your young children that, as Americans, they would rather stay in the United States with their grandparents or with a foster family than leave for a country they don't know could be hurtful for you to hear, such testimony would be further evidence that your deportation would cause them hardship.

Proof that any illness for which you or a family member is being treated in the United States, and evidence that the same treatment or medicine is either lacking or too expensive in your own country should also be given to the judge, supported by letters from doctors and pharmacists in the United States and the foreign country.

Provided they are either U.S. citizens or permanent residents, more distant relatives—

including the grandparents or the biological parents of your child, their aunts, uncles, or cousins, or your own brothers and sisters—may all testify that your departure would also be an extreme hardship to them and to the family in general.

If you have a boyfriend or girlfriend who is married to somebody else, it is not recommended that he or she testify either on your behalf, or on behalf of the child he or she had with you. Although adultery has been repealed from immigration law as proof of the lack of good moral character, many judges will not look with favor upon such situations.

Economic reasons. Although you are probably earning much more in the United States than you would earn in your own country, economic reasons are the least persuasive arguments against deportation. Economic hardship by itself has never been considered by the immigration court as sufficient reason to cancel deportation.

If you are receiving welfare, government subsidies, or any form of public assistance, you may have an even more difficult time receiving mercy from the judge. A judge is unlikely to grant you permission to stay in the United States permanently if you may be seen as a burden to the government.

Proof of regular and continuous employment is very important. Letters from your employers, past and present, detailing your employment history and your value as an employee; your most current pay stubs; and evidence of your work product, in the form of photos or newspaper articles, are all useful in demonstrating your contribution to the economic life of the nation.

You should have filed income tax returns for the past ten years, so submit copies as proof. This will show that, except for your illegal immigration status, you have been law-abiding. If you have not filed any tax returns because you do not have a Social Security number or because you have always been paid in cash, you should consult a tax expert at once. You may have to pay back taxes.

If you are in business for yourself, submit a financial statement from an accountant to the court, along with incorporation papers showing you as the major or only stockholder; photos of your business in operation; a letter from your bank giving your account history and the average balance of your business account; and any savings, stocks, and bonds certificates. Letters from your business partners and testimony in court explaining how the business would be affected if you were forced to leave it should also be presented during the hearing.

If you have invested in real estate, present proof of ownership, mortgage papers, and a letter from a real estate broker concerning how much your property would be worth if sold in the present market and how much financial loss this would cause you.

Obtain a copy of your credit history from any of the national companies such as Experian, TransUnion, or Equifax whose credit reports are consulted by banks. This will prove that you have no judgments pending from creditors.

Sociocultural reasons. Convince the court that you are in good standing in your community. Present letters from your church, temple, or mosque about your active membership, from your block or village association, from the Parent Teachers' Association, from volunteer organizations, and from people you have cared for or helped. All are important to show that your life in the United States has been intimately entwined with American society and that you have been a useful member of your community.

Letters from the union supervisor or from your co-workers explaining the kind of person you are and how valuable you are to them personally and in terms of work are also persuasive documents to present to the judge.

The judge will want to know whether you have any other forms of relief from deportation, whether you have any pending petitions submitted on your behalf by a relative or an employer, and why it is advantageous for the U.S. government to grant you permanent residence through an immediate cancellation of removal instead of waiting for the Priority Date of any other immigration petition that may be pending.

Psychological reasons. You will have to acquaint the judge with the social, cultural, and political situation in your country and how your family may be subjected to prejudice, bigotry, or ostracism.

If you have a child born outside of marriage, or who is of a different race or is physically handicapped, provide evidence of how such children are treated in your country. Explain how going back to your country would affect your emotional and psychological health, thereby affecting your U.S. citizen and permanent resident family members. Also explain how going back would directly affect the emotional or psychological health of any relative who is a U.S. citizen or a permanent resident. Testimony from an expert witness, such as a psychiatrist or a psychologist, would bolster your case.

If you have a child who is a U.S. citizen, explain that his or her inability to speak the language of your native country and removing him or her from relatives, friends, classmates, and school could cause him or her great psychological shock.

E. How to File

You and your lawyer must submit the following documents to the immigration judge, along with a filing fee of $100:

- Form EOIR-42A, Application for Cancellation of Removal for Permanent Residents, or Form EOIR-42B, Application for Cancellation of Removal and Adjustment of Status for Certain Nonpermanent Residents
- Form I-765, Application for Employment Authorization, with an additional filing fee of $180
- Form G-325A, Biographic Information
- documentary evidence as described in Section D, above
- two color photographs taken within 30 days of submitting the application, and
- a $70 fingerprinting fee.

The immigration judge will set a hearing date for your case—time enough for you and your lawyer to prepare and for USCIS to investigate your case. In the meantime, USCIS should issue you a work permit within 60 days from the date you filed the application for cancellation of removal. Be sure that USCIS has your correct address.

The hearing may not finish the first day. In fact, it may be postponed one or more times because the immigration court devotes only a few hours at a time to each case on its calendar. Unless you are being detained at the immigration jail, or your lawyer is particularly insistent, your case may take one or two years before it is fully heard and a decision is reached.

F. Approving Your Application

If the immigration judge approves your application for cancellation of removal, you will be granted permanent residence that day (if there are still visa numbers available for the current year).

Because you have shown that you have lived a productive and useful life in the United States all those years that you were living illegally, and that your deportation would be extremely hard for your American or lawful permanent spouse, child, or parents, the U.S. government wants you to remain in the United States legally.

Winning Is Not Enough

Even if an immigration judge decides to cancel your removal order, you could face a delay. Only 4,000 people each year are granted formal cancellation of removal. Immigration judges have the power to grant conditional or temporary cancellation of removal orders until the person becomes eligible. The removal proceedings will not be formally ended, and permanent residence will not be formally granted, until their waiting number is reached.

G. Additional Forms of Cancellation of Removal

There are two additional forms of cancellation of removal. One is for permanent residents (green card holders) who have become deportable or removable. The other is for people who have been subjected to extreme cruelty or battery by a spouse or parent who is a U.S. citizen or permanent resident while in the United States.

1. Permanent Residents

An immigration judge may cancel the removal of, and re-grant a green card to, a permanent resident if the person:

- has five years as a permanent resident
- has lived continuously in the U.S. for at least seven years after having been admitted in any status, and
- has not been convicted of an aggravated felony.

This relief will serve as a waiver of removal for many permanent residents who commit acts which make them deportable. See a lawyer for help with this (see Chapter 24).

2. Abused Spouse or Child

An abused spouse or child of a U.S. citizen or permanent resident may apply for cancellation of removal under different rules. In this case, the applicant must show that he or she:

- suffered physical abuse or extreme mental cruelty in the U.S. at the hands of a permanent resident or U.S. citizen who is or was their parent or spouse—or the applicant is the parent of such an abused child
- has been physically present in the U.S. for a continuous period of at least three years at the time of the application
- has had good moral character for at least the three-year period, and
- is not inadmissible due to a conviction for a crime involving moral turpitude or drugs, not inadmissible on national security or terrorism grounds or other specified grounds, and has not been convicted of an aggravated felony.

The applicant must also show that the removal would result in extreme hardship to the applicant, the alien's child, or the alien's parent (if the applicant is a child). Congress added this provision so that spouses and children who are victims of abuse by their petitioning relative would have a way to obtain status if they left the household of the abuser. Again, seek a lawyer's help with this type of application. Many nonprofits offer free or low-cost help. ■

Adjustment of Status

Getting a Green Card While in the United States

The term "adjustment of status" refers to the procedure for obtaining a green card while you're in the United States, by submitting forms to USCIS and attending an interview at a local USCIS office. It literally means you're changing your status from that of an undocumented person or a nonimmigrant visa holder to that of permanent resident. The alternate way to obtain a green card is through what's called "consular processing" (discussed in Chapter 19), in which you correspond with and attend interviews at an overseas U.S. embassy or consulate.

If you're living or staying in the United States right now, you might prefer the convenience of applying for your green card without leaving, using the adjustment of status process. Unfortunately, it's not that easy. Many people who are eligible for green cards—because they're family members of U.S. citizens or permanent residents, or fall into other immigration categories—are nevertheless not allowed to stay in the United States to get their green card. Read on to find out the possibilities and potential problems that surround adjustment of status.

This chapter will discuss:

- who is allowed to use the adjustment of status procedure (Section A)
- who doesn't qualify, and what effect this has on their efforts to immigrate (Section B), and
- if you qualify, what forms and application procedures you'll need to use (Section C).

How Do You Decide?

If you are eligible for both adjustment of status in the United States or consular processing abroad, it is usually best to choose adjustment of status because:

- you will save the expense of traveling back to your home country
- if your application to adjust your status is denied, you can remain and work in the U.S. while you appeal that decision
- if you go for consular processing and your application is denied, there is no right to appeal, and
- when adjusting status, there is no risk of being kept out for three or ten years due to past illegal stays in the United States.

A. Who Is Allowed to Use the Adjustment of Status Procedure

You are allowed to choose adjustment of status as your green card application method only if you fall into one of the following three categories:

- You are the immediate relative of a U.S. citizen and your last entry into the U.S. was done legally (see Section 1, below).
- Your last entry into the U.S. was done legally and you have remained in legal status ever since (see Section 2, below).
- You are "grandfathered in" under certain old laws because you had a visa petition on file before the laws changed (see Section 3, below).

In addition, you must not be inadmissible based on the "permanent bar." This bar applies to people who lived in the United States illegally for more than a year and then left or were deported, but who returned to the United States illegally (or were caught trying to). Such people will never be allowed to get a green card. See a lawyer if you believe this bar might apply to you.

1. Immediate Relatives Who Entered Legally

If you meet the following two criteria, you are one of the lucky few allowed to use the adjustment of status procedure:

- You are the immediate relative (spouse, parent, or minor, unmarried child) of a U.S. citizen.

- Your most recent entry to the United States was done legally, most likely using a visa (such as a tourist or a student visa), a visa waiver (in which you simply showed your passport and were admitted for a 90-day tourist stay), or some other entry document like a border crossing card. There are exceptions, however: You cannot adjust under this category if you entered as a crewman on a boat or plane, regardless of what visa you had, or you were in transit to another country without a visa (for example, changing planes in a U.S. airport).

Remember, this chapter discusses only procedures, not your underlying eligibility for a green card. Unless you've already completed the steps explained in another chapter—most likely one describing family- or lottery-based visas—you shouldn't be in this chapter. It's only for people with approved visa petitions or winning lottery letters who are now completing their green card application process.

EXAMPLE: Katerina is a foreign student from Germany who has used her student visa to enter the United States many times, most recently on her return trip after summer vacation. She is engaged to marry a fellow student named Mark, a U.S. citizen. Once they're married, Katerina will be an immediate relative, whose last entry to the U.S. was done legally. (In fact, it wouldn't matter if she let her student visa expire before applying to adjust status, though we don't recommend this method, since it means spending time in the U.S. illegally.) Katerina will be able to apply for her green card without leaving the U.S., using the adjustment of status procedure.

However, there's one major, and common, difficulty for some immediate relatives: Your use of the visa or visa waiver to enter the U.S. has to have been an innocent one, merely to study, travel, or whatever it was your visa was meant for. If instead you used the visa specifically for the purpose of getting yourself to the U.S. so you could adjust status, that's visa fraud, and will make you ineligible for a green card. Visas are meant to be used only for the limited purpose of coming to the U.S. for a temporary stay—any secret plans to stay permanently can be seen as a big problem.

EXAMPLE: While Sally was a foreign student in the Netherlands, she met Joost, and they became engaged. After Sally's studies ended, she returned to the United States. Joost stayed behind for a few months, to finish an architecture project. Because citizens of the Netherlands are not required to obtain visas to visit the U.S., Joost simply picked up his passport when he was ready, and flew to New York. He told the border official he was there to visit friends, and was let in. They got married at city hall the next week, and Joost immediately began preparing his green card application. Joost's actions could easily be considered visa fraud. Although technically, Joost would be able to use the adjustment of status procedure—in fact, he would probably have no problem submitting his full green card application—when the time comes for Joost's interview, the USCIS officer may question him closely about whether he intended to apply for the green card when he entered the U.S. If Joost can't come up with a good answer, his application will be denied. (There is a waiver Joost can apply for, with the help of an attorney, but it's hard to get.)

An unbelievable number of married couples make the same mistake that Sally and Joost did. A few get lucky and the immigration official who interviews them simply overlooks the problem. If you wait long enough after your entry to either get married or submit the green card application—hopefully two months, at least—you'll face fewer questions, because USCIS may presume you were thinking your plans over in between. And some people are able to convincingly explain that their intentions when entering the U.S. were truly just to visit (or do whatever their visa was intended for), but while here, they talked it over with their relative (or soon-to-be spouse) and decided that the immigrant should stay and apply for a green card.

2. People Who Entered Legally and Remain Legal

Even if you're not the immediate relative of a U.S. citizen, you're allowed to get a green card using the adjustment of status procedure if you meet all the following criteria:

- You entered the U.S. legally, most likely using a visa (such as a tourist or a student visa) or some other entry document like a border crossing card. There are exceptions, however: You cannot adjust under this rule if you entered using a visa waiver, you entered as a crewman on a boat or plane (regardless of what visa you had), or you were in transit to another country without a visa (for example, changing planes in a U.S. airport).
- You have never been out of legal status (your right to stay hasn't expired).
- You have never worked without INS or USCIS authorization.

Whether or not your permitted stay has expired is an important issue. If you were granted a tourist visa (B-2), for example, the visa itself may be valid for many years and allow multiple entries. However, the important issue is how long the border officials said you could stay on this particular trip. You'll find this information on a small white card called an I-94. If you've overstayed that date, and didn't get any extension or change of status, your status is now illegal, no matter how long your visa is good for. **Note to students:** Your I-94 may not have an expiration date, but may

simply say "D/S," which means "duration of status." In other words, you're allowed to stay in the U.S. as long as you continue your studies (and don't violate the other terms of your student visa).

Working without authorization is also a troublesome issue for many immigrants. Tourist and student visa holders, for example, are frequent violators of the work permit rules (tourists aren't allowed to work at all, and students can work only under limited circumstances).

EXAMPLE: Ahmed and Ali, two brothers age 24 and 26, come to visit their mother in the United States, where she lives as a permanent resident. A month into their six-month stay, their mother's U.S. citizenship finally comes through. Because the mother petitioned for the brothers some years ago, they can use their old Priority Date, and they find that they're immediately eligible for green cards in the family first preference category (see Chapter 9). But can they apply for adjustment of status? They entered legally, and their stay is still legal. However, Ali has picked up a part-time job in a local restaurant. Only Ahmed will be able to adjust status. Ali will have to return home and tried to get his green card through consular processing (where he may face questions about his illegal work).

Another problem that comes up for some applicants is the use of visa fraud to enter the United States. After waiting outside the United States for many years for their Priority Date to become current, many applicants figure they can simply get a visa to the U.S. and submit an adjustment of status application once they're here. Many of them are disappointed to find out they've just committed visa fraud. Again, visas are meant to be used only for the limited purpose of coming to the U.S. for a temporary stay, and your activities on that visa must remain within its purposes—visitor visa holders must act like tourists, student visa holders must act like students, and so on. Although immigration officials will sometimes look the other way, it's best to avoid the problem, stay in your home country, and finish your application through the local consulate.

EXAMPLE: Meijin filed visa petitions for her two children, aged 26 and 28, in the second preference category, many years ago. Their Priority Date finally becomes current, and they receive forms and information from the U.S. consulate in Beijing, China, near where they live. The older child, Guofeng, can't wait—he uses a tourist visa he already happens to have to enter the United States. He tells the border officials in San Francisco he's just coming to sightsee (otherwise they would have turned Guofeng around and sent him home). Guofeng submits a green card application. The application is denied, because Guofeng inappropriately used a tourist visa when his real intention was to stay permanently. His sister, Jinqing, stays home and files her paperwork with the U.S. consulate, and she succeeds in getting an immigrant visa and green card.

Not sure whether you can adjust status under these rules? If you have any doubts at all about whether you qualify to adjust status, consult a qualified immigration attorney. See Chapter 24 for advice on finding a good one.

3. People Who Qualify Under Old Laws

As you've seen, a number of people are barred from adjusting status, including people who entered the United States illegally, people who overstayed their visa or other permitted time, people who worked without authorization, people who entered while in transit without a visa, and crewpeople on planes or boats. However, there are two exceptions that help a few such people, based on changes in the laws over the years.

At one time, a law called "245(i)" allowed all people who were otherwise unable to adjust status to do so by paying a penalty fee. That law is now gone, but a few people who were around when the law was still in effect are allowed to make use of it. You can apply to adjust status under § 245(i) if you either:

- had an approvable visa petition or labor certification filed on your behalf before January 14, 1998 (it doesn't matter whether it was filed by the same person or employer as the one through whom you're now immigrating), or
- you had an approvable visa petition or labor certification filed on your behalf before April 30, 2001, so long as you were physically in the U.S. on December 21, 2000 (again, it doesn't matter whether it was filed by the same person or employer as the one through whom you're now immigrating).

EXAMPLE: Amina's father, a U.S. permanent resident, filed a visa petition on her behalf in 1996. She was in the U.S. on a student visa, but then overstayed her visa after graduation. Unfortunately, although the visa petition was approved, the father died before Amina could complete the green card application process. Amina's brother, a U.S. citizen, then files a visa petition for her. When her Priority Date becomes current (and assuming USCIS hasn't caught and deported her), Amina can use the approval notice from her father's 1996 petition to make her eligible to adjust status in the United States.

There is a financial catch to using these old laws to adjust status, however: You'll have to pay a penalty fee, currently $1,000.

B. People Who Can't Adjust Status at All

If you don't fall into any of these categories described above, you do not qualify to use adjustment of status. This means that someone who only recently became eligible to immigrate—for example, by marrying a U.S. citizen—but who entered the U.S. illegally, and had no visa petitions filed for him or her by any of the important 1998 or 2001 dates, will be ineligible to adjust status.

Unfortunately, this person is in a difficult trap, because if he or she has spent more than 180 days in the U.S. illegally, leaving the U.S. to try to apply through an overseas U.S. consulate could result in being barred from returning for three or ten years. See a lawyer if you're in this or a similar situation.

C. How to File

If you are one of the lucky people who can adjust status in the U.S., a number of picky rules control how and when you can submit your various application forms. Follow them exactly, so that you will be sure that your paperwork can be processed quickly and properly.

1. Whether You Need to Wait for Approval of Form I-130

Most people who are eligible to adjust status can do so only after receiving some official government statement about their basic eligibility for a green card; for example, USCIS approval of their Form I-130 visa petition, a State Department letter indicating they won the lottery, or a grant of political asylum (which can be used as the basis for a green card after one year). However, one exception allows certain applicants applying through family to turn this two-step application process into one step.

If you are the spouse, parent or minor child of an American citizen (an immediate relative), or if you are over 21 years old and the unmarried child of a U.S. citizen and you have maintained your legal status and never worked illegally and your Priority Date is current, then you can file the I-130 and adjustment of status paperwork at the same time. If you've already filed the I-130, file your adjustment application with either the approval or with a request for them to request the pending file be transferred.

If you are applying through a family member but do not match the description in the paragraph above, then your family member must file Form I-130 and accompanying documents at a USCIS Service Center first. (The procedures for I-130 submissions are explained in the various chapters of this book that apply to different types of eligibility for family members.) Only after the I-130 is approved and your Priority Date is current can you continue with your application.

2. Adjustment of Status Forms and Documents

To apply for adjustment of status, you must submit the following forms to USCIS:

❑ **Copy of government document proving your basic green card eligibility.** This might be an approved I-130 visa petition (unless you're a family member who can submit this petition together with the adjustment of status application as described in Section 1, above), a State Department letter notifying you that you've won the lottery, a grant of political asylum or refugee status, or the like. **Note:** If you're applying for registry, you need not have any such government document (see Chapter 16).

❑ **Proof that you're eligible to use the adjustment of status procedure.** What you use as proof depends on the reason you're able to adjust status. For example, if you're an immediate relative who entered the U.S. legally, a copy of your I-94 card from your passport would be sufficient. If you're claiming eligibility because you fall under old laws, you'll need to submit a copy of your old approved I-130 visa petition or labor certification. **Note:** If you're an asylee or refugee, or you're applying for registry, or you entered the U.S. on a fiancé visa (K-1, K-2, K-3, or K-4) and got married or met your other visa requirements, you don't need to worry about this; you're eligible to adjust status.

❑ **Form I-485, Application to Register Permanent Resident or Adjust Status.** This is the primary form used to adjust status, which collects information on who you are, where you live, and how you're eligible for a green card.

❑ **Form I-485 Supplement A.** Use this form only if you're applying to adjust status based on old laws (245(i)). Also remember to pay the penalty fee.

❑ **If you want permission to work: Form I-765.** Several months may pass before you're approved for a green card, during which time you can't work without getting permission. Use this form to ask permission (and don't forget to pay the fee that goes with it). You'll be given an Employment Authorization Document (EAD), which is an identification card with your photo. Even if you don't plan to work, this card is a handy way to prove who you are.

❑ **Form G-325A, Biographic Information.** This form gives the information on where you have lived and worked since you were 16 years old, for background investigation. (See the sample at the end of Chapter 7.)

❑ **Form I-864, Affidavit of Support.** (See the sample in Chapter 19.) If you're applying through a family member (not an employer or as an asylee or refugee), you must submit this sworn statement from the petitioner (a U.S. citizen or lawful permanent resident who is sponsoring you) who has sufficient income and who promises to support you and to refund the U.S. government certain types of public benefits if you must receive public assistance after receiving your permanent residence. Certain exceptions apply, however. You need not submit a Form I-864 if either the immigrant or the immigrant's spouse or parent has already worked in the U.S. for 40 quarters as defined by the Social Security system—about ten years. Nor do you need to submit the Form I-864 if the beneficiary is a child (adopted or natural born) who will become a U.S. citizen automatically upon entering the U.S. If you're exempt from the Affidavit of Support requirement due to one of these exceptions, you should fill out Form I-864W instead of the regular Form I-864. The latest year's tax returns (or IRS transcripts) of the citizen or permanent resident should be attached to the affidavit as proof of financial capacity (or up to three years' worth if it will strengthen your case). Proof of the sponsor's employment should also be attached. If your petitioner doesn't earn enough to meet the government requirements, you'll have to find an additional financial sponsor or another member of the sponsor's household who can add income and/or assets to the mix. If, on the other hand, you are the only person that your petitioner is sponsoring, and your petitioner can meet the sponsorship requirements based upon his or her income alone, he or she can use a shorter version of the form, called I-864EZ.

❑ **Job letter.** If you are working, you can submit a job letter from your employer in the United States stating your work history, when you started to work, whether your employment is permanent, and how much you earn along with a payroll statement showing your earnings.

If you are applying for a green card based on marriage, the job letter must include your marital status, name of spouse, and name and telephone number of person to be notified in case of an emergency.

Sample Job Letter

ABC Company
123 Main Street
Anytown, Anystate 12345

April 24, 200_
U.S. Citizenship and Immigration Services
26 Federal Plaza
New York, NY 10278

Dear Sir or Madam:

This letter is to certify that Jon Fratellanza has been employed by this company since March 2002 as a widget inspector.

His salary is $850/week and he is employed on a full-time, permanent basis. His prospects for continued employment with this company are excellent.

Our personnel records indicate that this employee is married. In case of emergency, his spouse, Danielle Fratellanza, must be notified at their home telephone: 111/222-3456. [Use this type of paragraph in a family-based application.]

Sincerely,

Milton Mutter

Milton Mutter
Personnel Director, ABC Company

❑ **Form I-693, Medical Examination of Aliens Seeking Adjustment of Status.** This must be filled out by a USCIS-approved doctor and submitted in an unopened envelope.

❑ **If you're applying as an asylee or refugee.** Proof that you've been physically present in the U.S. for at least a year, such as a letter verifying your employment, an apartment lease, or school records. You'll also need

to include evidence of any trips you've made outside the U.S. since gaining asylum. (Remember, if you've made any trips to the country from which you claimed asylum or refugee status, you've cancelled your eligibility and should see a lawyer.)

❑ **If you're applying as an asylee or refugee.** A copy of your birth certificate.

❑ **If you're applying for registry.** Proof that you have been in the U.S. since January 1, 1972, as described in Chapter 16.

❑ **Two color photographs.** They must be taken in passport style.

❑ **Filing fee.** USCIS charges fees for handling applications, based on which forms you submit. They regularly raise the fees, so check with USCIS for the latest before you turn in your application. As of the date that this book went to print, the fee to file Form I-485 is $325 if the petitioner is 14 years old or over, $225 if under 14 years old. Pay by money order or certified check made payable to DHS or USCIS. In addition, if you file Form I-485 Supp. A, you'll have to pay the penalty fee of $1,000 (see Section A). If you apply for a work permit (Form I-765), the fee is $180. Fingerprints ("biometrics") are an additional $70.

3. Submission Procedures

The procedures for submitting an adjustment of status application have changed a lot in recent years. In the past, you could ordinarily walk your application right into a local USCIS office. Now, however, you'll most likely have to mail your application to a service center or an out-of-state processing office. See the chart below for the appropriate address.

If you're applying based on:	Send your adjustment of status application to:
either a family relationship (for example, you're the spouse, widow, parent, or child of a U.S. citizen, or the spouse or child of a U.S. permanent resident); as the battered spouse or child with an approved Form I-360 petition; as a winner of the diversity visa lottery; as someone eligible for registry; as a Cuban adjustment applicant; or as an Amerasian	U.S. Citizenship and Immigration Services, P.O. Box 805887, Chicago, IL 60680-4120 (if you're using the U.S. Postal Service) or U.S. Citizenship and Immigration Services, 427 S. LaSalle, 3rd Floor, Chicago, IL 60605-1098 (if you're using a private delivery service instead of the U.S. Postal Service).
If you're applying based on: having held political asylum for at least one year	**Send your adjustment of status application to:** USCIS Nebraska Service Center, P.O. Box 87485, Lincoln, NE 68501-7485
If you're applying based on: having had refugee status for at least one year	**Send your adjustment of status application to:** USCIS Nebraska Service Center, P.O. Box 87485, Lincoln, NE 68501-7485

Travel Outside the U.S. Is Restricted

You or your minor children should not leave the United States while waiting for your adjustment of status interview without first applying for and receiving advance permission to reenter the United States. This is called "Advance Parole." You can apply for Advance Parole when you file your adjustment of status application or later, by submitting Form I-131 to the office handling your file. You must pay a fee (currently $170).

If you leave without this permission, USCIS will cancel your adjustment of status application. It will assume that your departure shows your lack of interest in receiving your green card in the United States and that you have abandoned your application.

Note that if you have been out of status for 180 days or more after April 1, 1997 before filing your green card application, you should not travel until your application is approved. In this case, according to USCIS interpretation, you must wait for three years to return to the United States—or ten years if you were out of status for over one year. Not even an Advance Parole document will protect you.

D. After You Apply

After you've submitted your adjustment of status application, USCIS should send you a receipt notice. This will confirm that your application contained everything it should have, and that you're now in line for an adjustment of status interview. If your application was incomplete, you will receive a letter indicating what's missing, and you should reply as soon as possible.

How long you'll have to wait for your adjustment of status interview depends on how backed up your local USCIS office is. (These interviews are held locally, at a different office than you submitted your application to.) Some months before your interview is scheduled, you'll be called in to have your fingerprints taken for your security checks.

During this wait, it's best not to take any long trips or move to a different address. USCIS won't give you much advance notice of your interview date.

E. Interview and Approval

Although USCIS makes some exceptions, it requires most applicants to attend an interview at a local USCIS office before approving them for permanent residence and a green card. You'll get a letter advising you of the interview date and location, and telling you what to bring along (normally a photo identification; originals of your birth certificate, passport, visas, and other documents you've submitted copies of in connection with your application, for the USCIS officer to view, not keep; and documents showing any changes in the information on your application, such as a new employer). If you're applying based on marriage, you'll also need to bring documents proving that your marriage is the real thing, such as copies of your home mortgage or lease, joint credit card statements, children's birth certificates, and more.

When bringing new documents, be sure to make copies of any that you don't want to leave with USCIS—they're usually happy with copies, particularly if they can view the original when you bring it. They're unwilling, however, to make photocopies for you, so you must either bring a copy or lose your original to the USCIS file.

If you don't speak English, you'll need to bring your own interpreter. You don't need to spend money on a professional—a friend or family member over 18 and a legal U.S. resident will do. But it's worth spending the money if you don't know anyone who's truly fluent in both English and your native language—your future is at stake here, and a little confusion may delay or destroy your hopes of getting a green card.

Arrive on time—then be prepared to wait.
Leave extra time for parking and passing through the security guard post at the USCIS office. Remember, this is a federal government building, so they'll X-ray your possessions and confiscate pocket knives or other illegal materials. If you arrive late, you will probably lose your chance to be interviewed that day, and go through major hassles getting USCIS to reschedule you.

At your interview, a USCIS officer will review your application, ask you some questions, and presumably approve you for a green card. Most of the questions will relate to what's already on your application, such as your current address, how you last entered the United States, and whether you have a criminal record or are otherwise ineligible for a green card. If you're applying based on marriage, be prepared to answer additional questions to prove that your marriage is the real thing, such as how you met, details of your wedding, and details about your house and your life together. Most interviews last about 20 minutes.

Answer the questions courteously and honestly—but don't volunteer extra information. Saying too much wastes the officer's time and may bring to light information that would have been better left unsaid.

If everything is in order, your application for adjustment of status should be approved. Your passport may be stamped with a temporary approval, good for one year, authorizing you to stay in the United States. If you are not approved at your interview, you will later be notified of the approval and requested to bring your passport to the nearest USCIS office.

Your green card—which is actually pink—will be sent by mail to your address in several weeks or months. Be sure to inform USCIS of any change of address, because your green card might not be forwarded to you by the post office. Even after you get your green card, you are obligated to send USCIS written word every time your address changes—see Chapter 23 for this and other important rules on keeping your right to a green card.

It's wonderful! You are now a lawful permanent resident who is authorized to work and stay in the United States legally.

⚠ **If your application is denied, consult an experienced immigration attorney.** Unless you have some other visa or legal status in the United States, your file will be transferred to the Immigration Court for removal proceedings. See Chapter 24 for advice on finding a good attorney.

Interview Tips for Spouses

If you are requesting an adjustment of status as the spouse of a U.S. citizen or permanent resident, USCIS will require a personal interview with you both before granting your application.

Bring copies of all the forms relevant to your application, along with evidence of a bona-fide marriage—such as wedding pictures. (See Chapter 7.)

If you've got solid documentary evidence of your real marriage, the officer is likely to ask only a few questions. If, on the other hand, the documents are weak or you and your spouse don't seem able to answer the questions about your marriage, you may be sent for what's called a "fraud interview." This means that you and your spouse will each separately meet with a different USCIS officer, who will ask each of you the same set of questions, and then check whether your answers match up. If you don't already have an attorney, this is a good time to ask that the interview be postponed, so that you can return with legal help.

Application to Register Permanent Resident or Adjust Status, Sample Form I-485 (page 1)

OMB No. 1615-0023; Expires 09/30/08

Department of Homeland Security
U.S. Citizenship and Immigration Services

**I-485, Application to Register
Permanent Residence or Adjust Status**

START HERE - Please type or print in black ink.

Part 1.   Information about you.

Family Name	Given Name	Middle Name
Michelski	Anda	M.

Address- C/O
Grun Michela

Street Number and Name	68 Watertown Boulevard	Apt. # 12

City
Erie

State	Zip Code
Pennsylvania	19380

Date of Birth *(mm/dd/yyyy)*	Country of Birth: Bulgaria
06/28/1978	Country of Citizenship/Nationality: Bulgaria

U.S. Social Security #	A # *(if any)*
128-46-9255	

Date of Last Arrival *(mm/dd/yyyy)*	I-94 #
11/04/2005	123 123 123

Current USCIS Status	Expires on *(mm/dd/yyyy)*
B-1	05/1/2006

For USCIS Use Only

Returned	Receipt

Resubmitted	

Reloc Sent

Reloc Rec'd

Applicant Interviewed

Part 2.   Application type. *(Check one.)*

I am applying for an adjustment to permanent resident status because:

a. ☑ an immigrant petition giving me an immediately available immigrant visa number has been approved. (Attach a copy of the approval notice, or a relative, special immigrant juvenile or special immigrant military visa petition filed with this application that will give you an immediately available visa number, if approved.)

b. ☐ my spouse or parent applied for adjustment of status or was granted lawful permanent residence in an immigrant visa category that allows derivative status for spouses and children.

c. ☐ I entered as a K-1 fiancé(e) of a United States citizen whom I married within 90 days of entry, or I am the K-2 child of such a fiancé(e). (Attach a copy of the fiancé(e) petition approval notice and the marriage certificate.)

d. ☐ I was granted asylum or derivative asylum status as the spouse or child of a person granted asylum and am eligible for adjustment.

e. ☐ I am a native or citizen of Cuba admitted or paroled into the United States after January 1, 1959, and thereafter have been physically present in the United States for at least one year.

f. ☐ I am the husband, wife or minor unmarried child of a Cuban described above in (e) and I am residing with that person, and was admitted or paroled into the United States after January 1, 1959, and thereafter have been physically present in the United States for at least one year.

g. ☐ I have continuously resided in the United States since before January 1, 1972.

h. ☐ Other basis of eligibility. Explain. If additional space is needed, use a separate piece of paper.

I am already a permanent resident and am applying to have the date I was granted permanent residence adjusted to the date I originally arrived in the United States as a nonimmigrant or parolee, or as of May 2, 1964, whichever date is later, and: *(Check one.)*

i. ☐ I am a native or citizen of Cuba and meet the description in (e) above.

j. ☐ I am the husband, wife or minor unmarried child of a Cuban, and meet the description in (f) above.

Section of Law
☐ Sec. 209(b), INA
☐ Sec. 13, Act of 9/11/57
☐ Sec. 245, INA
☐ Sec. 249, INA
☐ Sec. 1 Act of 11/2/66
☐ Sec. 2 Act of 11/2/66
☐ Other

Country Chargeable

Eligibility Under Sec. 245
☐ Approved Visa Petition
☐ Dependent of Principal Alien
☐ Special Immigrant
☐ Other

Preference

Action Block

To be Completed by
Attorney or Representative, **if any**
☐ Fill in box if G-28 is attached to represent the applicant.
VOLAG #

ATTY State License #

Form I-485 (Rev. 04/01/06)Y

Sample Form I-485 (page 2)

Part 3. Processing information.

A. City/Town/Village of Birth	Current Occupation
Sofia	Language teacher

Your Mother's First Name	Your Father's First Name
Anastasia	Liski

Give your name exactly as it appears on your Arrival/Departure Record (Form I-94)

Anda Michelski

Place of Last Entry Into the United States *(City/State)*	In what status did you last enter? *(Visitor, student, exchange alien, crewman, temporary worker, without inspection, etc.)*
JFK Airport, New York	
Were you inspected by a U.S. Immigration Officer? ☑ Yes ☐ No	Visitor

Nonimmigrant Visa Number	Consulate Where Visa Was Issued
1062745139652	Sofia

Date Visa Was Issued (mm/dd/yyyy) 7/2/2004	Gender: ☐ Male ☑ Female	Marital Status: ☐ Married ☑ Single ☐ Divorced ☐ Widowed

Have you ever before applied for permanent resident status in the U.S.?   ☑ No   ☐ Yes. If you checked "Yes," give date and place of filing and final disposition.

B. List your present husband/wife, all of your sons and daughters (If you have none, write "none." If additional space is needed, use separate paper).

Family Name	Given Name	Middle Initial	Date of Birth *(mm/dd/yyyy)*
Country of Birth	Relationship	A #	Applying with you? ☐ Yes ☐ No
Family Name	Given Name	Middle Initial	Date of Birth *(mm/dd/yyyy)*
Country of Birth	Relationship	A #	Applying with you? ☐ Yes ☐ No
Family Name	Given Name	Middle Initial	Date of Birth *(mm/dd/yyyy)*
Country of Birth	Relationship	A #	Applying with you? ☐ Yes ☐ No
Family Name	Given Name	Middle Initial	Date of Birth *(mm/dd/yyyy)*
Country of Birth	Relationship	A #	Applying with you? ☐ Yes ☐ No
Family Name	Given Name	Middle Initial	Date of Birth *(mm/dd/yyyy)*
Country of Birth	Relationship	A #	Applying with you? ☐ Yes ☐ No

C. List your present and past membership in or affiliation with every organization, association, fund, foundation, party, club, society or similar group in the United States or in other places since your 16th birthday. Include any foreign military service in this part. If none, write "none." Include the name(s) of organization(s), location(s), dates of membership, from and to, and the nature of the organization(s). If additional space is needed, use a separate piece of paper.

None

Sample Form I-485 (page 3)

Part 3. Processing information. *(Continued)*

Please answer the following questions. (If your answer is **"Yes"** on any one of these questions, explain on a separate piece of paper. Answering **"Yes"** does not necessarily mean that you are not entitled to adjust status or register for permanent residence.)

1. Have you ever, in or outside the United States:

    a. knowingly committed any crime of moral turpitude or a drug-related offense for which you have not been arrested? ☐ Yes ☒ No

    b. been arrested, cited, charged, indicted, fined or imprisoned for breaking or violating any law or ordinance, excluding traffic violations? ☐ Yes ☒ No

    c. been the beneficiary of a pardon, amnesty, rehabilitation decree, other act of clemency or similar action? ☐ Yes ☒ No

    d. exercised diplomatic immunity to avoid prosecution for a criminal offense in the United States? ☐ Yes ☒ No

2. Have you received public assistance in the United States from any source, including the United States government or any state, county, city or municipality (other than emergency medical treatment), or are you likely to receive public assistance in the future? ☐ Yes ☒ No

3. Have you ever:

    a. within the past ten years been a prostitute or procured anyone for prostitution, or intend to engage in such activities in the future? ☐ Yes ☒ No

    b. engaged in any unlawful commercialized vice, including, but not limited to, illegal gambling? ☐ Yes ☒ No

    c. knowingly encouraged, induced, assisted, abetted or aided any alien to try to enter the United States illegally? ☐ Yes ☒ No

    d. illicitly trafficked in any controlled substance, or knowingly assisted, abetted or colluded in the illicit trafficking of any controlled substance? ☐ Yes ☒ No

4. Have you ever engaged in, conspired to engage in, or do you intend to engage in, or have you ever solicited membership or funds for, or have you through any means ever assisted or provided any type of material support to any person or organization that has ever engaged or conspired to engage in sabotage, kidnapping, political assassination, hijacking or any other form of terrorist activity? ☐ Yes ☒ No

5. Do you intend to engage in the United States in:

    a. espionage? ☐ Yes ☒ No

    b. any activity a purpose of which is opposition to, or the control or overthrow of, the government of the United States, by force, violence or other unlawful means? ☐ Yes ☒ No

    c. any activity to violate or evade any law prohibiting the export from the United States of goods, technology or sensitive information? ☐ Yes ☒ No

6. Have you ever been a member of, or in any way affiliated with, the Communist Party or any other totalitarian party? ☐ Yes ☒ No

7. Did you, during the period from March 23, 1933 to May 8, 1945, in association with either the Nazi Government of Germany or any organization or government associated or allied with the Nazi Government of Germany, ever order, incite, assist or otherwise participate in the persecution of any person because of race, religion, national orgin or political opinion? ☐ Yes ☒ No

8. Have you ever engaged in genocide, or otherwise ordered, incited, assisted or otherwise participated in the killing of any person because of race, religion, nationality, ethnic origin or political opinion? ☐ Yes ☒ No

9. Have you ever been deported from the United States, or removed from the United States at government expense, excluded within the past year, or are you now in exclusion, deportation, removal or recission proceedings? ☐ Yes ☒ No

10. Are you under a final order of civil penalty for violating section 274C of the Immigration and Nationality Act for use of fraudulent documents or have you, by fraud or willful misrepresentation of a material fact, ever sought to procure, or procured, a visa, other documentation, entry into the United States or any immigration benefit? ☐ Yes ☒ No

11. Have you ever left the United States to avoid being drafted into the U.S. Armed Forces? ☐ Yes ☒ No

12. Have you ever been a J nonimmigrant exchange visitor who was subject to the two-year foreign residence requirement and have not yet complied with that requirement or obtained a waiver? ☐ Yes ☒ No

13. Are you now withholding custody of a U.S. citizen child outside the United States from a person granted custody of the child? ☐ Yes ☒ No

14. Do you plan to practice polygamy in the United States? ☐ Yes ☒ No

---

Sample Form I-485 (page 4)

Part 4.   Signature.   *(Read the information on penalties in the instructions before completing this section. You must file this application while in the United States.)*

Your registration with U.S. Citizenship and Immigration Services.

"I understand and acknowledge that, under section 262 of the Immigration and Nationality Act (Act), as an alien who has been or will be in the United States for more than 30 days, I am required to register with U.S. Citizenship and Immigration Services. I understand and acknowledge that, under section 265 of the Act, I am required to provide USCIS with my current address and written notice of any change of address within **ten** days of the change. I understand and acknowledge that USCIS will use the most recent address that I provide to USCIS, on any form containing these acknowledgements, for all purposes, including the service of a Notice to Appear should it be necessary for USCIS to initiate removal proceedings against me. I understand and acknowledge that if I change my address without providing written notice to USCIS, I will be held responsible for any communications sent to me at the most recent address that I provided to USCIS. I further understand and acknowledge that, if removal proceedings are initiated against me and I fail to attend any hearing, including an initial hearing based on service of the Notice to Appear at the most recent address that I provided to USCIS or as otherwise provided by law, I may be ordered removed in my absence, arrested and removed from the United States."

Selective Service Registration.

The following applies to you if you are a male at least 18 years old, but not yet 26 years old, who is required to register with the Selective Service System: "I understand that my filing this adjustment of status application with U.S. Citizenship and Immigration Services authorizes USCIS to provide certain registration information to the Selective Service System in accordance with the Military Selective Service Act. Upon USCIS acceptance of my application, I authorize USCIS to transmit to the Selective Service System my name, current address, Social Security Number, date of birth and the date I filed the application for the purpose of recording my Selective Service registration as of the filing date. If, however, USCIS does not accept my application, I further understand that, if so required, I am responsible for registering with the Selective Service by other means, provided I have not yet reached age 26."

Applicant's Certification.

I certify, under penalty of perjury under the laws of the United States of America, that this application and the evidence submitted with it is all true and correct. I authorize the release of any information from my records that U.S. Citizenship and Immigration Services (USCIS) needs to determine eligibility for the benefit I am seeking.

Signature	*Print Your Name*	*Date*	*Daytime Phone Number*
Anda Michelski	Anda Michelski	5/19/06	(314) 276-9440

NOTE: *If you do not completely fill out this form or fail to submit required documents listed in the instructions, you may not be found eligible for the requested document and this application may be denied.*

Part 5.   Signature of person preparing form, if other than above. (sign below)

I declare that I prepared this application at the request of the above person and it is based on all information of which I have knowledge.

Signature	*Print Your Full Name*	*Date*	**Phone Number** *(Include Area Code)*
			( )

Firm Name
and Address   *E-Mail Address (if any)*

Form I-485 (Rev. 04/01/06)Y Page 4

Application for Employment Authorization, Sample Form I-765

OMB No. 1615-0040; Expires 08/31/08

Department of Homeland Security
U.S. Citizenship and Immigration Services

**I-765, Application for
Employment Authorization**

Do not write in this block.

Remarks	Action Block	Fee Stamp
A#		
Applicant is filing under §274a.12 _____		

☐ Application Approved. Employment Authorized / Extended *(Circle One)*   until _____ (Date).
_____ (Date).

Subject to the following conditions: _____
☐ Application Denied.
  ☐ Failed to establish eligibility under 8 CFR 274a.12 (a) or (c).
  ☐ Failed to establish economic necessity as required in 8 CFR 274a.12(c)(14), (18) and 8 CFR 214.2(f)

I am applying for: ☑ Permission to accept employment.
  ☐ Replacement of lost Employment Authorization Document.
  ☐ Renewal of my permission to accept employment *(attach previous Employment Authorization Document).*

1. Name (Family Name in CAPS) (First)   (Middle)
MANZETTI   Julie   Anna

2. Other Names Used (Include Maiden Name)
Juliet Stefano

3. Address in the United States (Number and Street)   (Apt. Number)
280 Mosher Street

(Town or City)   (State/Country)   (ZIP Code)
Baltimore   Maryland   21216

4. Country of Citizenship/Nationality
Italy

5. Place of Birth (Town or City)   (State/Province)   (Country)
Verona   Italy

6. Date of Birth (mm/dd/yyyy)   **7.** Gender
12/23/1962   ☐ Male ☑ Female

8. Marital Status   ☑ Married   ☐ Single
  ☐ Widowed   ☐ Divorced

9. U.S. Social Security Number (Include all numbers you have ever used, if any)
none

10. Alien Registration Number (A-Number) or I-94 Number (if any)
A45678910

11. Have you ever before applied for employment authorization from USCIS?
☐ Yes (If yes, complete below)   ☑ No
Which USCIS Office?   Date(s)

Results (Granted or Denied - attach all documentation)

12. Date of Last Entry into the U.S.   (mm/dd/yyyy)
09/01/2005

13. Place of Last Entry into the U.S.
New York, New York

14. Manner of Last Entry (Visitor, Student, etc.)
Parolee

15. Current Immigration Status (Visitor, Student, etc.)
Parolee

16. Go to **Part 2** of the Instructions, Eligibility Categories. In the space below place the letter and number of the category you selected from the instructions. (For example, (a)(8); (c)(17)(iii); etc.)

Eligibility under 8 CFR 274a.12
(   ) (c) (9)

Certification.

Your Certification: I certify, under penalty of perjury under the laws of the United States of America, that the foregoing is true and correct. Furthermore, I authorize the release of any information that U.S. Citizenship and Immigration Services needs to determine eligibility for the benefit I am seeking. I have read the Instructions in **Part 2** and have identified the appropriate eligibility category in **Block 16.**

Signature	Telephone Number	Date
Juliet Manzetti	(301) 123-4567	May 25, 2006

Signature of person preparing form, if other than above: I declare that this document was prepared by me at the request of the applicant and is based on all information of which I have any knowledge.

Print Name	Address	Signature	Date

Remarks	Initial Receipt	Resubmitted	Relocated		Completed		
			Rec'd	Sent	Approved	Denied	Returned

f

Form I-765 (Rev. 04/01/06)Y

Consular Processing

Leaving the U.S. to Get a Green Card

The second type of government procedure for getting a green card (other than adjustment of status) is "consular processing." It means that the immigrant goes to a U.S. embassy or consulate to complete his or her green card application. Only after the consulate interviews and approves the immigrant for an immigrant visa can he or she enter the United States and claim permanent resident status.

Most immigrants will have no choice but to use consular processing as their application method. Immigrants who are overseas are almost all required to use consular processing, though many would love to enter the U.S. and finish their application there. However, with the exception of fiancés and people immigrating based on marriage (who can use a K-3 fiancé visa to enter the U.S. and then adjust status) most immigrants will only get themselves in trouble (for example, accused of visa fraud) if they try to enter the U.S. to finish their green card application.

Immigrants who are already in the United States may be required to use consular processing if they are not eligible to use the adjustment of status procedure described in Chapter 18. Unfortunately, this lack of choice creates a trap for immigrants who have lived illegally in the U.S. for 180 days or more. By leaving the U.S., they become subject to penalties for their illegal stay. Even if they otherwise qualify for a green card, the consulate must, under the law, bar them from reentering the U.S. for three years (if their illegal stay was between 180 days and one year) or ten years (for illegal stays over one year). See an attorney if you're in this situation—there is a waiver you can apply for, but it's hard to get approved.

This chapter will discuss the paperwork and other requirements involved in consular processing.

Remember, this chapter discusses only procedures, not your underlying eligibility for a green card. Unless you've already completed the steps explained in another chapter—most likely one describing family- or lottery-based visas—you shouldn't be in this chapter. It's only for people with approved visa petitions or winning lottery letters who are now completing their green card application process.

If You Have a Choice of Procedure

While the requirements for adjustment of status (getting a green card at a USCIS office) are rather restrictive, if you qualify, there are a number of advantages to that procedure over consular processing. If you are currently in the U.S., read Chapter 18 carefully to see whether you qualify to get a green card through adjustment of status.

A. How Your Case Gets to the Consulate

When your relative filled out your visa petition, or when you filled out your lottery application, your address or other information will have indicated to the U.S. government which consulate would be most convenient for you. After your visa petition has been approved or you've won the lottery, a central office known as the National Visa Center (NVC) will take care of transferring your file to the appropriate consulate. (Remember that if you're not an immediate relative but a "preference relative," you may have to wait several years before your Priority Date becomes current and your case is transferred to a consulate—see Chapter 5 for details.)

A lot has to happen, however, before the NVC transfers your case. First, the NVC will send you an Agent of Choice and Address form (DS-3032). This is a very simple form, indicating whether you have an attorney or not. You'll need to send this back to continue the process.

At the same time, if you're immigrating through a family member, the NVC will send that person a bill for processing the Affidavit of Support (Form I-864). (This is the form in which your family member promises to support you if necessary.) Again, that person will need to pay the bill (currently $70) for the process to continue.

After the NVC receives your Form DS-3032, it will send you a bill for the immigrant visa processing fee (currently $335 plus a $45 surcharge for security services).

Once you've paid this fee, the NVC will send you an instruction packet, including some forms for you to fill out and return to the NVC. Only after you've filled out and returned these forms (as described below) will your case be transferred to the U.S. consulate.

B. Forms and Documents You'll Need to Mail

Included in your instruction packet from the National Visa Center will be Form DS-2001, Notification of Applicant(s) Readiness (formerly "OF-169"), and Form DS-230 Part I, Application for Immigrant Visa and Alien Registration. Form DS-2001 is very short, simply asking you to confirm that you've prepared the various documents (such as your passport, photographs, and evidence of financial support) on the checklist that's in your instruction packet. Don't send these items in! Your statement that you've prepared these items is taken as a sign that you're ready for a visa interview as soon as it can be scheduled—and that you'll bring these various items with you.

The first part of Form DS-230 asks for information about your family and personal history, your past and present residences, places

of employment, and your membership in any organizations. Answer all questions as accurately as possible. (See the samples at the end of this chapter.)

Complete and mail these forms as soon as possible. Once the forms are received, government officers will begin a background security check.

If You're in the U.S. Now

Many people try to stay in the United States while they are waiting to be called for consular processing. But if you have no separate immigration status, then you are not entitled to work in the United States—and staying here is a violation of the law. You run the risk of being deported if USCIS decides to start removal proceedings against you (though they are likely to do so only if they happen to catch you, for example, in a workplace raid). And, if you have been in the United States for more than 180 days without USCIS permission, you could be prevented from reentering the United States for three years after you leave. If you spend one or more years out of status, you may not be eligible to return for ten years. In either case, you may require a lawyer and should consult Chapter 24.

C. Forms and Documents You'll Bring to Your Interview

Some of the forms and documents that you'll need to bring to your visa interview you should begin preparing right away (technically, before you send in Form DS-2001, though many people send the form in first anyway). These include the following, plus any others that the consulate specifically requests of you:

❏ current passports for you and for everyone in your family who is getting an immigrant visa (they must not expire earlier than six months after your interview date)

❏ birth certificates for you and for your spouse or children, with English translations

❏ a police clearance certificate for each person over 16 years of age from every country in which the person has lived for more than six months

❏ marriage certificate, death certificate, divorce or annulment decree—whichever shows your current marital status

❏ military record of any service in your country, or any country, including certified proof of military service and of honorable or dishonorable discharge

❏ certified copy of court and prison records if you have been convicted of a crime

❏ evidence of your own assets, including titles or deeds to any real estate, condominium, or co-op apartment, or bank account statements to show that you are not destitute and will not be a financial burden to the U.S. government

❏ if you are immigrating through a family petition, a job letter from your petitioner's employer in the United States that gives their work history and salary, and explains whether the employment is permanent (see the sample in Chapter 18), and

❏ Form I-864, I-864EZ, or Form I-134, both of them called Affidavit of Support. (See the samples of Form I-864 and I-134 at the end of this chapter. Notice that in our sample Form I-864, the sponsor didn't have enough income, and therefore had to add a Form I-864A in which his daughter, who lives with him, also promised to add her income to help the immigrant.) Which form you must submit depends on your situation. You must file Form I-864 if your petition is family-based (except K-1 fiancé visas). But if you are the only person that your petitioner is sponsoring, and your petitioner can meet

the sponsorship requirements based upon his or her income alone, he or she can use a shorter version of the form, called I-864EZ. On both Form 1-134 and I-864, a U.S. citizen or permanent resident promises to repay the U.S. government if you become impoverished and go on public assistance after you arrive in the United States. Your sponsor who fills out the form must also include financial documents, including an employer letter or other proof of income, his or her latest U.S. income tax returns and W-2s (or your sponsor can submit the last three years' returns, if it will strengthen his or her case), and bank statements or other proof of assets. In certain exceptional cases, however, a Form I-864 need not be filed. One of these is where the beneficiary is a child (adopted or natural born) who will become a U.S. citizen automatically upon entering the United States (see Chapter 11 for details). The other is where the beneficiary, or the beneficiary's spouse or parent, has worked 40 "quarters" (about ten years, as defined by the Social Security Administration) in the United States. If you're exempt from the Affidavit of Support requirement due to one of these exceptions, you should fill out Form I-864W instead of the regular Form I-864.

You will also be required to submit to fingerprinting, for a background check by the FBI and CIA. (See Chapter 22, Section F.)

You can begin assembling the rest of your interview materials after you receive from the consulate a final packet, which gives you the date of your interview with the chief of the Immigrant Visa Branch. On this form, you will also be directed to where you must go to get a required medical examination. During that exam, your blood will be tested and you will be X-rayed. You may be barred from immigrating if these tests show that you have a contagious disease of public health concern such as AIDS or tuberculosis, or if you have a severe mental disorder.

The remaining interview documents include:

❑ Three color photographs, passport style.

❑ Medical examination report.

❑ Form DS-230 Part II, Application for Immigrant Visa and Alien Registration (Sworn Statement). (See the sample at the end of this chapter.) Each applicant must submit one. After your interview, you must sign it in the presence of the U.S. consular officer.

❑ U.S. income tax returns. All those who have worked in the U.S. and intend to immigrate must present proof that they have filed income tax returns for every year they have worked, as reported on Form OF-230.

❑ Filing fees, if not already paid. The charge for a fiancé visa is $100.

⚠ **Unmarried Children Beware** If you are an unmarried son or daughter of a permanent resident or a U.S. citizen, and you marry before you have your immigration visa interview, be prepared for a shock: Your visa will be denied because you are no longer in the immediate relative or second preference category under which you were petitioned.

If you married after your visa interview but before you entered the U.S. with your immigrant visa, you may also be in serious trouble. Although you may be admitted into the United States because USCIS has no way of knowing that you are no longer eligible, the agency could discover this fact if you later apply to bring your spouse or try to become a U.S. citizen. It will not matter that you have been admitted as a permanent resident.

Removal proceedings will be started against you. You and your spouse will not be reunited in the United States. And you will eventually have to go back to your country and start all over again in the preference category of the married son or daughter of a U.S. citizen. You could completely lose your immigrant eligibility if your parent is only a green cardholder.

If you fall into this category, see an experienced attorney (Chapter 24 offers tips on finding one).

D. Your Visa Interview

The final step in obtaining your visa is to attend an interview with a U.S. consular official. Until the date of your interview, it's quite possible that neither you nor your petitioning spouse or family members (if any) will have had any personal contact with any immigration official. At last, you can deal with a real human being—for better and for worse.

With all the paperwork you've submitted by now, you might wonder why the interview is even necessary. However, the government views the interview as its opportunity to confirm the contents of your application after you've sworn to tell the truth. If you're applying based on marriage, it also allows them to ask personal questions designed to reveal whether your marriage is the real thing or a sham.

If you're being petitioned by a spouse or other family member, they're not required to attend the interview—but it's a good idea. After all, one of the main topics of discussion will be a form your family member filled out—the Affidavit of Support— showing his or her financial situation. If your family member can answer questions and confirm the contents of the affidavit in person, your case will be much stronger. And if yours is a marriage case, your spouse's willingness to travel and be with you at the interview is a good sign that your marriage is not a sham. Some, but not all, consulates also allow you to bring a lawyer, if you feel you need one.

To prepare for your interview, the most important thing is to review all your paperwork. Look at all the questions and answers on all the forms, including any ones that were submitted for you, by your U.S. family member. Though boring, this information is all important to the consular officials. Be alert for any inconsistencies and mistakes, and bring along any documents that will help correct them.

If you're applying through a spouse or fiancé, spend some time with him or her reviewing the details of how you met, how you've corresponded and visited each other or each other's families, and when and why you decided to get married. If already married, review the details of the wedding—number of guests, where it was held, what food and drink was served, and the like.

If you don't live in the same city as the consulate, it's a good idea to get there a few days in advance, particularly for purposes of getting your medical exam and photos done. Arrive early, in case there's a line. Consulates often schedule applicants in large groups, telling them all to arrive at the same time. And be careful of personal security outside the consulate—it's a common place for pickpockets and con artists to hang around. The interview itself will probably last 30 minutes.

Tips for the Interview

The most important thing to do is relax. Wear conservative but comfortable clothes. The interviewer will ask you only about information you have already given in response to questions on your immigration forms and other documents.

Answer all questions truthfully. If you cannot understand a question, be brave and ask for an interpreter. It is better to be embarrassed about not understanding English very well than to be denied your immigrant visa because you misunderstood the question.

E. Approval of Your Immigrant Visa

If everything is in order, if you have all the documents required, and if you are not inadmissible according to immigration law—you have no criminal record, terrorist affiliations or communicable disease, for example—your application for an immigrant visa should be approved.

You will be given a final document, your Immigrant Visa and Alien Registration, which bears your photograph and a stamp of approval. You will also be given your original Form DS-230,

supporting documents, and your X-rays. You will carry all these documents with you during your trip to the United States and give them to immigration authorities when you arrive.

Your immigrant visa is valid for six months, and you must arrive in the United States within those six months.

If you are unable to leave for the United States and your visa is about to expire, you may apply for an extension of your immigrant visa by means of an affidavit, or written statement signed before a notary public, explaining why you are unable to leave on time. But unless you have a very good reason, the U.S. Consulate will be reluctant to approve an extension.

F. Arriving in the United States

When you arrive at your U.S. port of entry, the U.S. citizens who were on the plane with you will be admitted in one line, while all the noncitizens will be queuing in another line.

When it is your turn, the immigration officer will take your immigrant documents and keep them—all but your X-rays—and make them part of your permanent record in the USCIS office. Your passport will be stamped to show that you have entered as a lawful permanent resident, and your Form I-94, Record of Arrival and Departure, will be stamped with an employment authorization, good for six months from your date of entry.

Your green card will be mailed to you within several weeks to months. You must inform USCIS if you change addresses, using Form AR-11, available in this book (but see the USCIS website for full instructions). You must tell them within ten days of your move or you can be deported. Besides, if you don't tell them, you may not receive your green card until you have made several trips to the USCIS office and filled out countless forms. See Chapter 23 for more information on keeping your right to a green card.

At last! You are now a bona fide immigrant—able to live and work legally in the United States. Welcome.

Notification of Applicant(s) Readiness, Sample Form DS-2001 (page 1)

FORM DS-2001 It won't be possible to schedule your Immigrant Visa
Appointment until you return this form signed along with the form DS-230 Part 1.

**CONSULATE GENERAL OF THE
UNITED STATES OF AMERICA**
Immigrant Visa Unit
**Av. Pres. Wilson, 147 – Centro
Rio de Janeiro – RJ – 20030-020**
Tel: 21-2292-7117   Fax: 21-2524-1972

www.consuladodoseua-rio.org.br
www.state.gov

Notification of Applicant(s) Readiness - Form DS-2001

Introduction   You, or your agent, may notify United States Consulate listed above that you
are ready for an interview by using this *DS-2001 form*. The form indicates
that you and your family members (if applicable) have obtained all the
necessary documents for the immigrant visa interview.
Note: Please read the *Instructions for the Immigrant Visa Applicants* before
completing this form.

**Document
Requirements**   Please obtain the original documents or certified copies listed in the
*Instructions for
Immigrant Visa Applicants* form, from an appropriate authority for yourself
and each family member who will accompany you to the United States. All
documents that pertain to your petition are required, even if they were
previously submitted to the INS with your petition.

1

Sample Form DS-2001 (page 2)

FORM DS-2001   It won't be possible to schedule your Immigrant Visa Appointment until you return this form signed along with the form DS-230 Part 1.

Signature   Please fill out the information below and sign.

ROM1234567899	Terese Maria Mancini
(Case Number)	(Complete Name-Please type or print)

108 Piazza d'Azeglio

Venice, Italy

(Mailing Address for Appointment Letter)

7/20/06	764-290-7645
(Date)	(Applicant's daytime phone number)
terese@mnm.com	alberto@bobs.com
Beneficiary's e-mail address	Petitioner's e-mail address

Sworn Statement:

I attest that I have all of the documents specified in the *Instructions for Immigrant Visa Applicants* which are applicable in my case, and I am prepared for immigrant visa interview.

Terese M. Mancini

(Applicant's signature – if minor, someone responsible for the minor should sign)

Where to send this form: Please send this form, along with DS-230 Part 1 (for each applicant), to the address of the United States Consulate listed in the heading of this letter.

Co/sep02

Application for Immigrant Visa and Alien Registration, Sample Form DS-230 Part 1 (page 1)

U.S. Department of State

OMB APPROVAL NO. 1405-0015
EXPIRES: 07/31/2007
ESTIMATED BURDEN: 1 HOUR*
(See Page 2)

APPLICATION FOR
IMMIGRANT
VISA AND ALIEN REGISTRATION

PART I - BIOGRAPHIC DATA

INSTRUCTIONS: Complete one copy of this form for yourself and each member of your family, regardless of age, who will immigrate with you. Please print or type your answers to all questions. Mark questions that are **Not Applicable** with "N/A". If there is insufficient room on the form, answer on a separate sheet using the same numbers that appear on the form. Attach any additional sheets to this form.

WARNING: Any false statement or concealment of a material fact may result in your permanent exclusion from the United States.

This form (DS-230 PART I) is the first of two parts. This part, together with Form DS-230 PART II, constitutes the complete Application for Immigrant Visa and Alien Registration.

1. Family Name	First Name	Middle Name
Mancini	Terese	Maria

2. Other Names Used or Aliases *(If married woman, give maiden name)*
   Terese Brabantio

3. Full Name in Native Alphabet *(If Roman letters not used)*
   n/a

4. Date of Birth *(mm-dd-yyyy)*	5. Age	6. Place of Birth		
		(City or town)	*(Province)*	*(Country)*
02/02/1973	33	Venice		Italy

7. Nationality *(If dual national, give both)*	8. Gender	9. Marital Status
Italian	☐ Male ☒ Female	☐ Single *(Never married)* ☒ Married ☐ Widowed ☐ Divorced ☐ Separated

Including my present marriage, I have been married _one_ times.

10. Permanent address in the United States where you intend to live, if known *(street address including zip code)*. Include the name of a person who currently lives there.

800 Broadway
Linderhurst, NY 11757

Telephone number: 212 222-2121

11. Address in the United States where you want your Permanent Resident Card (Green Card) mailed, if different from address in item #10 *(include the name of a person who currently lives there)*.

Telephone number:

12. Your Present Occupation
Freelance writer

13. Present Address *(Street Address) (City or Town) (Province) (Country)*
108 Piazza d'Azeglio
Venice, Italy
Telephone number: Home 764-290-7645   Office   none

14. Name of Spouse *(Maiden or family name)*	First Name	Middle Name
Mancini	Alberto	Ilario

Date *(mm-dd-yyyy)* and place of birth of spouse: 3/30/68, Los Angeles, CA

Address of spouse *(If different from your own)*:
800 Broadway
Linderhurst, NY 11757

Spouse's occupation: cook   Date of marriage *(mm-dd-yyyy)*:

15. Father's Family Name	First Name	Middle Name
Brabantio	Francisco	Noffo

16. Father's Date of Birth *(mm-dd-yyyy)*	Place of Birth	Current Address	If deceased, give year of death
08/02/1951	Venice, Italy	deceased	1989

17. Mother's Family Name at Birth	First Name	Middle Name
Gallo	Magdalena	Alcine

18. Mother's Date of Birth *(mm-dd-yyyy)*	Place of Birth	Current Address	If deceased, give year of death
04/24/1958	Venice, Italy	90 Piazza d'Azeglio, Venice, Italy	

DS-230 Part I
07-2004

**THIS FORM MAY BE OBTAINED FREE AT CONSULAR OFFICES OF THE UNITED STATES OF AMERICA
PREVIOUS EDITIONS OBSOLETE**

Page 1 of 4

Sample Form DS-230 Part 1 (page 2)

---

19. List Names, Dates and Places of Birth, and Addresses of **ALL** Children.

NAME	DATE *(mm-dd-yyyy)*	PLACE OF BIRTH	ADDRESS *(If different from your own)*
Giovana Moreno	6/01/2001	Florence, Italy	

20. List below all places you have lived for at least six months since reaching the age of 16, including places in your country of nationality. Begin with your present residence.

CITY OR TOWN	PROVINCE	COUNTRY	FROM/TO *(mm-yyyy)*
Venice		Italy	1969 present

21a. Person(s) named in 14 and 19 who will accompany you to the United States now.

Giovanna Moreno

21b. Person(s) named in 14 and 19 who will follow you to the United States at a later date.

22. List below all employment for the last ten years.

EMPLOYER	LOCATION	JOB TITLE	FROM/TO *(mm-yyyy)*
Self-employed	108 Piazza d'Azeglio Venice, Italy	Writer	Aug. 1995 present

In what occupation do you intend to work in the United States?_____Writer_____

23. List below all educational institutions attended.

SCHOOL AND LOCATION	FROM/TO *(mm-yyyy)*		COURSE OF STUDY	DEGREE OR DIPLOMA
Venice University, Italy	9/1996	6/2000	Linguistics	B.A.
Venice High School, Italy	9/1992	6/1996		Diploma
Venice Primary School	9/1980	6/1992		Certificate

Languages spoken or read:_____Italian, English_____

Professional associations to which you belong:_____Italian Writer's Guild_____

24. Previous Military Service   ☐ Yes   ☒ No

Branch:_____ Dates *(mm-dd-yyyy)* of Service:_____

Rank/Position:_____ Military Speciality/Occupation:_____

25. List dates of all previous visits to or residence in the United States. *(If never, write "never")* Give type of visa status, if known. Give DHS "A" number if any.

FROM/TO *(mm-yyyy)*	LOCATION	TYPE OF VISA	"A" NO. *(If known)*
Never			

SIGNATURE OF APPLICANT *Terese Mancini*	DATE *(mm-dd-yyyy)* 7/30/2006

Privacy Act and Paperwork Reduction Act Statements

The information asked for on this form is requested pursuant to Section 222 of the Immigration and Nationality Act. The U.S. Department of State uses the facts you provide on this form primarily to determine your classification and eligibility for a U.S. immigrant visa. Individuals who fail to submit this form or who do not provide all the requested information may be denied a U.S. immigrant visa. If you are issued an immigrant visa and are subsequently admitted to the United States as an immigrant, the Department of Homeland Security will use the information on this form to issue you a Permanent Resident Card, and, if you so indicate, the Social Security Administration will use the information to issue you a social security number and card.

*Public reporting burden for this collection of information is estimated to average 1 hour per response, including time required for searching existing data sources, gathering the necessary data, providing the information required, and reviewing the final collection. In accordance with 5 CFR 1320 5(b), persons are not required to respond to the collection of this information unless this form displays a currently valid OMB control number. Send comments on the accuracy of this estimate of the burden and recommendations for reducing it to: U.S. Department of State (A/RPS/DIR) Washington, DC 20520.

DS-230 Part I   **Page 2 of 4**

Affidavit of Support, Sample Form I-134 (page 1)

OMB No. 1615-0014; Exp. 04-30-07

U.S. Department of Homeland Security
Bureau of Citizenship and Immigration Services

I-134, Affidavit of Support

(Answer All Items: Type or Print in Black Ink.)

I, ___Sandra Leah Beach___ residing at ___114 Fulton St., Apt. 6E___
    (Name)   (Street and Number)

___New York___   ___NY___   ___10038___   ___U.S.A.___
(City)   (State)   (Zip Code if in U.S.) (Country)

BEING DULY SWORN DEPOSE AND SAY:

1. I was born on ___12/20/1981___ at ___Horseheads___   ___U.S.A.___
    (Date-mm/dd/yyyy)   (City)   (Country)

If you are **not** a native born United States citizen, answer the following as appropriate:

a. If a United States citizen through naturalization, give certificate of naturalization number _____

b. If a United States citizen through parent(s) or marriage, give citizenship certificate number _____

c. If United States citizenship was derived by some other method, attach a statement of explanation.

d. If a lawfully admitted permanent resident of the United States, give "A" number _____

2. That I am ___25___ years of age and have resided in the United States since (date) ___birth___

3. That this affidavit is executed on behalf of the following person:

Name (Family Name)	(First Name)	(Middle Name)	Gender	Age
Hollis	Nigel	Ian	M	27

Citizen of (Country)	Marital Status	Relationship to Sponsor
United Kingdom	Divorced	Fiancé

Presently resides at (Street and Number)	(City)	(State)	(Country)
123 Limestone Way #7	Penzance	Cornwall	U.K.

Name of spouse and children accompanying or following to join person:

Spouse	Gender	Age	Child		Gender	Age
Child	Gender	Age	Child		Gender	Age
Child	Gender	Age	Child		Gender	Age

4. That this affidavit is made by me for the purpose of assuring the United States Government that the person(s) named in item **3** will not become a public charge in the United States.

5. That I am willing and able to receive, maintain and support the person(s) named in item **3**. That I am ready and willing to deposit a bond, if necessary, to guarantee that such person(s) will not become a public charge during his or her stay in the United States, or to guarantee that the above named person(s) will maintain his or her nonimmigrant status, if admitted temporarily and will depart prior to the expiration of his or her authorized stay in the United States.

6. That I understand this affidavit will be binding upon me for a period of three (3) years after entry of the person(s) named in item **3** and that the information and documentation provided by me may be made available to the Secretary of Health and Human Services and the Secretary of Agriculture, who may make it available to a public assistance agency.

7. That I am employed as or engaged in the business of ___Executive Assistant___ with ___Helport Foundation___
                                                          (Type of Business)   (Name of Concern)

at ___87 W. 57th St.___   ___New York___   ___NY___   ___10039___
   (Street and Number)   (City)   (State)   (Zip Code)

I derive an annual income of *(if self-employed, I have attached a copy of my last income tax return or report of commercial rating concern which I certify to be true and correct to the best of my knowledge and belief. See instructions for nature of evidence of net worth to be submitted.)* $ ___45,000___

I have on deposit in savings banks in the United States $ ___8,000___

I have other personal property, the reasonable value which is $ ___7,500___

Sample Form I-134 (page 2)

I have stocks and bonds with the following market value, as indicated on the attached list, which I certify to be true and correct to the best of my knowledge and belief. $_____0_____

I have life insurance in the sum of $_____0_____

With a cash surrender value of $_____

I own real estate valued at $_____0_____

With mortgage(s) or other encumbrance(s) thereon amounting to $ _____

Which is located at _____

| (Street and Number) | (City) | (State) | (Zip Code) |

8. That the following persons are dependent upon me for support: *(Place an "x" in the appropriate column to indicate whether the person named is **wholly** or **partially** dependent upon you for support.)*

Name of Person	Wholly Dependent	Partially Dependent	Age	Relationship to Me
None				

9. That I have previously submitted affidavit(s) of support for the following person(s). If none, state **"None."**

Name	Date submitted
None	

10. That I have submitted visa petition(s) to the Bureau of Citizenship and Immigration Services (CIS) on behalf of the following person(s). If none, state none.

Name	Relationship	Date submitted
Nigel Ian Hollis	Fiancé	8/2/2006

11. That I ☐ intend ☒ do not intend to make specific contributions to the support of the person(s) named in item **3**. *(If you check "intend," indicate the exact nature and duration of the contributions. For example, if you intend to furnish room and board, state for how long and, if money, state the amount in United States dollars and state whether it is to be given in a lump sum, weekly or monthly, or for how long.)*

_____

_____

_____

Oath or Affirmation of Sponsor

I acknowledge that I have read Part III of the Instructions, Sponsor and Alien Liability, and am aware of my responsibilities as an immigrant sponsor under the Social Security Act, as amended, and the Food Stamp Act, as amended.

I swear (affirm) that I know the contents of this affidavit signed by me and that the statements are true and correct.

Signature of sponsor _____

Subscribed and sworn to (affirmed) before me this _____ **day of** _____, _____

at _____. **My commission expires on** _____

Signature of Officer Administering Oath _____ **Title** _____

If the affidavit is prepared by someone other than the sponsor, please complete the following: I declare that this document was prepared by me at the request of the sponsor and is based on all information of which I have knowledge.

| (Signature) | (Address) | (Date) |

Form I-134 (Rev. 06/17/04)N (Prior versions may be used until 09/30/04) Page 2

Affidavit of Support Under Section 213A of the Act, Sample Form I-864 (page 1)

OMB No. 1615-0075; Expires 09/30/06

**I-864, Affidavit of Support
Under Section 213A of the Act**

Department of Homeland Security
U.S. Citizenship and Immigration Services

Part 1. Basis for filing Affidavit of Support.

1. I, _Albert Ilario Mancini_   ,
am the sponsor submitting this affidavit of support because (Check only one box):

a. ☒ **I am the petitioner. I filed or am filing for the immigration of my relative.**

b. ☐ **I filed an alien worker petition on behalf of the intending immigrant, who is related to me as
my** _____.

c. ☐ **I have an ownership interest of at least 5 percent in** _____,
**which filed an alien worker petition on behalf of the intending immigrant, who is related to
me as my** _____.

d. ☐ **I am the only joint sponsor.**

e. ☐ **I am the** ☐ **first** ☐ **second of two joint sponsors.** *(Check appropriate box.)*

f. ☐ **The original petitioner is deceased. I am the substitute sponsor. I am the intending
immigrant's** _____.

For Government Use Only
This I-864 is from:
☐ the Petitioner
☐ a Joint Sponsor # _____
☐ the Substitute Sponsor
☐ 5% Owner
This I-864:
☐ does not meet the requirements of section 213A.
☐ meets the requirements of section 213A.
Reviewer
Location
Date *(mm/dd/yyyy)*
Number of Affidavits of Support in file: ☐ 1   ☐ 2

Part 2. Information on the principal immigrant.

2. Last Name
   Mancini

First Name   _Terese_   Middle Name   _Maria_

3. Mailing Address Street Number and Name *(Include Apartment Number)*
   108 Piazza D'Azeglio

City _Venice_   State/Province   Zip/Postal Code _99999_   Country _Italy_

4. Country of Citizenship   _Italy_

5. Date of Birth *(mm/dd/yyyy)*   _2-15-979_

6. Alien Registration Number *(if any)*   A- _none_

7. U.S. Social Security Number *(if any)*   _none_

Part 3. Information on the immigrant(s) you are sponsoring.

8. ☒ I am sponsoring the principal immigrant named in Part 2 above.

   ☒ Yes   ☐ No (Applicable only in cases with two joint sponsors)

9. ☒ I am sponsoring the following family members immigrating at the same time or within six months of the principal immigrant named in **Part 2** above. Do not include any relative listed on a separate visa petition.

Name	Relationship to Sponsored Immigrant	Date of Birth *(mm/dd/yyyy)*	A-Number *(if any)*	U.S.Social Security Number *(if any)*
a. Giovana Moreno	daughter	06-01-2001	none	none
b.				
c.				
d.				
e.				

10. Enter the total number of immigrants you are sponsoring on this form from **Part 3**, Items **8** and **9**.   ☐ | 2

Form I-864 (Rev. 01/15/06)N

Sample Form I-864 (page 2)

Part 4. Information on the Sponsor.

11. Name	Last Name Mancini		For Government Use Only
	First Name Albert	Middle Name Ilario	

12. Mailing Address	Street Number and Name *(Include Apartment Number)* 800 Broadway	
	City Lindenhurst	State or Province New York
	Country U.S.	Zip/Postal Code 11757

13. Place of Residence *(if different from mailing address)*	Street Number and Name *(Include Apartment Number)*	
	City	State or Province
	Country	Zip/Postal Code

14. Telephone Number *(Include Area Code or Country and City Codes)*
212-222-2121

15. Country of Domicile
U.S.

16. Date of Birth *(mm/dd/yyyy)*
03-30-1968

17. Place of Birth *(City)* Los Angeles	State or Province CA	Country U.S.

18. U.S. Social Security Number *(Required)*   222 - 22 - 2222

19. Citizenship/Residency

[X] I am a U.S. citizen.

[ ] I am a U.S. national (for joint sponsors only).

[ ] I am a lawful permanent resident. My alien registration number is A-_____

If you checked box (b), (c), (d), (e) or (f) in line 1 on Page 1, you must include proof of your citizen, national, or permanent resident status.

20. Military Service (To be completed by petitioner sponsors only.)

I am currently on active duty in the U.S. armed services.   [ ] Yes   [X] No

Sample Form I-864 (page 3)

Part 5. Sponsor's household size.

For Government Use Only

21. Your Household Size - DO NOT COUNT ANYONE TWICE

Persons you are sponsoring in this affidavit:

a. Enter the number you entered on line 10. ☐ 2

Persons NOT sponsored in this affidavit:

b. Yourself. **1**

c. If you are currently married, enter "1" for your spouse. ☐

d. If you have dependent children, enter the number here. ☐ ☐

e. If you have any other dependents, enter the number here. ☐ ☐

f. If you have sponsored any other persons on an I-864 or I-864 EZ who are now lawful permanent residents, enter the number here. ☐ ☐

g. OPTIONAL: If you have siblings, parents, or adult children with the same principal residence who are combining their income with yours by submitting Form I-864A, enter the number here. ☐ 1

h. Add together lines and enter the number here. **Household Size:** ☐ 4

Part 6. Sponsor's income and employment.

22. I am currently:

a. ☒ Employed as a/an _cook_.

Name of Employer #1 *(if applicable)* _Bob's Diner_.

Name of Employer #2 *(if applicable)* _____.

b. ☐ Self-employed as a/an _____.

c. ☐ Retired from _____ since _____.
        (Company Name)   *(Date)*

d. ☐ Unemployed since _____.
                              (Date)

---

23. My current individual annual income is: $ _20,000_
                                               (See Step-by-Step Instructions)

Sample Form I-864 (page 4)

24. My current annual household income:

    a. List your income from line 23 of this form. $ ___20,000___

    b. **Income you are using from any other person who was counted in your household size,** including, in certain conditions, the intending immigrant. (See step-by-step instructions.) Please indicate name, relationship and income.

Name	Relationship	Current Income
Beatrice Mancini	daughter	$ 46,000
		$
		$
		$

    c. **Total Household Income:** $ ___66,000___
    (Total all lines from 24a and 24b. Will be Compared to Poverty Guidelines--See Form I-864P.)

    d. [X] The persons listed above have completed Form I-864A. I am filing along with this form all necessary Forms I-864A completed by these persons.

    e. [ ] The person listed above, _____, does not need to
                                  (Name)
       complete Form I-864A because he/she is the intending immigrant and has no accompanying dependents.

25. Federal income tax return information.

    [X] I have filed a Federal tax return for each of the three most recent tax years. I have attached the required photocopy or transcript of my Federal tax return for only the most recent tax year.

    My total income (adjusted gross income on IRS Form 1040EZ) as reported on my Federal tax returns for the most recent three years was:

Tax Year		Total Income
2005	*(most recent)*	$ 20,000
2004	*(2nd most recent)*	$ 18,000
2003	*(3rd most recent)*	$ 17,500

    [ ] *(Optional)* I have attached photocopies or transcripts of my Federal tax returns for my second and third most recent tax years.

For Government Use Only

Household Size = _____

Poverty line for year

_____ is:

$ _____

Sample Form I-864 (page 5)

	For Government Use Only
Part 7. Use of assets to supplement income. *(Optional)*	

If your income, or the total income for you and your household, from line 24c exceeds the Federal Poverty Guidelines for your household size, YOU ARE NOT REQUIRED to complete this Part. Skip to Part 8.

Household Size =

_____

26. Your assets *(Optional)*

    a. Enter the balance of all savings and checking accounts. $ _____5,000_____

Poverty line for year

_____ **is:**

    b. Enter the net cash value of real-estate holdings. (Net means current assessed value minus mortgage debt.) $ _____none_____

$ _____

    c. Enter the net cash value of all stocks, bonds, certificates of deposit, and any other assets not already included in lines 26 (a) or (b). $ _____3,000_____

    d. Add together lines 26 a, b and c and enter the number here.   **TOTAL:** $ _____8,000_____

27. Your household member's assets from Form I-864A. *(Optional)*

Assets from Form I-864A, line 12d for

_____. $ _____

(Name of Relative)

28. Assets of the principal sponsored immigrant. *(Optional)*

The principal sponsored immigrant is the person listed in line 2.

    a. Enter the balance of the sponsored immigrant's savings and checking accounts. $ _____

    b. Enter the net cash value of all the sponsored immigrant's real estate holdings. (Net means investment value minus mortgage debt.) $ _____

    c. Enter the current cash value of the sponsored immigrant's stocks, bonds, certificates of deposit, and other assets not included on line a or b. $ _____

    d. Add together lines 28a, b, and c, and enter the number here. $ _____

The total value of all assests, line 29, must equal 5 times (3 times for spouses and children of USCs, or 1 time for orphans to be formally adopted in the U.S.) the difference between the poverty guidelines and the sponsor's household income, line 24c.

29. Total value of assets.

Add together lines 26d, 27 and 28d and enter the number here.   **TOTAL:** $ _____8,000_____

Sample Form I-864 (page 6)

Part 8. Sponsor's Contract.

Please note that, by signing this Form I-864, you agree to assume certain specific obligations under the Immigration and Nationality Act and other Federal laws. The following paragraphs describe those obligations. Please read the following information carefully before you sign the Form I-864. If you do not understand the obligations, you may wish to consult an attorney or accredited representative.

What is the Legal Effect of My Signing a Form I-864?

If you sign a Form I-864 on behalf of any person (called the "intending immigrant") who is applying for an immigrant visa or for adjustment of status to a permanent resident, and that intending immigrant submits the Form I-864 to the U.S. Government with his or her application for an immigrant visa or adjustment of status, under section 213A of the Immigration and Nationality Act these actions create a contract between you and the U. S. Government. The intending immigrant's becoming a permanent resident is the "consideration" for the contract.

Under this contract, you agree that, in deciding whether the intending immigrant can establish that he or she is not inadmissible to the United States as an alien likely to become a public charge, the U.S. Government can consider your income and assets to be available for the support of the intending immigrant.

What If I choose Not to Sign a Form I-864?

You cannot be made to sign a Form 1-864 if you do not want to do so. But if you do not sign the Form I-864, the intending immigrant may not be able to become a permanent resident in the United States.

What Does Signing the Form I-864 Require Me to do?

If an intending immigrant becomes a permanent resident in the United States based on a Form I-864 that you have signed, then, until your obligations under the Form I-864 terminate, you must:

-- Provide the intending immigrant any support necessary to maintain him or her at an income that is at least 125 percent of the Federal Poverty Guidelines for his or her household size (100 percent if you are the petitioning sponsor and are on active duty in the U.S. Armed Forces and the person is your husband, wife, unmarried child under 21 years old.)

-- Notify USCIS of any change in your address, within 30 days of the change, by filing Form I-865.

What Other Consequences Are There?

If an intending immigrant becomes a permanent resident in the United States based on a Form I-864 that you have signed, then until your obligations under the Form I-864 terminate, your income and assets may be considered ("deemed") to be available to that person, in determining whether he or she is eligible for certain Federal means-tested public benefits and also for State or local means-tested public benefits, if the State or local government's rules provide for consideration ("deeming") of your income and assets as available to the person.

This provision does **not** apply to public benefits specified in section 403(c) of the Welfare Reform Act such as, but not limited to, emergency Medicaid, short-term, non-cash emergency relief; services provided under the National School Lunch and Child Nutrition Acts; immunizations and testing and treatment for communicable diseases; and means-tested programs under the Elementary and Secondary Education Act.

Contract continued on following page.

Sample Form I-864 (page 7)

What If I Do Not Fulfill My Obligations?

If you do not provide sufficient support to the person who becomes a permanent resident based on the Form I-864 that you signed, that person may sue you for this support.

If a Federal, State or local agency, or a private agency provides any covered means-tested public benefit to the person who becomes a permanent resident based on the Form I-864 that you signed, the agency may ask you to reimburse them for the amount of the benefits they provided. If you do not make the reimbursement, the agency may sue you for the amount that the agency believes you owe.

If you are sued, and the court enters a judgment against you, the person or agency that sued you may use any legally permitted procedures for enforcing or collecting the judgment. You may also be required to pay the costs of collection, including attorney fees.

If you do not file a properly completed Form I-865 within 30 days of any change of address, USCIS may impose a civil fine for your failing to do so.

When Will These Obligations End?

Your obligations under a Form I-864 will end if the person who becomes a permanent resident based on a Form I-864 that you signed:

- Becomes a U.S. citizen;
- Has worked, or can be credited with, 40 quarters of coverage under the Social Security Act;
- No longer has lawful permanent resident status, and has departed the United States;
- Becomes subject to removal, but applies for and obtains in removal proceedings a new grant of adjustment of status, based on a new affidavit of support, if one is required; or
- Dies.

Note that divorce **does not** terminate your obligations under this Form I-864.

Your obligations under a Form I-864 also end if you die. Therefore, if you die, your Estate will not be required to take responsibility for the person's support after your death. Your Estate may, however, be responsible for any support that you owed before you died.

30. I, ___Alberto Ilario Mancini_____ ,

(Print Sponsor's Name)

certify under penalty of perjury under the laws of the United States that:

a.   I know the contents of this affidavit of support that I signed.

b.   All the factual statements in this affidavit of support are true and correct.

c.   I have read and I understand each of the obligations described in Part 8, and I agree, freely and without any mental reservation or purpose of evasion, to accept each of those obligations in order to make it possible for the immigrants indicated in Part 3 to become permanent residents of the United States;

d.   I agree to submit to the personal jurisdiction of any Federal or State court that has subject matter jurisdiction of a lawsuit against me to enforce my obligations under this Form I-864;

e.   Each of the Federal income tax returns submitted in support of this affidavit are true copies, or are unaltered tax transcripts, of the tax returns I filed with the U.S. Internal Revenue Service; and

Sign on following page.

Sample Form I-864 (page 8)

f. I authorize the Social Security Administration to release information about me in its records to the Department of State and U.S. Citizenship and Immigration Services.

g. Any and all other evidence submitted is true and correct.

31. _Alberto Ilario Mancini_ _____   _07_ / _06_ / _2006_

(Sponsor's Signature)   *(Date-- mm/dd/yyyy)*

Part 9. Information on Preparer, if prepared by someone other than the sponsor.

I certify under penalty of perjury under the laws of the United States that I prepared this affidavit of support at the sponsor's request and that this affidavit of support is based on all information of which I have knowledge.

Signature: _____   **Date:** _____ / _____ / _____

                                                           (mm/dd/yyyy)

Printed Name: _____

Firm Name: _____

Address: _____

Telephone Number: (_____) _____

E-Mail Address _____

Business State ID # *(if any)* _____

Attachment to Affidavit of Support

Department of Homeland Security U.S.Citizenship and Immigration Services	OMB# 1615-0075; Expires 09/30/06 **I-864P, Poverty Guidelines**

2006 Poverty Guidelines*
Minimum Income Requirement For Use in Completing Form I-864

For the 48 Contiguous States, the District of Columbia, Puerto Rico, the U.S. Virgin Islands, and Guam:

Sponsor's Household Size	100% of Poverty Line For sponsors on active duty in the U.S. Armed Forces who are petitioning for their spouse or child.	125% of Poverty Line For all other sponsors
2	$13,200	**$16,500**
3	16,600	**20,750**
4	20,000	**25,000**
5	23,400	**29,250**
6	26,800	**33,500**
7	30,200	**37,750**
8	33,600	**42,000**
	Add $3,400 for each additional person.	**Add $4,250 for each additional person.**

	For Alaska		For Hawaii	
Sponsor's Household Size	100% of Poverty Line For sponsors on active duty in the U.S. Armed Forces who are petitioning for their spouse or child	**125% of Poverty Line For all other sponsors**	100% of Poverty Line For sponsors on active duty in the U.S. Armed Forces who are petitioning for their spouse or child	**125% of Poverty Line For all other sponsors**
2	$16,500	**$20,625**	$15,180	**$18,975**
3	20,750	**25,937**	19,090	**23,862**
4	25,000	**31,250**	23,000	**28,750**
5	29,250	**36,562**	26,910	**33,637**
6	33,500	**41,875**	30,820	**38,525**
7	37,750	**47,187**	34,730	**43,412**
8	42,000	**52,500**	38,640	**48,300**
	Add $4,250 for each additional person.	**Add $5,112 for each additional person.**	Add $3,910 for each additional person.	**Add $4,887 for each additional person.**

Means-Tested Public Benefits

Federal Means-Tested Public Benefits. To date, Federal agencies administering benefit programs have determined that Federal means-tested public benefits include Food Stamps, Medicaid, Supplemental Security Income (SSI), Temporary Assistance for Needy Families (TANF), and the State Child Health Insurance Program (SCHIP).

State Means-Tested Public Benefits. Each State will determine which, if any, of its public benefits are means-tested. If a State determines that it has programs which meet this definition, it is encouraged to provide notice to the public on which programs are included. Check with the State public assistance office to determine which, if any, State assistance programs have been determined to be State means-tested public benefits.

Programs Not Included: The following Federal and State programs are *not* included as means-tested benefits: emergency Medicaid; short-term, non-cash emergency relief; services provided under the National School Lunch and Child Nutrition Acts; immunizations and testing and treatment for communicable diseases; student assistance under the Higher Education Act and the Public Health Service Act; certain forms of foster-care or adoption assistance under the Social Security Act; Head Start Programs; means-tested programs under the Elementary and Secondary Education Act; and Job Training Partnership Act programs.

* These poverty guidelines remain in effect for use with Form I-864, Affidavit of Support, from March 1, 2006 until new poverty guidelines go into effect in the spring of 2007.

Form I-864P (Rev. 02/21/06)N

Contract Between Sponsor and Household Member, Sample Form I-864A (page 1)

OMB No. 1615-0075; Expires 09/30/2006

Department of Homeland Security
U.S. Citizenship and Immigration Services

I-864A, Contract Between
Sponsor and Household Member

Part 1. Information on the Household Member. (You.)			For Government Use Only

			This I-864A relates to a household member who:
1. Name	Last Name Mancini		
	First Name Beatrice	Middle Name Stella	
2. Mailing Address	Street Number and Name *(include apartment number)* 800 Broadway		☐ is the intending immigrant.
	City Lindenhurst	State or Province New York	☐ is not the intending immigrant.
	Country U.S.	Zip/Postal Code 11757	
3. Place of Residence *(if different from mailing address)*	Street Number and Name *(include apartment number)*		
	City	State or Province	Reviewer
	Country	Zip/Postal Code	Location
4. Telephone Number	*(Include area code or country and city codes)* 212-222-2121		
5. Date of Birth	*(mm/dd/yyyy)* 03/06/1982		Date *(mm/dd/yyyy)*
6. Place of Birth	City State/Province Country Horseheads NY U.S.		
7. U.S. Social Security Number *(if any)*	206-45-9872		

8. Relationship to Sponsor (Check either a, b or c)

a. ☐ I am the intending immigrant and also the sponsor's spouse.

b. ☐ I am the intending immigrant and also a member of the sponsor's household.

c. ☒ I am not the intending immigrant. I am the sponsor's household member. I am related to the sponsor as his/her.

☐ Spouse

☒ Son or daughter *(at least 18 years old)*

☐ Parent

☐ Brother or sister

☐ Other dependent (specify) _____

Form I-864A (Rev. 01/15/06)N

Sample Form I-864A (page 2)

For Government Use Only

9. I am currently:

a. [X] Employed as a/an _____Legal secretary_____.

Name of Employer # 1 *(if applicable)* ___Wynken, Blynken & Nodd___.

Name of Employer #2 *(if applicable)* _____.

b. [ ] Self-employed as a/an _____.

c. [ ] Retired from _____ since _____.
(Company Name) *(mm/dd/yyyy)*

d. [ ] Unemployed since _____.
(mm/dd/yyyy)

10. My current individual annual income is: $__46,000__.

11. Federal income tax information.

[X] I have filed a Federal tax return for each of the three most recent tax years. I have attached the required photocopy or transcript of my Federal tax return for only the most recent tax year.

My total income (adjusted gross income on IRS Form 1040EZ) as reported on my Federal tax returns for the most recent three years was:

Tax Year		Total Income
2005	*(most recent)*	$ 46,000
2004	*(2nd most recent)*	$ 43,000
2003	*(3rd most recent)*	$ 27,000

[ ] *(Optional)* I have attached photocopies or transcripts of my Federal tax returns for my second and third most recent tax years.

12. My assets (complete only if necessary)

a. Enter the balance of all cash, savings, and checking accounts. $_____.

b. Enter the net cash value of real-estate holdings. (Net means assessed value minus mortgage debt.) $_____.

c. Enter the cash value of all stocks, bonds, certificates of deposit, and other assets not listed on line a or b. $_____.

d. **Add together Lines a, b, and c and enter the number here.** $_____.

Sample Form I-864A (page 3)

Part 2. Sponsor's Promise.	For Government Use Only

13. I, THE SPONSOR, _Alberto Ilario Mancini_ ,
(Print Name)

in consideration of the household member's promise to support the following intending immigrant(s)

and to be jointly and severally liable for any obligations I incur under the affidavit of support,

promise to complete and file an affidavit of support on behalf of the following ___2___ named
(Indicate Number)

intending immigrant(s) (see Step-by-Step instructions).

Name	Date of Birth (mm/dd/yyyy)	A-number (if any)	U.S. Social Security Number (if any)
a. Terese M Mancini	02-15-1979	none	none
b. Giovana Moreno		none	none
c.			
d.			
e.			

14. _Alberto I. Mancini_   _07_ / _06_ / _2006_
    (Sponsor's Signature)   *(Date--mm/dd/yyyy)*

Part 3. Household Member's Promise.

15. I, THE HOUSEHOLD MEMBER, _Beatrice Stella Mancini_ ,
(Print Name)

in consideration of the sponsor's promise to complete and file an affidavit of support on behalf of the

above ___2___ named intending immigrant(s):
(Number from line 13)

a. Promise to provide any and all financial support necessary to assist the sponsor in maintaining the sponsored immigrant(s) at or above the minimum income provided for in section 213A(a)(1)(A) of the Act (not less than 125 percent of the Federal Poverty Guidelines) during the period in which the affidavit of support is enforceable;

b. Agree to be jointly and severally liable for payment of any and all obligations owed by the sponsor under the affidavit of support to the sponsored immigrant(s), to any agency of the Federal Government, to any agency of a State or local government, or to any other private entity that provides means-tested public benefit;

c. Certify under penalty under the laws of the United States that all the information provided on this form is true and correct to the best of my knowledge and belief and that the Federal income tax returns submitted in support of the contract are true copies or unaltered tax transcripts filed with the Internal Revenue Service.

d. **Consideration where the household member is also the sponsored immigrant:** I understand that if I am the sponsored immigrant and a member of the sponsor's household that this promise relates only to my promise to be jointly and severally liable for any obligation owed by the sponsor under the affidavit of support to any of my dependents, to any agency of the Federal Government, to any agency of a State or local government, and to provide any and all financial support necessary to assist the sponsor in maintaining any of my dependents at or above the minimum income provided for in section 213A(s)(1)(A) of the Act (not less than 125 percent of the Federal poverty line) during the period which the affidavit of support is enforceable.

e. I authorize the Social Security Administration to release information about me in its records to the Department of State and U.S. Citizenship and Immigration Services.

16. _Beatrice Stella Mancini_   _07_ / _06_ / _2006_
    (Sponsor's Signature)   *(Date--mm/dd/yyyy)*

Form I-864A (Rev. 01/15/06)N Page 3

Application for Immigrant Visa and Alien Registration, Sample Form DS-230 Part II (page 1)

U.S. Department of State
APPLICATION FOR IMMIGRANT VISA AND
ALIEN REGISTRATION

OMB APPROVAL NO. 1405-0015
EXPIRES: 07/31/2007
ESTIMATED BURDEN: 1 HOUR*

PART II - SWORN STATEMENT

INSTRUCTIONS: Complete one copy of this form for yourself and each member of your family, regardless of age, who will immigrate with you. Please print or type your answers to all questions. Mark questions that are **Not Applicable** with **"N/A"**. If there is insufficient room on the form, answer on a separate sheet using the same numbers that appear on the form. Attach any additional sheets to this form. The fee should be paid in United States dollars or local currency equivalent, or by bank draft.

WARNING: Any false statement or concealment of a material fact may result in your permanent exclusion from the United States. Even if you are issued an immigrant visa and are subsequently admitted to the United States, providing false information on this form could be grounds for your prosecution and/or deportation.

This form (DS-230 PART II), together with Form DS-230 PART I, constitutes the complete Application for Immigrant Visa and Alien Registration.

26. Family Name	First Name	Middle Name
Mancini	Terese	Maria

27. Other Names Used or Aliases *(If married woman, give maiden name)*

Terese Brabantio

28. Full Name in Native Alphabet *(If Roman letters not used)*

n/a

29. Name and Address of Petitioner

Alberto Mancini
800 Broadway
Lindenhurst, NY 11757
Telephone number: (212) 222-2121

30. United States laws governing the issuance of visas require each applicant to state whether or not he or she is a member of any class of individuals excluded from admission into the United States. The excludable classes are described below in general terms. You should read carefully the following list and answer YES or NO to each category. The answers you give will assist the consular officer to reach a decision on your eligibility to receive a visa.

EXCEPT AS OTHERWISE PROVIDED BY LAW, ALIENS WITHIN THE FOLLOWING CLASSIFICATIONS ARE INELIGIBLE TO RECEIVE A VISA.
DO ANY OF THE FOLLOWING CLASSES APPLY TO YOU?

a. An alien who has a communicable disease of public health significance; who has failed to present documentation of having received vaccinations in accordance with U.S. law; who has or has had a physical or mental disorder that poses or is likely to pose a threat to the safety or welfare of the alien or others; or who is a drug abuser or addict. ☐ Yes ☒ No

b. An alien convicted of, or who admits having committed, a crime involving moral turpitude or violation of any law relating to a controlled substance or who is the spouse, son or daughter of such a trafficker who knowingly has benefited from the trafficking activities in the past five years; who has been convicted of 2 or more offenses for which the aggregate sentences were 5 years or more; who is coming to the United States to engage in prostitution or commercialized vice or who has engaged in prostitution or procuring within the past 10 years; who is or has been an illicit trafficker in any controlled substance; who has committed a serious criminal offense in the United States and who has asserted immunity from prosecution; who, while serving as a foreign government official and within the previous 24-month period, was responsible for or directly carried out particularly severe violations of religious freedom; or whom the President has identified as a person who plays a significant role in a severe form of trafficking in persons, who otherwise has knowingly aided, abetted, assisted or colluded with such a trafficker in severe forms of trafficking in persons, or who is the spouse, son or daughter of such a trafficker who knowingly has benefited from the trafficking activities within the past five years. ☐ Yes ☒ No

c. An alien who seeks to enter the United States to engage in espionage, sabotage, export control violations, terrorist activities, the overthrow of the Government of the United States or other unlawful activity; who is a member of or affiliated with the Communist or other totalitarian party; who participated in Nazi persecutions or genocide; who has engaged in genocide; or who is a member or representative of a terrorist organization as currently designated by the U.S. Secretary of State. ☐ Yes ☒ No

d. An alien who is likely to become a public charge. ☐ Yes ☒ No

e. An alien who seeks to enter for the purpose of performing skilled or unskilled labor who has not been certified by the Secretary of Labor; who is a graduate of a foreign medical school seeking to perform medical services who has not passed the NBME exam or its equivalent; or who is a health care worker seeking to perform such work without a certificate from the CGFNS or from an equivalent approved independent credentialing organization. ☐ Yes ☒ No

f. An alien who failed to attend a hearing on deportation or inadmissibility within the last 5 years; who seeks or has sought a visa, entry into the United States, or any immigration benefit by fraud or misrepresentation; who knowingly assisted any other alien to enter or try to enter the United States in violation of law; who, after November 30, 1996, attended in student (F) visa status a U.S. public elementary school or who attended a U.S. public secondary school without reimbursing the school; or who is subject to a civil penalty under INA 274C. ☐ Yes ☒ No

Privacy Act and Paperwork Reduction Act Statements

The information asked for on this form is requested pursuant to Section 222 of the Immigration and Nationality Act. The U.S. Department of State uses the facts you provide on this form primarily to determine your classification and eligibility for a U.S. immigrant visa. Individuals who fail to submit this form or who do not provide all the requested information may be denied a U.S. immigrant visa. If you are issued an immigrant visa and are subsequently admitted to the United States as an immigrant, the Department of Homeland Security will use the information on this form to issue you a Permanent Resident Card, and, if you so indicate, the Social Security Administration will use the information to issue you a social security number and card.

*Public reporting burden for this collection of information is estimated to average 1 hour per response, including time required for searching existing data sources, gathering the necessary data, providing the information required, and reviewing the final collection. In accordance with 5 CFR 1320 5(b), persons are not required to respond to the collection of this information unless this form displays a currently valid OMB control number. Send comments on the accuracy of this estimate of the burden and recommendations for reducing it to: U.S. Department of State (A/RPS/DIR) Washington, DC 20520.

DS-230 Part II   **PREVIOUS EDITIONS OBSOLETE**   **Page 3 of 4**

Sample Form DS-230 Part II (page 2)

g. An alien who is permanently ineligible for U.S. citizenship; or who departed the United States to evade military service in time of war. ☐ Yes ☒ No

h. An alien who was previously ordered removed within the last 5 years or ordered removed a second time within the last 20 years; who was previously unlawfully present and ordered removed within the last 10 years or ordered removed a second time within the last 20 years; who was convicted of an aggravated felony and ordered removed; who was previously unlawfully present in the United States for more than 180 days but less than one year who voluntarily departed within the last 3 years; or who was unlawfully present for more than one year or an aggregate of one year within the last 10 years. ☐ Yes ☒ No

i. An alien who is coming to the United States to practice polygamy; who withholds custody of a U.S. citizen child outside the United States from a person granted legal custody by a U.S. court or intentionally assists another person to do so; who has voted in the United States in violation of any law or regulation; or who renounced U.S. citizenship to avoid taxation. ☐ Yes ☒ No

j. An alien who is a former exchange visitor who has not fulfilled the 2-year foreign residence requirement. ☐ Yes ☒ No

k. An alien determined by the Attorney General to have knowingly made a frivolous application for asylum. ☐ Yes ☒ No

l. An alien who has ordered, carried out or materially assisted in extrajudicial and political killings and other acts of violence against the Haitian people; who has directly or indirectly assisted or supported any of the groups in Colombia known as FARC, ELN, or AUC; who through abuse of a governmental or political position has converted for personal gain, confiscated or expropriated property in Cuba, a claim to which is owned by a national of the United States, has trafficked in such property or has been complicit in such conversion, has committed similar acts in another country, or is the spouse, minor child or agent of an alien who has committed such acts; who has been directly involved in the establishment or enforcement of population controls forcing a woman to undergo an abortion against her free choice or a man or a woman to undergo sterilization against his or her free choice; or who has disclosed or trafficked in confidential U.S. business information obtained in connection with U.S. participation in the Chemical Weapons Convention or is the spouse, minor child or agent of such a person. ☐ Yes ☒ No

31. Have you ever been charged, arrested or convicted of any offense or crime?
(If answer is Yes, please explain) ☐ Yes ☒ No

32. Have you ever been refused admission to the United States at a port-of-entry?
(If answer is Yes, please explain) ☐ Yes ☒ No

33a. Have you ever applied for a Social Security Number (SSN)?	33b. **CONSENT TO DISCLOSURE:** I authorize disclosure of information from this form to the Department of Homeland Security (DHS), the Social Security Administration (SSA), such other U.S. Government agencies as may be required for the purpose of assigning me an SSN and issuing me a Social Security card, and I authorize the SSA to share my SSN with the INS.
☐ Yes Give the number _____ ☒ No	
Do you want the Social Security Administration to assign you an SSN (and issue a card) or issue you a new card (if you have an SSN)? You must answer "Yes" to this question and to the "Consent To Disclosure" in order to receive an SSN and/or card. ☒ Yes ☐ No	☒ Yes ☐ No
	The applicant's response does not limit or restrict the Government's ability to obtain his or her SSN, or other information on this form, for enforcement or other purposes as authorized by law.

34. WERE YOU ASSISTED IN COMPLETING THIS APPLICATION? ☐ Yes ☒ No
(If answer is Yes, give name and address of person assisting you, indicating whether relative, friend, travel agent, attorney, or other)

DO NOT WRITE BELOW THE FOLLOWING LINE
The consular officer will assist you in answering item 35.
DO NOT SIGN this form until instructed to do so by the consular officer

35. I claim to be:
☐ A Family-Sponsored Immigrant
☐ An Employment-Based Immigrant
☐ A Diversity Immigrant
☐ A Special Category *(Specify)* _____
(Returning resident, Hong Kong, Tibetan, Private Legislation, etc.)

☐ I derive foreign state chargeability under Sec. 202(b) through my _____

☐ Preference: _____
☐ Numerical limitation: _____
(foreign state)

I understand that I am required to surrender my visa to the United States Immigration Officer at the place where I apply to enter the United States, and that the possession of a visa does not entitle me to enter the United States if at that time I am found to be inadmissible under the immigration laws.

I understand that any willfully false or misleading statement or willful concealment of a material fact made by me herein may subject me to permanent exclusion from the United States and, if I am admitted to the United States, may subject me to criminal prosecution and/or deportation.

I, the undersigned applicant for a United States immigrant visa, do solemnly swear (or affirm) that all statements which appear in this application, consisting of Form DS-230 Part I and Part II combined, have been made by me, including the answers to items 1 through 35 inclusive, and that they are true and complete to the best of my knowledge and belief. I do further swear (or affirm) that, if admitted into the United States, I will not engage in activities which would be prejudicial to the public interest, or endanger the welfare, safety, or security of the United States; in activities which would be prohibited by the laws of the United States relating to espionage, sabotage, public disorder, or in other activities subversive to the national security; in any activity a purpose of which is the opposition to, or the control, or overthrow of, the Government of the United States, by force, violence, or other unconstitutional means.

I understand that completion of this form by persons required by law to register with the Selective Service System (males 18 through 25 years of age) constitutes such registration in accordance with the Military Selective Service Act.

I understand all the foregoing statements, having asked for and obtained an explanation on every point which was not clear to me.

_____
Signature of Applicant

Subscribed and sworn to before me this _____ day of _____ _____ at: _____

_____
Consular Officer

THIS FORM MAY BE OBTAINED FREE AT CONSULAR OFFICES OF THE UNITED STATES OF AMERICA

DS-230 Part II   Page 4 of 4

Private Bills

It's Not What You Know, It's Who You Know

You may have heard of people who became permanent residents by means of a private bill passed by the U.S. Congress. However, such cases are rare. You must have very special circumstances—and very strong political ties—to get a private bill passed.

Look into the possibility of a private bill where the law is against you, but your case has strong humanitarian factors. Private bills succeed when an injustice can be corrected only by a special act of the U.S. Congress.

A. What Is a Private Bill?

A private bill is the last resort of a desperate alien facing deportation—a special urging by high-level U.S. politicians to allow you to stay in the U.S. legally. Currently, very few private bills are filed on behalf of aliens. Fewer than 100 private bills have been successful during each of the past several years.

B. How a Private Bill Is Passed

A private bill must be sponsored by one or more members of the House of Representatives and one or more members of the Senate who urge that one individual be given special consideration in being allowed to become a permanent resident or get citizenship.

Like a law, a private bill has to be introduced in both houses of Congress. It then has to be recommended favorably by the Judiciary Committee to which it has been assigned in both houses, after having been favorably reported by the Subcommittee on Immigration of both houses.

Both houses of Congress must approve the bill during a regular session. The president of the United States must then sign it into law.

Thus, if you are an alien facing deportation, you will have to go through the eye of a needle before getting your private bill passed by Congress and signed by the president. In short, hiring the best immigration lawyer in town will give you a better chance to obtain a green card than will the private bill route. ∎

Inside the Immigration Bureaucracy

The Land of Oz

All too often, when you submit an application to U.S. Citizenship and Immigration Services (formerly called the INS), you expect to receive an official reply within a week or two. But a month may pass, then two—and still no reply arrives. You would like to find out why your application is delayed, but each time you contact the USCIS office, you are simply told to be patient and wait—that your paperwork is "being processed," or "pending."

But there are a number of things you can do to be sure that your dealings with USCIS move as smoothly and efficiently as possible. Those options are explained in this chapter.

A. Understanding the USCIS Culture

USCIS is just one branch of a huge agency, the Department of Homeland Security (DHS). The people working in USCIS reflect the workforce of any other government bureaucracy. These workers can generally be divided into two kinds: those who are earnest and conscientious in doing their jobs, and those who are at their posts in body but not in spirit. You take the luck of the draw as to which kind of bureaucrat will be handling your application or answering your questions.

Although USCIS is governed by law (the Immigration and Nationality Act, Code of Federal Regulations, and Operational Instructions), how these controlling rules and laws are applied depends upon USCIS office workers, who have their own cultural and social biases.

For example, you may be confronted with an immigration officer whose cultural background is anti-immigrant, and who detests dealing on a daily basis with people who do not speak English, who speak with an accent, or who look, dress, or even smell differently from what he or she thinks of as "ordinary" Americans. This bias may make the worker grumpy, officious, intimidating, unhelpful, unreasonable, discourteous, or downright infuriating.

Furthermore, USCIS is not very phone-accessible, and the people at its national information line aren't well-informed about local office procedures. This can make the agency seem faceless and impersonal.

Visiting USCIS Offices in Person

The only USCIS offices that you can visit in person are the district or field offices. Each U.S. state usually has one or two such offices (though in a few cases, you'll have to travel to another state). To find the office that serves you, go to www.uscis.gov and click on "Services Field Office Addresses and Information" (in the left-hand column). You'll eventually find your way to the Web page that your USCIS field office (or your regional service center, application support center, or other facility) maintains on the USCIS website. These are useful not only for finding street addresses and contact information, but also for answers to frequently asked questions and other useful information.

It used to be a major headache to visit a USCIS field office in person. To ask even a simple question about a form or a pending case, you often had to line up very early in the morning and wait half a day just to be seen by an officer. Nowadays, however, the USCIS InfoPass system allows you to go to http://infopass.uscis.gov and make an appointment. The appointment system is very slick—it can communicate in 12 different languages—and appointments are usually scheduled within a few days or weeks of the request. Best of all, you don't have to show up at USCIS until a few minutes before your appointment, and USCIS says that most visits last less than an hour!

B. Where to Go

Whenever a situation arises where you feel an immigration officer is being unreasonable, go up the chain of command and appeal to the worker's supervisor. Insist on speaking with the supervisor personally. You can even do this in the middle of an appointment or interview. If that's not possible, try to obtain the supervisor's telephone number to call and explain what happened—or write a detailed letter of explanation. Be clear on what action was taken by the worker and what you want the supervising officer to do.

Because the DHS is a bureaucracy with many departments and branches, it is easy to get mixed up in a game of finger-pointing in which each person with whom you speak claims that the problem is not his or her fault.

The most important bit of knowledge you can learn is the exact section where your application is pending or where you are directing your inquiry.

- The USCIS District or Field Office is open to the public for forms and information and also handles some (but not all) green card applications. Most states have at least one.
- The USCIS Regional Service Center is a processing facility that you cannot normally visit, but to which you may be required to send your visa petition or green card application, depending on your eligibility category. There are four service centers nationwide. You can check on the status of applications that you've filed with the service centers by telephone (see the phone number on your receipt notice) or online at https://egov.immigration.gov/cris/jsps/index.jsp.
- The National Benefits Center (NBC) was recently created to handle administrative case processing burdens formerly borne by local USCIS district or field offices. Many kinds of petitions and applications that used to be filed directly with local offices are now filed with a Lockbox facility located in Chicago, Illinois. The lockbox performs fee deposits, issues receipts, and handles initial data entry.

After receiving cases from the Lockbox, the NBC completes all necessary pre-interview processing of Form I-485 applications (including conducting background security checks, performing initial evidence review, and other tasks). Then NBC forwards the case files to local field offices for a final interview (if applicable) and decision. It's now more important than ever to understand which cases are filed at the NBC. For more information about the NBC, visit www.uscis.gov/graphics/fieldoffices/nbc/aboutus.htm.

- Immigration and Customs Enforcement (ICE) is the enforcement arm of the DHS. Its investigators check on whether both employers and employees have complied with the immigration laws. They do surveillance, make arrests, and issue orders to show up for deportation or exclusion hearings before the Immigration Court.
- The Detention Section is in charge of detaining all aliens caught by ICE or apprehended at the airport or the border.
- The Naturalization Section is responsible for deciding which aliens are eligible for citizenship and who qualifies as a citizen of the United States.
- The Litigation Section is the legal arm of the DHS and represents the government during hearings involving an alien before the Immigration Court and the federal and state courts. It also counsels the other sections of the DHS on legal matters.
- The Immigration Court (also called the Executive Office of Immigration Review), which was part of the INS until 1987, is now a separate bureaucracy.

Consult an expert. Note that if you are under removal proceedings in court, or facing other complications described in this chapter, it may be risky to proceed on your own. Consult an experienced immigration attorney for advice. (See Chapter 24.)

C. Tips for Filing Your Applications

USCIS loses a surprising number of applications, or the documents and checks that came with them. To protect yours, and to make sure they get through the system as smoothly as possible, follow the tips below.

1. Submitting Applications by Mail or Courier

After you've filled out your application forms, assembled the needed documents, and written the checks, you'll be eager to submit it to USCIS. Most applications must be submitted by mail. But don't just pop yours in the nearest mailbox. Take all applications and other immigration papers to the post office, and send them by certified mail with return receipt requested. Keep complete copies for your files—even copy the checks.

Sending applications via couriers such as FedEx or DHL is also a good way to make sure you have proof of its arrival. However, make sure the USCIS office is equipped to accept this form of delivery. Some don't at all, because a live person has to be there to sign for the package. Others designate a special address for such deliveries, which you can find on the USCIS website (www.uscis.gov).

When your application first arrives at a USCIS office, the clerical staff will first examine your papers to see if everything is in order. Your papers will likely be returned to you if you:

- did not enter your full name, including middle name
- did not sign your application or other papers requiring a signature
- signed a name different from that shown on your attached birth certificate
- did not enclose the correct filing fee
- left some questions unanswered, or
- forgot to include some documents.

When your papers are returned, there should be a letter included with them, telling you what information was incorrect or missing. You will usually have a chance to correct what was wrong and send back your documents and check or money order.

When your documents are in order, USCIS will accept your submission and will send you a receipt notice telling you the minimum time you'll have to wait for a decision.

If your application needs to be submitted in person—such as an application for employment authorization or advance parole—the USCIS worker to whom you are assigned will tell you whether or not your application is properly filled out and documented. You will have the opportunity to correct your answers right then and there. The USCIS worker will then direct you to pay the filing fee to the cashier, who will give you a receipt. Be sure to keep the receipt in case you need to use it as proof of filing.

If you move, take extra precautions. As you may know, all changes of address must be reported to USCIS within ten days, using Form AR-11. However, if you've got an application going through the USCIS system, this is just the beginning. You must also tell the office handling your application about your new address, or it won't find out. (Send a letter.) But don't count on your letter making its way into your file—USCIS is notoriously bad about keeping track of these things. Ask the U.S. post office to forward your mail, and if possible, stay in touch with the new people living in your old house or apartment to see whether anything from USCIS has arrived.

Some people even postpone moves until after their cases are finished processing! This might seem extreme, but if your or your loved one's immigration situation is the most important thing in your life, it's worth considering. Experienced immigration lawyers will tell you that anytime a file has to go from one USCIS field office to another (as is often the case when you move), bad things can happen, from unanticipated and lengthy delays to filings that "disappear" in the system. If you know you are going to move in the coming weeks or months and you have a case you want to file, consider waiting until after you have moved before filing the case.

2. Some Applications Can Be Filed Online ("e-Filing")

USCIS recently instituted an e-filing program for some (but not all) petitions and applications. USCIS says that the benefits of e-filing include your being able to file petitions and applications from anywhere with an Internet connection, pay your fees with a credit card or directly through your checking or savings account, and get immediate confirmation that your application has been received by USCIS.

However, the program as it currently exists is somewhat cumbersome—for example, you must still mail photocopies of documents such as birth certificates and passports. USCIS promises that the program will improve over time. If you're a procrastinator, or you worry about whether every "i" has been dotted and "t" crossed in your paperwork, you might especially appreciate the "instant confirmation" feature of e-filing. More information about e-filing is available at www.uscis.gov/graphics/formsfee/forms/eFiling.htm.

3. Faster, "Premium" Processing May Become Available

With USCIS's Premium Processing Service, 15-calendar day processing is available to people filing certain applications who are willing to pay the premium processing fee (currently $1,000). Unfortunately, only a few kinds of cases are currently eligible for premium processing, and none of them are covered in this book. (It's mainly available for petitions by companies on behalf of important workers.) However, USCIS has plans to make the service more widely available in the future.

Not only do premium processing cases get sent to special mailing addresses, but dedicated phone number and email addresses are available for use solely by premium processing customers. Requests for premium processing are filed using Form I-907.

More information about premium processing—including the latest news on which types of applications it's available for—can be found at www.uscis.gov/graphics/aboutus/repsstudies/h1b/premprsv.htm.

4. Always Use Your Alien Number

There are two kinds of numbers by which the DHS identifies every person who comes in contact with it. The first one, an A followed by 8 numbers—for example: A93 465 345—is given to those who apply for adjustment of status to become permanent residents (see Chapter 18) or who have a removal case. It's called an "Alien Registration Number" or "A Number."

The second type of number USCIS assigns starts with the initials of your district or of the Regional Service Center followed by ten numbers—for example: WSC 1122334455 or EAC 9512345678—and is given to applications submitted there, to track them through processing.

Once your immigration papers are accepted by USCIS, its computer system verifies whether you have ever been assigned an alien number or whether the alien number you wrote on your application is the right one for you.

The clerk then checks the computer files, looking for all the names you may have used, your date and place of birth, and your parents' names. The clerk will confirm the alien number you wrote on your application, or if you have other alien numbers previously assigned, will note them on your application so that all your files can be consolidated under one alien number. If you do not have a previous alien number, the clerk will give your file a new one.

Keep a record of your immigration case number, because any time you have a question to pose to USCIS, it will ask you first for your number. And if you send letters—for example, asking why your case is taking so long—you must include your A number or processing number.

5. Use One Check for Each Filing Fee

Occasionally you may find yourself submitting more than one petition or application at the same time. For example, in a marriage case where your spouse is here in the U.S., you can file Form I-130 and Form I-485 simultaneously. Or, you may file applications for your spouse and your stepchild in the same envelope. In any of these situations, resist the temptation to combine all the filing fees into a single check.

If you submit separate, individual checks for each filing fee, then if you make a mistake on the check (for example, you forget to sign it, or you make it for the wrong amount), USCIS will reject only the filing that is affected by that check. But if you submit a single check covering all fees, you will ruin all of the filings at once if you make a mistake.

It's a pain to have to write more than one check for forms and applications being submitted in the same package, but most of the time it's worth it.

6. Looking at Your File

If you need to see your immigration records, or to have a copy of a document you submitted, you can do so by filing Form G-639, Freedom of Information/Privacy Act Request. Request a current form from the nearest USCIS office or download it from the USCIS website (www.uscis.gov). Mark your envelope "Freedom of Information Request." Send it to the following address: National Records Center, FOIA/PA Office, P.O. Box 648010, Lee's Summit, MO 64064-8010.

Although USCIS has promised that it will answer a Freedom of Information/Privacy Act Request within ten days, it usually does not live up to its promise. If you have not heard from USCIS within one month after requesting to see your file, write and let them know that you are aware that it has a mandate to respond to these requests within ten days.

D. Inquiring About Delays

If you're waiting for an appointment or a decision on an immigration petition or application, you're likely to be frustrated. Action by USCIS and the State Department usually takes longer than anyone thinks it should. The question is, how long is too long? To some extent, this depends on the office you're dealing with.

For U.S. consulates, you'll have to ask other people in your country, or contact the consulate directly, to find out its normal schedule. Some consulates post such information on their websites, which you can access via the U.S. State Department website at www.state.gov (on the home page, click "Travel and Business," then "Visas," then "Visas for Foreign Citizens," then "Locate a Consular Office").

You can find out just how backed up the various USCIS offices are by going to the USCIS website at www.uscis.gov. Click "Immigration Services and Benefit Programs," then "National Customer Service Center," then (buried within the text) "Case Status Service." You'll be brought to a page where you can choose to request information on your own application, if it's with a service center and you have a receipt notice. If this doesn't work, or if you're simply told that your case is "pending," take a look at the link under the heading "Obtaining a List of Processing Dates." Here, you'll find out the dates of applications filed by other people like you—and can at least see whether they're still dealing with people who applied before you, or seem to have skipped over you and are dealing with people who applied after you.

In general, however, if you are waiting for an initial receipt, such as one for an I-129F or I-130 visa petition filed with a USCIS Service Center, six weeks is the longest you should wait. After that, write a letter like the one below. (Telephoning is rarely a good option, because it's impossible to get through, and when you do, you typically find yourself speaking to someone who isn't anywhere near your file.)

Didn't get a receipt? Don't fret, if you paid by check. Ask your bank for a copy of your canceled check. Your case number (and A number, if applicable) will be printed on it. This gives you a way to verify whether your case made it into the system. Next, let USCIS know that you didn't receive a receipt notice, by calling the customer service center at 800-375-5283. (It's important to do this, because not having gotten a receipt notice can mean USCIS made a mistake in data entry that could cause you not to receive the decision in your case after it's been made.) Your telephone call will go much more smoothly now that you're able to tell them the case number or A number that you got from your canceled check.

Sample Letter for No Receipt Notice

222 Snowy Road
Buffalo, NY 14221
716-555-1313
March 22, 2006

Department of Homeland Security
U.S. Citizenship and Immigration Services
Vermont Service Center

75 Lower Welden St.
St. Albans, VT 05479

RE: Petitioner: Charlie Citizen
       Beneficiary: Greta German
       Delayed receipt notice

Dear Sir/Madam:

I filed an I-130 visa petition for the above-named beneficiary on January 14, 2006. According to my certified mail receipts, the petition arrived in your office on January 16 (a copy of the notice is enclosed). It has now been over six weeks and I have not gotten a receipt notice from you.

Please advise me of the status of my visa petition at the above address or phone number. I look forward to your response.

Very truly yours,

Charlie Citizen

Charlie Citizen
Enclosed: Copy of return receipt

After you get a receipt notice, it should tell you how long you can expect to wait for an actual decision from USCIS. If weeks go by after that date has come, send another letter, like the one below.

Sample Letter for Delayed Decision

344 Noview Drive
Fremont, California 9000
510-555-1122
September 31, 2006

USCIS California Service Center
P.O. Box 10130
Laguna Niguel, CA 92607-0130

RE: Petitioner: Joe Citizen
         Beneficiary: Tana Tanzanian
         Processing number: WAC 01-555-54321

Dear Sir/Madam:

I filed a visa petition for my wife, the above-named beneficiary on May 1, 2006. According to your receipt notice, which I received on June 1, 2006, I could expect a decision within 90 days. A copy of that notice is enclosed.

Approximately 120 days have now passed, and I have received neither a decision nor any requests for further information from you.

Please advise me of the status of my visa petition at the above address or phone number. I look forward to your response.

Very truly yours,

Joe Citizen

Enclosed: Copy of USCIS receipt notice

Avoid the temptation to be rude. Keep your letters courteous, clear, and to the point. Demonstrate that you're well organized, and that you know exactly when USCIS or the State Department received your materials, and when you should have gotten an answer.

When writing letters, be careful to send them to the last office that you heard from. Remember, your file will, over the course of your immigration application, be transferred between various offices—and they won't take responsibility for transferring your letters of inquiry to the right place.

As with every document in your immigration case, make copies of your inquiry letters for your files. Answers to such letters usually take six weeks or longer. If you don't get an answer, write another, more urgent letter. Keep writing until you get results—or until it's no longer worth your time and you decide to hire an attorney. Attorneys can't always get results any faster than you could on your own, but they do—especially if they're members of AILA—have access to a few inside fax lines or phone numbers, which can help them make inquiries.

E. Speeding Up Processing in Emergencies

An emergency may arise where you need an action expedited or your immigration papers approved very quickly. For example, your wife may still be abroad because your petition for her is not yet approved, when she is stricken with a rare disease for which the only treatment is found in the United States.

Normally, USCIS is unwilling to bend its rules and act outside the standard operating procedures. But if your case truly deserves an exception from the general rule, and you approach the right USCIS worker in the right way, you may get a satisfactory resolution because there is a humanitarian reason to grant your request. It enables USCIS to show its human side.

But it is sometimes difficult to locate that human side.

First of all, be resigned to the fact that there are two kinds of USCIS workers: One makes a decision strictly according to the letter of the law, and the other exercises discretion when appropriate and makes a decision according to the spirit of the law.

You may get the best help if you write a letter explaining your situation, attaching documents to substantiate why immediate action is necessary.

As mentioned earlier, when the USCIS worker fails to respond to your inquiry or denies your request, try to go up the chain of command and speak with the supervisor.

If your request for immediate action is still denied unjustly, you may have to hire a lawyer to help put the pressure on. As a last resort, the lawyer may file a case of mandamus in the federal district court to force USCIS to act on your request.

Sample Letter to Supervisor

Leona Burgett, Supervisor
USCIS Office
Anytown, Anystate 12345
August 12, 200_

Dear Ms. Burgett:

My file number is A 12345678 and I have an adjustment of status application pending in your office.

I received a letter from my mother with a certification from the hospital that my father suffered a heart attack and his prognosis is dim. I filed for advance parole two days ago, but my application was denied. The USCIS worker said he believed that the certification from the hospital was fraudulently obtained, and did not accept my mother's letter because it was not translated into English.

Yesterday, I returned with a translation of the letter and my affidavit explaining that in our remote hometown, the most modern equipment available is a manual typewriter, on which some letters may be crooked or spaces may be skipped. The USCIS worker said that my advance parole will still be denied regardless of my explanations that my father is truly very ill.

I am married to a U.S. citizen and have been law-abiding—except for overstaying in this country until submitting my adjustment of status application.

Please help me with my advance parole request.

Sincerely,
Max Haxsim
Max Haxsim

F. Reporting Wrongdoing

Sometimes, a USCIS worker's actions may be truly reprehensible, involving gross incompetence, immoral conduct, or unlawful behavior—for instance, asking for a bribe, either before or after doing what the worker is supposed to do. In such cases, report the misdeed to the head of the particular USCIS office.

Your letter should specify the name of the USCIS worker, if known. If you did not ask for the name or the USCIS worker refused to answer, describe him or her. You also should indicate the time, date, and manner of misconduct and the names of any witnesses.

Although your complaint may lead to an investigation where you may be asked to repeat your facts in front of an investigator or an administrative judge, do not be afraid or unwilling to get involved. The officer's abusive behavior is not likely to stop, and many more people are likely to be injured by it unless you take action.

Sample Letter

USCIS
Department of Homeland Security
[use local address]
 April 15, 200_

Dear Investigating Officer:

This is a complaint against a male USCIS officer who refused to give me his name. He is Caucasian of medium build, has gray hair, and wears eyeglasses.

I spoke with this officer on Tuesday, April 5, 200_, at 10:00 a.m. on the 8th floor of the USCIS office in New York. He demanded a hundred extra dollars in cash before approving my request for advance parole.

When I refused to pay the additional money, he said that although all my paperwork was in order, he would have to deny the request since I wasn't willing to "pay what it took to get the wheels in motion."

Alfred Beiz, a paralegal at the law firm of Dias & Associates, was standing in line behind me, waiting to file some papers, and overheard the officer's remarks. Mr. Beiz is willing to file an affidavit swearing to the conversation he heard.

I request that you promptly investigate my charge against this officer, and inform me about what action is taken.

Thank you for your attention.

With my best regards,

Ali Mufti

Ali Mufti

Sometimes, They Surprise You

While it's important to make your dissatisfaction known about a USCIS officer's bad or abusive behavior, the contrary should also be true. If you are served by a USCIS worker who goes the extra mile to be helpful, by all means write to the worker's office and let them know that there is an outstanding worker in their midst.

It may encourage more workers to deliver superlative service to the public.

Immigration Forms: Getting Started

Paper, Paper, Everywhere

The most important part of obtaining a green card is the paperwork. The key to getting one is to pay very close attention to the immigration forms and other documents you submit as evidence to the U.S. government.

A. Don't Give False Answers

There is one primary rule to keep in mind while answering the questions on the immigration forms: Honesty Is the Best Policy.

For example, if you have been previously married, acknowledge this and provide the documents to prove that your previous marriage ended by divorce, annulment, or the death of your spouse.

If you have children by a previous marriage, or you have had any children while you were unmarried, list all of them on the immigration form, together with their correct names and dates of birth as shown on their birth certificates.

If the immigration form requests such information, be sure to list all your brothers and sisters, whether they are full-blood siblings, half-brothers or half-sisters, stepbrothers or stepsisters.

Once you submit the immigration forms, it is very difficult to change your answers. If you attempt later changes, you run the risk of having your petition denied.

EXAMPLE: Suppose you never told your American husband that you had an illegitimate child. For this reason, you do not mention this child in your immigration papers. Later on, you decide to reveal the truth to your husband. If you want to petition for an immigrant visa for the child you left behind in your country, you will have a hard time convincing USCIS that you had a child prior to your marriage.

1. Criminal Penalties

Aside from the difficulty of trying to convince the U.S. officials that an omission was an honest mistake, you also run the risk of being prosecuted for obtaining entry by a "willfully false or misleading representation or willful concealment of a material fact." In simple terms, you could be accused of lying on the immigration forms. Or you may be accused of filing documents that do not belong to you.

If you are found guilty of committing these offenses, you may be imprisoned for as long as five years or fined as much as $10,000, or receive both forms of punishment. If you received your green card by a fraudulent marriage, the punishment is more severe.

2. Civil Penalties

There are also civil penalties for those who "forge, counterfeit, alter, or falsely make any document" to satisfy a requirement of immigration law.

If you are found guilty, you can be fined $250 to $5,000 for each fraudulent document that you have in your possession or have already submitted to USCIS. In addition, if you are an alien, you may be excluded from entering the United States or, if you are already there, you may be removed or deported.

B. Check for Current Forms and Fees

The law and the rules on immigration procedures change frequently. Using old, outdated forms may cause your immigration petition to be delayed or, worse—denied. And if your immigration papers are filed with the wrong fee, they will be returned; this will further delay your legal entry as an immigrant.

Therefore, before mailing any immigration applications, take the time to request the most recent forms and to double check the filing fees with the local USCIS office or with an American consulate in your country of residence, whichever is most convenient.

If you have access to the Internet, you can check fees and request forms—or download most of them—from the USCIS website at www.uscis.gov.

C. Tips for Filling Out Forms

A number of immigration forms ask for the same kinds of identifying information—your name, address, identification numbers. While the answers may often seem obvious, USCIS requires that they be phrased in specific ways.

1. Your Family Name

When an immigration form asks you to fill in your name, write the complete name that you were given on your birth certificate or the name written in your passport, whichever document is required. Add your full middle name (if you have one), even if the form asks only for your middle initial. USCIS asks all applicants to add this for security check purposes, and may delay your application if you don't.

If the name on your birth certificate is not your name at present, explain the difference in a letter and submit the corresponding documents that show the change.

EXAMPLE: If you are a woman named Jane who is using the surname of your husband, John Smith, as your family name, write your husband's surname—that is, Jane Smith.

On the space that says "other names used," write your maiden name and any other names you have used—that is, Jane Doe.

If you were married previously, write your previous married name on that space. Attach your marriage certificate or divorce decree.

2. Your Address

Your address, as far as USCIS is concerned, is the place where you receive mail. The post office is very important in your immigration relationship because everything from USCIS will come by mail—notice of approval of petition, notice of incomplete submission, notice of interview, notice of proceedings, and your green card.

If the mail carrier does not deliver mail in your locality, rent a post office box. However, some USCIS forms ask not only for your mailing address but also for your actual address. In that case, write the exact address or location of your home or c/o—meaning "in care of"—the person you are living with.

3. Your Social Security and Alien Registration Numbers

The Social Security number requested on immigration forms is issued by the United States government, not by your country's own Social Security administration.

An alien registration number is issued by USCIS (or, formerly, the INS). If you have not been assigned one or both of these numbers, write "none" in the space provided on the immigration forms.

Answer Every Question

Answer all questions and do not leave a line on the form blank unless it clearly directs you to do otherwise. If the question being posed does not apply to you, write "not applicable" or, if you do not have a number or document, write "none." If you do not know the answer, write "not known." If you fail to answer all questions, processing your forms is likely to be delayed while USCIS sends them back and asks for more complete information.

D. When Additional Proof Is Required

USCIS requires specific proof to be submitted along with the answers on many of its forms, because you are entitled to a green card only when you can prove by convincing documentation that you meet specific qualifications. You can go a long way toward eliminating delays and confusion if you take the time to be sure your additional proof is accurate and complete.

Using the Department of State Documents Finder

Ever wonder how to get a birth certificate in Belarus or a divorce certificate in Djibouti? Go to http://travel.state.gov/visa/reciprocity/index.htm and find out. This tremendously helpful website tells you how to get documents you need for immigration cases (like proof of military service or lack of a police record) or replace documents you thought you had but can't lay your hands on. If you really can't get a certain document (such as a birth certificate), the website will give you suggestions on alternatives.

1. Proving a Family Relationship

As requested on the immigration forms, you must provide copies of documents to prove that a relationship permits you to apply as a family-based immigrant. If you do not submit the right documents, your materials will be returned and the whole process will be delayed.

You must have the official documents. To prove a family relationship, you must have the original birth certificate, marriage certificate, or death certificate issued by the civil registry of your country with the official government seal, stamp, or ribbon attached, depending on how official documents are marked in your country. Nongovernmental documents, such as church or hospital certificates, are usually not sufficient. Although you won't mail the originals in, you'll probably be asked to show them to USCIS at your interview.

Use your fingers to verify the indentation of the government seal that is embossed or pressed into the paper. USCIS will often assume that a document without such a seal is fraudulent.

If you have lost the documents, you can request certified copies from your government for an additional charge. Be sure these copies also have the official government seal.

USCIS has to carefully examine the documents people present. Some unscrupulous people create counterfeit documents to show relationships that do not exist, such as father and son or brother and sister, or to show educational attainment, such as school transcripts or diplomas, that they have not earned.

You must write or type the following statement on the back of each photocopy:

> Copies of documents submitted are exact photocopies of unaltered original documents, and I understand that I may be required to submit original documents to an immigration or consular official at a later date.

Include your signature and date of signature. There is no need to have your signature verified by a notary public.

Do Not Send Your Originals

Make a copy of your original document—and send the copy to USCIS. Things often get lost in the mail. And added to that, the USCIS offices are busy places crowded with many people and even more documents, so things can get lost there, too. USCIS often makes no effort to return originals to you, and takes no responsibility if they are lost. Keep the originals of your documents in a safe place—one that's fireproof if possible. Then show it to the consular or USCIS officer at your interview.

If you don't have the official document. Sometimes, you cannot get your original documents because of war, destruction of the civil registry, your government's prohibition on emigration, or simple oversight or ignorance.

In such cases, family relationships such as parent-child, brother-sister, or husband-wife can be proved by what is called secondary evidence—a combination of documents that may not come from the civil registry, but which nevertheless prove a relationship.

- Church records, for example, can sometimes be submitted. A baptismal certificate will show the parents' names and the date and place of birth of the child.

- Annotations in a family Bible, old letters, school records, or data from a relevant government census are other types of secondary evidence.

- USCIS may also accept the sworn statements, or affidavits, of two people who have witnessed your birth, your marriage, the death of a spouse, or whatever event you need to prove. The statement should include the witnesses' names and addresses, their relationship to you or your family, and why and how they know about the alleged event. The strongest evidence is from witnesses who were present at the event you need to prove.

For example, if you never had a birth certificate or you could not obtain a copy, an affidavit written by your sister could read as written below.

Sample Affidavit

My name is Jane Doe, and I am the older sister of John Doe.

I live at 123 Middle Abbey Street, Dublin, Ireland.

I was seven years old when my brother, John Doe, was born to our mother, Carolyn Doe, on July 4, 1930, at our home in Cork, Ireland. I remember the midwife coming to our house and I was sent outside to play. After it got dark, my brother was born and they called me inside to see him.

This affidavit is submitted because the civil registry in Cork was burned in 1932 and my brother's birth certificate was lost when the family moved to Dublin in the same year.

Signature: _____

Signed and sworn to before me on March 1, 200_
[Notary Stamp]

The witnesses have to swear to the truth of their statements before a notary public—a person who is authorized by the state to verify signatures. You can find a notary by looking in the telephone book, although most banks have one on staff. Most notaries will charge for their services, so it may be worthwhile to shop around for the one with the most reasonable charge. If required by the U.S. embassy in your country, the affidavits must be sworn to before the U.S. consular official, who will also charge a slight fee for the service.

You may need to submit your own affidavit stating why you cannot obtain the original documents and what efforts you have made to try to do so.

USCIS may further investigate your family relationship, or request that you and your relative undergo blood tests or give additional testimony. An investigation may even be conducted in the neighborhood in which you lived in your native country.

Before it confers an immigration benefit, the U.S. government must be certain that the person immigrating into the United States is truly the child, brother, sister, husband, or wife—and not the niece, nephew, aunt, uncle, cousin, or friend—of the U.S. citizen or permanent resident petitioner.

Documents in Languages Other Than English

If the documents you are submitting are not in English, have them translated accurately. An English summary of the document is not enough—although you do not have to hire a professional translator to do the job. Somebody who has competent knowledge of both English and the language in which the documents are written should be able to do the translation.

The translator must attach the following statement to the translated document and sign and date it:

I hereby certify that I am competent to translate this document from (the foreign language) to English and that this translation is accurate and complete to the best of my knowledge and ability.

2. Proving an INS or USCIS Approval

In some situations, you may have an application or petition that has been approved by the formerly named INS or USCIS, but need further action because:

- you lost the approval notice or you need a duplicate
- the U.S. embassy or consulate that originally received the approval notice closed down or you simply could not go to your home country, and another U.S. consulate is willing to process your immigration visa and needs to be officially notified, or
- you need USCIS to notify the U.S. consulate in your country that you became a green card holder in the United States so that your spouse and children can receive visas to join you.

In any of these circumstances, you must file Form I-824, Application for Action on an Approved Application or Petition, with the USCIS office that approved the original application or petition. The filing fee was $200 at the time this book went to print.

If you have a copy of the approval, make a copy of that and send or bring it to the USCIS office to help in locating your case.

3. Proving U.S. Citizenship

A U.S. citizen has the right to bestow permanent resident status on a spouse, parent, child, brother, sister, fiancée or fiancé, and widow or widower. But USCIS must first see documents proving the person's U.S. citizenship.

The following are accepted as proof:

- a birth certificate showing the place of birth to be any of the 50 states of the United States, Puerto Rico, the U.S. Virgin Islands, or Guam
- a valid U.S. passport issued for a full five or ten years
- a baptismal certificate with the seal of the church showing the place of birth and date of baptism, which must have occurred within

two months after birth, if the birth certificate cannot be obtained

- affidavits of two U.S. citizens who have personal knowledge of the petitioner's birth in the United States, if neither the birth nor the baptismal certificate can be obtained
- the certificate of naturalization from someone who has become a citizen by naturalization and who files a petition for a relative within 90 days of the date of naturalization
- Department of State Form FS-240, Report of Birth Abroad of a Citizen of the United States, which proves American citizenship for someone born abroad, and
- the certificate of citizenship issued by the INS or USCIS, which is also adequate proof that someone is a U.S. citizen born abroad.

4. Proving U.S. Lawful Permanent Residence

As a green card holder, you have the right to petition for your spouse and unmarried children, by submitting proof that you are a permanent resident. Although USCIS has your file and alien registration number in its records, you must still present your green card, or submit a copy of it if you are sending your immigration papers by mail.

The official name of your green card is Alien Registration Receipt Card Form I-551. Only the Form I-551 will be recognized as proof of lawful permanent residence.

If your green card is lost or not available, your passport—bearing the USCIS rubber stamp showing lawful admission for permanent residence and your alien registration number—is acceptable proof of your permanent resident status.

E. Submitting Photographs for Identification

Because good, accurate photographs are essential to ensure that a person is correctly represented for immigration purposes, the USCIS has imposed a number of strict specifications for the photographs and the poses it will accept. Essentially, it's the same style as required for U.S. passports.

While it is not essential to hire a professional photographer to take USCIS photos, it may be tough to comply with the picky requirements for size, lighting, and clarity. If you or a friend attempt to take the photos on your own, be sure to take a couple rolls of film—and to read the requirements first.

If, as is normally the case, you're asked to submit more than one photo, the photos must be identical—you can't just take a few photos that look quite similar and submit them.

Want more detail on the photo requirements? Visit the State Department website at www.state.gov. Under Travel and Business, click "Passports (U.S. Citizens)," then "Guide for Professional Photographers" (scroll down the left-hand column).

1. The Photographs

The overall size of the picture, including the background, must be at least 51 mm (2 inches) square.

The photographs must be in color—with no shadows, marks or discolorations on them. The background must be white or off-white; it is not acceptable to be photographed against a patterned or colored background. There must be good lighting; the photo must not appear too light or too dark. And the final image must be original, not retouched in any way.

2. The Image

The image on the photo—total size of the head—must be 25 to 35 mm (1 inch to $1^3/_8$ inches) from the top of the hair to the bottom of the chin.

Your eyes must be between $1^1/_8$ inches to $1^3/_8$ inches (28 mm and 35 mm) from the bottom of the photo.

Your face should be pictured from the front, with eyes open. Be sure that no jewelry or hats are worn—unless the headwear is required by your religion. Your facial expression should be natural—smiling is not necessary.

Before You Put Anything in the Mail

Whenever possible, it is best to file immigration papers personally, in case there are questions about your answers or your documents. However, many immigration offices allow you to file only by mail. Before mailing any immigration documents, make copies for your own records.

Submit your papers using certified mail, return receipt requested. This way, you will get confirmation that your papers were received.

F. Fingerprinting Requirements

USCIS requires fingerprinting to accompany a variety of applications, including permanent residence, asylum, and naturalization, among others. Fingerprints are generally reviewed by the FBI and CIA to determine an applicant's actual identity and to determine whether the person has a criminal background that would make him or her inadmissible. USCIS will also check to see whether you've submitted previous applications under a different name.

If the application you are filing requires fingerprinting, you should include a fee (currently $70, check or money order) made out to USCIS for the cost of fingerprinting. This is in addition to any fees for the application itself.

USCIS will usually contact you within 90 days by letter, telling you when you should go to a USCIS-authorized site for fingerprinting. You will be given directions and a specific week within which you must appear at the fingerprinting site.

If you cannot make it during your appointed time, you can ask to be rescheduled. At some locations, USCIS is also developing mobile fingerprinting vans that will make it easier for people who live outside major urban areas to comply with the fingerprinting requirements.

If you live abroad and are filing your application outside the United States, you may be fingerprinted at a U.S. consulate or military installation. The fee is $85.

G. Keep Your Own File

For your own records, make copies of everything that you submit to the U.S. government, including the immigration forms and the supporting documents. Also make a copy of the receipt USCIS issues to you after you pay the filing fee.

After you have made copies and mailed your immigration papers (certified mail, return receipt requested), or after you have personally submitted them to USCIS, keep your own copies and original documents in a safe place. You will need them again when you are called to receive your immigrant visa at the American embassy or when you attend your personal interview for your green card at USCIS.

Also, like any other bureaucracy, USCIS does sometimes misplace files. It will save you a lot of headache and heartache if you can show that you have already filed the application with USCIS by presenting a copy of the documents filed, the receipt from USCIS, and your certified check or money order. ■

Keeping, Renewing, and Replacing Your Green Card

When Your Green Card Is Lost, Stolen, or Cancelled

Now that you have finally obtained that plastic card giving you the right to stay and work in the United States without any hassle, and to leave and return without applying for a visa, make sure you don't you lose the card—or your right to it.

If all goes as it should, your green card will give you the right to live in the United States for as long as you want to. However, you need to protect this right by taking such measures as telling USCIS when you move, not spending too long outside the United States, and not becoming inadmissible or deportable. You should also make sure to renew your green card on time and replace it if it's lost.

⚠ Think about applying for U.S. citizenship.
After a certain number of years with a green card (usually five, but less for some people), you can apply for U.S. citizenship. This is a much more secure status—you'll be able to travel for longer periods of time, are safe from deportation, and will gain the right to vote. Start planning now: If you wait until five years go by to start thinking about citizenship, you may discover that there was something you needed to do (or something you did that you shouldn't have done) while you were waiting, that will end up setting you back. For complete guidance, see *Becoming a U.S. Citizen: A Guide to the Law, Exam & Interview,* by Ilona Bray (Nolo).

A. Renewing or Replacing Your Green Card

Whether your green card is lost or expires and needs to be renewed, the U.S. Citizenship and Immigration Services (USCIS) requires that you file Form I-90, Application to Replace Permanent Resident Card. (See the sample at the end of this chapter.)

The filing fee is currently $190, plus $70 for fingerprints. Where to file Form I-90 gets a bit complicated depending on why you are filing it, so the best thing to do is visit USCIS's website at www.uscis.gov/graphics/formsfee/forms/i-90.htm for the most up-to-date procedures. Consider e-filing this form in order to avoid any confusion about how to proceed. (See instructions for e-filing in Chapter 21.)

You can also use Form I-90 to get a new green card when:

- your name has been changed, due to marriage or divorce, in which case you must include a copy of your marriage or divorce certificate and your old card
- you turn 14 years of age; USCIS requires that you change your green card for a new one
- you receive an incorrect card with an erroneous name, birthdate, photo, or date of entry
- you never received your green card, or
- your green card is blue, Form I-151; these old cards were issued during the 1960s and 1970s and expired on August 2, 1996, because of their lack of security features, giving opportunities for fraud.

You must swear that all the answers you give when applying for a green card are correct. If you knowingly falsify or conceal a material fact, or use any false document in submitting the application, you may be fined up to $10,000, imprisoned for up to five years, or both.

You should receive your new green card (Form I-551) within 30 to 45 days after USCIS receives your paperwork and filing fee.

B. When the Immigration Authorities Can Take Away Your Card

As a green card holder, you are expected to be law-abiding. Because you were not born with the right to stay in the United States and have not yet been naturalized, the immigration laws put certain restrictions on you that do not apply to U.S. citizens.

1. Failing to Report a Change of Address

The immigration law says that an alien who fails to give written notice to USCIS of a change of address can be deported or removed from the United States. Not only that, the alien could be charged with a misdemeanor and if found guilty, fined up to $200, imprisoned up to 30 days, or both.

The alien would have to convince the immigration judge during removal hearings that failure to notify USCIS of an address change was reasonably excusable or was not willful.

Therefore, to avoid any possible problem whenever you move to a new address, mail Form AR-11 (available at USCIS offices or on the USCIS website at www.uscis.gov) to:

> Department of Homeland Security
> U.S. Citizenship and Immigration Services
> Change of Address
> P.O. Box 7134
> London, KY 40742-7134

There is no fee for filing this form.

2. Failing to Maintain a Residence in the United States

You became a permanent resident presumably because you intend to live in the United States. If you live outside the United States for more than 12 months, it will appear to the immigration authorities that you do not intend to make your home in America.

It is wise to be gone for no more than 180 days. This will decrease your risk of losing your green card and help ensure that your admission at the airport or other port of entry is as free of trouble as possible.

Otherwise, when you return after your year abroad, the border officials may put you into re-moval proceedings to determine whether you have lost the right to live in the United States as a perma-nent resident. Your green card may be taken away.

But you can do something to help avoid such a situation. If you know in advance that you may not be able to return to the United States within

a year's time, you can apply for a reentry permit by mailing the following to the USCIS Nebraska Service Center (get the address from the USCIS website) at least 30 days before you intend to depart, along with a filing fee (currently $170):

- Form I-131, Application for Travel Document (see the sample at the end of this chapter)
- a copy of your green card (front and back), and
- two photographs (see Chapter 22, Section E, for details).

USCIS will mail a reentry permit to the address in the United States you have indicated on your application.

You can protect your right to your green card. The best way to do this is to understand what you might do that could lead the authorities to decide that you have lost or abandoned your permanent residence status. In determining this, they look at your intentions about your permanent residence when you leave the United States. If your intent is to be gone temporarily, then you should be able to maintain your status.

Since the U.S. government cannot know your real intent, it will look at things such as:

- your purpose in leaving
- whether your purpose is consistent with a temporary absence
- whether you still have a job, home, or family in the United States, and
- the duration of your trip.

Getting a reentry permit before you leave is good evidence that you intend to return to the United States to continue living. It also means that the authorities cannot rely solely on the length of your absence to determine that you have lost your permanent residence status. However, since they can still look at other facts in your life, you should maintain as many ties to the United States as possible—even if you get a reentry permit.

If you have to go abroad before you receive the permit, you can request that the permit be delivered to your address overseas or, if the mail in your country is not reliable, through the United States embassy or consulate in your country.

However, you must be physically present in the United States when you file the application. If you have been outside of the U.S. for four out of the past five years, the permit will be issued for only one year. And if you have been out of the U.S. for that amount of time, you can also expect to receive intense questions at the airport about whether you have maintained your legal residence in the United States.

If a reentry permit is issued, it is good for two years.

3. Explaining Your Failure to Reenter the United States

If you stay longer than the two years allowed by the reentry permit, or if you stay longer than one year without applying for the reentry permit, you will jeopardize your immigration status.

Upon arriving at the port of entry, the officials will question you on your right to return as a green card holder. Therefore, you must be ready to present proof of why you did not return to the United States within the time expected.

Illness. A permissible delay could be due to your own serious illness or to that of a close relative, especially if the illness started after you left. Convincing evidence of the illness would be copies of a doctor's written diagnosis, medical bills, prescriptions, and letters to you from friends.

Death. A death in the family could be another reason for delay. Bring with you copies of the death certificate, letters from the court or lawyer on settlement of the estate, life insurance letters concerning distribution of the insurance proceeds, and a court order dividing property of the deceased.

Business reasons. Setting up or closing down a business enterprise could also be a valid reason for delay. Be ready to show bank statements; a contract of sale, invoices, letters from the bank, and letters from your business partners, your lawyer, and your accountant.

In other words, if you are detained at the airport for a more thorough questioning, you must be ready to convince the officer that you had a very good reason for not returning to the United States when expected. If the immigration officer is still not convinced, you will have another chance to explain your case before the immigration judge at your hearing.

Insist on your right to a hearing. Too often, the officer applies the third degree, and the scared green card holder signs away his or her green card rights. Once you do this, it is very difficult to get a second chance to explain your side before the immigration court. Your status will most likely automatically revert to that of a nonimmigrant—and you will have to repeat the process of getting a green card all over again.

However, if you were coerced or forced to sign away your rights, contact an immigration attorney, who may be able to help you fight to keep your green card.

4. Becoming Inadmissible

Grounds of inadmissibility are conditions that the immigration authorities can legally use to keep you from entering the United States. You had to prove that you weren't inadmissible (that is, hadn't committed any crimes, didn't have any serious illnesses, and weren't likely to need public assistance) in order to get your green card. But these same grounds apply to you every time you leave the United States and try to return. Even with your green card, you could be refused reentry. If one of these grounds applies to you, however, you may be able to get it waived. (See Chapter 4.)

5. Becoming Removable

In addition to the grounds of inadmissibility described above, the immigration laws list grounds of removability. These are actions or circumstances that can cause you to lose your right to the green card and be placed in removal proceedings in the

United States. If you lose, you could be deported back to the country you came from.

The grounds of removability are too complex to explain in detail here. We have already discussed one of them, namely your obligation to report your changes of address to USCIS. In general, however, you need to make sure not to violate any immigration or criminal laws and not to get involved with any organizations that the U.S. government believes to be terrorist.

For a complete list of the grounds of removability, see I.N.A. § 237 or 8 U.S.C. § 1227.

Application to Replace Permanent Resident Card, Sample Form I-90 (page 1)

OMB No. 1615-0082; Expires 06/30/09

Department of Homeland Security
U.S. Citizenship and Immigration Services

**I-90, Application to Replace
Permanent Resident Card**

START HERE - Please type or print in black ink.	**FOR USCIS USE ONLY**

Part 1. Information about you.

Family Name	Given Name	Middle Initial
Cosmin	Mihaita	

U.S. Mailing Address - C/O

Ravin Cosmin

Street Number and Name	Apt. #
8383 Kew Gardens	4001

City

Queens

State	ZIP Code
New York	11415

Date of Birth(Month/ Day/Year)	Country of Birth
October 2, 1951	Romania

Social Security #	A #
112-64-5793	A24-070-502

FOR USCIS USE ONLY

Returned	Receipt
Resubmitted	
Reloc Sent	
Reloc Rec'd	

☐ Applicant Interviewed

Status as _____ Verified by _____

Class _____ Initials _____

FD-258 forwarded on _____

I-89 forwarded on _____

I-551 seen and returned _____

Photocopy of I-551 verified _____ (Initials)
_____ (Initials)

_____ Name   _____ Date

Sticker # _____ (ten-digit number)

Part 2. Application type.

1. My status is: (check one)

a. ☑ Permanent Resident - (Not a Commuter)

b. ☐ Permanent Resident - (Commuter)

c. ☐ Conditional Permanent Resident

2. Reason for application: (check one)
I am a Permanent Resident or Conditional Permanent Resident and:

a. ☑ My card was lost, stolen or destroyed.

b. ☐ My authorized card was never received.

c. ☐ My card is mutilated.

d. ☐ My card was issued with incorrect information because of a USCIS administrative error.

e. ☐ My name or other biographic information has changed since the card was issued.

I am a Permanent Resident and:

f. ☐ My present card has an expiration date and it is expiring.

g. ☐ I have reached my 14th birthday since my card was issued.

h. 1. ☐ I have taken up Commuter status.

h. 2. ☐ I was a Commuter and am now taking up residence in the U.S.

i. ☐ My status has been automatically converted to permanent resident.

j. ☐ I have an old edition of the card.

Part 3. Processing information.

Mother's First Name	Father's First Name
Silvia	Claidus
City of Residence where you applied for an Immigrant Visa or Adjustment of Status	Consulate where Immigrant Visa was issued or USCIS office where status was Adjusted
Bucharest, Romania	U.S. Consulate, Bucharest
City/Town/Village of Birth	Date of Admission as an immigrant or Adjustment of Status
Bucharest	October 31, 2000

Action Block

**To Be Completed by
Attorney or Representative, if any**
☐ Fill in box if G-28 is attached to represent the applicant

VOLAG# _____

ATTY State License # _____

Form I-90 (Rev. 10/26/05)Y

Sample Form I-90 (page 2)

Part 3. Processing information (continued):

If you entered the U.S. with an Immigrant Visa, also complete the following:

Destination in U.S. at
time of Admission   New York, New York

Port of Entry where
Admitted to U.S.   JFK Airport

Are you in removal/deportation or recission proceedings?   ☑ No   ☐ Yes

Since you were granted permanent residence, have you ever filed Form I-407, Abandonment by Alien of Status as Lawful Permanent Resident, or otherwise been judged to have abandoned your status?   ☑ No   ☐ Yes

If you answer yes to any of the above questions, explain in detail on a separate piece of paper.

Part 4. Signature. *(Read the information on penalties in the instructions before completing this section. You must file this application while in the United States.)*

I certify, under penalty of perjury under the laws of the United States of America, that this application and the evidence submitted with it is all true and correct. I authorize the release of any information from my records that U.S. Citizenship and Immigration Services needs to determine eligibility for the benefit I am seeking.

Signature	Date	Daytime Phone Number
Mihaita Cosmin	January 6, 2006	718-675-4892

Please Note: If you do not completely fill out this form or fail to submit required documents listed in the instructions, you cannot be found eligible for the requested document and this application may be denied.

Part 5. Signature of person preparing form, if other than above. *(Sign below)*

I declare that I prepared this application at the request of the above person and it is based on all information of which I have knowledge.

Signature	Print Your Name	Date	Daytime Phone Number

Name and Address of Business/Organization (if applicable)

Application for Travel Document, Sample Form I-131 (page 1)

Department of Homeland Security
U. S. Citizenship and Immigration Services

OMB No. 1615-0013; Expires 11/30/07

I-131, Application for Travel Document

DO NOT WRITE IN THIS BLOCK		FOR USCIS USE ONLY (except G-28 block below)
Document Issued	**Action Block**	**Receipt**

Document Issued
☐ Reentry Permit
☐ Refugee Travel Document
☐ Single Advance Parole
☐ Multiple Advance Parole
Valid to: _____

If Reentry Permit or Refugee Travel Document, mail to:
☐ Address in Part 1
☐ American embassy/consulate at: _____
☐ Overseas DHS office at: _____

☐ Document Hand Delivered
On _____ By _____

To be completed by Attorney/Representative, if any.
Attorney State License # _____
☐ Check box if G-28 is attached.

Part 1.   Information about you. *(Please type or print in black ink.)*

1. A #	2. Date of Birth *(mm/dd/yyyy)*	3. Class of Admission	4. Gender
24-070-502	10/02/51	Spouse of U.S. citizen	Male ☒ Female ☐

5. Name *(Family name in capital letters)* — COSMIN   *(First)* — Mihaita   *(Middle)*

6. Address *(Number and Street)* — 8383 Kew Gardens   Apt. # — 4001

City	State or Province	Zip/Postal Code	Country
Queens	New York	11415	USA

7. Country of Birth	8. Country of Citizenship	9. Social Security # *(if any.)*
Romania	Romania	123-44-5555

Part 2.   Application type *(check one).*

a. ☒ I am a permanent resident or conditional resident of the United States and I am applying for a reentry permit.

b. ☐ I now hold U.S. refugee or asylee status and I am applying for a refugee travel document.

c. ☐ I am a permanent resident as a direct result of refugee or asylee status and I am applying for a refugee travel document.

d. ☐ I am applying for an advance parole document to allow me to return to the United States after temporary foreign travel.

e. ☐ I am outside the United States and I am applying for an advance parole document.

f. ☐ I am applying for an advance parole document for a person who is outside the United States. *If you checked box "f", provide the following information about that person:*

1. Name *(Family name in capital letters)*   *(First)*   *(Middle)*

2. Date of Birth *(mm/dd/yyyy)*	3. Country of Birth	4. Country of Citizenship

5. Address *(Number and Street)*   Apt. #   Daytime Telephone # *(area/country code)*

City	State or Province	Zip/Postal Code	Country

INITIAL RECEIPT _____   RESUBMITTED _____   RELOCATED: Rec'd. _____ Sent _____   COMPLETED: Appv'd. _____ Denied _____ Ret'd. _____

Form I-131 (Rev. 10/26/05) Y

Sample Form I-131 (page 2)

Part 3. Processing information.

1. Date of Intended Departure *(mm/dd/yyyy)*	2. Expected Length of Trip
12/15/2006	13 months

3. Are you, or any person included in this application, now in exclusion, deportation, removal or recission proceedings? [X] No [ ] Yes *(Name of DHS office):*

If you are applying for an Advance Parole Document, skip to Part 7.

4. Have you ever before been issued a reentry permit or refugee travel? *for the last document issued to you):* [X] No [ ] Yes *(Give the following information*

Date Issued *(mm/dd/yyyy):*   Disposition *(attached, lost, etc.):*

5. Where do you want this travel document sent? *(Check one)*

a. [X] To the U.S. address shown in **Part 1** on the first page of this form.

b. [ ] To an American embassy or consulate at: City: Country:

c. [ ] To a DHS office overseas at: City: Country:

d. If you checked "b" or "c", where should the notice to pick up the travel document be sent?

[ ] To the address shown in **Part 2** on the first page of this form.

[ ] To the address shown below:

Address *(Number and Street)*	Apt. #	Daytime Telephone # *(area/country code)*

City	State or Province	Zip/Postal Code	Country

Part 4. Information about your proposed travel.

Purpose of trip. *If you need more room, continue on a seperate sheet(s) of paper.*	List the countries you intend to visit.
To visit my dying brother and assist with the settlement of his estate.	Romania

Part 5. Complete only if applying for a reentry permit.

Since becoming a permanent resident of the United States (or during the past five years, whichever is less) how much total time have you spent outside the United States?

[X] less than six months   [ ] two to three years
[ ] six months to one year   [ ] three to four years
[ ] one to two years   [ ] more than four years

Since you became a permanent resident of the United States, have you ever filed a federal income tax return as a nonresident, or failed to file a federal income tax return because you considered yourself to be a nonresident? *(If "Yes," give details on a separate sheet(s) of paper.)*   [ ] Yes [X] No

Part 6. Complete only if applying for a refugee travel document.

1. Country from which you are a refugee or asylee:

If you answer "Yes" to any of the following questions, you must explain on a separate sheet(s) of paper.

2. Do you plan to travel to the above named country?	[ ] Yes	[ ] No

3. Since you were accorded refugee/asylee status, have you ever:
a. returned to the above named country?   [ ] Yes [ ] No
b. applied for and/or obtained a national passport, passport renewal or entry permit of that country?   [ ] Yes [ ] No
c. applied for and/or received any benefit from such country (for example, health insurance benefits).   [ ] Yes [ ] No

4. Since you were accorded refugee/asylee status, have you, by any legal procedure or voluntary act:
a. reacquired the nationality of the above named country?   [ ] Yes [ ] No
b. acquired a new nationality?   [ ] Yes [ ] No
c. been granted refugee or asylee status in any other country?   [ ] Yes [ ] No

Form I-131 (Rev. 10/26/05) Y Page 2

Sample Form I-131 (page 3)

Part 7. Complete only if applying for advance parole.

On a separate sheet(s) of paper, please explain how you qualify for an advance parole document and what circumstances warrant issuance of advance parole. Include copies of any documents you wish considered. *(See instructions.)*

1. For how many trips do you intend to use this document? ☐ One trip ☐ More than one trip

2. If the person intended to receive an advance parole document is outside the United States, provide the location (city and country) of the American embassy or consulate or the DHS overseas office that you want us to notify.

City

Country

3. If the travel document will be delivered to an overseas office, where should the notice to pick up the document be sent:

☐   To the address shown in **Part 2** on the first page of this form.

☐   To the address shown below:

Address *(Number and Street)*   Apt. #   Daytime Telephone # *(area/country code)*

City   State or Province   Zip/Postal Code   Country

Part 8. Signature. *Read the information on penalties in the instructions before completing this section. If you are filing for a reentry permit or refugee travel document, you must be in the United States to file this application.*

I certify, under penalty of perjury under the laws of the United States of America, that this application and the evidence submitted with it are all true and correct. I authorize the release of any information from my records that the U.S. Citizenship and Immigration Services needs to determine eligibility for the benefit I am seeking.

Signature   Date *(mm/dd/yyyy)*   Daytime Telephone Number *(with area code)*

Mihaita Cosmin   11/04/2006   718-675-4892

Please Note: If you do not completely fill out this form or fail to submit required documents listed in the instructions, you may not be found eligible for the requested document and this application may be denied.

Part 9. Signature of person preparing form, if other than the applicant. *(Sign below.)*

I declare that I prepared this application at the request of the applicant and it is based on all information of which I have knowledge.

Signature   Print or Type Your Name

Firm Name and Address   Daytime Telephone Number *(with area code)*

Fax Number *(if any.)*   Date *(mm/dd/yyyy)*

How to Find and Work With a Lawyer

If It Is Possible, As Far As It Depends on You, Live at Peace With Everyone.
                                        Romans 12:18

Although this book's philosophy is to help you understand the immigration law and procedures, your situation may be too complicated for you to handle on your own—particularly if you've spent time in the U.S. illegally, have a history of drug use or criminal activity, or fit any of the other problem scenarios described in this book. Or you may be unable to get USCIS to respond to a request for action on your application. It may become necessary to hire a lawyer or other immigration professional for help. This chapter gives you valuable tips on where to find help—and what to do once you find that help.

A. Where to Look for a Lawyer

A bad lawyer is worse than a thief. Good lawyers are worth their weight in gold. Look carefully to find a good, competent, honest lawyer who will help you with your immigration problems without charging you a hefty fee up front and a huge hourly fee as your case proceeds.

You can go a long way toward ensuring that you get the best lawyer possible by spending some time and effort before you hire him or her. There are a number of good places to begin your search.

1. Immigration Groups

Organizations that specialize in helping people with immigration problems may be able to answer your questions, to represent you in your case, or to refer you to an experienced immigration lawyer if the group does not take on individual cases. Ask your local USCIS office or church, mosque, or temple for referrals.

2. Friends and Relatives

Ask your friends and relatives about their own experiences with their immigration lawyers—whether they were satisfied with the representation,

with the competency, with the fees charged, and with their personal rapport with their attorney. Never choose a lawyer simply because he or she was the relative or classmate or friend of your brother or sister or best friend, without having an idea of the lawyer's competency or track record.

3. Embassies or Consulates

Your own embassy or consulate may have a list of immigration lawyers to recommend to you. Normally, your country's consular officers have your interests at heart and would not recommend a lawyer who is incompetent, a rogue, or a cheat.

4. Ads in Ethnic Newspapers

Your own ethnic newspapers and journals usually have an array of immigration lawyers offering their services directly through advertisements. But beware—anyone can buy ad space. Be sure to investigate the lawyer's reputation on your own. Ask your friends. Check with the local bar association or with immigration support groups in the area.

5. Lawyer Referral Groups

Although the local bar association and other lawyer groups may offer referral services, there is often little or no screening of lawyers listed in these services. The only qualification may be that no malpractice case has been filed against the lawyer.

The American Immigration Lawyers Association (918 F Street NW, Washington, DC 20004; telephone: 202-216-2400; fax: 202-783-7853; website: www.aila.org) operates a lawyer referral service. The lawyers who participate in the service are usually competent and knowledgeable.

Nolo also offers a lawyer directory for certain parts of the U.S., where lawyers have a chance to describe their philosophy and services, at http://lawyers.nolo.com.

Beware of the Bad Guys

Nonattorney practitioners, visa consultants, immigration pseudo-experts, travel agents, people posing as attorneys, and nonprofit organizations not authorized by U.S. Citizenship and Immigration Services (USCIS) to represent aliens before USCIS—all of them litter the immigration marketplace.

Some of them provide good advice. But for the most part, be wary—especially if they promise you a green card without any hassle for a certain amount of money. Aside from the fact that it is unlawful to practice law without being admitted by the state bar association, there is no way you can check on these individuals' expertise and nowhere to complain if their services are poor. Many imcompetent consultants prey on immigrants and then simply pack up and move when too many people catch on to them.

Report any wrongdoers to the attorney general's office in your state so that they will be forced to stop victimizing unsuspecting immigrants.

B. Deciding on a Particular Lawyer

Once you have a referral to a lawyer—or even better, several referrals—contact each and see whether he or she meets your needs.

A law firm may have a good reputation on immigration practice, but the lawyer assigned to handle your case is the lawyer responsible for the success or failure of your case. Base your decision about whether to hire an individual on the rapport you feel with him or her—not just on a law firm's reputation.

1. The Initial Interview

Start by asking for an appointment. The office may try to screen you by asking you to first discuss your immigration problem over the phone, because the lawyer may not handle cases such as yours.

When you do find a lawyer who agrees to meet with you, go to the meeting with the thought in mind that you are interviewing him or her—not the other way around. It will be you who decides whether or not you want to hire that particular lawyer to handle your case.

Rely on your instincts when you first interview the lawyer. Does he or she seem competent, knowledgeable, fair, efficient, courteous, and personable? It would be unfortunate and unwise for you to feel uneasy every time you are in contact with your lawyer while paying him or her your hard-earned money.

2. Consultation Fees

Some lawyers may not charge you an initial consultation fee, but most immigration lawyers charge between $50 and $200, depending on the city where you live, the expertise of the lawyer, and how long the interview lasts. When you ask for an appointment, also ask whether a consultation fee is charged and how much it is. Also ask how long the lawyer has been in immigration law practice and how many cases like yours the attorney has handled.

If you take a few minutes to get organized before you go to the lawyer, 30 minutes to an hour should be enough time to explain your situation and get at least a basic opinion of what the lawyer can do for you and what that help is likely to cost. Bring with you:

- your passport
- Form I-94
- a copy of any immigration forms you may have filled out and correspondence received from the INS or USCIS, and
- documents you may need to prove family relationships, such as husband and wife or parent and child. (See Chapter 22, Section D1.)

3. Dealing With Paralegals and Assistants

Because the practice of immigration law usually involves filling out a great number of forms, the lawyer may hire a paralegal or secretary who interviews you to get many of the answers needed to complete your paperwork.

The paralegal or secretary becomes your contact person. At the initial interview, ask permission to interview the paralegal who will be working on your case, too, so that you have an idea of how comfortable you will be in dealing with the assistant. Ask whether he or she is supervised and whether he or she normally gives the forms to the lawyer for review before submitting them to the U.S. government.

C. Paying the Lawyer

Some organizations specializing in immigration may take your case *pro bono,* meaning they will provide a lawyer to handle your case without asking for any money or for only a small amount to cover expenses. However, due to limited resources and great demand, they may not be able to accept your immigration case and may only be able to tell you what your legal options are and advise you about whether you seem to have a strong case. These groups may refer you to a list of attorneys they feel would be representing you in the same spirit of service as they do and whose fees would be reasonable.

1. Types of Fee Arrangements

Most lawyers are guided by the principle that Time is Money. Many will charge for their work based on quarter-hours, so that if you call and spend ten minutes on the telephone, you will be charged for a minimum of 15 minutes of work. Unless you are completely satisfied that your lawyer is honest, you may be opening yourself up to paying into a bottomless money pit in legal fees when you agree to pay the lawyer according to an hourly charge.

If you agree to the per-hour billing rate—usually unwise unless you are in a deportation or exclusion proceeding due to grave criminal conduct or some other complicated case—request a schedule of legal work to be done and a maximum you will pay for each task.

If the case is simple, as usually is the case with an immigration petition for relatives, you may be charged a flat fee, from several hundred to a few thousand dollars. And if the lawyer agrees, you can pay the fee in installments during the period it takes to process your immigration papers.

2. Get It in Writing

Most disagreements between lawyers and clients involve fees, so be sure to get all the details involving money in writing—either the per hour billing rate or flat maximum fee—how often you will be billed, and how the attorney will handle any funds you may have deposited in advance to cover expenses.

D. Managing the Lawyer

A great many complaints against lawyers have to do with their failure to communicate with their clients. Your lawyer may be the one with the legal expertise, but the rights that are being pursued are yours—and you are the most important person involved in your case. You have the right to demand that your lawyer be reasonably available to answer your questions and to keep you posted on your case.

You may need to put some energy into managing your lawyer.

1. Carefully Check Every Statement

Each statement or bill should list costs that the lawyer has paid or that you are expected to pay. If any one lacks sufficient detail for you to verify that it complies with your written fee agreement, call your lawyer and politely demand that a new, more detailed version be sent before you pay it. Don't feel as though you're being too pushy by demanding more detail: The laws in many states actually require thorough detail in lawyers' billing statements.

2. Educate Yourself

By learning the most you can about immigration laws and what to expect during the procedure, you'll be able to monitor your lawyer's work and may even be able to do some legwork, make a suggestion, or provide information that will move your case along faster.

Unfortunately, USCIS and the State Department are bureaucracies and oftentimes, a case is simply held up until the slow-grinding wheels of procedure get through it. However, if an immigration application is proceeding much more slowly than your lawyer initially told you it would, then ask your lawyer whether it would make sense to contact the appropriate office and find out the reason for the delay.

3. Keep Your Own Calendar

Note when papers and appearances are due in court. If you rely on your lawyer to keep your case on schedule, you may be unpleasantly surprised to find that an important deadline has been missed. And your immigration status may be put in jeopardy. Call or write to your lawyer at least a week before any important deadline in your case to inquire about plans to meet it.

4. Maintain Your Own File

Never give away original documents connected with your case; keep the originals for your own files and give only copies to your lawyer. USCIS will accept copies of the original documents. Also, ask for a copy of every letter and application your lawyer sends to USCIS. By having a well-organized file of your own, you'll be able to

discuss your case with your lawyer intelligently and efficiently—even over the telephone.

Being well-informed will help keep your lawyer's effectiveness up and your costs down, especially if your lawyer is working on an hourly basis, in which case telephone consultations are less expensive than office visits.

Also, your lawyer cannot hold your immigration files ransom in case you decide to change legal counsel, because you have copies of everything the office file has on your case.

In any event, you have a right to promptly receive a copy of your file. The attorney may ask you to sign or produce a written authorization and transfer request.

E. Firing a Lawyer

Change lawyers if you feel that's necessary. If the relationship between you and the lawyer you chose doesn't seem to be working out, or if you feel that your case isn't progressing as it should, think about asking another lawyer to take over.

If you get upset every time you talk to your lawyer because he or she does not seem to understand what you are saying about your case, or will not take the time to listen, you will save yourself both money and mental anguish if you look for someone else to represent you.

But be clear with the first lawyer that you are taking your business elsewhere, and immediately put your decision in writing. You could end up receiving bills from both lawyers—both of whom will claim they handled the lion's share of your case. Before you pay anything, be sure that the total amount of the bills does not amount to more than you agreed to pay. Do not be embarrassed to negotiate with your lawyer. If you have a contingency fee arrangement, it is up to your new lawyer and former lawyer to work out how to split the fee.

What to Do About Bad Legal Advice

Take prompt action against any behavior by a lawyer that appears to be deceptive, unethical, or otherwise illegal. A call to the local bar association, listed in the telephone directory under Attorneys, should provide you with guidance on what types of lawyer behavior are prohibited and how to file a complaint.

Still, in most states, groups that regulate attorneys are biased toward lawyers. Unless the lawyer's conduct is plainly dishonest or he or she has abandoned your case, you will probably not get much satisfaction. However, sometimes the threat of filing a complaint can move your lawyer into action. And if worst comes to worst, filing a formal complaint will create a document that you'll need should you end up later filing a lawsuit against a lawyer for malpractice.

■

Index

W

CATALOG

...more from Nolo

BUSINESS

	PRICE	CODE
Business Buyout Agreements (Book w/CD-ROM)	$49.99	BSAG
The CA Nonprofit Corporation Kit (Binder w/CD-ROM)	$69.99	CNP
California Workers' Comp: How to Take Charge When You're Injured on the Job	$34.99	WORK
The Complete Guide to Buying a Business (Book w/CD-ROM)	$24.99	BUYBU
The Complete Guide to Selling a Business (Book w/CD-ROM)	$24.99	SELBU
Consultant & Independent Contractor Agreements (Book w/CD-ROM)	$29.99	CICA
The Corporate Records Handbook (Book w/CD-ROM)	$69.99	CORMI
Create Your Own Employee Handbook (Book w/CD-ROM)	$49.99	EMHA
Dealing With Problem Employees	$44.99	PROBM
Deduct It! Lower Your Small Business Taxes	$34.99	DEDU
Effective Fundraising for Nonprofits	$24.99	EFFN
The Employer's Legal Handbook	$39.99	EMPL
Essential Guide to Federal Employment Laws	$39.99	FEMP
Form a Partnership (Book W/CD-ROM)	$39.99	PART
Form Your Own Limited Liability Company (Book w/CD-ROM)	$44.99	LIAB
Home Business Tax Deductions: Keep What You Earn	$34.99	DEHB
How to Form a Nonprofit Corporation (Book w/CD-ROM)—National Edition	$49.99	NNP
How to Form a Nonprofit Corporation in California (Book w/CD-ROM)	$49.99	NON
How to Form Your Own California Corporation (Binder w/CD-ROM)	$59.99	CACI
How to Form Your Own California Corporation (Book w/CD-ROM)	$34.99	CCOR
How to Write a Business Plan (Book w/CD-ROM)	$34.99	SBS
Incorporate Your Business (Book w/CD-ROM)	$49.99	NIBS
Investors in Your Backyard (Book w/CD-ROM)	$24.99	FINBUS
The Job Description Handbook	$29.99	JOB
Legal Guide for Starting & Running a Small Business	$34.99	RUNS
Legal Forms for Starting & Running a Small Business (Book w/CD-ROM)	$29.99	RUNSF
LLC or Corporation?	$24.99	CHENT
The Manager's Legal Handbook	$39.99	ELBA
Marketing Without Advertising	$20.00	MWAD
Music Law (Book w/CD-ROM)	$39.99	ML
Negotiate the Best Lease for Your Business	$24.99	LESP
Nolo's Guide to Social Security Disability (Book w/CD-ROM)	$29.99	QSS
Nolo's Quick LLC	$29.99	LLCQ
The Performance Appraisal Handbook	$29.99	PERF
The Small Business Start-up Kit (Book w/CD-ROM)	$24.99	SMBU
The Small Business Start-up Kit for California (Book w/CD-ROM)	$24.99	OPEN
Starting & Running a Successful Newsletter or Magazine	$29.99	MAG

Prices subject to change.

	PRICE	CODE
Tax Deductions for Professionals	$34.99	DEPO
Tax Savvy for Small Business	$36.99	SAVVY
Whoops! I'm in Business	$19.99	WHOO
Working for Yourself: Law & Taxes for Independent Contractors, Freelancers & Consultants	$39.99	WAGE
Working With Independent Contractors (Book w/CD-ROM)	$29.99	HICI
Your Crafts Business: A Legal Guide (Book w/CD-ROM)	$26.99	VART
Your Limited Liability Company: An Operating Manual (Book w/CD-ROM)	$49.99	LOP
Your Rights in the Workplace	$29.99	YRW

CONSUMER

	PRICE	CODE
How to Win Your Personal Injury Claim	$29.99	PICL
Nolo's Encyclopedia of Everyday Law	$29.99	EVL
Nolo's Guide to California Law	$24.99	CLAW

ESTATE PLANNING & PROBATE

	PRICE	CODE
8 Ways to Avoid Probate	$19.99	PRAV
Estate Planning Basics	$21.99	ESPN
The Executor's Guide: Settling a Loved One's Estate or Trust	$34.99	EXEC
How to Probate an Estate in California	$49.99	PAE
Make Your Own Living Trust (Book w/CD-ROM)	$39.99	LITR
Nolo's Simple Will Book (Book w/CD-ROM)	$36.99	SWIL
Plan Your Estate	$44.99	NEST
Quick & Legal Will Book (Book w/CD-ROM)	$19.99	QUIC
Special Needs Trust: Protect Your Child's Financial Future (Book w/CD-ROM)	$34.99	SPNT

FAMILY MATTERS

	PRICE	CODE
Always Dad	$16.99	DIFA
Building a Parenting Agreement That Works	$24.99	CUST
The Complete IEP Guide	$34.99	IEP
Divorce & Money: How to Make the Best Financial Decisions During Divorce	$34.99	DIMO
Divorce Without Court	$29.99	DWCT
Do Your Own California Adoption: Nolo's Guide for Stepparents and Domestic Partners (Book w/CD-ROM)	$34.99	ADOP
Every Dog's Legal Guide: A Must-Have for Your Owner	$19.99	DOG
Get a Life: You Don't Need a Million to Retire Well	$24.99	LIFE
The Guardianship Book for California	$34.99	GB
A Legal Guide for Lesbian and Gay Couples	$34.99	LG
Living Together: A Legal Guide (Book w/CD-ROM)	$34.99	LTK
Nolo's IEP Guide: Learning Disabilities	$29.99	IELD
Parent Savvy	$19.99	PRNT
Prenuptial Agreements: How to Write a Fair & Lasting Contract (Book w/CD-ROM)	$34.99	PNUP
Work Less, Live More	$17.99	RECL

	PRICE	CODE

GOING TO COURT

	PRICE	CODE
Beat Your Ticket: Go To Court & Win! (National Edition)	$21.99	BEYT
The Criminal Law Handbook: Know Your Rights, Survive the System	$39.99	KYR
Everybody's Guide to Small Claims Court (National Edition)	$29.99	NSCC
Everybody's Guide to Small Claims Court in California	$29.99	CSCC
Fight Your Ticket & Win in California	$29.99	FYT
How to Change Your Name in California	$29.99	NAME
Nolo's Deposition Handbook	$29.99	DEP
Represent Yourself in Court: How to Prepare & Try a Winning Case	$39.99	RYC
Win Your Lawsuit: A Judge's Guide to Representing Yourself in California Superior Court	$29.99	SLWY

HOMEOWNERS, LANDLORDS & TENANTS

	PRICE	CODE
California Tenants' Rights	$27.99	CTEN
Deeds for California Real Estate	$24.99	DEED
Every Landlord's Legal Guide (National Edition, Book w/CD-ROM)	$44.99	ELLI
Every Landlord's Guide to Finding Great Tenants (Book w/CD-ROM)	$19.99	FIND
Every Landlord's Tax Deduction Guide	$34.99	DELL
Every Tenant's Legal Guide	$29.99	EVTEN
For Sale by Owner in California	$29.99	FSBO
How to Buy a House in California	$29.99	BHCA
The California Landlord's Law Book: Rights & Responsibilities (Book w/CD-ROM)	$44.99	LBRT
The California Landlord's Law Book: Evictions (Book w/CD-ROM)	$44.99	LBEV
Leases & Rental Agreements	$29.99	LEAR
Neighbor Law: Fences, Trees, Boundaries & Noise	$26.99	NEI
Renters' Rights (National Edition)	$24.99	RENT

IMMIGRATION

	PRICE	CODE
Becoming A U.S. Citizen: A Guide to the Law, Exam and Interview	$24.99	USCIT
Fiancé & Marriage Visas (Book w/CD-ROM)	$34.99	IMAR
How to Get a Green Card	$29.99	GRN
Student & Tourist Visas	$29.99	ISTU
U.S. Immigration Made Easy	$39.99	IMEZ

MONEY MATTERS

	PRICE	CODE
101 Law Forms for Personal Use (Book w/CD-ROM)	$29.99	SPOT
Chapter 13 Bankruptcy: Repay Your Debts	$39.99	CHB
Credit Repair (Book w/CD-ROM)	$24.99	CREP
How to File for Chapter 7 Bankruptcy	$29.99	HFB
IRAs, 401(k)s & Other Retirement Plans: Taking Your Money Out	$34.99	RET
Solve Your Money Troubles	$19.99	MT
Stand Up to the IRS	$29.99	SIRS

	PRICE	CODE

PATENTS AND COPYRIGHTS

	PRICE	CODE
All I Need is Money: How to Finance Your Invention	$19.99	FINA
The Copyright Handbook: How to Protect & Use Written Works (Book w/CD-ROM)	$39.99	COHA
Copyright Your Software (Book w/CD-ROM)	$34.95	CYS
Getting Permission: How to License and Clear Copyrighted Materials Online and Off (Book w/CD-ROM)	$34.99	RIPER
How to Make Patent Drawings	$29.99	DRAW
The Inventor's Notebook	$24.99	INOT
Nolo's Patents for Beginners	$24.99	QPAT
Patent, Copyright & Trademark	$39.99	PCTM
Patent It Yourself	$49.99	PAT
Patent Pending in 24 Hours	$34.99	PEND
Patenting Art & Entertainment: New Strategies for Protecting Creative Ideas	$39.99	PATAE
Profit from Your Idea (Book w/CD-ROM)	$34.99	LICE
The Public Domain	$34.99	PUBL
Trademark: Legal Care for Your Business and Product Name	$39.99	TRD
Web and Software Development: A Legal Guide (Book w/ CD-ROM)	$44.99	SFT
What Every Inventor Needs to Know About Business & Taxes (Book w/CD-ROM)	$21.99	ILAX

RESEARCH & REFERENCE

	PRICE	CODE
Legal Research: How to Find & Understand the Law	$39.99	LRES

SENIORS

	PRICE	CODE
Long-Term Care: How to Plan & Pay for It	$19.99	ELD
Social Security, Medicare & Goverment Pensions	$29.99	SOA

SOFTWARE

Call or check our website at www.nolo.com for special discounts on Software!

	PRICE	CODE
Incorporator Pro	89.99	STNC1
LLC Maker—Windows	$89.95	LLP1
Patent Pending Now!	$199.99	PP1
PatentEase—Windows	$349.00	PEAS
Personal RecordKeeper 5.0 CD—Windows	$59.95	RKD5
Quicken Legal Business Pro 2007—Windows	$109.99	SBQB7
Quicken WillMaker Plus 2007—Windows	$79.99	WQP7

Special Upgrade Offer

Save 35% on the latest edition of your Nolo book

Because laws and legal procedures change often, we update our books regularly. To help keep you up-to-date, we are extending this special upgrade offer. Cut out and mail the title portion of the cover of your old Nolo book and we'll give you 35% off the retail price of the New Edition of that book when you purchase directly from Nolo. This offer is to individuals only.

ORDER 24 HOURS A DAY @ www.nolo.com
Call 800-728-3555 • Mail or fax the order form in this book

Order Form

Name

Address

City

State, Zip

Daytime Phone

E-mail

Our "No-Hassle" Guarantee

Return anything you buy directly from Nolo for any reason and we'll cheerfully refund your purchase price. No ifs, ands or buts.

☐ Check here if you do not wish to receive mailings from other companies

Item Code	Quantity	Item	Unit Price	Total Price

Method of payment

☐ Check   ☐ VISA

☐ American Express

☐ MasterCard

☐ Discover Card

Subtotal	
Add your local sales tax (California only)	
Shipping: RUSH $12, Basic $9 (See below)	
"I bought 3, ship it to me FREE!"(Ground shipping only)	
TOTAL	

Account Number

Expiration Date

Signature

Shipping and Handling

Rush Delivery—Only $12

We'll ship any order to any street address in the U.S. by UPS 2nd Day Air* for only $12!

* Order by noon Pacific Time and get your order in 2 business days. Orders placed after noon Pacific Time will arrive in 3 business days. P.O. boxes and S.F. Bay Area use basic shipping. Alaska and Hawaii use 2nd Day Air or Priority Mail.

Basic Shipping—$9

Use for P.O. Boxes, Northern California and Ground Service.

Allow 1-2 weeks for delivery.

U.S. addresses only.

For faster service, use your credit card and our toll-free numbers

Call our customer service group Monday thru Friday 7am to 7pm PST

 Phone
1-800-728-3555

 Fax
1-800-645-0895

 Mail
Nolo
950 Parker St.
Berkeley, CA 94710

Order 24 hours a day @ www.nolo.com

Get the Latest in the Law

Nolo's Legal Updater
We'll send you an email whenever a new edition of your book is published! Sign up at **www.nolo.com/legalupdater**.

Updates at Nolo.com
Check **www.nolo.com/update** to find recent changes in the law that affect the current edition of your book.

Nolo Customer Service
To make sure that this edition of the book is the most recent one, call us at **800-728-3555** and ask one of our friendly customer service representatives (7:00 a.m. to 6:00 p.m. PST, weekdays only). Or find out at **www.nolo.com**.

Complete the Registration & Comment Card ...
... and we'll do the work for you! Just indicate your preferences below:

- -

Registration & Comment Card

NAME _____ DATE _____

ADDRESS _____

CITY _____ STATE _____ ZIP _____

PHONE _____ EMAIL _____

COMMENTS _____

WAS THIS BOOK EASY TO USE?   (VERY EASY)   5   4   3   2   1   (VERY DIFFICULT)

☐ Yes, you can quote me in future Nolo promotional materials. *Please include phone number above.*

☐ Yes, send me **Nolo's Legal Updater** via email when a new edition of this book is available.

Yes, I want to sign up for the following email newsletters:

    ☐ **NoloBriefs** (monthly)
    ☐ **Nolo's Special Offer** (monthly)
    ☐ **Nolo's BizBriefs** (monthly)
    ☐ **Every Landlord's Quarterly** (four times a year)

☐ Yes, you can give my contact info to carefully selected partners whose products may be of interest to me.

GRN 7.0

NOLO

Nolo
950 Parker Street
Berkeley, CA 94710-9867
www.nolo.com

YOUR LEGAL COMPANION